OTHER BOOKS BY YVONNE YOUNG TARR

The Great East Coast Seafood Book

The GREAT EAST COAST SEAFOOD Book

Yvonne Young Tarr

Illustrations by Pat Stewart

Vintage Books • A Division of Random House • New York

A Vintage Original, July 1982

First Edition

Copyright © 1982 by Accabonac Creative, Inc.

All rights reserved under International and Pan-American Copyright Conventions. Published in the United States by Random House, Inc., New York, and simultaneously in Canada by Random House of Canada Limited, Toronto.

Poems by Isaac McLellan are reprinted from Poems of the Rod and Gun. *A copy of the book is in the Long Island Collection of the East Hampton Free Library.*

Library of Congress Cataloging in Publication Data

Tarr, Yvonne Young.

The great East Coast seafood book.

Includes index.

1. Cookery (Seafood)   2. Seafood—Atlantic States.

I. Title.

TX747.T37   641.6′9   81-52921

ISBN 0-394-75325-9   AACR2

Manufactured in the United States of America

Book design: Elissa Ichiyasu

COVER AND TEXT ILLUSTRATIONS
BY PAT STEWART

*I dedicate this book
with love to my mother and father,
Margaret and Elwood Young.*

ACKNOWLEDGMENTS

With many thanks to: The East Hampton Baymen's Association and particularly Arnold Leo, their secretary, for information and encouragement, not to mention fish for testing;

Dorothy T. King of the Long Island Collection, East Hampton Free Library, for help in locating the old poetry included herein; George Sid Miller, Sr., and Jarvis Woods for their tales, well told, of life in old East Hampton; the many others: from New England to the Carolinas—friends, fish-boat captains and crews, haul seiners, etc., who told me their fish stories, filled in the spaces where my own experience was spotty, and in general made this rather difficult task easier; Random House editor Alexandra Halsey, copy editor Cordelia Jason and designer Elissa Ichiyasu for their expert assistance in making this book possible;

And, once more, a very special thank you to my long-time friend and editor, Ruth Grossman, for her accuracy, patience, skill and dedication— without her this book could not have been written.

CONTENTS

◆ ◆

PART THREE: FISH AND NUTRITION

◆ ◆

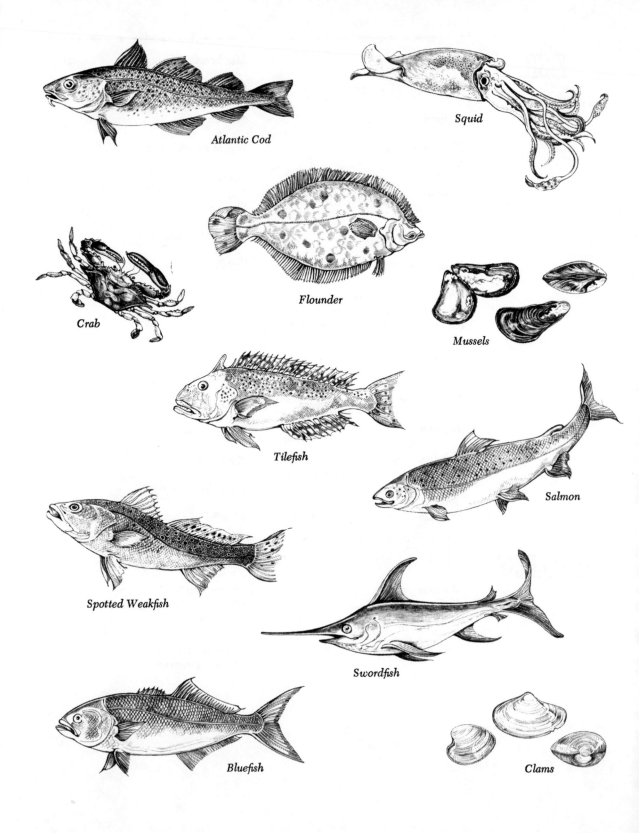

Atlantic Cod

Squid

Flounder

Crab

Mussels

Tilefish

Salmon

Spotted Weakfish

Swordfish

Bluefish

Clams

Mackerel

Eel

Herring

Tuna

Ray

Scallops

Porgy

Sea Robin

Whelk

Striped Bass

Lobster

INTRODUCTION

Twilight blue-snapper fishing at the tip of beach where Gerard Drive reaches out and nearly touches the sandy finger of Louse Point. To the left the sky folds and ripples from rose to mauve to that tender gray of the gulls that tip and cry not four feet over our heads. Two silent figures are already fishing the riptide, where we know the snappers wait for smaller fish disoriented from the curling turbulence where sweet water meets salt. One angler faces Louse Point, the other casts toward Gardiner's Island, where the nips of the snappers are usually most frequent. His bait box is open in precisely that foot of pebble beach we have come to think of as our own. Good manners prevail. We station ourselves at a respectable distance. There is no sound other than the tic-tic-tic-tic of the ratchet as our friend reels in his flashy Day-Glo silver lure. No one chatters. The unwritten rule.

The shore to our right lines Accabonac Bay, called simply "the Creek" by those "Bonackers" whose ancestors harvested these rich underwater gardens. This "creek" glides a mile or so to my right, barely waist-high at low tide. It slips past Louse Point, surrounds Tick Island and laps at the fields that meander back to my vegetable garden. I can see my kitchen window if I really try. The land is low here, no more than a brush-wide purple shadow across the bottom of the huge canvas of blazing sky. Barely a breath of wind mars the glaze of the water, but high above, the air currents have slashed the clouds into shreds of colors as brilliant as bolts of Chinese silk thrown carelessly from one side of the horizon to the other. Color shimmers over the water before us, thinner than oil slick, so fragile it breaks in half-circles around the pebbles at our toes, so delicate my fishing line slices it in half to reveal the black depths beneath. Occasionally in the absolute quiet a gull laughs, tearing the stillness. The swift black skimmer silently slits the bay with his lower mandible, luring tiny fish to the surface for his evening tidbit. The sky darkens to a fluorescent fuchsia, silhouetting Tick Island and a solitary great blue heron that spears a fish with a flash of his pointed beak, tosses it in the air, catches it and gulps it down in perfect sync with his reflection. His schedule agrees with ours. It's well past dinner time. Our rival angler folds his tackle box and calls it a night. We move into his place and snag our snappers, one-two-three-four-five-six.

In my yard I clean the gleaming silver swimmers, then dig their remains into my garden to enrich the soil. While I'm about it I pull a few onions, break off some sage and thyme, and fill my two pockets with crisp knobs of Brussels sprouts. Later we feast on pan-fried snappers with onions, potatoes with herbs, and the buttery sprouts. We drink a wine with the sturdy depth of salt air. For dessert I toast a few freshly baked ladyfingers, sprinkle them with kirsch, top them with dollops of clotted cream and fistfuls of raspberries from a friend's bushes.

The moon is nearly full now and is resting on the sliver of land beyond the bay between the blinking red lights of the Napeague Towers. The moon glow rolls across Gardiner's Bay to the Accabonac, where fine dark horses bend their necks, still chewing the sweet grasses. Living here, we feel we are in accord with the ecology of the island. We take from the land and the waters only what we can consume, and that in moderation. We enrich the land at least in proportion to that richness which we glean from it. We pledge ourselves to the preservation of the fragile ecological equation. We are, like the heron, the skimmer, the horses, the gulls, the snappers, a natural part of the living land.

Few seasonal vacationers realize when they visit our thin edge of island how many winter families linger here when icy winds rip the foam-crests from the waves and slash across the wetlands, bending marsh grasses double into the semifrozen ripples of high-tide water. Then, when cold, mean gusts whip the beaches into sand-haze, resident Hamptonites, like stubborn snow birds, face into the storm to wait out winter gales. We persistent few have a special feeling for our bays and creeks and inlets, our shingled houses, our windmills and fences, our creeks and ponds and kettle holes and dreens.

This East End of Long Island isn't a sleek and chic resort to us. Eight months a year it is, rather, a lonely rural outpost where, just a few feet from our windows, fishermen still wrest a living from waters that sometimes killed, but yet gave nourishment and pleasure to their ancestors. Here, farmers still sow winter wheat and plow under crops of green manure to prepare the earth for those endless rows of potato plants summer visitors find flowering here.

How long you've lived in the Hamptons isn't counted by summers, but by winters. And to native Bonackers, whose early relatives came down in ships from New England centuries ago to settle this slice of paradise, even if you winter in the Hamptons you are, and will be to your dying day, a "year 'round summer resident." No matter. We on this thirty-mile island-within-an-island, separated from the rest of the 118 miles of Long Island by the Shinnecock Canal, are alone with history, and beauty, and nature, and, for better or for worse, with one another. Farther from Manhattan than many natives of New Jersey, Delaware and Connecticut, we have a feeling—perhaps no longer fashionable but for that no less real . . . we love with an almost embarrassing passion this green and sandy place in which we live our lives. We plant our gardens, snare our fish, and in a quiet offhand way take care of one another. Our overgrown herbs, our gooseberries, our surplus catch, our beach-plum jam, our hospitality—we share.

This book reflects my personal way of living, of cooking and of eating. As dissimilar as this coastal life-experience may be to that of urban, suburban and inland families, it is far from unique. Up and down our great seacoasts this lifestyle is repeated. Many Eastern Shore folks along the inlets and creeks of Maryland's and Virginia's Chesapeake Bay, New England's Down-Easterners, shore dwellers along Delaware and the two Carolinas share an existence enlarged, expanded and sweetened by exposure to the wonders of field and shore, bay and sea.

It is because I live in this remarkable and precious place that I have put this particular book together in this particular way. Here I am constantly aware of the rise and fall of tides, of the surf crashing with muffled roars of power, then meekly rippling its way to my sneakers. This mysterious liquid dimension around me is a broth teeming with miracles of swimming ingredients. With these being mine for the taking, I have turned away almost entirely from red meat to a table laden with fishy stews and simmering stocks, of smoky seafood sausages, shark-tail steaks and divers manners of finny pleasures.

From my first days as part-time Hampton angler and resident, through hammering, hurricane-tossed fishing trips, to yesterday's victorious bout with a raging fifteen-pound blue right off Napeague beach, I have kept notes on every fish I've snagged, where and when I've hooked him, how I've cooked him and a multitude of other fascinating (to me) fishy facts. Those scribblings, numerous notes from coastal camping trips, plus a decade of research and experimentation, have resulted in this book. In fish cooking, a somewhat inexact science, there are many ways to skin a fillet, as well as many ways to serve one. Grandma's favorite pickled scallop, Madame Prunier's gourmet excess, a sea captain's prize-winning chowder, are all valid entries here. The rule is: if it tastes good, it is good —enjoy it.

I frequently encounter large amounts of one variety of fish at a time, depending upon what's in season, how they're biting and what price they're bringing at the Fulton Fish Market. If a certain fish is plentiful but demand is lagging, I sometimes inherit fifty pounds or more at a time. Besides hours of tedious cleaning and filleting, this means dreaming up new recipes, variations on those recipes, and even variations on the variations—probably just what you are called upon to do when the fisherperson in your family has been particularly lucky. For the most part, the following are recipes as I've cooked them—some are down-home favorites, many reflect my world-wide cookbook testing sprees. A few recipes of East End friends and New England and Eastern Shore acquaintances (more than a few of them cookbook authors) are also included for your pleasure. Use all of these as they appear here, mix and match them, change them to accommodate the ingredients you have on hand—in other words, make them your own. Happy fishing, eating, and living.

The Great
East Coast Seafood
Book

THE SPRINGS FISHERMAN HAS HIS SAY

Well, the fishin' hasn't changed too much from the old times. There isn't as many fish as there used to be, but everything is bigger, so they get more. You get what I mean? You got more equipment to work with, so therefore you get the same many fish, sometimes more. Used to be that you could catch all the fish you wanted. But you couldn't take care of 'em, see, 'cause you'd have no ice and so on, no trucks to cart 'em home. So you just took what you could handle. Now you take all you can get. I think the fish runs in cycles. An old fisherman I knowed, Mike Brown . . . had traps out to Montauk there . . . four generations ago. He said some years they wouldn't catch no blowfish, and other years they'd be loaded up with them. They don't know where they all come from. Well, it's like the Lord takes care of all so's not to get the earth overpopulated, you know.

In the old days things were harder. A little harder. The fish train left Montauk around about six-thirty and went on down the line. They loaded box after box, car after car of fish. The railroad cars used to have these wooden boxes t' ship 'em in. You packed the fish in the box, an' threw ice on 'em. After that there was a trucking concern in Patchogue that used to come on 'round and pick up in front of your house in trucks with hard rubber tires. Now we take 'em to Stuart's. An' in Bridge-hampton and in Montauk they got places there they ship 'em from. We pack 'em in these cardboard boxes now, an' ice 'em up, and we ship 'em to the market. The market takes out so much for the ice and so much for the boxes and freight and sends us what's left.

But before . . . it wasn't so easy. Every fisherman had an ice house. You see, we used to, when the bay froze over or the creek froze over, we'd take teams of horses and take out the ice to the ice house. What they would do, they would saw it. Go out there and saw it into cakes. Take a pitchfork and throw it in the wagon. Then we'd throw it out by hand. The only time you really got cold was when it was snowing and your hands would be wet. If it was froze all the time, then you didn't feel it. They'd load the ice into these ice houses with salt hay on the sides and cover it all up with more salt hay. In the morning, first thing they'd do is uncover some ice and chop it up, put it in bags 'n take it down when they'd go fishing.

They'd have ice about all summer here. Until East Hampton Ice Company commenced t' make their own ice from Hook Pond, you know, in East Hampton. They'd have it in cakes and put it in these big silos and

3

peddle it around all summer long. But when they formed their ice company there at the railroad station where they made ice, then these fishermen . . . Hell, soon as theirs was gone, they didn't worry about sawing it. Too much trouble. They all just went over to buy.

But nothin' was too easy then. Cod-fishin' you rowed oars in the old days. Out in a big dory, long-linin'. Had to row out a mile 'n a half. Put three men in a boat, an' row out, an' set your net, set the trawl and then go back an' get 'em. That's real fishin'. 'Course years ago there were a lot of fish, so's you didn't have to go so far and didn't have to do so much, you know. People didn't want to make a thousand dollars a day. If they made twenty-five or thirty dollars a week they was happy. They had a livin', an' all they wanted, 'n when that was gone, they'd go again. Now everybody's crazy. If they make a hundred dollars a day they want to make two hundred a day. If they get two they want to make four.

They used to make the nets up themselves then too. Even now you can't buy 'em just right. If you do it's not what you want. Just make 'em yourself. Different-size mesh for different fish. You can buy the right size, but after you buy it you got to hang it, got to have the ropes to hold it, have to put leads on it, corks onto it. Depends on what you're goin' to make. The traps are practically about all the same design. Some got little different ideas, you know, but the main design is all one thing, one design.

The fish come along shore 'cause they're looking for feed or somethin' to eat 'n they follow the bait. The bait goes in toward shore, 'n the fish goes in too. They come along 'n hit your net. Well, it's natural for the fish to go offshore, it's natural for his safety, you know. So you figure your net. You put it just the right place offshore, 'n they hit that leader an' they go offshore again. An' when they do they go off your net again, followin' that little hole gettin' smaller and smaller an' smaller 'n they get in an' they can't get out. They don't turn back. They're always goin' offshore, you see. Offshore. Except for strip-ed bass, he'll go inshore just as quick as he'll go offshore. But most of the fish go offshore.

You go out to the traps according to the tide. Every six hours the tide changes, see. You got two, three hours when it's slack water. You try to figure on gettin' that slack water, 'cause it's easier to work that way. You lift one trap today and one tomorrow and so on. Now poles are gettin' scarce. You've got to have something that's tall and straight and not too big . . . oak, hickory. There's not too much hickory around. You cruise around the woods findin' one here and there.

I still take the traps out in June or July. The shoal traps—the big deep traps set for butterfish and porgies—you can leave 'em all summer. All fall. Take 'em out in November—when the water gets warm in the summertime the fish go offshore, see, an' you don't get any. So it's better to take the trap out an' bring it home and wait for next year than to play around with it. After the shoal traps are out, then most fellows go porgyin'. Handlinin'. You got to get the knack of it. They're funny little fish. You get the knack of it and you can pull 'em in quite fast sometime. Use chum, see, to keep 'em around the boat. Bunker for chum. You grind 'em up an put 'em in a chum pot. That keeps the fish there. Keeps 'em bitin'. You got to wait 'till you feel 'em there. They don't grab big. They just nibble, you know.

Then summertimes some of the fellows they go clammin' . . . soft clammin', hard clammin'. Different things. Couple years ago there was good musselin'. And everybody goes crazy scallopin', come scallop season. It's hard work, yeah. But everybody's into it 'cause it's good money. Used to get a dollar a quart for 'em and tickled to death to get it. Now they get ten dollars. Yeah, there's a lot of work to fishin'. You've gotta keep a-jumpin' t' live on it today. You gotta keep goin' from one thing to another. You have traps in a couple a months, then you've got to do somethin' else. Then you go scallopin', then you go eelin'. Anything. You keep jumpin' from one thing to another. Get up before the sun does, lots of mornings. Get goin' before sunrise. Gotta lift nets early in the morning. If you don't the crabs get into 'em. It's not easy, you see. Not an easy life. But, you know, when you go out there in the mornin', you get the sunrise . . . It's beautiful. You just think, just how fortunate you are to have such a wonderful place to go. I love it out there. Just me an' the Lord visit together . . . go along together. It's quiet. It's peaceful. Yeah. Very relaxin'. Very relaxin'.

Part One

A·L·L A·B·O·U·T

F·I·S·H

KEEPING
FISH FRESH

Essential to excellent fish cookery is the freshness of the fish. Ideally, if your fish is to be a triumph when you present it at the table it should be dressed and cooked within minutes of being flipped from the water. Unfortunately, the reality for most of us is somewhat short of ideal. Whether we are angler-cooks who prize the one that didn't get away or city fish lovers who haunt fish markets in search of perfect specimens to grace urban menus, hours and even days often elapse before actual feasting can begin. The perishability of this highly prized foodstuff—more dependent than any other on freshness for fine texture and flavor—stems from the nature of its flesh, which is marvelously adapted to its cold deep-water environment, but highly susceptible to warmer surface temperatures. The myth that fish is fresh just because you caught it yourself is just that—a myth. To preserve its excellence, once your fish has left its aquatic home it must remain well chilled from hook to cooking pot.

If the fish you eat are the fish you catch, you can preserve their delicate, fresh-caught flavor by following a few simple rules:

1. Kill your fish by stunning them and/or breaking their backbones by placing your gloved thumb in their mouths and snapping their heads back just as soon as you take them from your hook. This prevents these beautiful creatures from a slow, gasping death and in the long run provides less-bruised, better-quality fish flesh for your table. Never use a stringer or one of those metal mesh bags designed to keep fish alive in the water. These not only bump the fish about and prolong their suffering

but the warm surface water promotes sogginess as well as bacterial growth, causing the fish to spoil more rapidly.

Promptly gut your fish, rinse them well, scrape out as much blood as possible, wipe them dry and place them on ice. This immediate cleaning is essential. As soon as a fish dies its powerful digestive enzymes begin to attack and destroy its own flesh. Most larger fish, particularly tuna and shark, are more tasty if bled. To bleed your fish, cut off the tail and hang tailside down.

2. When surf fishing, gut your fish as you catch them and pack them in canvas-covered boxes or in burlap bags. If seaweed is handy, use it to layer with the fish as extra insurance that your catch will stay fresh. Sprinkle the containers from time to time with sea water; evaporation will keep the fish cool.

3. If you decide to bring an ice chest along on your fishing expedition (and this is a good idea), pack it with shaved or crushed ice rather than with ice cubes or a large ice cake. Fish stay fresher when ice is heaped up and over them so that more body surface comes into direct contact with the ice. Drain the ice chest frequently. Fish soaked in water become soft and water-logged. If you have chosen to fillet your fish at dockside, be sure to slip your fillets into plastic bags before settling them into the ice for the trip home.

4. Although it's best to cook or process your fish immediately, they will remain edible if kept in the coldest part of your refrigerator for up to three to five days, provided, of course, that you have cleaned and wrapped them properly. Unwrapped or carelessly covered fish not only dry out quickly in the refrigerator but may transfer odors to other foods as well. Be sure to cover your catch tightly with moisture-proof paper or place it in a bowl tightly covered with plastic wrap before storing it in the refrigerator, even if you plan to use it within a few hours. If your fishing trip has been a stunning success, and you bring home more provisions than you or your refrigerator can immediately deal with, treat your family and/or friends or prepare and wrap the fish for the freezer and freeze at once as directed in Freezing Fish.

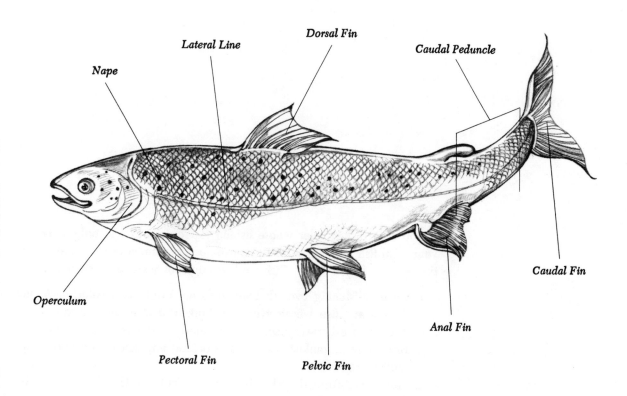

Nape

Lateral Line

Dorsal Fin

Caudal Peduncle

Operculum

Pectoral Fin

Pelvic Fin

Anal Fin

Caudal Fin

BUYING FISH

If you are a fish fancier whose fishing expeditions extend only as far as your local fish market, make these eye-nose-and-touch tests to make sure the fish you buy is fresh. Fish fresh enough for your table should have:

1. Clear, glistening eyes that are bulging, bright and colorful. Avoid buying any fish whose eyes look sunken or dull and milky.
2. A clean, fresh fragrance, smelling more of the sea than of fish.
3. Bright-red or pinkish gills. Leave behind any fish whose gills are a dullish gray-brown.
4. Shiny, well-formed scales that adhere tightly to the skin.
5. Skin that is neither slippery nor slimy.
6. Firm flesh. Don't be afraid to touch the skin or press the fish with your fingertips—if the flesh does not spring back, or if the fish seems limp when held by its head or tail, avoid it; it is a veteran of the display case.

Cut fish are a little more difficult to judge, but in general, if your store displays whole fish that pass the "fresh test" given above, it's probably safe to assume that the steaks and fillets purveyed there are equally fresh. If you have any doubts, look for the following:

1. General good looks, with no yellowing or browning around the edges.
2. Firm, moist texture. A fillet should not flake when held up, nor should it have any trace of slime.

3. The nice sweet smell that signals freshness. By-pass any fillet or steak with a strong fishy or unpleasant odor.

BUYING FROZEN FISH

Much of the catch harvested by professional fishermen is commercially flash-frozen soon after it is hauled from the water, allowing fish fanciers who live far from a fresh supply to enjoy the same culinary adventures and nutritional advantages available to seaside residents. The best frozen fish is similar in flavor and texture to the fresh, and is comparable in appearance and food value. Here's what to look for when buying frozen products:

1. A solidly frozen package, without too much air space.
2. A package free of frost and ice crystals.
3. Contents that reveal no sign of the discoloration or white patches that indicate freezer burn.

FISH BUYER'S DICTIONARY

Fish are marketed in a number of forms. In general, these are determined by the shape, skeletal structure and keeping qualities of the different species, but other influences also come into play—tradition, size and the cooking method called for by your recipe.

The following will help you ask for exactly what you want and understand exactly what you are being offered at your fish market.

Whole or **round** fish are those marketed just as they come from the water. These include not only small fry of large fish but fish such as the whitebait varieties, that keep well without being dressed, and fish that conveniently never grow beyond single-portion size (whiting, for example).

Drawn fish are whole fish that have been scaled and gutted and have usually had their gills removed before being shown in the display case.

Dressed fish are drawn fish whose heads, tails and fins have been removed. If the fish is too large to be baked or poached it may also be split or cut into serving-size pieces. Small varieties of fish are *pan-dressed* (rather than merely "dressed"), which means they are handled the same way as above except that the tails may be left on and the backbones removed. These fish are by tradition sautéed or deep-fried.

Steaks are cross-cut portions taken from the mid-sections of large dressed fish. A steak may vary in thickness from ¾ to 1½ inches, and its only bone is a small section of backbone. Steaks are usually broiled, baked, steamed or poached.

Fillets are severed from both sides of most fish in single meaty slabs cut lengthwise and free of the backbone and rib cage. They contain no bones or waste, although the skin may be left on. Fillet size varies with the size of the fish and may range from a few ounces to several pounds. A **butterfly fillet** is two single unskinned fillets—that is, both sides of a fish cut free from the skeletal structure but joined together at the top by an uncut flap of flesh and skin.

Fingers are narrow boneless pieces of fish cut from fillets or steaks. Like the more uniform, commercially packaged frozen fish sticks, fingers are intended for deep-frying or tempura but work beautifully in Seviche and in other recipes as well.

HOW MUCH TO BUY: For an *average* serving of the meatier cuts—fillets, steaks and fingers—⅓ pound of fish is generally adequate, although heartier diners will probably need ½ pound per serving. When buying dressed fish, ½ pound per person is about right for a delicate appetite, but to make sure you have enough to go around when purchasing a whole, round or bony fish, better plan on buying from ¾ to one pound per person.

WHEN TO BUY AND HOW TO STORE: Quality is highest—and prices lowest— when a particular fish is in season. Your fish dealer can be an excellent guide in these matters and, having sold you fresh fish, will doubtless wrap your purchase in moisture-proof paper so that it stays fresh and cold until it can be safely deposited in the coldest part of your refrigerator. Once it is there, leave the fish in its original wrappings, or cover tightly with plastic wrap as you would if you had caught the fish yourself, and use, if possible, the same day, since fish in city markets are generally a day (or more) old when you purchase them.

CLEANING AND DRESSING FISH

Probably the least appealing aspect of fish cookery is the sometimes intimidating job of dressing the fish you catch yourself or are blessed with by angler friends. Before I began research on this book I'll admit that I often side-stepped my share of fish-cleaning chores. I told my husband that I had already mastered the art on our many camping trips and that my contribution was to be preparing these deep-sea treasures . . . more than enough work, it seemed to me. But once I began in earnest to hook my own fish in quantity and to collect specimens from professional trap fishermen, haul seiners, charterboat captains and amateur anglers, I realized that cleaning could provide a fascinating insight into how much, when and on what fish feed; when spawning takes place and other finny facts. From that day to this, I do the cleaning and dressing myself, even when I buy fish from my fishermen friends. Whole fish are less expensive in the long run, and if you save the heads and bones for stock, salvage the roe, and dig the rest into your garden, not a penny's worth need be wasted.

Cleaning and dressing your fish yourself (whether self-caught or purchased) might never become your favorite pastime, but you're sure to feel a great deal of satisfaction as you gain proficiency. As with any other culinary technique, the way to learn is to have a go at it. Practice—abetted by the right tools—makes perfect every time. When you're fishing in deep waters much of the preliminary work can—and should—be performed in the boat. If you must clean and dress your fish at home, neatness and convenience do count. Layer several thicknesses of newspaper on your work surface and as each fish is cleaned, fold up the remains in a few sheets of newspaper and set it aside. (Don't forget to save the heads and bones for stock.)

TOOLS

Nothing facilitates cleaning and dressing, or makes you feel and perform more like an expert, than a thin good-quality, exquisitely sharp, flexible filleting knife. For most surf and bottom fish, a stainless- or carbon-steel 6- to 8-inch blade is ideal. A carbon-steel blade has the advantage of being easier to use and to sharpen, but it does rust easily, and in seaside areas this is a consideration. Whatever knife you choose, be sure that it feels balanced in your hand and take care to keep its cutting edge razor-sharp with frequent honing.

There are other tools that are useful but not essential. While anything from a large soupspoon to a table knife will easily divest most fish of their scales, store-bought scalers ranging from the simplest serrated kind to electric varieties that shave a fish in seconds are available to help speed the process. By giving you a good grip on the edge of a fillet, a skinning tool lets you peel off most fish's skin as easily as opening a can of sardines, but an ordinary pair of pliers will still be necessary when you're tackling the tougher, thicker skins of the likes of eels. A skinning board, with a clip at one end to secure the fish's tail, also expedites the job by freeing both your hands.

SCALING

Hold the fish firmly by the head, and starting at the tail, use your scaling tool to scrape the scales at a 45-degree angle against the grain all the way to the head, paying particular attention to the areas around the fins and throat. If you're performing this first step at home (particularly indoors), it's best to place the fish in water in a large pan or sink. Loose fish scales are much less apt to decorate your walls and ceiling if you submerge the fish while doing the job. Then, too, since scales are much more difficult to remove once they begin to dry, this *brief* soak is sure to make the job easier.

CLEANING AND DRESSING

Note: While the method described below is suitable for most species, there are a few fish which, for anatomical or other reasons, need to be handled differently. For directions on cleaning and dressing bottlefish, eels, shad, mackerel, skate, dogfish, monkfish and sea robins, see these individual sections.

If the fish has not been gutted, begin by cutting along the entire length of the belly from the vent to the head (A). (A bit of extra effort may be needed to get through the pelvic fin area.) Make a slanting cut behind the head and pectoral fins downward (B). Bend the head down, snapping the backbone, then continue the downward pull and most of the entrails will follow. Remove remaining entrails and scrape the area around the backbone to clean out any blood.

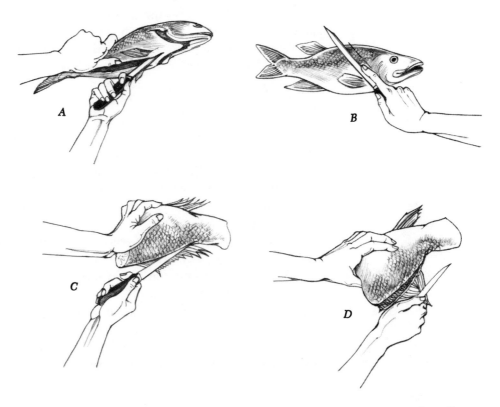

If you choose to leave the head on your fish, you must cut out the gills, which impart a bitter flavor. Or you may remove both the head and gills together by cutting through the fish just above the collarbone. When working with a large fish, this is facilitated if you cut through to the backbone on both sides first, then break this bone by bending the fish head over the edge of a cutting board or table. Cut through and trim away any ragged flesh.

Once the head and entrails have been removed, the fish is considered "dressed" and, except for a rinse under cold running water, is ready to grace any number of fish dishes. Pan-fish (small or miniature fish that will fit into a frying pan) are most often sautéed or deep-fried in a whole or nearly whole condition and are ready for cooking at this point. Really large fish, however, usually need further preparation.

The fish tail may be cut off or left on. If the tail is to be removed, cut through the skin in a semicircle around the caudal peduncle (the point where the tail joins the body), then bend and break the bone as above. Fins should be removed by cutting through the surrounding flesh (C) and, using pliers if necessary, jerking the fin backward toward the tail (D) so that the root bones at the base of each fin come free at the same time. If you trim off the fin with shears or a knife, these sharp base-bones will be left in the meat. Because the pectoral and pelvic fins are attached to large rigid bones that separate easily from the meat after cooking, some people prefer not to remove these or the graceful and decorative dorsal fin from a large fish that is to be served whole. The last step before cooking is to rinse and scrape the cavity free from all dark, unattractive or inedible material, wash the fish well under cold running water and pat it dry.

If you intend to stuff the fish, you may also remove the backbone and rib cage. To do this, widen the ventral opening at the head end, slide your knife between the rib cage and flesh on each side of the fish right up to the backbone, then cut the backbone free and detach the whole bony structure. The cleaning and dressing process outlined above is satisfactory for all round fish.

The same instructions pertain when preparing a whole flatfish for the table, but the order in which they are performed is a bit different. Begin by scaling and detaching the fins as directed above. When you cut off the head, the entrails will usually follow. Rinse well inside and out and wipe dry. To stuff a cleaned flatfish, simply slit the flesh on the belly (white) side in a straight line from the neck area to the tail, leaving the backbone intact. Holding the knife flat, cut from this slit along the bone toward the edge of the fish on each side to form two pockets.

STEAKING

Very large fish, those too unwieldy to cook whole or too thick for fillets, may be turned into steaks. First dress the fish by gutting and scaling it, then cut off its head. Leave the skin on to hold the flesh together while it cooks. It's easily removed afterward. Lay the fish on one side on your work surface and slice completely through the body at ¾- to 1¼-inch intervals, according to your preference or your recipe directions. I always cut fish steaks ¾- to 1-inch thick—seldom thicker or thinner. Thinner steaks are cooked through before they have a chance to brown nicely, and thicker ones dry out on top before the centers are sufficiently cooked.

Unless the fish is on the small side, or you're lucky enough to hit squarely between the vertebrae with each slice, you will need some assistance in cutting through the backbone. There are several options— a cleaver, meat saw or frozen-food knife will each do the trick, but I prefer placing a sturdy knife on the backbone and firmly tapping the back of the blade with a mallet. Often you will be left with a tail section too small to yield adequate steaks. In this case, cook the piece as you would any fairly large chunk of fish, or turn the meat into fillets.

FILLETING

This method is suitable for most round surf and bottom fish 2 to 3 pounds and over. No gutting is necessary, and unless you prefer to serve your fillets unskinned, you may by-pass the scaling process as well. As a general rule sport fish have thin, palatable skin that thickens somewhat as they increase to trophy size. Let your preference or your recipe be your guide when deciding whether to skin or not to skin the fish you cook. If you're storing your fish in the refrigerator or freezer, remember that unskinned fillets remain moist longer and freeze more successfully.

TO FILLET ROUND FISH, I: Hold the fish firmly on its side, its tail toward you. Make a cut all the way down the backbone (A) alongside the dorsal fin from the head to the tail, then make one cut behind the head and pectoral fins to the bone. Make another cut across the caudal peduncle (the point where the tail joins the body), holding the knife flat and cutting forward from the tail until you reach the abdominal cavity. Now place your knife along the backbone and with a slight sawing motion (and turning the wrist gently back and forth if you encounter resistance) slice the meat away from the ribs and backbone (B). Be careful not to cut into the viscera. Lift off the entire fillet in one piece, then turn the fish over and repeat the procedure on its other side. It sounds easy, and with a little practice it is. As you become more adept you will, with the flick of your wrist, be able to free the fillet in what seems to be a single stroke of the knife. But that takes a while.

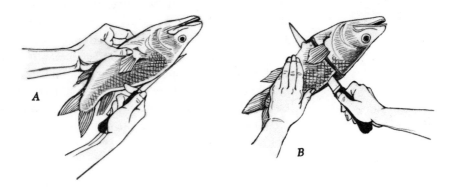

TO FILLET ROUND FISH, II: An alternate technique, and one that beginners seem to conquer more easily, is the "outline" method.

Outline the fillet by cutting just behind the gills from the backbone to the belly, then, with the sharp point of your knife, make a cut from the back of the head all along the backbone to the tail. Cut across the caudal peduncle at the base of the tail. Make a very shallow cut from the anal vent forward and then from the vent to the tail. Do not cut into the viscera. With your knife flat and beginning at the tail, slide your knife along the backbone and with a slight sawing motion (and turning the wrist gently back and forth if you meet resistance) slice the meat away from the backbone and ribs. Lift off the fillet and repeat the process with the other fillet.

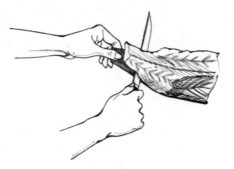

To skin the fillet, place it skin-side-down on the work surface. Holding it by the tail end, cut through to the flesh; then, with the tail end of the skin secure between your thumb and forefingers, flatten your knife and work the blade down to the other end of the fillet, pulling the skin as you push the knife. Beginners might find that a sharp, flat, broad-bladed, not too flexible knife is easier to use here than a thin, flexible filleting knife. Once you gain proficiency, almost any sharp knife will do.

TO FILLET FLATFISH: Place the fish eye-side-up on your work surface and make a shallow cut just down to the backbone (don't cut into these bones). Follow the natural line you'll see running down the center of the fish (A). Now make a slightly slanting cut behind the head to the first cut from the top of the head to the bottom of the chin (B). Flatten your knife and slide it along one side of the backbone to the tail and out to the edge of the fish (C), stopping when the knife meets the resistance of the line of small bones that radiate out to the edge of the fish. Cut along these bones to free the fillet (D). Turn the fish around and use the same procedure to free the second fillet. Turn the fish over and repeat the process to free the final two fillets.

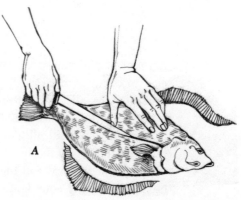

A

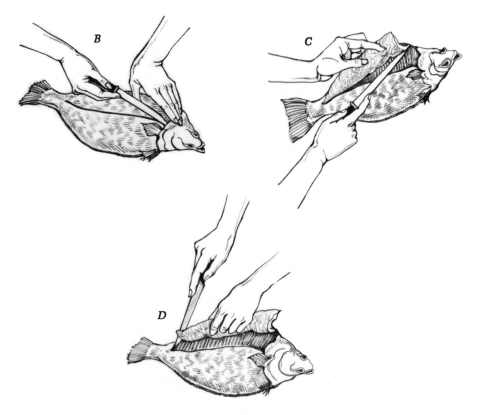

TO MAKE A DOUBLE BUTTERFLY FILLET FOR PLANKING OR STUFFING A ROUND FISH: Begin by scaling the fish. Cut off the fish's head at a point just behind the pectoral fins, then remove as much of the entrails as possible. Make a long cut along one side of the dorsal fin, then flatten the knife against the ribs and backbone and scrape and cut away the bones without severing the belly skin, which must be kept intact to hold the fillets together. Cut through the anal fin all the way to the tail. The whole spine and rib cage are now attached to the remaining fillet. Begin again by making another cut on the other side of the dorsal fin and cut the meat away from the ribs as before. Discard the bones, rinse the two fillets joined by the belly skin and pat dry. Plank or stuff.

TO FILLET FISH WITH TOUGH, TENACIOUS SKIN: When filleting fish with skin that is difficult to remove, monkfish, for example, it's best to get this chore out of the way prior to filleting.

To begin, make a shallow cut with a knife along the fish's back from a point just behind the head to the tail, keeping to one side of the dorsal fin. Make a shallow vertical cut behind the head and pectoral fins, along the belly to the tail and across the point where the tail meets the body back up to meet the cut you made along the backbone. You've now outlined the fillet.

Using the tip of the knife, pry up a bit of skin at the juncture of the two points behind the head, then holding the head firmly, pull the skin off. If the skin will not yield to pulling alone, work it off by alternately pulling and slicing where skin and flesh join, then fillet as above.

To fillet extra-large fish, you may remove the skin beforehand and then fillet as above, but if the skin is at all tractable the filleting process is easier to manage with it on. First, using the same principle as in filleting flatfish, cut through to the backbone in a vertical cut made just behind the gill cover. Next, slice through the flesh along the backbone, lifting it as you go; continue lifting and slicing until the belly side of the fillet is reached, then cut through the skin to free the fillet.

FISH COOKERY
METHODS

Veteran fish cooks develop a second sense when it comes to judging whether the fish they happen to be preparing is perfectly baked, poached or whatever. It's done by eye, by instinct . . . by experience. And even then, a nudge with a finger or a flake with the tines of a fork is an almost automatic double-check. Until that instinct takes over, a good many beautiful specimens may be over-, or under-, cooked.

One of the great culinary innovations in recent years has been the discovery that excellent results in fish cookery can be achieved when the fish is measured at its thickest point, then cooked at a rate of 8 to 10 minutes' cooking time per inch, with an appropriate amount of cooking time added for any fractions included in the measurement. This theory, known as the Canadian timing or cooking method, is the outgrowth of experimentation and testing by the Department of Fisheries of Canada and popularized in this country by James Beard. For generations of cooks intimidated by the experienced-eye or test-and-flake method of assuring that fish is perfectly cooked, the Canadian idea seems nothing short of revolutionary.

It's wonderfully easy. All that it involves is a ruler and some simple arithmetic. It applies equally to whole fish, pieces of fish, steaks, and fillets and (with minor modifications) to every cooking method—broiling, baking, deep frying, sautéing, braising and/or poaching. (If you prefer fish slightly underdone, as I do, figure 7 to 8 minutes per inch.)

If it is a whole fish that is to be cooked, simply lay it on its side on a flat surface, measure its thickest point in inches (plus fractions) and allow 8 to 10 minutes of cooking time per inch. Pieces of fish, steaks, fillets, and even rolled fillets may be measured in the same way, no matter what cooking method is planned. For example, a fish that measures 2½ inches thick should be cooked for 20 to 25 minutes, no more; a ½-inch fillet needs a mere 4 to 5 minutes.

The Canadian timing rule works well with frozen fish, too, and saves time besides, because there is no need to thaw the fish in advance. Instead, all you need do is measure the frozen fish or portion as you would its fresh counterpart, then double the cooking time by figuring 15 to 20 minutes per inch rather than 8 to 10.

From an aesthetic point of view, the nice thing about the Canadian theory is that by virtually eliminating guesswork, it also does away with the need to frequently poke, pry, lift or otherwise mar your fish in order to determine its degree of doneness. Cook by any of the methods given in this section, and as long as you follow the Canadian timing rule (and your oven thermometer is properly adjusted) your fish should arrive at the table with its natural beauty and flavor intact.

BROILING

Whole or split fish and steaks or fillets ¾ to 1 inch thick may be broiled. Preheat the broiler, then measure the thickness of the fish or pieces of fish to be cooked. Arrange on a greased broiling pan and baste with melted butter, oil or basting sauce. Broil 2 to 4 inches from the heat, allowing 8 to 10 minutes of cooking time per inch. If the fish is frozen, set the broiling pan farther away from the heat and increase cooking time to 15 to 20 minutes per inch. When the fish browns lightly on one side, turn and baste the other side until done.

Thicker cuts of fish are less apt to dry out under the broiler than thinner ones, but on the other hand, very thick cuts of a dense fish like cod are better off being baked since broiling these can produce a somewhat leathery finished dish. If you do decide to broil thin fillets (and I don't recommend it), there is no need to turn them during cooking, but be sure to set them at least 4 inches from the heat. Since fillets are often uneven in thickness, it's a good idea to tuck under any thin edges when arranging the fish on the greased broiling pan. This makes them uniform in thickness and ensures even cooking. Measure their thickness *after* turning the edges under, and cook 8 to 10 minutes per inch.

Steaks may be prepared for broiling by dusting with flour and dotting well with butter or simply basting with melted butter or oil. Place these on a well-greased broiling pan, measure at their thickest part and broil about 2 inches from the heat, figuring 8 to 10 minutes per inch of thickness, turning only once and basting frequently throughout cooking. When calculating the time needed to cook fish steaks, you may want to allow them to cook a longer time after turning than before, to ensure that they will emerge from the broiler nicely browned on top.

Whole fish may be broiled with or without their heads, although I feel a headless fish is a rather pathetic sight. Aside from beauty, leaving the head on is insurance that more of the cooking juices will stay where you want them . . . in your fish. Dust the fish lightly with flour and grease on one side with butter or oil. Place greased-side-up in the broiling pan. Set small fish 3 inches from the heat, larger fish at least 6 inches away. Broil for 8 to 10 minutes per inch of thickness, adding an appropriate amount of time for fractions, basting frequently with butter, oil, lemon juice or wine and turning once.

When broiling a split fish, be sure to leave the backbone in—to ensure extra juiciness and flavor. Set the fish skin-side-down on a greased broiling rack. Dust with flour and arrange pieces of butter over the top, or brush with melted butter or oil, and broil 2 to 3 inches from the heat. Cook without turning for 8 to 10 minutes per inch of thickness, basting frequently.

GRILLING OUTDOORS

As delicious as fish tastes indoors, fish cooked on an outdoor grill is somehow even more spectacular. A really fine investment is one of those hinged grills for keeping whole fish, steaks, or fillets intact as they cook over the coals. Grease it well, then preheat briefly before setting in the fish.

Prepare the fish for grilling by dusting lightly with flour and brushing with melted butter, oil or sauce. Measure the fish at its thickest part, then broil as you would indoors: 8 to 10 minutes per inch for fresh fish, 15 to 20 minutes per inch for frozen. Be sure to baste frequently during cooking so that the fish does not dry out.

BAKING

Baking is an excellent way to prepare fish. Generally this is best done in a very hot (450 degrees F.) oven and usually without turning, since the heat surrounds the fish. Measure the fish or piece of fish at the thickest point, and bake for 8 to 10 minutes per inch; be sure to include appropriate time for fractions. Allow 15 to 20 minutes per inch if the fish is frozen. When baking stuffed fish, take the fish's measurements *after* stuffing, then bake according to the Canadian timing rule. If the recipe directs you to cook the fish in a good deal of sauce or in foil, you will need to increase cooking time by an additional 5 minutes per inch. Bake your fish as plain or as fancy as you wish. Baste with butter or oil and serve with a plain lemon wedge, or richly stuff your fish, mantle it with a tantalizing sauce, and serve it side-by-side garden-fresh vegetables or tender summer fruits. For those on fat- or salt-free diets—or for those who simply believe that less is more when it comes to fish—plain lemon or lime juice sprinkled over as a basting sauce will give excellent results. From a decorative point of view you may wish to cover the eye of the fish with a slice of stuffed olive.

PAN-FRYING OR SAUTÉING

Small whole fish, as well as serving-size fillets or smaller fish pieces, are suitable for this cooking method. These are usually cooked through when they reach a golden brown on both sides but the Canadian rule also works here. Measure the fish at its thickest point, then sprinkle with salt and pepper or dust with seasoned flour. Using a skillet large enough to hold all the pieces without crowding, heat ¼ inch butter or oil—or equal amounts of the two—until sizzling. Arrange the fish or fish pieces in a single layer and cook over brisk heat for 8 to 10 minutes per inch of thickness until golden brown on both sides, turning once about halfway through the cooking time. Pan-fried fish may also be dipped in thin batter or dusted lightly with flour, then dipped in beaten egg and finally in bread crumbs before frying.

DEEP-FRYING

In your deep-fryer, heat to 375 degrees F. enough fat to cover the fish. Measure the fish at its thickest point, then blot dry with paper towels, dredge in flour, dip in beaten egg and roll in cracker or bread crumbs (or follow recipe directions). Place in the frying basket and cook in the hot fat for 8–10 minutes per inch of thickness. Drain briefly on paper towels and sprinkle with salt and pepper to taste before serving hot.

When frying a large amount of fish, fry only as many pieces at one time as the deep-fryer can comfortably hold without crowding, and be sure that the temperature of the fat returns to 375 degrees F. before adding the next batch.

Deep-frying is one method in which it is not advisable to cook frozen fish without first thawing and thoroughly blotting dry. The contrast between the boiling oil and ice-cold fish might lower the temperature of the oil to below proper frying level, producing inferior results, and the water content just might cause dangerous splattering.

BRAISING

This cooking method, which calls for browning food in fat, then cooking it slowly in a small amount of liquid, is not usually associated with fish cookery, although it produces excellent results. Braising can take place on top of the stove or in the oven, but it is always accomplished at low heat. In braising, the fish may be arranged over sautéed julienne vegetables, then topped with bacon, salt pork or a little vegetable oil. Add red or white wine or a mixture of either of these with water or stock to a level halfway up the sides of the fish and quickly bring to a boil. Counting from the time of the boil, cook the fish over low heat, or in a 350 degrees F. oven, for 8–10 minutes per inch of thickness plus any fraction thereof. Be sure to baste the fish frequently with its cooking liquid.

After the fish is braised for the required amount of time, arrange it on a platter and keep it warm. Reduce the cooking liquid to 2 cups over high heat and use to prepare a sauce. Serve the fish with a little of the sauce spooned over, the rest of the sauce served separately. If you wish, cover the eye of the fish with a stuffed-olive slice.

POACHING

No matter what the poaching liquid, the Canadian formula for measuring the fish at its thickest point, then poaching it for 8–10 minutes per inch, still applies. Simply bring to a boil enough water, milk, court bouillon or fish stock to cover the fish, then add the fish to the pan. Lower the heat immediately so that the liquid barely boils—or "shivers"—and count the timing from that point on. Figure 8–10 minutes per inch plus fractions for fresh fish, 15–20 minutes per inch for frozen. If the recipe directs that the fish be cooled in the poaching liquid, use the shorter cooking times given to prevent overcooking the fish.

The foolproof way to make sure your whole fish stays whole after poaching is to use a professional fish poacher—an elongated pot made of aluminum tin-plate or stainless steel lined with a rack with handles at either end—which permits you to lift out the fish intact when cooking is over. These pots come in several different lengths and are designed to accommodate one large striped bass, for instance, or several smaller fish at one time.

If you're unwilling or unable to spend the rather outrageous sum these fish poachers now cost there are two inexpensive substitutes. Heat the cooking liquid in a roasting pan large enough to hold the fish you wish to cook. Make a sling of double cheesecloth long enough to cradle your fish and also extend over the ends of the pan. Fold the cheesecloth ends on top of the fish while it cooks. When you are ready to transfer the fish to the platter use the cheesecloth ends as handles to gently lift the fish out. Or arrange one cup each sliced onion, celery and carrot on one half of a piece of heavy-duty aluminum foil a little more than twice the length of your fish. Bend up the edges and pour in one cup of white wine. Seal the edges securely and bake in a preheated 450° oven for 8 to 10 minutes per pound. No matter how the fish is cooked a nice decorative touch is to cover the fish eye with a slice of stuffed olive.

There you have it, the most scientific fish-cooking method yet devised . . . a wonderful beginners' guide. I must confess that I poke and peek at my fish, even cajole and talk to them, and resort to the fork-flake test when I'm in doubt. But the Canadian method does reassure the not-so-sure fish cook until confidence and instinct take over.

STEAMING

Clean and scale fish; rinse and dry well. Rub lightly with salt, inside and out. Place finely cut scallions, or other ingredients as directed in your recipe, on a shallow, ovenproof dish—a Pyrex pie plate, for example. Arrange the fish on top. Bring several inches of water to a boil in a large pan or wok. Place a rack an inch or two above water level, set the dish on it, cover the pan or wok and steam 8 to 10 minutes per pound for whole fish, 10 to 15 minutes for ¾-inch thick steaks or fillets, and 6 to 8 minutes for thin fillets.

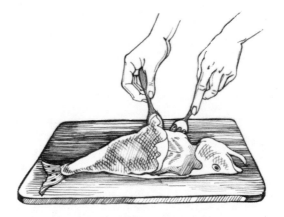

To serve poached fish: Lift portions of flesh from bones with serving fork and spoon.

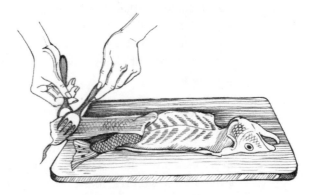

To skin: Grasp skin with serving utensils and gently pull away from flesh, toward tail.

PRESERVING
FISH

SALT FISH

Colonial Hamptonites brought with them food-preservation methods popular in seventeenth-century Europe. Many of the skills imported with the settlers were admirably suited to the abundance of fish they found swarming in North Atlantic waters. Pickle Salting and Dry Salting are two techniques that have changed little since those early years when Lion Gardiner first cast an eye on his beautiful Gardiner's Island. I've seen them used, however, only in fishing camps in Northern Canada. These are presented here more as historical curiosities than as practical procedures.

PICKLE SALTING: This is a preservation process in which fish are salted down in layers in a watertight container and then cured in the liquid (called pickle) that collects around them. The salty product is not to everyone's taste, but the method does keep fish like cod, pollock, mackerel, striped bass, salmon, mullet, herring, alewife and shad edible for long periods of time by gradually withdrawing moisture from their flesh. The traditional receptacle is the old-fashioned, well-seasoned wooden barrel, or a large stoneware crock. If you're processing only a few fish, an institutional-size glass mayonnaise jar or unchipped, oversize enamel clam steamer will do nicely.

Scale the fish; dress small fish by cutting them down the back, leaving the belly portion intact; fillet larger fish without skinning them, but leave on the collarbones to make the pieces easier to handle. To permit the salt to penetrate thicker fillets more deeply, make ½-inch-deep cuts about 2 inches apart on the flesh side, without cutting through to the skin.

Wash the fish thoroughly and, to rid them of blood, soak them for 30 to 40 minutes in a weak salt solution (make by mixing ½ cup pickling or kosher salt with one gallon of water), then drain 15 minutes. Give the bottom of the container a sprinkle of salt, then dredge each fish in salt, rubbing it into the slashes. Pack the fish skin-side-down in layers facing in perpendicular directions with as much salt as will cling to them. Keep the layers as level as possible . . . if necessary, put 2 small fish together to equal a larger one.

The amount of salt you will need will vary. Pickling or dairy salt goes farther than kosher salt. More salt is needed in summer than in winter. Fat fish should be more heavily salted than lean ones. In general, a light pickle will require about one pound of salt to each 10 pounds of fish; for a heavier pickle, 3 pounds of salt for the same amount of fish will be about right.

Set a clean plate or board on top of the fish and weight it down with clean, round stones or a casserole filled with cans of produce. The pickle will form automatically. The length of time needed for curing, for the salt to thoroughly penetrate the fish, cannot be predicted with any exactness—thin fillets may be ready in a couple of days—fatter fish may require 10 days; fine weather means a shorter cure—stormy weather usually prolongs the time the fish must stay in the brine.

When the center of the thickest fish is thoroughly infused with salt, remove the fish and scrub them under running water with a stiff brush. For long-term storage, repack them in the container with a light sprinkling of salt between the layers. Refill the container with a saturated solution made by mixing one cup of salt with one gallon of water, then store in a cool, dark place. Pickle-salted fish will keep as long as 9 months after a heavy cure, provided the temperature in the storage place stays cool. Remove and change the brine solution after three months, unless signs of fermentation—bubbles or scum—show up earlier. In this case change the brine immediately. To use the fish, soak for 8 to 12 hours in fresh water.

DRY SALTING: Dry salting is a process similar to, but even older than, pickle salting. Here, lean, fresh salt-dredged fish (classically cod) are layered alternately with additional salt, but the pickle that forms is drained and pressed off. After an initial curing period of a week or 10 days, the fish are scrubbed free of salt and then hung in a shady place to dry thoroughly in the open air.

This preservation method is risky because chances for success are so dependent on fair weather. Only the freshest fish should be used, and these should be readied for salting as soon as possible after catching and carefully handled at every step along the way.

Prepare the fish by scaling and filleting as you would for pickle salting, or scale and split them, removing the backbone; in either case, leave the collarbone intact. Scrub well under running water, then allow to soak for 20 minutes in a brine made by dissolving one cup of salt in one gallon of fresh water. Drain well.

Dredge the fish in pickling salt and stack them in staggered layers on a raised wooden platform or in a container with holes in the bottom and on the sides to permit the pickle that forms to drain off. Take care to pile fish only 12 layers high and to stack all fish skin-side-down except for those in the top layers. Sprinkle salt generously between the layers (you will need a total of about one pound of salt for each 4 pounds of fish). Cure fish in shade loosely covered with cheesecloth.

Depending on the size and thickness of the fish but principally on the weather, the cure will take from 1 to 2 weeks. A succession of fine days with low humidity will expedite the process. During this time shield the fish from insects and other marauders by moving them indoors each night. Press out as much moisture as possible before repiling them outside the next day.

When the curing process is over, scrub the fish to remove all salt residue, then drain for 20 minutes. Make a drying stack by stapling or nailing wire mesh to a wooden frame. Place this in an airy open shed with good cross-ventilation, out of direct sunlight.

Set the fish on the racks skin-side-down, and turn them three or four times the first day. Stack them inside each night in 2-foot-high piles off the floor, especially if the weather is damp or an overnight dew is expected. See that the fish are always arranged skin-side-down except for the top layer, and weighted evenly to press out any liquid.

To dry properly, the fish will need at least six days of shaded exposure to the open air in good weather. To test whether the drying has been sufficiently long, squeeze the fleshiest part of a fish between thumb and forefinger. If no imprint remains, you may wrap the fish individually in waxed paper, pack into wooden boxes and store in a cool, dry place.

Dried salted fish will need to be soaked in liquid—fresh water or milk—before it can be used. The amount of time this will take depends on how heavily it was salted during the cure. In general, a lightly salted piece of dried fish should be soaked for 12 hours, while a stiffly dried, very salty fish will need a full 24 hours or even more.

PICKLED FISH

I can think of no finer palate-tickler than pickled fish. The tender, slightly chewy texture, the sharp prickle of vinegar and pickling spice, the satisfying subtaste of salt, the illusive sweetness, the crunch of onion rings, the winey sauces, to my mind combine to produce a near-perfect eating experience.

While in general pickling refers to curing foods with salt in amounts sufficient to draw out moisture (dry salting) or soaking in concentrated salt and water solution (brining), the pickled fish of culinary legend always involves vinegar as well.

Almost any foodfish can be pickled, but members of the herring tribe—Atlantic, blueback, alewife and shad—seem to be the heavy favorites, with mackerel, mullet, salmon, eel, and such shellfish as oysters, clams, mussels and scallops close runners-up.

BASIC PICKLED FISH

The basic recipe for pickling your own fish or shellfish will require the same pure pickling or kosher salt and fresh drinking water indispensable in dry salting or brining, plus distilled *white* vinegar, customary because of its purity and standardized acetic acid content. Have on hand also a variety of pickling spices and fresh or dried herbs, sugar and such vegetables as onions, garlic and carrots.

You'll need a large stoneware crock or wide-mouthed gallon-size glass jar, or plastic bucket; a sharp supple knife for cleaning the fish; a wide-mouthed, earthenware crock or several glass jars (canning jars are ideal) for storing the fish after pickling; and such standard culinary amenities as a large stainless-steel pot for cooking the brine or fish (or both), a wooden spoon or two for mixing ingredients, glass graduates or cups for measuring them, and so on.

To ready whole herring for pickling—scale, behead and gut the fish, taking care to remove the dark streak that runs along the backbone. Or substitute fillets if you prefer. Wash the fish thoroughly and drain well, then pack loosely in a crock or jar. Mix together a brine made up of ¾ cup pickling salt and 2 cups distilled white vinegar for each quart of water used. Pour this over the fish, making sure there is enough liquid to completely cover. Place in a cool (40 to 50 degrees F.) storage space to soak for at least 48 hours—considered the safe minimum—or up to 7 days. As is so often true, experience is the last important ingredient—and the most difficult to obtain.

Now for the tricky part. Knowing just when to whisk your fish from the brine depends on the size of your fish, the temperature of the liquid and so on. The aim is to keep the fish immersed long enough to cure them, but not so long that the skin begins to wrinkle or lose color. Should either of these problems develop, immediately remove the fish from the brine.

Once the fish have undergone the initial pickling they may be further processed as your recipe indicates. Simply freshen by soaking in cold water for 10 hours, or overnight, before using.

If you prefer not to use the fish at once, keep them for 3 weeks by storing as follows: Repack the fish in the crock or jar more tightly than before, scattering salt between the layers. Cover with a diluted brine—¾ cup pickling salt and 2 cups of distilled white vinegar mixed with 2 quarts of water. Cover and store in a cool place until needed. Do not use rubber jar rings, which deteriorate when they come into contact with vinegar. Make sure to freshen the pickled fish by soaking in cold water for 10 hours or overnight before using.

PICKLED FISH WITH ORANGES

◆

To prepare 6 to 7 pounds of fish

Follow directions for Basic Pickled Fish.

Cut fish into bite-size pieces and pack in jars in layers alternating with crumbled bay leaves and peeled, sliced onions, mustard seeds and black peppercorns. Arrange several seedless orange slices and pieces of cinnamon stick attractively around the sides of each jar. Dissolve 2 tablespoons sugar in 1½ cups water and 3 cups white vinegar, pour over fish and refrigerate 48 hours before using.

HAMPTON'S-GARDEN PICKLED FISH WITH HERBS

◆

To prepare 6 to 7 pounds of fish

Follow directions for Basic Pickled Fish.

Cut fish into bite-size pieces and pack in jars in layers alternating with crumbled bay leaf, minced fresh dill, rosemary and thyme. For 30 minutes, simmer 3 cups white vinegar, 2 tablespoons sugar, 1 tablespoon each whole black peppercorns, mustard seeds, allspice and cloves and 2 teaspoons mustard seeds. Cool the liquid and pour over the fish. Refrigerate 36 hours before serving with dollops of Crème Fraîche.

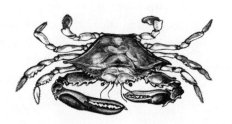

QUICK AND EASY ROLLMOPS

◆

8 Salt herrings
Milk
3 Tablespoons prepared mustard
⅔ Cup minced onion
1 Sweet onion, peeled, sliced and
    separated into rings

16 Small sweet pickles
2 Cups white vinegar
¼ Cup minced parsley
1 Teaspoon dried thyme
2 Teaspoons each whole peppercorns
    and cloves

Soak the herrings in milk overnight. Fillet without skinning and spread each fillet with a teaspoon each mustard and minced onion. Roll up around a small sweet pickle and tie with string. Arrange in a crock and cover with the onion rings.

Bring to a boil the remaining minced onion, the vinegar, parsley, thyme and spices. Pour the hot marinade over the fish and refrigerate for 3 days, turning once or twice a day.

MY FAVORITE PICKLED SALT HERRING

◆

Yield: About 4 quarts

7 Large whole salt herrings, with
    milt or roe, if possible
3½ Cups distilled white vinegar
1 Cup water
1 Tablespoon each black or white
    peppercorns and coriander seeds

4 Medium-size onions, peeled and
    very thinly sliced
2–3 Bay leaves, finely crumbled
1 Whole dried hot chili pepper
1 Cup sour cream

Place herrings in a deep ceramic casserole, crock or jar and cover with cold water. Partially cover and refrigerate for several days, or until the herrings are as salty as you like them, changing the water several times and rinsing the fish well each time. Drain the fish well and clip off fins and tails with kitchen scissors.

Make a very shallow cut from the anal opening forward and carefully remove the insides. Set the milt or roe aside and discard viscera, etc.

Cut the fish into 2-inch pieces.

Bring the vinegar, water and spices to a boil in a glass, stainless-steel or unchipped enamel pan. Boil 5 minutes. Add onion rings and fish and remove from the heat. Cool to room temperature. Remove the onions from the vinegar mixture with a slotted spoon. Place the chili pepper in the ceramic casserole, crock or jar in which the fish were soaked. Arrange half the onion rings and fish on pepper. Sprinkle with crumbled bay leaves. Top with remaining fish and onion rings. Press the creamy milt from their sacs and stir milt into the vinegar mixture. Pour over the fish and onions. Cover with several layers of waxed paper and/or a lid. Invert several times during the next 48 hours if container is watertight. If not, repack the fish once, making sure the top pieces are on the bottom. Serve fish chilled with the onions and a sauce made by stirring ¼ cup pickling liquid into 1 cup sour cream.

SAUCED HERRING

◆

Yield: 2 dozen herring

24 *Small herrings, cleaned*
2½ *Cups white wine*
1 *Cup tomato juice*
2 *Cups white vinegar*
2 *Tablespoons kosher salt*
3 *Medium-size carrots, scraped, notched and sliced*
4 *Medium-size onions, peeled and thinly sliced*
3 *Sprigs each fresh dill and parsley*
1 *Bay leaf*
1 *Tablespoon each fresh, minced sage and thyme (or 1 teaspoon dried)*
18 *Peppercorns*

Arrange the herrings in a single layer in stainless-steel pan (or two) large enough to hold them. Bring the remaining ingredients to a boil in a stainless-steel or glass saucepan and boil until the vegetables are barely tender. Pour this boiling marinade over the herrings and cook for 10 minutes over very low heat so that the liquid barely "shivers." Arrange the fish in a dish, pour the marinade over and arrange the vegetables attractively on top. Chill overnight. Garnish with very thin lemon slices and serve cold.

PICKLED SALMON, OR GRAVLAX

◆

Scandinavians relish a raw, salt-and-sugar-cured salmon they call *gravlax*. This combination of ingredients and pickling time is most pleasing to me. Experiment, if you like, with more or less salt or sugar, more or less pickling time—until you find the combination that suits your taste. Serve accompanied by the butter-fried fish skin (cut in strips), Mustard Gravlax Sauce, chopped fresh dill, thinly sliced cucumbers, lemon wedges and tiny tumblers of aquavit.

2 *1- to 1½-pound centercut scaled but unskinned salmon fillets*
½ *Cup each salt and sugar*
10–12 *Large sprigs fresh dill*
20 *Coarsely crushed white peppercorns*

Wipe dry the 2 fillets, then rub on all sides with an equal mixture of salt and sugar. Layer the sprigs of dill and the peppercorns between the cut sides of the fillets and tie together loosely on either end with string, then cover the fish with a double thickness of aluminum foil and weight down lightly with unopened cans. Refrigerate for 4 hours.

Pour off the accumulated liquid, rub the outsides of the fillets with more salt and sugar mixture, cover with plastic wrap, weight the fish down lightly again and refrigerate for 2 to 3 days, turning twice. Just before serving, remove the string and skin, cut the fish into thin diagonal slices and serve cold.

SEVICHE

Seviche (pronounced seh-veech-ee) is a delicate, fresh-tasting fish dish traditionally marinated in fresh citrus juices instead of vinegar. In this easiest of all pickling methods, seafood is immersed in lemon or lime juice until it is quite literally "cooked" by the citric acid . . . turned firm, snowy white and unusually delicious within 24 hours. The dish originated in Peru, where the classic seafood combination is *corvina*, a kind of weakfish, and bay scallops. In the Hamptons I've experimented with very nearly every native fish, excluding blowfish. As with so many ethnic favorites there is no standard recipe, but there are standard ingredients. You may use almost any lean fish (and even a few fatty ones), lemon or lime juice, sliced onion rings, black peppercorns, red pepper flakes, and bay leaves. Vary the amounts of basic ingredients and add additional spices and flavorings to suit yourself or follow one of the recipes below. In either case, be sure to allow your Seviche to marinate in the refrigerator in a stoneware or glass container for at least 5 or 6 or up to 24 hours. Drain and serve as an hors d'oeuvre.

SPRINGS SEVICHE I

◆

Yield: Enough to serve 6

Traditionally lime juice alone is used, but I've experimented with citrus combinations with fine results.

1½ Pints scallops

½ Cup fresh lime juice

2 Each lemons and oranges, juiced

4 Small white onions, peeled, sliced and separated into rings

1 Teaspoon sugar

1½ Teaspoons salt

White pepper

Tabasco

2 Tablespoons olive oil

Cover the scallops with the lime, lemon and orange juice. Press the onion rings over the top. Cover the dish and refrigerate 5 to 6 hours, or overnight, turning the fish once or twice. Add remaining ingredients except oil and refrigerate one hour longer. Add oil and serve with drinks or on cupped lettuce leaves as a first course.

SEVICHE II
◆

1½ Pounds flounder fillets
⅓ Cup fresh lime juice
3 Lemons, juiced
2 Teaspoons each salt and sugar
1½ Teaspoons pepper
3 Medium-size tomatoes, peeled,
    seeded and coarsely chopped
1 Avocado, peeled, pitted and cut
    into ½-inch cubes

4 Scallions, each with 3 inches of
    green tops, chopped
1 Tablespoon each fresh coriander or
    parsley, minced
Tabasco to taste
2 Tablespoons olive oil

Cut the fish into 1-inch cubes and marinate in the citrus juices for 5 to 6 hours. Stir in remaining ingredients except oil and marinate at least one hour longer. Add oil and serve.

For a nice variation to the above, add 2 canned jalapeño chilies and ¼ cup pimento, both minced. Omit the Tabasco.

HAWAIIAN LORNI LORNI
◆

This is a Hawaiian friend's South Seas version of Seviche.

1½ Pounds salmon fillets, cut into
    long, narrow strips
4 Limes, juiced
2 Oranges, juiced
4 Scallions, each with 2 inches of
    green tops, thinly sliced

Salt and pepper to taste
Tabasco (a generous amount)
2 Tablespoons salad oil
1 Lime, cut into thin slices

Marinate the salmon 5 to 6 hours in lime and orange juices. Drain and combine with the remaining ingredients except the oil. Chill several hours. Add oil and serve on lettuce surrounded by lime slices.

AKU AKU SEVICHE
◆

In Thor Heyerdahl's fascinating account of his first South Seas adventure on Aku Aku, he mentions a marinated fish concoction put together by a friendly cannibal. The original combination of ingredients—fish, coconut milk, lime juice and sea water—so intrigued me that I tried it out before I finished reading the book. This is an easy version that doesn't involve such hard-to-get ingredients as the coconut milk or seawater; however, if these are available, by all means use them.

12 Very small, thin flounder or
    fluke fillets
5 Limes, juiced
2 Oranges, juiced
1 Tablespoon sea salt

2 Tablespoons canned coconut cream
Tabasco sauce
4 Small white onions, peeled and
    very thinly sliced

Score the fillets without cutting through and cover them with the citrus juices. Refrigerate overnight. Add the salt, coconut cream and Tabasco and cover with the separated onion rings. Cover and refrigerate 6 hours longer, then taste and add more salt, coconut cream and Tabasco to suit your taste. Refrigerate again overnight. When the fish is white all the way through, drain and serve on lettuce leaves topped with onion rings.

SPICY PICKLED OYSTERS

◆

Yield: 3 dozen oysters

Plump oysters, red-hot and tart, wake up appetites and accompany drinks with aplomb.

36 Oysters
¼ Cup water
1 Tablespoon lemon juice
½ Teaspoon salt
¾ Cup olive oil
2 Large cloves garlic, peeled and crushed

½ Teaspoon Szechwan peppers
2 Jalapeño chili peppers, seeded, cut into thin slivers and drained well
⅓ Cup mild vinegar

Simmer the oysters in the water, lemon juice, salt and oyster juices for one minute. Strain and reserve juices. Discard any bits of shell and fry the oysters in the hot oil one minute on each side. Remove with a slotted spoon and set aside. Add the garlic, Szechwan peppers and chili peppers to the oil in the pan and fry for 2 minutes. Place oysters, oyster juices, vinegar and peppered oil in a jar. Cover and refrigerate overnight, turning the jar occasionally to pickle evenly. Serve at room temperature on individual small wooden skewers or large toothpicks.

GARDINER'S BAY SWEET AND SOUR PORGIES

◆

Yield: Enough to serve 6

Cornstarch
12 Very small porgy fillets or 6 small ones cut in half lengthwise
Oil for deep-frying
½ Cup white wine vinegar

¼ Cup soy sauce
3 Tablespoons sugar
2 Teaspoons dry red pepper
1 Onion, peeled, vertically sliced and separated

Work cornstarch into the fish flesh and deep-fry in hot oil until crispy and light brown. Drop the hot fish into the mixed vinegar, soy sauce, sugar, red pepper and onion and refrigerate for not less than one hour and not more than 3 days.

OLD COUNTRY POTTED ANCHOVIES

◆

Yield: 24 fish

These small fish are very tart and spicy—a terrific addition to a summer buffet. And they keep for months in the refrigerator.

2 Dozen whole fresh anchovies, or
   other very small fish, cleaned
¾ Cup kosher salt
4 Tablespoons whole cloves
3 Tablespoons whole allspice

3 Tablespoons sugar
Cider vinegar
Sour cream (optional)
Scallions with 3 inches green top

Preheat oven to 350 degrees F.

Clean the fish as for pan-frying, as directed on page 16. Roll them in salt and pack tightly in an ovenproof casserole, sprinkling the spices in as you go along. Dissolve the sugar in enough vinegar to cover the fish. Pour this over, then cover the pot and bake for 6 hours. Refrigerate. Serve the fish as they are or with sour cream mixed with finely chopped scallions.

PATCHOGUE DEVILED HERRING

◆

6 Herrings (8–10 inches long), cleaned
1 Tablespoon each whole cloves,
   black peppercorns, mace and dried
   red pepper

½ Cup minced celery
¾ Cup each white vinegar and water

Preheat oven to 350 degrees F.

Arrange the herrings in an ovenproof baking dish large enough to hold them in a single layer. Bring remaining ingredients to a boil, boil 5 minutes and pour over the fish. Bake 8 minutes. Cool in the liquid. Refrigerate several hours or overnight. Serve cold in the liquid.

SWEET AND SOUR HERRING

◆

Follow directions for Deviled Herring but add one cup light-brown sugar to the marinade prior to boiling and boil 3 minutes longer (8 minutes altogether).

ESCABÈCHE OF SMALL FISH

◆

In Spain the small fish used are generally fresh anchovies or sardines, but you may use whatever is available.

2 Pounds very small fresh fish (any
   one variety)
Flour
2 Cups oil
Salt to taste
2 Large cloves garlic, peeled
1 Medium-size carrot, scraped,
   scored and thinly sliced

1 Cup white vinegar
½ Cup white wine
2 Small, hot red peppers
¼ Teaspoon dried thyme
1 Bay leaf

Dry the fish, dust with flour and fry in the smoking oil until golden. Remove from the pan, drain, arrange in an attractive serving dish and sprinkle with salt to taste. Reheat the oil, add the garlic and carrot and fry 2 to 3 minutes. Lower the heat somewhat, add remaining ingredients and cook at a low boil for 10 minutes. Pour the marinade and vegetables over the fish and chill overnight or up to 2 weeks. Serve at room temperature as an hors d'oeuvre.

SMOKED FISH

Rarely have I enjoyed an in-depth food-testing spree as much as I have experimenting with the smoky delicacies in this book. There is something positively magical about turning ordinary fish into burnt-umber works of culinary art. No matter how humble your ingredients, no matter how unsure your technique, most likely the smoke will work its small miracle to produce absolutely beautiful, thoroughly professional-looking and -tasting masterpieces. If your aim is to impress guests, this trick will do it every time.

Hot smoking is my favorite because it's a snap to do even on an apartment terrace, takes only a couple of hours, and the fish remain succulent and moist under their golden cloaks. But for country dwellers, particularly those who live along the coast where fish are available, cold smoking is equally intriguing and a good deal more lasting. Drying is the oldest of all food-preservation techniques, but smoking has been a major means of preserving protein foods ever since it first dawned on Neolithic cooks that smoke from the smudge pots burning under their drying racks not only speeded drying but produced foods greatly improved in flavor and texture. Although modern refrigeration methods and a readily available fresh-food supply have made superfluous the smokehouse that was once a necessity on every American farm, dedicated do-it-yourself gourmets are discovering the ease of preparing and joy of eating their own tawny, smoked-to-perfection meat, fish and game.

As mentioned, there are two ways to smoke food: the hot-smoking and the cold-smoking techniques. Both of these continue a curing and flavoring process that usually begins with dry salting or soaking in brine. The difference between them is the temperature at which the food is smoked and the length of time the food must remain in the smoker.

Hot smoking is really smoke cooking, since high temperatures—120 to 180 degrees F.—result in end products that need little or no further cooking or preparation. Unfortunately, hot-smoked foods, although delicious and wonderfully simple to prepare, cannot be kept for any length of time. Dine on them at once, or refrigerate them for use within a few days as you would ordinary leftovers. (Some foods may be preserved for future enjoyment by freezing or canning them, but neither process is really applicable for smoked fish, since home-canning them can be dangerous and freezing generally results in a soggy, unpleasant finished product.)

In cold smoking, the food is exposed to smoke temperatures ranging from 70 to 90 degrees F. for varying periods of time. It is a curing rather than a cooking process. How long a food will keep after being cold-smoked depends on two important factors: the strength of the brine or amount of salt in which it was dried before smoking; and, more importantly, the length of time—hours, days, weeks—the food was kept in the smokehouse. Generally, the longer the exposure to smoke at low temperatures, the greater the keeping qualities of the food.

What actually takes place during smoking is that the smoke produces chemicals that penetrate deep into the foods to give them their characteristic color and flavor. In long periods of cold smoking, these same chemicals also kill off or effectively neutralize the yeasts, molds and bacteria that would otherwise cause the food to spoil.

PREPARING FISH FOR SMOKING

The first rule here, as in any fish cooking, is to buy the freshest fish possible, or to catch your own and store it properly. Follow the suggestions on pages 9 to 14 for keeping your catch fresh or for choosing peak specimens from your fish dealer. Handle the fish very carefully at every step of the cleaning and dressing process, and be sure to keep them refrigerated right up until the time curing begins.

There are several ways to prepare fish for smoking. Once the initial cleaning—scaling and gutting—is out of the way, fish may be left whole if small, or if large, split, cut into chunks, steaks or fillets. Fish weighing less than one pound may be "gibbed" (a small cut is made just below the gills, and gills and guts together are pulled out, leaving the body otherwise intact). I like the look of a whole, smoked fish but if you don't, by all means—off with their heads!

If behead you must—when preparing small fish, do so without removing the bony collarbone just beneath the gills. This makes an ideal "handle" through which an S-hook or steel wire can be threaded, should you wish to hang up the fish at any point during processing. Bigger fish may be split along the back and flattened slightly, leaving the belly skin to hold the two sides together. It is best not to remove the skin from any fish or piece of fish intended for the smokehouse, since this not only helps hold the flesh together but diminishes shrinkage.

FUELS FOR SMOKING: Hardwoods are the only ones to use. While wood from fruit trees—apple, pear and cherry—have the most flavorful smoke, wood from almost any tree that sheds its leaves in winter will work very well. Avoid soft, resinous woods like pines, spruce, hemlock, balsam, cedar, etc., that keep their needles all year long. These impart an unpleasant flavor. Remove the bark from birch wood so that the tiny carbon and pitch particles do not cling to your smoker and its contents. The wood you burn may be small twigs, chips, shavings or sawdust and, since the idea is to generate dense smoke rather than heat, whatever you use need not be completely dry. Use kindling or charcoal to start the fire, then as soon as this reaches the glowing-ember stage, smother it with any of the above. If the fire should flare up too much during the process, dampen the fuel slightly.

OTHER EQUIPMENT FOR THE SMOKEHOUSE: In addition to the sharp knife or knives essential to the proper cleaning and dressing of fish, other items you will need are:

· An assortment of large, nonmetallic containers for curing the fish. These may be glass, earthenware or plastic.
· An oven thermometer. Smoking temperatures are hard to control, but with this important piece of equipment you will at least know whether they are too low or too high.
· Wooden or plastic spoons for preparing or stirring brine mixtures. Do not use metal spoons, which may react with the brine ingredients.
· Materials for suspending fish during drying or smoking. Steel wire hangers bent into S-hooks and string or twine are all suitable.

It may not sound easy—but it is.

HOT SMOKING

There are a number of small, convenient-to-use hot smokers on the market and, since the process is so easy, most of these perform well. Follow directions for brining and drying given on page 44 in the cold smoking section (but cut the times in half), then further consult the directions for use that accompany your smoker. These generally involve building a wood fire under a pan of water designed to moderate temperature and catch any fats. Foods are placed on racks or hooks above the water.

COLD SMOKING

Cold smoking is a three-step process comprised of brining, drying and smoking.

BRINING: Brining consists of presoaking the fish in a mixture of salt, seasonings and water, or lightly rubbing a mixture of dry salt and seasonings over the surface of the fish. Either cure will reduce the moisture content of fish flesh, help curb the formation of or destroy microorganisms that cause spoilage, and supply flavor.

Commercial smokehouses use a salinometer (salt-measuring instrument) for consistent quality when brining their products, but in lieu of this, a brine strong enough to counter spoilage organisms can be produced simply by adding 1½ cups pickling or kosher salt to each gallon of water used.

The length of time the fish needs to be kept in the brine depends on the size and thickness of the fish being cured, as well as how salty you want the end product to be. This, like the combination of flavoring ingredients that goes into making up a brine, is a matter of personal taste and can be varied simply by increasing or decreasing the amount of time the fish remains in the brine. A short soaking—about 30 minutes for a very thin fillet—will produce a mild cure. Fish or pieces of fish that are one-inch thick will reach a medium cure in 2 to 3 hours. In general, you may figure on 1 to 4 hours of brine cure for fillets, steaks or split fish, 5 hours or more for fish over 5 pounds. These brining times, incidentally, apply only to lean, non-oily fish. When curing fat fish such as herring, mackerel, salmon, sturgeon, dogfish and so on, increase brining time by 25 percent. Reduce brining time by 25 percent if you score thick pieces of fish with a knife to speed penetration.

In dry curing, the dry-cure mixture is lightly rubbed over all sides of the fish, both inside and out, to form a thin coating. The fish is then cured in the refrigerator for 5 to 8 hours, total time depending here, as in brining, on thickness and desired degree of saltiness.

When long-term storage is not a consideration, you can greatly improve the flavor of your smoked fish by using a marinade instead of a brine or dry cure. Experiment with lime, lemon (or other fruit juice), vinegar or wine combined with water, sugar, olive oil, garlic and other herbs and spices, but whatever combinations you use, keep the following suggestions in mind:

1. Use only pickling or kosher salt.
2. The ideal brine is a salt solution in a ratio of 1½ cups pickling or kosher salt to each gallon of water.
3. Prepare only one particular type of fish at a time and, ideally, fish of nearly the same size.

4. Make sure that each piece of fish being brined is completely submerged for the required time. Weight the batch down, if necessary, with a plate topped with clean stones kept for this purpose or a casserole filled with cans of tinned produce. If soaking time required extends past two hours, turn the pieces at this point or stir the mixture thoroughly with a wooden spoon.
5. Keep both fish and brine cool. Refrigerate the fish in the container or, if the container is too large, surround it with ice.

DRYING: Drying is the next step in the smoking process. Remove each piece of fish from the brine, give it a light rinse in fresh water, and then set it aside to dry thoroughly. Drying may take place in a cool, shaded, screened-in outdoor area if the day is fine, or indoors in a dry room or garage if the weather is bad or likely to be. You may hang the fish up for drying, or arrange it skin-side-down on wire racks, but be sure in either case that air can circulate freely around each piece or fish. An electric fan will considerably speed the indoor drying process. When drying out-of-doors, be sure to keep the fish protected from sun and insects at all times.

Generally, the drying process takes several hours and is complete when a shiny "skin" or pellicle forms over the entire surface. Fish smoked before they are totally dry will require a longer period in the smoker to reach the desired texture and flavor, and there is a possibility the surface may look blotchy rather than sleek and glossy.

SMOKING: It is a good idea to have a low, smoldering fire going in the smokehouse or smoker well before the fish are transferred there. Ideally, fish should go direct from drying racks to smoking racks, where temperatures ranging from 70 degrees F. to 85 degrees F. are already being maintained.

When the aim in cold smoking is to preserve the fish for a long period of time rather than merely flavor it, smoke temperatures should not be permitted to go above 85 degrees F. Keep an eye on the thermometer. Cold smoking preserves fish by slowly and steadily removing all moisture to vastly increase keeping qualities, so a light smoke should be constantly present. It is far better to err on the side of too much smoking than take a chance that your fish may not be properly smoked.

Nibble a sample from time to time to see if your fish has reached the color, texture and smoky flavor that please you. If this happens before curing time is up, continue the drying by keeping the fire going without generating any smoke. On the other hand, if the fish is sufficiently dry but lacking in color and smoky taste, heap extra hardwood on the fire to quickly produce additional smoke.

In general, the keeping qualities of cold-smoked fish are directly proportional to the length of smoking time. Fish properly cold-smoked for 24 hours will usually keep about two weeks; those exposed to temperatures below 90 degrees F. for two days will be safe to eat for four weeks; three to five days' exposure will preserve a catch from two to six months.

While fish cold-smoked for several days will keep at room temperature for a period of time, it's safest to wrap each fish or piece individually in plastic wrap or aluminum foil and store at 32 to 40 degrees F.

HOW TO BUILD A SMOKEHOUSE: In order to cold smoke fish, you will need a smokehouse. This may be simple or elaborate, store-bought or home-constructed. An electric smoker is efficient, reliable, and can be used for hot smoking as well as cold smoking, but most models can only handle small amounts of food at one time and all require electricity to operate. If you are at all handy, you can easily build your own smokehouse using relatively inexpensive materials.

Cold smoking works best on the old-time smokehouse principle of burning the fire at some distance from the food, so that by the time the smoke reaches the food, most of the heat has already been dissipated. Ideally, then, a smokehouse consists of three basic units: a fire pit in which the fire is kept going, a smoke chamber where the food is smoked, and a tunnel to connect the two.

The fire pit may be simply a hole in the ground lined with good-size rocks or a much more carefully designed structure. Dig it about 2 to 2½ feet deep, about 10 to 12 feet away from where the smoke chamber is to go and on the side from which the prevailing winds are most likely to come. Give the pit a cover of some kind—a piece of sheet metal is ideal, although a wooden board covered with flattened tin cans will also do—to act as a damper to regulate air intake and control the size of the fire in the pit. Leave an opening about 6 inches in diameter on one side of the pit for the smoke tunnel connection.

The reason for putting the smoke tunnel underground is to cool the smoke en route to the smoke chamber. To construct the tunnel, dig a trench about 6 inches wide from the fire pit to where the smoke chamber will be and line it with stovepipe or terra-cotta tile, using an elbow section of pipe, if necessary, to complete the connection. Place boards over the pipe or tile, then refill the trench with earth to ground level.

The type of smoke chamber you end up with will probably depend on what you happen to have on hand. Successful smokers have been made from old chests of drawers, large metal trunks or kitchen cabinets, clean 50-gallon metal drums, new oversize metal garbage cans, and the old-time, one-door type of refrigerator—in short, anything but a wooden barrel, whose staves may dry out and open after prolonged exposure to heat. Should you eventually decide to make smoking fish a permanent part of your culinary repertoire, you might even want to invest in materials for a sturdier structure—one of tin- or aluminum-lined plywood, for instance, or even a masonry smoking shed.

A smoke chamber should be large enough to accommodate the products being smoked, plus a door or opening for easy access. It should also be equipped with some kind of draft control that can be opened or closed as necessary. Other essential features are crosspieces or hooks for hanging fish or shelves or trays to hold them during the smoking process. The best material for any of these fixtures is stainless steel, but in any case be sure that you do not use galvanized wire, copper or brass—these metals give off noxious oxides during smoking.

STUFFING SAUSAGE CASINGS

Soak salted natural casings (available at most fine butcher shops or meat counters) in warm water for 30 minutes, changing the water several times. Insert one or two fingers into one end of each casing to separate the sides. Hold under warm running water to rinse. If casing has an inner membrane, remove it. Drain on paper towels.

BY HAND: Slip wet casing over the spout of your funnel and slide the entire length up onto spout. Pack sausage ingredients into funnel spout with the handle of a wooden spoon. When sausage mixture reaches the end of the spout, pull casing out one inch and tie off with white thread. Stuff casings loosely (cooking expands the filling). Tie off in preferred lengths.

BY MACHINE: Slip open end of wet casing over outside of the stuffer nozzle of your mixer or grinder. Force sausage mixture through to end of tube. Pull out one inch of casing and tie off with white thread. Stuff casings loosely (cooking expands the filling). Tie off in preferred lengths.

EAST END SEAFOOD SAUSAGES

◆

Yield: About 2 dozen medium size—3-inch— or 3 dozen smaller— 2-inch—sausages

These are so delicately delicious, so versatile a main ingredient about which to build an array of imaginative dishes, that you'll wonder why they are so difficult to find anywhere except in your own backyard.

3 Pounds chilled firm white fish like monkfish, sand shark, whiting, perch, etc.

1 Pound cooked, shelled and cleaned shrimp (optional)

½ Teaspoon each saffron threads, white pepper, nutmeg and thyme

1 Medium onion, peeled and coarsely chopped

1 Tablespoon each salt and slightly crushed coriander seeds

¼ Pound cold, sweet butter, cut in ½-inch pieces

1 Cup dry white bread crumbs

¾ Cup finely crushed ice

Natural casings (available at most fine meat markets)

In your food processor or blender, whirl 1½ pounds of the fish into purée or paste. Scrape into a bowl and refrigerate. Purée the saffron, pepper, nutmeg and thyme with the onion and knead or cut into the puréed fish. Coarsely chop the remaining fish and the shrimp and mix well with the fish-spice purée and the additional spices. Refrigerate overnight.

The next day, knead the bread crumbs, the butter and the ice into the fish mixture. Stuff sausages by hand as directed on page **47** or use the coarse blade to extrude the sausages into moist casings. Tie off in the size you prefer. Smoke as directed.

SESAME SEAFOOD SAUSAGES: Omit the saffron and coriander from the East End Seafood Sausage recipe and substitute 2 tablespoons sesame oil and ½ cup sesame seeds blended to a paste with 3 tablespoons vegetable oil.

SZECHWAN SEAFOOD SAUSAGES: Omit the saffron and the white pepper from the East End Seafood Sausage recipe and add instead 1½ tablespoons Szechwan peppercorns and 2 large, peeled cloves of garlic, both finely crushed.

CURRIED SEAFOOD SAUSAGES: Omit the saffron, white pepper and coriander from the East End Seafood Sausage recipe and substitute 2 tablespoons curry powder mixed to a paste with 3 tablespoons vegetable oil.

HERBED SEAFOOD SAUSAGES: Omit the Szechwan peppercorns from the Szechwan Seafood Sausages and substitute instead 3 tablespoons each fresh rosemary and thyme leaves (or 1 tablespoon dried) and 2 teaspoons coarsely ground fresh black pepper.

SMOKED ROE
◆

Here in the Hamptons, roe in season is easy to come by. The hot-smoking process turns it into a pâté-like spread that's marvelous on toasted rye croutons or thin slices of French bread. The flavor and texture here are so subtle that a too-crunchy or highly seasoned cracker will shatter the effect.

Any roe may be smoked.* Each will produce a slightly different but equally luscious product. Simply wrap roe in bacon to protect and flavor it and hot smoke alone (or without the bacon, tucked in the cleaned fish) for 1½ to 2 hours.

Wrap roe from the thicker end to the slimmer one, leaving a little space in between to allow the smoke to penetrate.

* I don't recommend blowfish roe, since this is considered by some to be poisonous.

FREEZING FISH

Although there is no denying that frozen fish is not quite the equivalent of fresh, when your success as an angler begins to overwhelm your capacity to cook and consume your catch, or when a particular fish is in season and less expensive, freezing becomes eminently practical. Properly packaged and stored at o degrees F. or below, many fish will retain a good deal of their texture and fresh, sweet taste for as long as 6 to 9 months. The secret lies in understanding "proper packaging" and how it applies to the various fish you may encounter in Northeastern coastal waters.

Best candidates for long-term freezing are lean fish with firm white meat. Dark-fleshed fish (bluefish, mackerel, tuna and the like) also freeze well, but since their oil content is high they will be fresher-tasting if their freezer stay is limited to three months or less. Even lean, white fish will quickly decline in quality in the freezer if the following special precautions are not taken.

1. Whether freezing your fish whole or in pieces, as steaks or fillets, be sure to carefully trim away any streaks of blood or dark-red patches. These areas are the first to develop off-flavors in your freezer.

2. It is a good idea to give your fish or piece of fish a 30-second dip in chilled brine (⅔ cup of salt mixed with one gallon ice water) before wrapping. This commercial freezing technique helps prevent darkening during storage and also keeps drip during thawing and cooking to a minimum. When freezing fish in containers (see below), a milder salt-solution—⅓ cup of salt to each gallon of water—is superior to water as a freezing medium, particularly for those specimens with high oil content.

3. The ultimate flavor and quality of your frozen fish depends on the freezer protection you give them. Suitable packaging is any material or procedure that will insulate the fish against the harmful effects of those double demons, freezer burn (caused by moisture loss) and rancidity (caused by exposure to air).

4. Freeze fish in amounts that your freezer can handle efficiently and still remain at o degrees F. or below. Fish must freeze rapidly to retain peak quality. If too many packages are placed in the freezer at the same time, or if these packages are stacked, the necessary quick-freezing may be slowed, and unpleasant changes in texture and flavor may take place.

5. Mark each package or container to indicate kind of fish and date frozen, number of servings, etc. Always use the oldest packages first.

PACKAGING: Fish should be packaged for the freezer in the forms and amounts that best fit your family's needs. Cleaning and dressing your catch—turning it into steaks, fillets or pieces—means that valuable freezer space can be saved.

Ideal freezer wrap is any airtight, moisture-proof material that is also pliable enough to be molded to the fish and strong enough to be puncture- and tear-proof. The aim is not only to eliminate all air from the package but to make sure that none can creep back in during storage.

Of the many moisture-proof and air-resistant wraps, the most effective seem to be heavyweight aluminum foil, coated or laminated freezer papers, and transparent polyethylene film, saran, and polyester films, all of which are either self-sealing or easily secured by freezer tape or wire twists.

To package, begin with a piece of wrap that is considerably larger and wider than the fish or portion to be packaged. Fold snugly over the fish, smoothing with your hands to force out as much air as possible, then seal the seam with a double fold and fold the ends neatly under. Secure with freezer tape, if necessary. When freezing fish in plastic bags, be sure to squeeze out as much air as possible before applying the seal.

Another popular long-term freezing technique is the ice-block method. Place the whole fish or fish portion in a rigid container and add ice water or a chilled mild brine, as directed, to within one inch of the top (the fish must be completely covered). The top space allows for expansion during freezing. Eliminate any air bubbles by running a knife blade around the edges of the container, then cap with top or other airtight covering. Fish frozen this way get double protection—isolated in their beds of ice and secured against evaporation by an airtight seal, they are practically impervious to air or accident. Standard freezer containers with their tight-fitting, snap-on lids are ideal for this, but clean milk cartons, or plastic grocery-product containers, make equally good receptacles.

THAWING: Individual frozen fish or portions may be cooked without thawing by doubling the cooking time as directed in the Canadian cooking method. If your fish has not been dressed, or if you plan to stuff, bread or deep-fry it, thawing is necessary. Thawing is also required when fish are frozen in an ice block as described above. To prevent loss of freshness and flavor, defrost your small fish or fish portions in the refrigerator 24 hours in advance of cooking. (Larger fish or portions may take two days.) Never defrost your fish at room temperature, or the natural proteins will leach away as the ice melts. And remember, even partially frozen fish kept at room temperature deteriorate more quickly than fish kept chilled.

Fish that you plan to stuff or bread need be defrosted only to the point where they are easy to handle. To thaw ice-encased fish, run cold water over the container until contents slide out, then replace under running cold water until the fish is ice-free on the outside. If your recipe requires complete defrosting, place your fish back in its empty container, re-cover with the lid, and set in cold water to within an inch or so from the top. On no account should the fish be allowed to sit directly in water for any length of time, or its flesh will turn soft and unappetizing. Once a fish has been defrosted, it should *never* be refrozen.

FREEZING SHELLFISH

Should you be blessed with an abundance of shellfish, or merely want to postpone eating your catch until a later date, freezing is practical providing you freeze only shellfish that are very fresh and have been refrigerated right up to the moment of freezer preparation.

To freeze raw clams or oysters, shuck and place them, along with their liquor, in serving-size freezer containers, leaving ¼-inch headroom in each pint and ½-inch headroom in each quart. To freeze lobster and crab meat, prepare as you would for using fresh, but cook in a brine made by combining ⅓ cup salt with one gallon water. Remove from the shell when cool, pack into serving-size portions and cover with brine, leaving headroom as above, then seal and freeze. Scallops may be prepared for freezing as you would any fish fillet.

Store frozen shellfish at 0 degrees F. or below, and use within 2 to 3 months. Like fish, shellfish should always be allowed to thaw in the refrigerator.

ICE GLAZING: Ice glazing, a popular commercial process designed to preserve the fresh-caught goodness and flavor of frozen fish, can easily be duplicated at home if freezer settings are kept at 0 degrees or below. The advantage of this method over freezing in containers is that it takes less space.

Clean and dress the fish as for other kinds of freezer storage, arrange in a single layer on a baking sheet or tray (the fish must not touch), cover loosely with aluminum foil or other moisture-proof wrap and freeze one or two trays at a time. As soon as the fish or fish pieces are solidly frozen, quickly dip them one at a time in ice water. A thin coat of ice should immediately form. Repeat this process two or three times until the ice glaze thickens, then, handling each carefully to keep the ice glaze intact, wrap the fish separately and return to 0 degrees or below.

Part Two

R·E·C·I·P·E·S

THE FISHING TOURIST (ON LONG ISLAND) 1892

Taken all in all, I much doubt if there is any locality where the angler may enjoy his favorite pastime with the same luxurious ease as on Long Island. . . . There is no more pleasant or profitable way of spending a two weeks' vacation than to take a horse and wagon, fill it with provender and equipments, and make a round trip of the entire Island, stopping at the various fishing-grounds by the way. The roads are for the most part good; and when the tourist has passed through Babylon, Jerusalem, and Jericho, and left the western half of the island behind him, he will find himself among a community living in primitive simplicity, who have possessed the land for nearly two centuries and a half—upright, God-serving, well-to-do farmers, who go barefoot and eat with silver spoons— men who have seldom traveled beyond the limits of the townships in which they were born, whom cares of state do not perplex, and whose ancestors were the original purchasers of the land from the aboriginal owners, and with whom they always lived in peace. There he will find a remnant of the Indian tribes themselves, and discover traces of their ancient burial grounds and fortifications. He will discover a nomenclature new and strange, and curious geological freaks; ponds with no visible outlets that rise and fall with the tides; sand-hills one hundred feet high that shift with every gale that blows; fantastic cliffs and singular tongues of land; groups of islands, between which the ocean currents set like a mile-race; skeletons of wrecks imbedded in the beach; graveyards with one hundred head-stones sacred to entire ships; crews who perished on the strand.

For fishing Montauk Point is decidedly a region of the first water. Of striped bass and blue fish, in their season, there literally seems to be no end. On a reef near the lighthouse, there have been taken with the net, in the autumn, as many as a thousand bass in a single night; but all along the ocean shore, the bass and blue fish are taken by trolling with an ivory or leaden squid; and, what I have never known elsewhere, both these fish are taken here continually by "heaving and hauling," while standing on the beach. On these occasions the squid is covered with an eel skin, and you throw the bait directly in the surf. The sport is rather laborious but nothing could be better to expand the chest, and there is certainly something quite novel in the idea of dragging your prize by main strength, directly on the smooth white shore. In this manner, on one occasion, I saw two fishermen capture a cart-load of fish in less than one hour, ranging in weight from six to twenty pounds. Another mode of

fishing with the hand-line is to float along the shore in a surf-boat, throwing the bait into the surf as before, while the boatman keeps the little craft in a proper and safe position. The only trouble is, that if you happen to be caught by one of the big waves at the moment of breaking, you may be instantly swamped and drowned. In your excitement, however, you are apt to forget all this; and especially is this the case when, through the pure water, you see the huge fish darting to and fro between the great boulders, which seem to cover the bottom of the ocean immediately around Montauk Point. Black fish, sea bass and paugies, flounders and codfish, may also be taken in this vicinity; but they are not much sought after, when the bass and blue fish are about. Indeed, so abundant are all these varieties, that, during the summer, you may see, at all times of day, a fleet of fishing smacks floating in bird-like beauty upon the neighbouring waters.

. . . A peculiar and fortune-favored people are the Long Islanders, who know how to enjoy life in a quiet way, and do have an unusual variety of its good gifts convenient to their hands. . . . The fertile belt of land which girts the island yields of its abundance—its grain-fields, its gardens, its orchards, and its live-stock. Water-fowl and fresh-water fish throng its ponds and streams, and the broad salt marshes afford an excellent shooting-ground for sportsmen. Beyond them the ocean rolls up its surf on the outer beach, while within the sheltered bays the most delicious fish and shell-fish are found in profusion. The long, level roads offer the rarest opportunities for driving and trotting, and the bays for bathing, boating and yachting.

The James Slip Ferry connects with the Long Island Railroad at Hunter's Point, and the Grand and Roosevelt Ferries with the South Side Railroad. The entire journey to Greenport is made in about four hours.*

◆ ◆

* In 1982 the trip by rail takes three hours . . . an improvement of one hour per hundred years.

AMERICAN
INDIAN DISHES

When the British colonists began to populate the Eastern seaboard of America during the seventeenth century, they found to their surprise that the native inhabitants had considerable cooking skills. These Atlantic Coast Indians were an agricultural people who not only ate a more varied fare than the average European, but were inventive cooks who utilized to the fullest the bounty afforded both by their fertile farmlands and an abundant wilderness.

Not surprisingly, part of this bounty came from the surrounding sea and salt marshes. One seventeenth-century account listed more than two hundred kinds of edible fishes that could be taken with little effort from fertile Long Island and Connecticut waters. Fish so fine, so bountiful that "at the turning of the tyde . . . such multitudes . . . could be seen that . . . it seemed one might goe over their backes dri-shod."

If the deep waters fairly boiled with fish only slightly smaller than sea monsters, the peaceful shallows yielded countless shellfish, including giant crabs a foot long and 6 inches wide and lobsters nearly 6 feet in length (although a contemporary Dutchman remarked of one such giant, "Those a foot long are better for serving at table").

So valuable a food source did the Indians consider our Long Island shores that entire villages visited the shellfish beds on a regular basis to wade in the pure waters of the bays and collect great quantities of fish and shellfish that they cooked in many creative ways. A surprising number of the seafood dishes—and cooking methods—they devised have passed virtually unchanged into the American cooking repertory.

That quintessentially American, ever-popular seaside event, the clambake, undoubtedly originated as the shore-dwelling Indian's solution to the problem of feeding a crowd without benefit of fire-resistant pots or pans. The Indians dug a deep pit in the sand, lined it with stones, started a fire at the bottom, layered fish, shellfish, unshucked ears of corn and sweet potatoes in their jackets over the hot stones—all neatly tucked in between layers of freshly gathered seaweed—then covered the food over with more seaweed and sand and slowly steamed it to perfection. The technique—and ingredients—the Indians used have scarcely changed from that day to this.

Another fish-cookery method the Indians resourcefully designed to make up for the absence of flameproof pots was the trick of broiling foods at the end of sweet sapling sticks, a technique often described as the forerunner of the barbecue. All along the seacoast, Indian tribes found this a convenient way to cook fish, particularly the eels that were so popular.

As a seaside population, the Indians of the East Coast produced their own creditable version of chowder, probably utilizing nut milks and butters. As befitted an agricultural people whose farming skills were far superior to those of sixteenth- and seventeenth-century Europeans, they knew how to combine the fish and shellfish they took from the salt marshes and bays with the harvest of vegetables and seasonings they reaped from their fertile fields or foraged for in marsh and woodland. An Iroquois favorite, for instance, was a fish soup known as *u'nega'gei'*, prepared by boiling fish of any kind in a quantity of water (brought to the boiling point by dropping heated stones into a leakproof vessel), removing the fish and stirring in coarse corn siftings to the desired consistency. In season, wild onions and other freshly gathered greens would add their woodsy flavors. Botanist John Bartram described the contents of three great kettles of corn soup "or thin hominy" served at an Iroquois feast in 1743, as soup "with dry'd eels and other fish boiled in it."

Fish of different kinds might also be added in season to the local variation of succotash, the universal Indian dish found in its different manifestations from coast to coast. We tend to think of sweetened corn and lima beans as the only ingredients used by the Indians in preparing this nourishing mixture, and very often this was true, but "succotash" in the language of the Narragansett Indians also meant "fragments," and Indian cooks generally treated the dish as a stew that included whatever happened to be on hand. Since fish was most often handy, into the pot it went to be cooked underground with the vegetables.

Just as they knew the ways of animals in the forests and how to trap them, the Indians knew the best places to fish and used the same fishing techniques that commercial fishermen use today. They constructed weirs and traps from reeds and vines, many of which were designed to stay in place year after year. They also used hooks and lines and nets to catch fish, and were incredibly adept at spearing fish with wooden poles sharpened at one end. These were thrown, according to one astonished English observer, "after the maner as Irishmen cast dartes," from rowboats or while wading in shallow waters.

Among the immense colonies of bivalves lining Long Island bays and inland waters, oysters were the great favorites, followed closely by clams. The Indians preferred the softshells but also relished skimmers and hardshells. The shells of Quahogs—from the Narragansett Indian *poquaûhock* —were used for wampum beads and belts. They also enjoyed periwinkles and, to a somewhat lesser extent, mussels.

The East Coast Indians had learned, probably through hard experience, the dangers of eating their shellfish raw and, in fact, most tribes overcooked them, boiling the freshly gathered oysters, clams and mussels for 5 or 6 hours. The Pilgrims, on the other hand, were not so cautious during their first encounter with America's vast seafood resources. Suffering from scurvy and malnutrition and ravenous for fresh food after their three-month Atlantic crossing, the Mayflower passengers fell upon the raw clams and "very fat" mussels they found in Provincetown Harbor. The mussels they ate during this first landfall before their eventual landing at Plymouth ". . . [caused] all to cast and scoure," but these very bivalves found in profusion along Massachusetts Bay were the foods that later sustained the starving settlers during their first devastating winter in America. City-dwellers all, the Pilgrims had neglected to bring with them the hooks and nets they needed for fishing, and were reduced to foraging along the shore for their food supply—primarily the abundant clam that they consumed in such quantity that first year that these were given the nickname "Pilgrim's bread."

Our early colonists could not have survived without the Indians' help, and wisely, the Pilgrims sought and signed a treaty that first spring with the Massachusetts Bay tribes—guaranteeing not only peace but the benefit of the Indians' wilderness expertise. The Pilgrims' famous Indian benefactor Squanto showed them how to build weirs and traps to catch alewives during their annual spring spawning runs, and also taught them the Indian practice of using surplus fish as fertilizer—three fish to each hillock laid out spokewise, their heads to the center—for their cornfields. They learned their lessons well, and eventually these early colonists ate a greater variety of fish than we eat today, cooking them mostly in Indian ways.

BAKED BLUEFISH WITH CORNMEAL AND NANNYBERRY STUFFING

◆

Yield: Enough to serve 6-8

1 *6–7-pound Bluefish*

1 *Large leek, well washed and coarsely chopped*

2 *Tablespoons Nut Butter (or cow's butter)*

1 *Cup nannyberries (wild raisins from a spring-flowering viburnum) or currants*

1 *Cup fine corn meal*

3 *Cups cold fish stock (or water)*

1 *Cup sunflower seeds, toasted*

Clean the fish, remove the backbone but leave the skin intact (see page 18). Heat the nut butter or cow's butter in a large nonstick pan. Stir the leeks over medium heat until wilted, add the berries and corn meal and cook, stirring, for 5 minutes. Pour in 2 cups of the stock and cook over medium heat, stirring frequently for 30 minutes, or until the stock is absorbed. Stir in the sunflower seeds and stuff the fish with half the corn-meal stuffing.

Preheat the oven to 350 degrees F.

Spread the remaining stuffing over the bottom of an ovenproof dish that is just large enough to hold the fish. Arrange the fish in the center. Sprinkle ½ cup fish stock over the corn-meal stuffing and bake the fish until done (following directions on page 23), basting occasionally with the remaining ½ cup of stock. Serve as is or with your favorite sauce or butter.

DEEP-FRIED CODFISH AND UNPEELED POTATO BALLS

◆

Many colonial recipes originated with the Indians, as this one may have, since these natives usually disdained peeling vegetables (a nice idea since the peels not only add an interesting flavor, but increase the nutritional content as well). However, if the original recipe was an Indian one, the potatoes used were undoubtedly sweets, the great Northeastern Indian staple. The white potato reached these shores through a circuitous route by way of England from its South American place of origin.

2 *Pounds cod, with skin and bone removed*

3 *Cups unpeeled potatoes, diced*

2 *Cups water*

⅛ *Teaspoon pepper*

3 *Tablespoons Nut Butter*

2 *Teaspoons each minced fresh parsley and marjoram*

Salt to taste

Oil for deep-frying

Boil the cod, potatoes and water in a tightly lidded pot until the potatoes are tender and the fish flakes. Drain well and mash vigorously with the pepper, butter and herbs. Season to taste with salt. Roll into one-inch balls and deep-fry until golden. Drain and serve hot or cold.

NUT BUTTER

◆

The Northeast Indians kept no domesticated animals before the settlers came, and so their nut butter was extracted by grinding or pounding nuts to a paste to produce something akin to a coarse peanut butter. Nut oils, when they were needed, were also obtained this way. Since both cow's butter and nuts are readily available to us, the following tasty, but not authentic, product is recommended for use in these recipes.

Whirl in food processor, blend or grind ½ cup shelled walnuts or hickory nuts. Work into ¼ pound sweet butter. Refrigerate immediately.

SHINNECOCK SHAD WITH MELTED BONES

◆

Yield: Enough to serve 6

The long cooking tenderizes thinner bones and leaves the fish strangely sweet.

1 3–4-pound whole shad, cleaned
3 Cups water
½ Cup cider vinegar
1 Large whole leek, trimmed, well washed and coarsely chopped
2 Tablespoons Nut Butter

Salt and pepper
Bacon slices
1 Cup heavy cream
½ Cup shelled and toasted pumpkin or sunflower seeds

In a large enamel or stainless-steel pan, simmer the fish in the water and vinegar for 15 minutes. Reserve the liquid. Scrape away and discard skin over the center portion of the fish.

Preheat oven to 225 degrees F.

Scatter the leek in the bottom of a heavy roasting pan large enough to hold the fish, arrange the shad on top, pour in ½ cup fish-cooking liquid and season with the butter, salt and pepper. Cover the skinned area with bacon slices placed edge to edge. Cover the pan tightly and bake 5 hours, basting frequently with the reserved fish liquid.

Transfer the fish to a heated platter, discarding the bottom skin in the process. Discard any fish skin in the pan and purée the leeks with the fish juices.

In a small saucepan cook the purée over medium-low heat until it is reduced to 1¼ cups. Add the cream and simmer until the sauce is nicely thickened. Spoon a little sauce over the fish and sprinkle with the toasted seeds. Serve the remaining sauce separately.

STEAMED SHAD WITH MELTED BONES

◆

1 3–4-pound whole shad, cleaned
Salt and pepper to taste
1½ Cups dry white wine or stock
Water
1 Cup each chopped celery, carrot
  and onion

Garlic cloves, peeled and minced
2 Small bay leaves, crumbled
1 Tablespoon cornstarch

Rinse and dry the fish, rub inside and out with salt and pepper and arrange on a rack in a roasting pan with a tight-fitting lid. Add wine and just enough water so that it does not touch the fish. Sprinkle vegetables over fish, cover the pan with aluminum foil and fit on the lid. Steam over low heat for 5 hours, basting frequently. To serve, transfer fish to a heated platter and keep warm. Strain the liquid in the pan, reduce it to 1 cup, stir in the cornstarch mixed with ¼ cup cold water until lump-free, and continue stirring over medium heat until sauce is thick and smooth. Serve with the fish.

FISH AND SHELLFISH, RAW AND NEARLY SO

On this island paradise where a fish can grace a plate only moments after it last flips its tail in the bright-blue bay, it is only natural, I suppose, that fish-eaters here should undercook their treasures . . . or not cook them at all. It's inevitable that a hungry scalloper should pop a raw scallop into her cheek straight from the shell or that a cook should pilfer the silk-thin slivers left against the backbone when a fillet is severed from the fish stunned into final rest only seconds before. Even fish that toughen slightly under the flame are most often butter-tender in their natural state . . . with no fishy odor, or for that matter, no fishy taste.

Which brings us to Sashimi, to Sushi . . . in fact to eating raw, or nearly raw fish. (Seviche is actually cooked with fruit juice rather than flame.) While testing this book I've cleaned, scaled, filleted and otherwise dealt with all of the creatures mentioned herein. Every fish, shellfish, mollusk and echinoderm (sea urchin) I've cooked, I've also nibbled raw, and while a few are totally off-putting uncooked—monkfish, for example, quivers like Jell-O and chews like blubber (not precisely a dazzling duo of qualities)—most fish are exquisite uncooked.

Sashimi is perhaps the raw fish dish most familiar to Americans, thanks to the sudden proliferation of Japanese restaurants on these shores. Traditionally served in Japan as a separate course, in our country it is most frequently offered as a go-with for drinks or occasionally as a first course or entree. Since there is no cooking involved, the trick here is to cut each fish in the particular way that will best bring out its unique texture and delicate flavor while producing a bite-size tidbit easily managed with chopsticks, hors d'oeuvre picks, fingers or forks.

For example:
- Very firm, very dense squid are cut into small, flat, scored squares or threads.
- Dense, tightly constructed fish like the tuna are sliced or cubed (*kaku giri*).
- Looser-textured but still-firm fish like the porgy are cut into thin slices (*usu zukuri*).
- Fish with moist, more fragile texture are cut into ¼-inch-thick flat slices (*hira zukuri*).
- Very tender fish such as flounder, which tend to fall apart easily, are cut into ¼-inch-thick threads (*ito-zukuri*) or very thinly sliced (*hirame-usuzukuri*).

These cuts are the rule but there are exceptions. A general guide, if you just want to try raw fish in the most uncomplicated way, is to skin firm to medium-firm fish fillets, cut them lengthwise into long, 1½-inch-wide pieces, then cut them across on a *slight* slant (salmon is cut at a greater slant) to form bite-size pieces. Cut moist fish into nearly transparent flat slices about one inch wide and 2 inches long or into ¼-inch strips.

The fish used must be exquisitely fresh . . . hooked and cleaned and immediately iced not more than 24 hours prior to eating. They must be deeply chilled but never frozen (not even partially) or the wonderful, subtle flavor will leach away as they defrost.

Present the fish beautifully in interesting combinations of texture, color and shapes, on unsprayed garden leaves, ferns etc., garnish with attractively cut vegetable flowers, shreds or ribbons and serve with a soy-sauce-based dipping sauce.

And remember:

- Fish or shellfish to be consumed raw should be taken only from unpolluted waters.
- Weakfish and other members of the drum family (*Sciaenidae*), which includes kingfish and various croakers and drums, are susceptible to and may harbor trematode parasites which are not known to be harmful to humans. On the other hand, fresh-water fish should never be eaten raw, since certain dangerous cestode- and nematode-related diseases can result from eating these uncooked fish.

Although many fish are excellent when served raw, the ones listed on the opposite page are a few of my own favorites.

- salmon
- tuna
- porgy
- striped bass
- flounder

- fluke
- mackerel
- halibut
- black sea bass
- squid

SASHIMI DIPPING SAUCE

◆

Yield: 1 cup

This will keep almost indefinitely if refrigerated.

1 Cup soy sauce
1 Teaspoon wasabi (horseradish)
*   powder (Add additional wasabi if*
*   a hotter sauce is desired.)*

Water
1 Grated white daikon radish
*   (optional)*

Mix the soy sauce with the horseradish powder mixed with enough water to form a thick paste. Stir in the daikon radish. Each guest picks up a piece of fish with chopsticks (or a small fork) and dips it into the sauce.

VARIATION: Add grated fresh ginger to taste. Omit the wasabi if you prefer. Experiment with combinations of ingredients to create your own dipping sauces. There should be at least one salty substance and one spicy one.

SESAME DIPPING SAUCE

◆

½ Cup each soy sauce and
*   Worcestershire sauce*
Sesame oil to taste

Mix well. Use as a dip for Sashimi.

SWEET AND SALTY DIPPING SAUCE

◆

½ Cup mirin (a heavy, sweet Japanese
*   cooking wine) or sherry with*
*   1 teaspoon sugar*

½ Cup soy sauce
½ Cup sake
3 Drops Tabasco sauce

Boil the mirin, soy sauce and sake until syrupy. Stir in the Tabasco. Use as a dip for Sashimi.

AN UNUSUAL PREPARATION FOR FLOUNDER AND FLUKE

◆

The delicate flatfish are seldom served raw in this country but are excellent *au naturel*. Remove the fillets from the fish, leaving the head, the tail and the dorsal fin intact. Arrange the fish frame on a bed of dill or fern fronds, dark-side-up. Cut the flesh into paper-thin, nearly transparent ribbons, each about 1½ inches long. Starting at the tail, arrange these pieces in overlapping layers, ending at the back of the head. The result should resemble rows of wide wavy scales. These are best lifted from the frame with chopsticks and dipped in sauce; however, a small fork or a sturdy toothpick will work nearly as well.

1 Medium-size fresh, chilled flounder or fluke, cleaned and filleted	Dipping sauce
	4 Radish roses
Dill branches or fern fronds	8 Carrot flowers

Prepare the fish as described above. Refrigerate until serving time.

SUSHI

Second cousin to Sashimi is Sushi, another superb Japanese raw-fish dish, this one served in concert with balls of warm or cold vinegared rice and bits of seaweed. While cold rice with raw fish may sound like a gastronomic experience to avoid at all costs, it is actually a delicate and intriguing treat.

Prepare fish and your choice of dipping sauces as directed for Sashimi. Serve on ovals of Sushi Rice.

SUSHI RICE

◆

Yield: About 3 dozen rice ovals

3 Cups rice	Finely shredded daikon radish
3½ Cups water	Finely grated fresh ginger
1 Cup Japanese sweet rice vinegar	Bits of dried seaweed
½ Cup sugar	Small strips of raw cucumber, peeled
Wasabi	and seeded

Stir the rice into the boiling water, allow to return to the boil, then cover, lower the heat and simmer for 15 minutes or until tender. Meanwhile boil the vinegar and sugar together until syrupy. Mix the rice into the vinegar syrup and chill quickly in a flat dish. Press the rice between your palms into ovals about 2 inches by 1 inch by ½ inch thick. Arrange on arugula or other flat leaves on a lacquered tray, brush with wasabi, top with strips of fish, and garnish with radish, ginger, seaweed and cucumber.

RAW SHELLFISH

Eating raw oysters and clams, those treasures of the sand flats, has long been an accepted indulgence, particularly to those in close touch with the shore, but for some reason that most delicate of all shellfish, the raw scallop, has been overlooked. For this reason I've included clams on the half shell and oysters on the half shell in their respective sections, where you would expect to find them, but I've slipped the raw scallop recipes in here, where you might happen across them when you're looking for new ideas and feeling adventurous.

SCALLOPS AU NATUREL

◆

Yield: Enough to serve 6

If possible, acquire a few dozen bay scallop shells, scrub them well and save them for these recipes.

1 Pint scallops
2 Lemons, cut into 12 wedges, each
   ¼-inch thick

Tabasco sauce

If you've gathered the scallops yourself, run your knife inside the shell (an easy matter, since scallops don't "clam up"), loosen the white adductor muscle, remove it and set it aside. Repeat the process until you have one pint. You may use the body of the scallop, which, while unattractive, is perfectly edible, for Scallop Pie. Rinse the firm, white scallops, drain them and place 1 or 2 in each scrubbed bay scallop shell with a thin sliver of lemon. If you like, sprinkle a couple of drops of lemon juice and a drop of Tabasco over each before you arrange them on a bed of ice on a large tray.

SCALLOPS WITH BLACK CAVIAR

◆

Yield: 2 dozen hors d'oeuvres

This is an outrageously extravagant morsel to nibble with drinks . . . but who deserves it more than you do? Once again you'll need 2 dozen small, scrubbed bay scallop shells or, if this is to be a first course, medium-sized bay scallop shells. Sea scallop shells will be too large.

1 Pint scallops (adductor muscles only)
1 Lemon, sliced into 16 ½-inch-
   thick wedges

Black caviar (Red caviar gives a less
   subtle effect)

Place 1 or 2 scallops in each shell with a sliver of lemon and ¼ teaspoon caviar. Arrange on a bed of ice. Squeeze the lemon over and slurp the seafood from the shell.

ROES

When it comes to delicacies, virtually no food can surpass the elite status of several of the various fish roes. Best known of these, of course, come from sturgeon (sumptuous black caviar), salmon (gorgeous red caviar) and shad (lovely, delicate off-white shad roe). In addition, many other fish produce excellent edible roes, including those you might find at the end of your line in East End waters—cod, haddock, mullet, flounder, mackerel, bluefish, weakfish, smelt, herring, alewife, sea robin and white perch.

Roe is the name given to the two sets of immature eggs found during the spawning season in the ovaries of female fish and also generally applied to the long white gonads of the male fish, known as "white roe" or "milt."

While color and size of the roes may vary with the species and size of the fish, they are best when the unripe eggs are 1) clearly visible through the membrane covering; 2) are of overall uniform color and size; and 3) are neither too compact and small nor too well-developed.

Roe found in the body cavities of small fish such as herring or smelt are frequently cooked right along with the fish, but larger roes are usually cooked separately.

Fresh roes meant to be served whole always need careful handling—when being separated from the fish and during storage and cooking—so that the membranes containing the eggs remain intact.

First, rinse these carefully to remove all bloodstains. Many recipes traditionally call for poaching all roes for a few minutes before further cooking them to firm and prevent breaking as well as to shorten cooking time for thicker roes, but this step is not really necessary if the roe is handled gently and sautéed over very, very low heat for a long period of time. For beginners, this poaching can be the cause of severe burns. If even a minuscule hole in the membrane allows water to seep in among the eggs, these can explode as they heat, splattering hot fat over the cook as well as the kitchen. A too-high cooking temperature can result in similar problems. If you do poach roe first, just prior to sautéing (or even if you don't), prick each here and there with a pin, taking care not to tear the membrane.

PECONIC FLOUNDER ROE DIP

◆

Yield: Enough to serve 6 to 8

When I clean fish in spawning season I'm especially careful to make only a very shallow slit from the anal vent forward in case there's a treasure of roe inside (about 7 out of 10 times I'm rewarded for my trouble). Unless I'm smoking the roe with the fish, I often prepare it in this unusual but really tasty way. Try it with any except blowfish roe.

6 *Flounder roe (or other roe to make 2½ cups)*
1½ *Tablespoons butter or vegetable oil*
4 *Anchovy fillets*
1 *Small onion, peeled and cut in quarters*
1 *Large clove garlic, peeled*
1 *Cup sour cream*
Salt and pepper to taste
Croutons or toast points or zucchini slices

Dry the roe well and sauté in the butter about 8 minutes on each side or until roe is cooked through. Cut into one-inch pieces and remove membranes. In blender or food processor, whirl the roe, anchovies, onion and garlic only until ingredients are well incorporated. Add the sour cream and seasoning and whirl a few seconds more—just long enough to mix. Chill the dip and serve it in a bowl surrounded by croutons, toast points or very thin slices from tender young zucchini. If you must use crackers, choose only delicately flavored ones so as not to mask the subtle flavor and texture of the roe.

SPRINGS ROE AND EGGS WITH TRUFFLES

◆

Yield: Enough to serve 4

Truffles are culinary gems, priced accordingly; therefore I seldom include them in any but the most elegant recipes—and then only when no other ingredient can substitute for them.

This dish is very rich, very unusual, and is unmistakably improved by the startling rich blackness and unique texture/flavor of truffles.

By no means disdain the recipe if truffles are beyond your budget. The basic ingredients provide ample rewards even without those almost priceless black jewels.

1 Cup roe ⎫	2 Teaspoons water
1 Cup milt ⎬ or 2 cups of either	½ Teaspoon truffle liquid
4 Tablespoons butter	1 Black truffle, peeled and sliced
2 Tablespoons peeled and minced	A sprinkle of cayenne pepper
shallots	Salt to taste
4 Eggs	Buttered crustless toast quarters

Sauté the roe and/or milt for 10 minutes in 2 tablespoons butter heated in a nonstick pan. With a flat turner, turn the roe/milt carefully. Sauté 10 minutes more or until cooked through.

In another pan, heat 2 tablespoons butter and sauté shallots until transparent. Beat the eggs with the water and truffle liquid, add to the pan and cook without stirring for one minute. Stir the eggs, then cook without stirring for one minute more. Continue this method of cooking until the eggs are still moist but beginning to firm. Do not overcook the eggs. Remove the membranes from the roe and slice. Add the warm roe/milt, truffle slices, cayenne and salt and stir gently only once. Do not mix the ingredients.

Arrange 4 toast quarters on each of 4 small china plates (points toward the center of the plates). Spoon the roe and eggs onto the center of the toast points and serve immediately.

BASIC ROE/MILT SALAD
♦

Yield: Enough to Serve 6

This is a rather basic recipe from which many variations may stem. I've suggested a few, but by all means mix, match and experiment on your own.

1½ Cups roe ⎫	1 Tablespoon minced fresh dill
1½ Cups milt ⎬ or 3 cups of either	Lemon juice, cayenne and salt to taste
Diluted fish stock	Sauce Mayonnaise
2 Tablespoons peeled and minced	
shallots	

Simmer the roe/milt in a bit of diluted fish stock until it feels rather firm and is cooked through. Do not overcook. Drain the roe/milt and chill well. Discard membrane, drain again, cut into slices and toss lightly with shallots, dill, lemon juice, cayenne and salt and enough mayonnaise to moisten.

CURRIED ROE/MILT SALAD: Substitute one tablespoon minced chutney and curried Sauce Mayonnaise for the dill and plain mayonnaise in Basic Roe/Milt Salad.

HERBED ROE/MILT SALAD: Substitute one teaspoon each minced fresh thyme and rosemary for the dill, and Tarragon Mayonnaise for Sauce Mayonnaise in Basic Roe/Milt Salad.

OPEN-FACE TOMATO ROE/MILT SALAD SANDWICHES: Place one piece crustless bread or toast on each of 6 plates. Top with Sauce Mayonnaise, buttercrunch lettuce, Basic Roe/Milt Salad, 2 thin slices of tomato and a sprinkle of minced dill. Serve cold.

OPEN-FACE ROE/MILT SALAD MIMOSA: Place one piece crustless bread or toast on each of 6 plates. Top with Sauce Mayonnaise, buttercrunch lettuce, Basic Roe/Milt Salad, sieved hard-cooked egg yolk and one rolled anchovy fillet.

HERBED OPEN-FACE ROE/MILT SALAD SANDWICH: Place one piece crustless bread or toast on each of 6 plates. Top with Tarragon Mayonnaise, buttercrunch lettuce, Herbed Roe/Milt Salad, several thin slices peeled cucumber and a grind of black pepper.

HERBED ROE/MILT SALAD IN AVOCADO

◆

Yield: Enough to serve 6

Herbed Roe/Milt Salad
3 Ripe avocados with seeds and
   peel removed

Tarragon Mayonnaise
3 Large pitted black olives

Spoon Roe/Milt Salad into the hollows of the avocados; top each with Tarragon Mayonnaise and half an olive.

ROE/MILT SALAD IN TOMATO SHELLS

◆

Yield: Enough to serve 6

6 Small- to medium-size tomatoes
Basic Roe/Milt Salad

Anchovy Mayonnaise
Lettuce leaves

Cut tops from tomatoes and scoop out pulp. Turn tomato shells upside down on paper towels to drain. Discard seeds and juice, finely chop pulp and drain well. Mix drained tomato pulp with Roe/Milt Salad, spoon into tomato shells, set each on a lettuce leaf and top with Anchovy Mayonnaise.

CURRIED ROE/MILT SALAD WITH CANTALOUPE

◆

Yield: Enough to serve 6

6 *Buttercrunch lettuce leaves*
Curried Roe/Milt Salad

24 *Thin, peeled cantaloupe slices*
Curry Mayonnaise

Arrange lettuce leaves on each of 6 plates, spoon Curried Roe/Milt Salad into the center of each and decorate each plate with 4 slices cantaloupe. Top with Curry Mayonnaise.

CURRIED ROE/MILT DIP

◆

Curried Roe/Milt Salad
⅓ *Cup sour cream*

⅓ *Cup Curry Mayonnaise*
Salt to taste

Lightly mash the salad. Mix all ingredients, chill well and serve with crackers or raw vegetable sticks.

HERBED ROE/MILT DIP

◆

Herbed Roe/Milt Salad
⅓ *Cup sour cream*

⅓ *Cup Tarragon Mayonnaise*

Lightly mash the salad. Mix all ingredients, chill well and serve with crackers or raw vegetable sticks.

ANCHOVY ROE/MILT DIP

◆

Basic Roe/Milt Salad
⅓ *Cup sour cream*

⅓ *Cup Anchovy Mayonnaise*
3 *Minced anchovy fillets*

Lightly mash the salad. Mix all ingredients, chill well and serve with crackers or raw vegetable sticks.

CROUSTILLES SAINT-MICHEL

◆

Yield: 6 sandwiches

This variation on a French theme is an interesting addition to a country brunch.

12 *Slices fine white bread with*
  crusts trimmed
1 *Recipe Curried Roe/Milt Salad or*
  Herbed Roe/Milt Salad

1 *Recipe Enriched Sauce Velouté*
Butter

Spread 6 slices of the bread with either of the Roe/Milt salads bound with Sauce Velouté instead of mayonnaise. The filling should be stiff, not runny. Top the filling with the remaining bread slices and fry to golden in foaming butter, turning once. Serve immediately.

VEGETABLE-ROE (OR MILT) STUFFING

◆

Try this rich fish filling whenever roe is available to you in some quantity. Use to stuff delicate fish (whiting, for example), to roll up in flounder fillets or even to fill cooked artichoke bottoms.

1 Large carrot, scraped and sliced
3–4 Tablespoons butter
2 Cups roe or milt
2 Shallots, peeled and finely chopped
¾ Cup each finely chopped celery and mushrooms

⅛ Teaspoon each thyme and marjoram
A pinch of nutmeg
Salt and pepper to taste
Fine bread crumbs

Simmer the carrot in water to cover for 5 minutes. Drain and finely chop. Melt 3 tablespoons butter in a large skillet and simmer the roe 10 minutes on each side or until not quite cooked through (do not increase the heat or the roe may pop and splatter). Remove from the pan, discard membranes, and coarsely crumble or chop roe. Add the shallots, celery, mushrooms, carrots and seasonings to the pan; sauté until the shallots are tender, adding more butter if needed. Stir in the roe and a sprinkle of bread crumbs if the stuffing does not hold together.

HAM AND ROE (OR MILT) STUFFING

◆

This recipe is the basis for a very tasty filling for any rather bland, non-oily fish. Increase the proportion of roe to bread crumbs if you are fortunate enough to have additional roe.

3 Tablespoons butter
1½ Cups blackfish, sea robin or flounder roe or milt
1 Shallot, peeled and finely chopped
1 Cup finely chopped ham

1 Cup bread crumbs
¼ Teaspoon each thyme and marjoram
Salt and pepper to taste
Fish stock or water

Melt the butter in a large skillet and simmer the roe 10 minutes on each side, or until not quite cooked through (do not increase the heat or the roe may pop and splatter). Add the shallot and continue to cook for 5 minutes. Remove the roe from the pan and stir in the ham, bread crumbs and seasonings. Remove membranes, coarsely chop or crumble the roe and stir it into the stuffing along with enough stock or water to moisten slightly.

HAM, ROE AND VEGETABLE STUFFING: Follow directions for Ham and Roe (or Milt) Stuffing above, but in place of half the bread crumbs add ½ cup each chopped green pepper and mushrooms when you add the shallot.

ON LONG ISLAND SOUND

I wander daily by thy shore,
Thy rocky shore, Long Island Sound,
And in my little boat explore,
The secrets of thy depths profound,
I trace the great brown rocks far down,
O'er which the salt tides ebb and flow,
Encrusted with their rugged shells,
Rocks where ribbon'd seaweeds grow,
And there the glancing fish I view,
The weakfish and the dusky bass,
The bergalls and the blackfish schools,
And silvery porgees as they pass.

Fast-anchor'd in my swinging boat,
The welcome nibble to await,
I feel the sheepshead at the line,
The sea-bass tugging at the bait,
And as I gaze across the wave,
I see the shining sturgeon leap,
Springing in air with sudden flash,
Then splashing, plunging to the deep,
I see the porpoise schools sweep by,
In sportive gambollings at their play,
Puffing and snorting as they rise,
Wheeling and tumbling on their way,
And never wearied is my gaze,
As o'er the blue expanse it roams,
Viewing the endless billows roll,
White-crested with the yeasty foams.

FISH

AS YOU LIKE IT: This book is designed to help you deal with all of the superb fish and shellfish residents along our great Northeast seacoast and to provide you with a wide variety of recipes for these so that you need never again wonder what on earth to do with the fish you have on hand. For those who feel that less is more when it comes to dining, who prefer to stay with the basics, particularly when those basics are as outstanding as fish and shellfish, this book provides a cookbook within a cookbook. Included here are not only the ABC's of perfect fish preparation but twenty-two fresh-tasting chilled sauces and eighteen simple and compound butters to flavor your fish, shellfish and steamed garden vegetable combinations, simply but wonderfully well.

The health-promoting qualities of fish have, quite rightly, been highly touted (see Fish and Nutrition, page 355). Fish *is* good for you—fathoms lower in cholesterol (and calories) than most meats, sky-high in protein and loaded with vitamins and minerals. For readers who choose to, or must, lower the fat content in their diets, Baking (page 26), Poaching (page 28) and Steaming (page 29), using nonfatty bastes, are the recommended fish-cooking techniques. Continue this *nouvelle* trend toward lighter eating by serving the fish with a squeeze of fresh citrus juice, one or more vegetable purées, and/or a garnish of julienne vegetables. Vegetarians who eat fish but not dairy products will find many recipes that follow may be prepared with oil rather than butter without altering the final results too drastically.

The more adventurous cook, as well as one who enjoys (as I do) just browsing through cookbooks, will find some four hundred regional, ethnic and classic recipes to pique his or her appetite and imagination. By all means do try the sauce from one dish with the fish from another. More than half the fun of cooking is using your creativity to satisfy your own cravings precisely how and when you wish. Whether you opt for simplicity of menu or Victorian excess, no matter how you sauce, slice, butterfly, fillet, steak or flake it, when correctly prepared, fish is delicious.

ANCHOVIES

These flashy, slim little fish with oversize eyes and wide, underslung mouths, while not indigenous, do dart in and about Long Island waters. There are actually eight anchovy species in Atlantic waters, all primarily inhabitants of middle and southern Atlantic regions, but quick-silvery schools of three of these species stray hereabouts often enough to make them a commercially important catch.

- Bay anchovy (*Anchoa mitchilli*), also known as anchovy whitebait and common anchovy, a three- to four-inch translucent silver fish with large, loose scales.
- Striped anchovy (*Anchoa hepsetus*), a bit larger and slimmer than the bay anchovy. Gray-green with yellow highlights and dark spots, sporting a prominent, bright-silver band that runs from gills to tail.
- Silvery anchovy (*Anchoviella argyrophanus*), bright silver all over and even more streamlined than the striped anchovy.

Anchovies differ from the silversides and other baitfish in having a single dorsal fin and a deeply forked tail. The favored item in their diet is plankton, in search of which they can be found both offshore and inshore and even, on occasion, in brackish waters.

ANCHOVIES AS FOOD: Anchovies are not much utilized fresh despite their similarity to whitebait species—a pity, since these are at least as tasty as whitebait, especially when fried.

PAN-FRIED FRESH ANCHOVY

◆

Follow directions for cleaning (page 16) and pan-frying (page 26) small whole fish. Serve with the flavored butter or sauce of your choice.

DEEP-FRIED FRESH ANCHOVY

◆

Follow directions for cleaning (page 16) and deep-frying (page 27) small, whole fish. Serve with the sauce that suits your fancy.

ESCABÈCHE OF ANCHOVY

◆

Yield: 2 dozen fish

2 Dozen whole fresh anchovies, cleaned
Flour
Vegetable oil for deep-frying
4 Small onions, peeled and sliced
1 Carrot, scraped and sliced
6 Cloves garlic, peeled and crushed
½ Cup olive oil
1 Cup vinegar

½ Cup water
1 Tablespoon sugar
1 Teaspoon salt
2 Tablespoons each of fresh minced thyme, fennel leaves and marjoram
1 Bay leaf
6 Hard-cooked eggs, shelled and quartered
¼ Cup small pimento strips

Clean the fish as for pan-frying (see page 16), wipe them dry and dust with flour. Deep-fry in hot vegetable oil for a few minutes until golden brown. Remove from the oil, drain well and arrange in a deep earthenware dish.

Sauté the onions, carrot slices and garlic until the oil turns yellow. Add the olive oil, vinegar, water, sugar, salt and herbs, bring to a boil, then lower the heat and simmer the marinade for 15 minutes. Pour this over the fish and marinate for at least 24 hours. Serve cold or at room temperature, garnished with egg quarters and pimento.

FRESH ANCHOVY SALAD, ORIENT POINT

◆

Yield: Enough to serve 4 to 6

2 Dozen whole, fresh anchovies
Flour
Vegetable oil for frying
3 Warm new potatoes, diced
3 Tablespoons warm white wine
2 Hard-cooked eggs, shelled and coarsely chopped
3 Scallions, with 3 inches green tops, chopped

3 Tablespoons olive oil
1 Large clove garlic, peeled and crushed
2 Tablespoons lemon juice
1 Tablespoon each chopped thyme and marjoram
Salt and freshly ground black pepper to taste
2 Tablespoons capers, drained

Clean the fish as for pan-frying (see page 16), wipe them dry and lightly dust with flour. Fry in vegetable oil until golden brown on both sides. Flake the meat from the bones in as large pieces as possible and toss with the potatoes and wine. Let stand 15 minutes. Add the eggs and scallions. Shake the olive oil, garlic and lemon juice together. Sprinkle this over the salad with the thyme, marjoram and seasonings. Toss lightly again, garnish with capers and serve at room temperature.

ANCHOVY EYE

◆

Yield: Enough to serve 4 to 6

This is a simple, attractive and particularly tasty cocktail nibble. Serve surrounded with small toast points for guests to use to dip first into the egg yolk, then the onion and finally the anchovy.

18 Home-salted or canned anchovy fillets, drained and finely chopped
1 Medium-size onion, peeled and finely chopped

1 Large uncooked egg yolk
1 Teaspoon finely chopped fresh thyme or parsley
Freshly ground black pepper

Arrange the anchovies in a circle around the edge of a small plate. Make a circle of onion within the anchovy ring. Carefully place the unbroken egg yolk in the center. Sprinkle with thyme or parsley and a little pepper. Serve at once so the egg yolk does not become "leathery."

◆ ◆

SEA-BASS

Wide off Long Island's yellow beach
Where fisher's plummet scarce may reach
Deep-sunken in the depths of brine
Where sea-weeds all the rocks entwine
Where kelp its beaded ribbon flings
And the black mussel closely clings
And sea-dulse their long tresses flaunt
There the dark sea-bass makes his haunt

And where the Sound outspreads its plain
Extended to the tossing main
Off Orient Point and green Plum Isle
Where the Gut currents chafing boil
Where Gardiner's Island and Gull-rocks
Breast and repel the ocean shocks
There goes the fisher with his boat
Above the sunken ledge to float
Skilful to take with baited line
The sable sea-bass of the brine

I love to stand on rocks that throw
Deep shadows on the tides below
And note the varied life that sweeps

The salt abysses of the deeps
The sword-fish and the spouting whale
The porpoise tumbling in the gale
The dolphin and the grampus dark
The sharp-finn'd, man-devouring shark
The blue-fish leaping as they pass
The strip'd and pearl-enamell'd bass

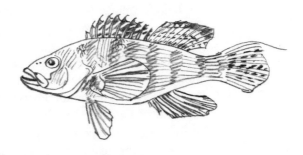

BLACK SEA BASS

Centropristis striatus

Plain or fancy, this firm, lean, sweet-fleshed fish (family *Serranidae*) is delicious. Hereabouts this fish is sometimes called blackfish, which leads to confusion, since this is also the name for tautog. When you're buying fish, be sure it's sea bass you're getting if sea bass you desire.

This big-mouthed true sea bass (not to be confused with the freshwater black bass, which is really a member of the sunfish family) sports a mean-looking, spiny, black-and-white-striped dorsal fin with a large black spot on the last dorsal spine. Its body color is overall black or very dark brown with lighter flecks; the tail fin is slightly rounded, with the top ray characteristically extended. The average fish weighs 1½ to 3 pounds, but larger specimens may reach 5 to 8 pounds. Juveniles have a black lateral line.

BLACK SEA BASS AS FOOD: An excellent table fish with delicately flavored, firm white flesh—which is most likely the result of dining almost exclusively on shellfish—this bass may be served many ways—deep-fried, steamed, in vegetable casseroles, or in soups and chowders. It is a particular favorite of New York's Chinese chefs, who steam and serve it with Fermented Bean Sauce.

Cook the fish whole after gutting and scaling or skinning it, or fillet and scale or skin. To facilitate removal of the dorsal fin, cut through the skin on both sides and lift it out; the other fins should give you no trouble. Scrape out any blood pockets in the body cavity.

HABITS, HABITAT AND SEASON: Black sea bass are bottom-feeders in clear, hard-bottomed waters that range 10 to 80 feet or so during spring and summer, slipping away to deeper offshore areas when the air turns nippy and waters chill. They prefer the subaqueous mysteries of wrecks, piers and dock pilings—anywhere barnacles and mussels abound—or rocky bottoms teeming with crabs and small fish. Spawning takes place offshore in late spring.

This big-mouthed fish visits Hamptons waters from May until September. But when the delicate days of summer linger into a mild autumn, bass, like other itinerant East Enders, may delay their departure until the end of October. Best bass angling is in July in the surf or in inland waters such as bays, inlets and channels where depths run 20 to 40 feet. Larger specimens seem to prefer deeper waters, underwater wrecks and the like.

STEAMED WHOLE BLACK SEA BASS WITH CLAMS AND MUSHROOMS

◆

Yield: Enough to serve 4

A steamed whole fish seems an impressive culinary achievement but is not at all difficult to prepare.

1 2½-pound whole black sea bass, cleaned and scaled

Salt

5 Scallions with 3 inches green tops, chopped

2 Tablespoons each sherry and soy sauce

½ Teaspoon each salt and sugar

2 Teaspoons peanut oil

¼ Teaspoon sesame oil

3 Dried black mushrooms, soaked and shredded

8 Scrubbed softshell clams (or others)

Rinse the fish, wipe it dry and cut 2 diagonal parallel slashes on both sides to the bone over the rib cage. Rub lightly with salt (inside and out). Scatter half the scallions in a shallow ovenproof dish and arrange the fish on top. Mix the sherry, soy sauce, salt, sugar, peanut and sesame oil. Spoon the sauce over the fish. Press the remaining scallions over the fish with the mushrooms (most pieces will fall off). Steam, as directed on page 29, until the fish barely flakes. Ten minutes before the fish is ready to serve, arrange the clams around it and continue steaming.

WHOLE BLACK SEA BASS WITH FERMENTED BLACK BEAN SAUCE

◆

Yield: Enough to serve 4

1 2½-pound whole black sea bass, cleaned and scaled
Salt
3 Scallions with 3 inches green tops, chopped
1 Tablespoon fermented black beans, soaked 10 minutes in cold water
1 Large clove garlic, peeled and crushed
2 Tablespoons soy sauce
2 Teaspoons peanut oil
½ Teaspoon each sugar and salt
2 Slices fresh ginger root, peeled and shredded
¼ Teaspoon sesame oil (optional)
3 Scallions with 3 inches green tops

Rinse the fish, wipe it dry, and cut 2 diagonal parallel slashes to the bone over the rib cage on both sides. Rub lightly with salt (inside and out) and place the fish in a shallow ovenproof dish on a rack in a fish poacher, wok or other pan. Crush the beans and garlic together, then stir in all remaining ingredients except 3 whole scallions. Spoon sauce over the fish. Cut the scallions into ¼-inch slices and press over the fish, then cover and steam for 30 minutes or until the fish barely flakes. Serve immediately.

BATTER-FRIED BLACK SEA BASS WITH SCALLIONS

◆

Yield: Enough to serve 6

24 Pencil-thin scallions, each with 3 inches green tops
6 Fillets black sea bass
¼ Cup each flour and cornstarch
1 Large egg
Water
Oil for deep-frying
1 Bunch parsley, well washed and dried
¼ Cup soy sauce
½ Teaspoon grated fresh ginger root

Cut the white parts of the scallions into one-inch lengths. Chop the green tops.

Dry the fillets thoroughly. Beat the flour, cornstarch and egg together and beat in, a little at a time, enough water to produce a batter that flows nicely but does not run off the fillets.

Dip each fillet in batter and deep-fry in hot oil until golden brown. Arrange on a heated platter and keep warm. Quickly deep-fry the scallion pieces and the parsley, heap around the fish and serve immediately with soy sauce flavored with ginger on the side and small bowls of rice garnished with chopped scallion tops.

STIR-FRIED BLACK SEA BASS WITH SNOWPEAS AND ASPARAGUS

◆

Yield: Enough to serve 4 to 6

2 Pounds black sea bass fillets, cut against the grain in ¼-inch slices
1 Tablespoon cornstarch
3 Tablespoons sherry
2½ Tablespoons oil
½ Teaspoon salt
1 Clove garlic, peeled and crushed
1 Cup Chinese cabbage, thinly sliced
3 Water chestnuts, thinly sliced

12 Snowpea pods, stemmed
6 Asparagus spears, scraped and cut into 1-inch slices
4 Slices fresh ginger root, peeled and minced
½ Cup Fish Stock
⅛ Teaspoon sugar
2 Scallions, coarsely chopped
2 Cups hot cooked rice

Mix the cornstarch, sherry and ¼ teaspoon salt and toss with the fish. Heat 1½ tablespoons oil with the remaining ¼ teaspoon salt and the garlic and stir-fry the cabbage, chestnuts, snow peas and asparagus for one minute. Remove the vegetables with a slotted spoon and set aside. Heat the remaining oil, add the ginger and stir-fry the fish very carefully, to keep them from breaking, 3 minutes or until the fish barely flakes. Remove the fish with a slotted spoon, place in the center of a serving platter and keep warm. Return the vegetables to the wok, add the Fish Stock and sugar and boil for 2 minutes. Pour this around the fish. Sprinkle with scallions. Stir together at the table and serve with a little rice.

SOUTH-SEAS SAILOR SEA BASS

◆

6 Black sea bass fillets
Salt and white pepper to taste
2–2½ Cups fresh or dried coconut
2 Cups heavy cream

2 Mangoes or 1 papaya, peeled, seeded and cut into ½-inch thick slices
¼ Cup finely chopped macadamia nuts

Sprinkle the fillets with salt and pepper, arrange in a buttered ovenproof serving dish and refrigerate. Bring the coconut and cream to a boil, remove from the heat and let cool for 25 minutes. Squeeze the coconut and cream through cheesecloth and discard the dry pulp. Drain off any liquid around the fish and pour the cream over. Bake in a preheated 350-degree oven 15 minutes or until the fish flakes. Arrange the fruit around the fillets, sprinkle with the nuts and slide under the broiler for a few seconds until flecked with brown. Serve immediately.

SEASIDE BLACK SEA BASS

◆

Yield: Enough to serve 6

6 Sea bass fillets
Salt and pepper to taste
3 Tablespoons butter
2 Shallots, peeled and minced
½ Cup white wine
¾ Cup Fish Stock (or clam juice)
12 Oysters, shucked

12 Cooked shrimp, peeled and de-veined
12 Mussels, well scrubbed
12 Scallops in the shell, well scrubbed
1 Recipe Sauce Velouté

If scallops in the shell are available, the fluted shells add a nice touch. (Yes, the entire body of this shellfish is edible.) Sprinkle the fish with salt and pepper. Melt the butter in a large pan and arrange the fillets over the shallots. Add the white wine and the Fish Stock and bring to a boil, then lower the heat and simmer until the fish flakes. Remove the fillets from the pan, arrange on an ovenproof platter and keep them warm. Simmer the oysters in the Fish Stock until the edges curl (about 2 minutes), then drain and arrange them around the fish along with the shrimp. Allow the mussels and scallops to open in the simmering Fish Stock and arrange them attractively around the fish. Reduce the stock to 3 tablespoons and stir this into the Sauce Velouté. Mask the fish and oysters with the sauce (be sure to spread ½ teaspoonful over each mussel and scallop), then glaze under the broiler.

VARIATION I: Poach 6 fillets as directed in Seaside Black Sea Bass and keep them warm. Drain well and cover with Sauce Aurore. Sprinkle with grated Parmesan cheese and slide under the broiler until nicely flecked with brown. Serve immediately.

VARIATION II: Poach 6 fillets as directed in Seaside Black Sea Bass. Drain and chill. Drain again and arrange on serving platter or plates. Mask with Sauce Ravigote, Sauce Gribiche or Sauce Rémoulade. Serve cold garnished with a border of sieved egg yolks. Place one thin lemon or lime slice on or near each fillet. Serve cold.

STRIPED BASS

Roccus saxatilis

Also called rockfish (though not of the rockfish family), lunkers or linesider. Old-timers refer to this beauty as stripe-ed bass or simply striper. The premier salt-water fish of the Northeast, more fished for than any other, striped bass is a great game fish, an exquisite food fish and, to the commercial fisherman, one of the most important sources of protein taken from the sea.

STRIPED BASS AS FOOD: If there is a cooking method that striped bass does not take to with ease . . . I can't think of it. Broil it, bake it, fry it, poach it, steam it, simmer it in stews or chowders, charcoal-broil it, pickle it, smoke it. Serve it up with or without sauces, spices or elaborate garnishes. Striped bass is wonderful any way. The lean white meat is even terrific uncooked (see page 64). It is perfect for Sashimi (the fish most preferred for this in New York City's Japanese restaurants) and served as Seviche it defies description.

The most important factor in dining upon striped bass in any of its magnificent guises is freshness. When buying, follow the guide on page 12 and remember the meat should be silvery in appearance and have a fresh, shiny look.

The fish can be scaled and gutted and served whole, with or without the head and tail, dressed and cut into steaks, or scaled and/or skinned and filleted.

In fact there is only one drawback to eating striped bass—because the fish spawn in Hudson River waters extremely high in the toxic chemicals PCBs (polychlorinated biphenyls), the State Department of Environmental Conservation has recommended that children under age twelve not eat stripers and that adult intake be limited to one portion per week. It is to be hoped that when the Hudson responds to cleanup measures now under consideration this warning may be rescinded.

DESCRIPTION: A ruggedly handsome fish, olive-green to gray-green above with silvery sides, fading to delicate silvery-white on the belly. The most characteristic markings—and those that give the fish its name—are 7 or 8 narrow longitudinal stripes that run horizontally along the back and sides of the elliptical body. The topmost stripes tend to be most distinct, especially in older fish, becoming less prominent toward the belly.

The striper has two dorsal fins of about the same height, the forward one spiny, the rear one consisting of soft, even rays. The anal fin is preceded by several stiff rays, and the tail is distinctly forked.

Although record catches of stripers weighing in at over 100 pounds have been recorded (the record is 125 pounds), "lunkers" in the 50- or 60-pound class are about as big as anyone catches today. Stripers 2 feet long (minimum keeping size in New York State is 16 inches) weigh from 7 to 10 pounds; a 3-foot striper is a respectable catch at 20 pounds.

HABITS, HABITAT AND SEASON: Although most striped bass are anadromous (salt-water fish which enter fresh-water tidal rivers and estuaries to spawn) and migratory (moving up the Eastern seaboard as water temperatures warm in spring), there are also local populations which take shorter journeys between estuaries and tidal rivers and bays or sounds, wintering in a semidormant state and those that live landlocked in fresh water. The great majority, however, are hatched in the Chesapeake and Delaware bays and do not leave these waters until they are two years old and from 10 to 15 inches long. Of the countless millions of bass that migrate toward our shores, only a fraction actually reach Long Island waters. The commercial catch in Delaware, Maryland and Virginia accounts for more than 50 percent of the bass leaving that area, a great many more are caught before they reach Coney Island and a tremendous number pass us by completely on their way to New England.

Spawning takes place in spring, peaking from April to June. Striped bass are voracious but unpredictable feeders. Squid, shrimp, crabs, marine worms, soft clams, mussels, American eels, and various small fish all may be gulped down at one time, spurned at another. Eating patterns also vary with age—younger "school stripers" are active, aggressive hunters; older fish are more solitary, content to lurk near food sources and wait for prey to come to them.

There are two big runs of striped bass in the East End. The spring run begins in May and lasts for a few weeks, then lapses into sporadic catching until the fall run starts in September to last for two or three months. According to old-timers, legendary catches were made in the past at the eastern end of Long Island at Christmas time, but no one really knows where, when, how many, how soon or how late in the season these fish may appear or disappear.

WHERE TO CATCH: Most promising locations are those where food sources are likely to be abundant . . . in the churning surf, on rock-studded beaches, rocky jetties, sea walls, mussel and other shellfish beds, underwater marine vegetation areas, and inlets through which baitfish frequently pass on their way from one area to another. Other possibilities are sandy beaches, points of land and sand bars near inlets, and mouths of tidal rivers and estuaries. Time of day is important, too: since many of the striper's favorite delicacies are awake and stirring only at night, the period from an hour or so before sunset to an hour or so after sunrise is the best time to fish.

HOW TO CATCH: Surf-casting, surf-fishing on the bottom, fishing from jetty or shore, trolling from boats, boat casting—methods are numerous, and each has its share of ardent advocates. Because the striper is so unpredictable, and quite the biggest and most challenging gamefish found just offshore in East End waters, anglers must be ingenious in both locating their whereabouts and then figuring out what will tempt this cagey fish to dine.

Tackle: Medium tackle setup is generally most effective. Use your conventional surf rod and revolving reel or surf spinning combination, with at least a 20- to 30-pound test. No need for a wire leader when casting with lures, but if you're casting or bottom-fishing with natural or live bait, a short leader helps, since food is often taken deep.

Baits: A list of preferred foods is lengthy, and the fish will even oblige at times by going after artificial lures that resemble any of these natural favorites, but just when (and where) they will take what is often puzzling. As they work their way north in spring and into fresh-water tidal rivers and estuaries to spawn, try bloodworms. Later on in the season, bucktail jigs, metal squids, eel skins, plastic eels, or diving and popping plugs are favored, as are such natural baits as skimmer clams, sand eels, squid, bunkerfish, herring or alewives. "Live-lining," or using live bait such as live eel, hooked through lips or tail, or a live alewife, mackerel or menhaden, also has merit. When in doubt about what stripers are taking at any particular time, quiz your fellow anglers, ask the expert at your local tackle shop or fishing station or read the fishing column of the local newspaper.

The striper's aim is to try to throw the hook, so keep the tension on. Set the hook solidly with an upward lift of your rod tip, and let your fish play out the line. Allow the flexibility and resiliency of the rod to take up slack when the fish reverses direction, and you'll eventually wear your opponent down. Be sure to bring along a gaff when out for stripers; if you're lucky a net may be far too small.

The vast schools of striped bass that carpeted waters when North America's first settlers sailed through the Chesapeake Bay in 1607 have vanished, but this fish is still one of the most popular gamefish (along with the bluefish) and, in the hierarchy of anglers, is the one that gives most personal satisfaction and social cachet. To insure that there will still be viable populations of striped bass in years to come, however, various seacoast states, under the aegis of the National Marine Fisheries Council, are being encouraged to work out cooperative fishery management plans for the species within their territorial waters, which extend 12 miles out to sea. New York State has a management program of sorts, prohibiting the taking of any striped bass smaller than 16 inches from tip of snout to fork of tail, but there is no limit on maximum size. Other states have more restrictive laws, including a catch limit.

Once you land your striped bass, gut it and put it on ice as soon as possible, especially during warm weather. If ice isn't handy, cover the fish with a tarpaulin or cloth and wet it down from time to time. Striped bass do stay safe to eat longer than most softer-fleshed fish (weakfish and bluefish, for instance), but immediate icing best preserves the superb texture and flavor. Stripers are also easier to scale if you get to it immediately after catching; however, if you intend to fillet and skin your catch, don't bother with this.

Size may mean a great deal to anglers in fishing competitions, but stripers that make the best table fare are those in the 5- to 8-pound range.

MONTAUK WHOLE YOUNG STRIPER, DEEP-FRIED

◆

Weigh your fish and figure on ½-pound to 1-pound portions, depending on your guests' appetites, to see how many it will serve

There are few gourmet triumphs that can compare with this excellent dish.

1 Whole 16–18-inch striped bass, cleaned and scaled
Salt
3 Tablespoons each cornstarch and flour

Sherry
Soy sauce
1–2 Tablespoons minced scallion (optional)

Rinse the fish, wipe it dry and cut 3 parallel slashes on both sides over the rib cage (not too close to the tail). Rub lightly with salt inside and out. Mix the cornstarch and flour with enough sherry to make a paste. Cover the entire fish with the paste. Hold the fish by the tail and drop in deep fat heated almost to smoking over high heat. Fry for one minute on each side, then lower the heat to medium and fry 4 to 6 minutes on each side. Raise the heat to high once more and fry one minute on each side. Carefully make a thin cut behind the head to the bone. If the flesh flakes it is done.

The fish is marvelous unembellished, but if you would enjoy a sauce, mix equal parts sherry and soy sauce with the scallion.

FLAMBÉED WHOLE STRIPED BASS WITH DRIED HERB BRANCHES

◆

Figure ½ pound to 1 pound per serving

1 Whole striped bass, cleaned and scaled
Branches of dried herbs (thyme, basil, sage, fennel, rosemary)

3–4 Tablespoons cognac

Broil the fish following directions for broiling, page 24. Arrange small branches of herbs, one kind or a variety, on a flameproof platter or shallow baking sheet covered in foil. Place the broiled fish on these and cover with additional branches. Sprinkle with warm cognac and ignite in front of your family or guests. Allow the herb branches to burn down completely so that their flavors permeate the fish. Serve immediately.

BROILED WHOLE BASS WITH TWO HOT SAUCES

◆

Figure ½ pound to 1 pound per serving

1 *Whole striped bass, cleaned and scaled*
6 *Thin lemon slices*
6 *Pimento-stuffed olive slices*

1 *Recipe Sauce Nantua*
1 *Recipe Herb Hollandaise*

Broil the fish as directed on page 24. Garnish with lemon slices centered with olive slices. Serve immediately. Pass the sauces in two sauce boats.

BROILED WHOLE BASS WITH TWO COLD SAUCES

◆

Figure ½ pound to 1 pound per serving

1 *Whole striped bass, cleaned and scaled*
6 *Hard-cooked egg slices*
6 *Slices pitted black olives*

6 *Capers*
1 *Recipe Tomato-Cream Sauce*
1 *Recipe Green Goddess Dressing*

Broil the fish as directed on page 24. Garnish with egg slices centered with black olive slices, centered with capers. Serve immediately. Pass the sauces in a double sauce boat if one is available.

BAKED STRIPED BASS FILLETS WITH FLAVORED BUTTER

◆

Striped bass is superb baked (see page 26) and served with very nearly any flavored butter, but my favorites are Lemon Butter, Caviar Butter, Maître d'Hôtel Butter and Tarragon Butter.

BRAISED STRIPED BASS WITH SHELLFISH

◆

Allow ½ pound to 1 pound per serving

Fish are seldom braised, but this method of cooking is eminently suitable, particularly when a large whole fish is involved. Sautéed crayfish with their tails shelled are particularly attractive and delicious served as a garnish with the fish, but cooked, shelled shrimp and/or steamed mussels in their shells are also excellent.

1 *Large whole striped bass*
Salt and pepper
1 *Carrot, sliced*
2 *Onions, peeled and sliced*
Bouquet garni
Dry white wine

Fish Stock
Hot, cooked crayfish, shelled shrimp and/or mussels
1–2 *Recipes Sauce Cardinal (optional)*

Preheat the oven to 250 degrees F.

Rinse the fish, dry it well and rub it, inside and out, with salt and pepper. Scatter the carrot, onions and bouquet garni in the bottom of a fish poacher with a rack. Set in the fish, cover with the lid and bake for 15 minutes. Add white wine and fish stock until the liquid reaches not quite halfway up the fish. Bring just to a boil on top of the stove, then place in the oven and cook until the fish tests done, basting the top of the fish frequently with the liquid. Arrange the whole fish on a heated platter, surround it with hot crayfish, shrimp or mussels and serve with your favorite sauce (mine is Sauce Cardinal) made with some of the strained and reduced Fish Stock.

HOT POACHED BASS WITH TWO HOT SAUCES

◆

Clean, scale and poach fish as directed. Remove the skin but do not remove the head and tail. Arrange the fish on a platter and drain well. Decorate with alternate bands colorful Sauce Aurore and Parsley Sauce (pages 327–328). Place a set of criss-crossed 2-inch pimento strips on each band of sauce. Serve immediately with the remaining hot sauces passed separately.

CHILLED POACHED BASS WITH TWO CHILLED SAUCES

◆

Clean, scale and poach fish as directed. Chill. Remove the skin but do not remove the head or tail. Arrange the fish on a platter with thinly sliced ripe tomatoes. Spoon a few tablespoons Sauce Vinaigrette (page 324) over all and decorate with 6 thin lime slices. Pass the remaining Vinaigrette and chilled Sauce Gribiche.

STUFFED STRIPED-BASS SKIN

◆

Yield: Enough to serve 6

For fish without fuss, try this easy-to-serve recipe. Your food processor does the work in seconds.

1 3-pound striped bass
1 Ounce smoked ham, coarsely chopped
4 Scallions, with 2 inches green tops, minced
6 Water chestnuts, peeled
6 Shrimp, peeled and coarsely chopped
4 Dried black mushrooms, soaked and coarsely chopped

1 Tablespoon ice water
1 Tablespoon each oil and soy sauce
2½ Teaspoons cornstarch
½ Teaspoon sugar
⅛ Teaspoon each salt and pepper
Oil for frying
¼ Cup each sherry and soy sauce, mixed together

Scale the fish and carefully cut the skin away from the body so that each side comes off in one large piece. Cut the head and bones away from the flesh and reserve for stock. Cut the flesh into one-inch pieces and mince with the ham, scallions, chestnuts, shrimp and mushrooms. Work in the water, oil, soy sauce, cornstarch, sugar, salt and pepper. If the mixture seems too dry, mix in an additional teaspoon or two of ice water to form a moist filling that is stiff enough to hold its shape.

Flatten the fish skin on your work surface. Spread the fish mixture on one piece of skin, leaving ½-inch margin around all edges. Top with the other fish skin and fasten with toothpicks. Heat ¼ cup oil in a large skillet (a nonstick one is best) and carefully transfer the stuffed fish to it. Fry 2 minutes, then carefully turn and fry until the skin next to the pan is golden brown. Turn once more and fry until the stuffed fish feels firm to the touch and is cooked through, adding more oil if necessary to prevent sticking.

Serve immediately with the mixed sherry and soy sauce.

SPRINGS BASS AND MUSSEL SALAD

◆

Yield: Enough to serve 6

3 *Pounds chilled poached striped bass*
  with skin and bones removed
5 *Scallions, with 3 inches green tops,*
  minced
¾ *Cup finely chopped celery*

1 *Recipe Sauce Vinaigrette*
1 *Bunch watercress, well washed*
1 *Recipe Mussels in Curry Mayonnaise*
3 *Hard-cooked eggs, shelled and sliced*

Flake the fish and toss it with the scallions, celery and Sauce Vinaigrette. Arrange watercress on a serving platter with stems pointing in. Spoon the salad around the platter, leaving a 2-inch border of watercress and an empty space in the center of the platter about the size of a saucer. Heap the mussels in the center and surround them with egg slices. Serve lightly chilled.

BLACKFISH

Tautoga onitis

Considered an underutilized fish by commercial East End fishermen because of scanty demand, the blackfish is as superb a food buy as you're likely to encounter in these days of accelerating prices. This member of the Wrasse tribe (*Labridae*) has family traits that include a long, continuous dorsal fin, a ventral fin that sits immediately below the pectoral fins, a rounded forehead and thick lips that cover powerful canine teeth, useful in nibbling the bivalves that make up the fish's main food source.

BLACKFISH AS FOOD: Although blackfish are at their tastiest prior to spawning, they are at all times an excellent eating fish, with lean, silver-gray flesh that turns white and fairly firm after cooking. Rather bland in taste, probably due to the fish's preference for mollusks, the meat lends itself to "dressing up" with piquant sauces, crisp frying or stewing in chowders and fish soups, since it does not easily fall apart. The tough skin may be removed after cooking, but a better method is to freeze the fish only until the skin stiffens and then remove it with a sharp knife. (In either case, leave the head and tip of the tail unskinned and intact.)

DESCRIPTION: A chunky, dark, thick-bodied fish, mostly gray-brown to brown but occasionally black with brown or black smudges on its back and sides. The underbelly and chin are pale, with colors ranging from tan to white. In general, size runs from one to 5 pounds, but many taken in East End waters weigh in at 8 to 10 pounds.

HABITS, HABITAT AND SEASON: Blackfish prefer shallow inshore waters of up to 60 feet, where oysters, clams, barnacles, mussels and/or snails abound.

These fish visit the East End from May through October—give or take a week or two, depending upon the weather. They move into deeper waters and become more lethargic when cold weather sets in.

HOW TO CATCH: Try any bottom-fishing method, using light but sturdy tackle (a fairly stiff boat pole is ideal). For surf-fishing, use a lightweight conventional surf rod with one or two standard blackfish hooks or hooks of Virginia type, sizes 2 to 7, depending on the size of fish you hope to catch. Use a bank-type sinker that just holds the bottom, attached with string rather than directly to the line. Blackfish usually dine around obstructions of some kind, and this way only your sinker, instead of your

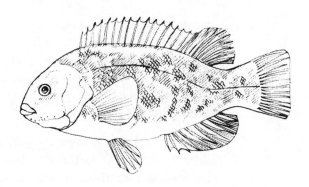

whole rig, will be lost should your line snag. At any rate, be prepared with extra hooks and sinkers when setting out for blackfish.

Bait: Skimmer clams, mussels, periwinkles, fiddler and green crabs are all popular with East End fishermen. Leave crabs whole or cut them in half and push your hook through. When using clams or mussels, crack a hole in the shell and attach the hook. Many anglers swear by this, since bergalls, traveling companions of blackfish and also incorrigible bait stealers, are less likely to filch bait because their teeth aren't strong enough to crush the shells.

Blackfish aren't particularly shy, but they are a bit crafty and almost as adept as bergalls at denuding a hook. Be patient; blackfish like to nibble a bit first, and pulling up too soon may cause them to lose interest. Give your fish time to swallow the bait, then set the hook smartly when the tugs become harder. Once your fish is hooked, be prepared for some sharp maneuvering . . . rushing under rocks or zooming in-between pilings. This is a tricky and courageous fish that you will probably have to wear out before landing—if you manage to land him at all.

BERGALL

Tautogolabrus adspersus

This Wrasse family member is also known as cunner, perch or chogset.

BERGALL AS FOOD: A century ago, when specimens running as large as 2 to 3 pounds were common to Long Island's waters, bergalls were a popular catch. While still abundant, bergalls taken from the same waters today weigh in at much less, and commercial fishery, as a consequence, has declined. Bergall meat is very tasty cleaned, scaled and pan-fried, although its blue tint may disincline some. Unlike blackfish, bergall need not be skinned.

DESCRIPTION: Smaller and more slender than blackfish, but of similar shape, this hard-bodied fish averages 3 to 6 inches and one-half pound. Bergalls have the same sharp, protruding teeth as blackfish, but their lips are thinner and their snouts are more pointed. Color varies with diet and habitat. Skin tones range from reddish-brown to black to bluish beneath the gills.

HABITS, HABITAT AND SEASON: Bergalls are traveling companions of blackfish and correspond to them in seasonal appearances and food tastes. Fish for and cook them as you would blackfish.

STUFFED BLACKFISH, HAMPTON BAYS

◆

Yield: Enough to serve 4 to 6

Since blackfish, with their tightly overlapped, black-edged scales, are hard to clean, freeze them skin deep only or place the cleaned fish under the broiler for a minute or two on each side, then scrape away and discard the skin over the fillets, scales and all.

1 Large, cleaned, whole blackfish either scaled or with skin removed as directed above
3 Tablespoons butter

1 Recipe Ham and Roe Stuffing
6–8 Lemon slices
6 Large pimento-stuffed olives, sliced
1 Recipe Sauce Aurore

Rub the fish with 2 tablespoons softened butter, fill the cavity with stuffing, then arrange in a shallow pan on a piece of heavy-duty aluminum foil long enough to fold up at the ends. Bake at 325° F. following directions on page 26 until fish flakes. Baste with butter. Lift the fish, in the foil, out of the pan, slide it onto a platter, then carefully pull away and discard the foil.

Garnish the fish with a row of lemon slices down the middle of the skinless top fillet. Edge this row on either side with olive slices. Serve immediately with Sauce Aurore.

STUFFED BLACKFISH WITH TOMATO-NUT TOPPING

◆

This is an elegant dish for a very special occasion. The crunchy topping is Oriental in origin but lends itself admirably to Western cuisine.

Follow directions for Stuffed Blackfish, Hampton Bays, but prior to baking, spread the skinless top section with Tomato-Nut Topping. When fish tests done, remove from oven and pipe one recipe Duchesse Potatoes around the fish. Quickly brown the potatoes under the broiler. Serve immediately.

PAN-FRIED BLACKFISH WITH FRUIT

◆

Yield: Enough to serve 6

1½ Pounds blackfish fillets
½ Teaspoon salt
1 Egg, beaten
1 Tablespoon cornstarch
Oil for frying
4 Scallions, with 2 inches green tops, cut in 1-inch pieces

2 Tablespoons each soy sauce and sherry
4 Canned pineapple rings cut in eighths (save the juice)
2 Cups mixed cubed fruit (peaches, papaya, mango, etc.)
6 Slices peeled kiwi fruit

Rinse and dry the fillets. Beat the salt, egg and 2 teaspoons cornstarch together. Dip the fillets in the batter and fry them in 3 tablespoons hot oil until golden on both sides. Transfer fish to a hot platter and keep warm. Stir-fry scallions for one minute. Mix one cup pineapple juice, the soy sauce and sherry with one teaspoon cornstarch, add to scallions and stir over medium heat until thick and smooth. Stir in fruit. Pour over fish, garnish with kiwi slices and serve immediately.

POACHED WHOLE BLACKFISH, SAUCE AMÉRICAINE

◆

Allow ½ pound per serving

Pearly, bland blackfish flesh shows off a superior sauce to advantage. If you were fortunate enough to obtain your fish for a nominal amount, why not splurge on this very special sauce?

1 Recipe Sauce Américaine
1 Large blackfish, cleaned and skinned

Court Bouillon
2 Teaspoons chopped chives

Prepare Sauce Américaine. Poach the fish in Court Bouillon, as directed on page 28. Arrange the fish on a platter. Spoon a little sauce over the meaty skinless portion and sprinkle with chives. Serve the remaining sauce on the side.

BLACKFISH FILLETS À LA MEUNIÈRE

◆

Yield: Enough to serve 6

Simply delicious with garden vegetables and silvery fine-kerneled corn on the cob fresh from Hampton fields.

6 Small blackfish fillets
Salt and pepper to taste
4 Tablespoons butter

2 Lemon wedges
1 Tablespoon coarsely chopped parsley

Rinse, dry and lightly season the fillets with salt and pepper. Fry to golden in 2 tablespoons hot butter, turning once. Arrange on a heated platter and sprinkle with lemon juice and parsley. Quickly swirl the remaining butter in the pan until it is *slightly* browned and nutty in flavor. Pour the hot butter over the fish and serve immediately, while the butter is still foaming.

PAN-FRIED BLACKFISH FILLETS WITH FRIED TOMATOES

◆

Yield: Enough to serve 6

6 Blackfish fillets
6 Medium-size tomatoes
2 Tablespoons each butter and oil
2 Eggs beaten with 1 teaspoon salt

1½ Cups fine white bread crumbs
2 Tablespoons minced fresh thyme (or chives)

Rinse and dry the fillets. Cut the tomatoes into ½-inch slices. Drain well. Heat one tablespoon each butter and oil in each of two large skillets (preferably the nonstick kind). Dip the fillets first in beaten egg, then in bread crumbs, and fry to golden, turning once. While these are frying, quickly dip the tomato slices first in egg and then in bread crumbs and fry to golden in the second pan, turning once. Surround the fillets with the tomatoes and sprinkle with thyme or chives.

STIR-FRIED BLACKFISH WITH LILY BUDS AND SHRIMP

◆

Yield: Enough to serve 6

2½ Pounds blackfish fillets
2 Tablespoons cornstarch
3 Tablespoons water
½ Cup Fish Stock
3 Tablespoons soy sauce
2 Tablespoons sherry
2½ Tablespoons oil

½ Teaspoon salt
15 Dried lily buds, soaked and cut in two
3 Scallions, each with 2 tablespoons green tops, minced
1 Dozen shelled and cleaned shrimp
2–3 Cups hot cooked rice

Rinse the fish fillets, dry them well and cut against the grain into ½-inch slices. Mix 1½ tablespoons cornstarch and water and carefully toss with the fish pieces, taking care not to break them. Mix the Fish Stock, soy sauce, sherry and remaining ½ tablespoon cornstarch.

Heat the oil and salt and gently stir-fry the fish for 3 minutes. Add the lily buds, scallions and shrimp and stir-fry 3 minutes more or until fish flakes. Transfer the fish, lily buds and shrimp to a heated serving platter and keep warm. Add the Fish Stock mixture to the pan and cook, stirring constantly, until thick and smooth. Pour over the fish, lily buds and shrimp and serve immediately with small bowls of rice.

BLACKFISH AND SCALLOPS IN SHELLS

◆

Yield: Enough to serve 6 as a first course or light lunch accompanied by a salad and simple dessert

. . . Put it in a scallop shell, and there you'll cook it very well.

1 Cup bay scallops
3 Cups cooked blackfish*, flaked
1 Recipe Duxelles
A pinch or two of powdered marjoram and thyme

Salt and pepper to taste
1 Recipe Sauce Mornay
3 Tablespoons finely grated cheese
Melted butter

Preheat oven to 500 degrees F.

Poach the scallops or sauté in butter for 2 minutes. Toss the fish and duxelles together and season with the salt, pepper and herbs. Spoon into 6 scallop shells, dot with scallops and mask with Sauce Mornay. Sprinkle each with cheese and melted butter. Bake just until lightly browned. Serve immediately

VARIATION: Substitute for the scallops one cup cooked artichoke bottoms cut into ½-inch cubes.

* Reduce the cooking liquid and use some in the Sauce Mornay.

BLACKFISH AND ANCHOVY SALAD, GARDINER'S BAY

◆

Yield: Enough to serve 6

2 Pounds blackfish fillets
10 Salted flat anchovies, cut in ½-inch pieces and drained
3 Small white onions, peeled, thinly sliced and separated into rings
Salt and pepper to taste

1 Recipe Sauce Vinaigrette à la Moutarde
6 Buttercrunch lettuce leaves
1½ Tablespoons capers, drained
2 Hard-cooked eggs, sieved

Poach the fillets as directed on page 28. Chill. Flake the fish coarsely with a fork. Gently toss with the anchovies, onion rings, salt and pepper, and sauce. Arrange on lettuce leaves in a shallow serving bowl (cut glass is nice) or on a small serving platter. Sprinkle capers in the center, garnish with a border of sieved egg and serve immediately.

CHILLED POACHED WHOLE BLACKFISH WITH FISH-STUFFED HARD-COOKED EGGS

◆

Allow ½ pound per serving

This makes a most attractive star attraction for a cold buffet.

1 Large blackfish, cleaned and skinned
Court Bouillon
1 Bunch watercress, well washed
1 Recipe Basic Fish-Filled Hard-
    Cooked Eggs

1 Recipe Anchovy Mayonnaise
2 Tablespoons finely chopped parsley

Poach the fish in the Court Bouillon as directed on page 28. Chill. Arrange the watercress around the outside of a platter with stems toward the middle. Set the fish in the center and surround with the stuffed eggs. Spoon a little mayonnaise over the skinless portion of the fish and sprinkle parsley over this and the eggs. Serve chilled. Pass the remaining Anchovy Mayonnaise separately.

• •

THE BLUEFISH

. . . First from West India seas they came
Haunting the Cuban coast
Cruel as Spanish buccaneers
A fierce, rapacious host
But now by Northern seaboard shores
Their murderous way they take
From Mexic Gulf to Labrador
Wherever billows break
The weaker tenants of the main
Flee from their rage in vain
The vast menhaden multitudes
They massacre o'er the flood;
With lashing tail, with snapping teeth
They stain the tides with blood . . .

• •

Some years there wasn't no bluefish. When I was a kid, you couldn't hardly steal bluefish. They was here since the Indians was here, they were, but there was a time when I was a boy when there was none. When I was first fishing with father, if we got a bluefish we just took him home and eat 'im right away. Yes, sir, that's how rare they were.

Those Bluefish'll eat anything. Even eat blowfish. An' they're real killers. Small bait'll drive onshore even, to get away from him. Last year the bluefish was full of blowfish. Little blowfish. They et the whole blowfish, they'll eat anything.

• •

BLUEFISH

Pomatomus saltatrix

Although an absolutely first-rate food fish, the "blue" is perhaps even more highly prized as a gamefish because of its evil disposition and the savage fury of its feeding habits. Only the needle-toothed piranha of South America (to which blues may have an ancient link) equals this tasty table fish in lust for blood. Known as the "chopping machine of the sea," or simply "chopper," no other species can come close to the blue for sheer gluttony and wastefulness. Voracious almost to the point of madness, they often empty inland waters of smaller fish simply by making an appearance—sometimes actually beaching these small fry as they flee in terror before them. But to give this devil its due, few fish provide more succulent table fare, nor are many scrappier, trickier, more dynamic or better appreciated by anglers than are these.

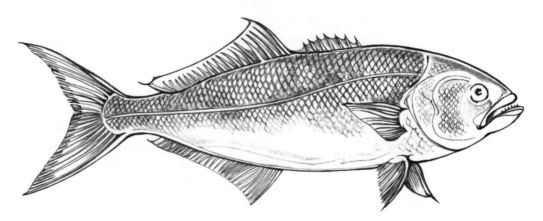

DESCRIPTION: The Bluefish family consists of a single species with distinctive blue- to blue-green or blue-gray color above, fading away to silvery-white on the belly. Young bluefish, called snappers (so special that they rate a section of their own in this book), are a richer blue, with a more distinctive metallic sheen. The bluefish is easily recognized by its large rounded head and deeply forked tail and that most outstanding feature, the mouthful of strong canine teeth that line its upper jaws. Its flesh is somewhat soft and may have an oily taste if the fish has dined primarily on menhaden.

Blues are a migratory species, appearing progressively later in the year as they travel farther north up our Atlantic seacoast in their mysterious wanderings from as far south as Argentina, Brazil and the Gulf of Mexico to as far north as Nova Scotia and as far afield as the Mediterranean Sea, Africa, Madagascar, Australia and New Zealand. Schools, more tightly packed than those of striped bass, usually consist of fish of nearly the same size, since their younger brothers and sisters, nieces and nephews, are all as appealing to adult blues as are the mackerel, herring and menhaden on which they traditionally feed.

BLUEFISH AS FOOD: Freshness is the key here. Unless dressed and refrigerated shortly after being taken from the water, your prize blue will spoil rapidly. High in oil content, blues are among the "fishiest" of local fishes, probably because of their preference for the strong-flavored oily menhaden. Snappers prefer a more delicate menu—mollusks, crustaceans and small inshore fishes—and are consequently sweeter.

To prepare bluefish for broiling or baking, remove the skin if you wish, then cut away the dark strip of meat that runs along the midline. This strip, characteristic of all fast-swimming marine fishes (tuna and mackerel, too), is very nutritious but somewhat bitter. It can be easily excised by making a shallow V-cut along the entire length on both sides with a very sharp, thin knife.

Because this is an oily fish, it is best baked or broiled with as little additional fat as possible. Tomatoes, onions, wine and citrus juice are frequently used in bluefish recipes because they help cut the oily taste.

Freshly caught small snappers need only be gutted and scaled before pan-frying. Here, of course, as in any frying process, some fat is needed to prevent the fish from sticking to the pan. Larger snappers can be filleted butterfly-style, then stuffed and baked. For more specific broiling, baking and frying information, measure the thickness of your fish or fillet and consult the instructions on page 23.

HABITS, HABITAT AND SEASON: Bluefish generally arrive in East End offshore waters in May but rarely work their way into more shallow bays and inlets until just before June, to remain through October. First to make their debut in the spring are "snappers" (under one pound), snapper-blues (one to three pounds), and small to medium-size blues (3 to 5 pounds). Most sport-caught blues appear a little later and range from about 6 pounds to 10 or 12, but the really big blues (up to 14 pounds and called "gorillas" or "alligators") generally appear late in August and continue through October. Once cold weather hits, lowering water temperatures to 58 or 60 degrees or so, blues perfunctorily depart for warmer regions. The two weeks prior to this leave-taking is usually prime angling time both for snappers and larger fish. With bluefish, however, there seems to be no really hard-and-fast rule. No rhyme or reason.

WHERE FOUND: Big blues seem not to be too choosy about depths, except that the heftier fish seem to prefer the deeper waters. One day you may find them at 25 feet, the next they may be taking bait near the bottom at 150-foot depths or even deeper. When blues are feeding near the surface you'll know it by the silver showers of spray boiled up by frantically jumping baitfish, or by blood slicks on the waters where these "choppers" have been rampaging. In the surf, the blues' own favorite hunting grounds seem to be where two tidal currents meet and disorient prey.

HOW TO CATCH: In Long Island waters alone, catching techniques vary radically with the location, with chumming generally preferred in southern areas, trolling dominating at Montauk and jigging generally favored off Orient Point. The best tackle for catching these formidable opponents seems to be a medium-caliber boat or all-purpose conventional tackle, with lighter-tackle rigs used during the spring run or when bay-fishing. In either case, be sure to attach a single-stand wire leader to terminal tackle before putting on hook or lure; with those wicked, razor-sharp teeth blues can (and probably will) bite through anything else.

Hooks: Use No. 5/0 through 8/0, depending on the size of the fish you're going for. Eagle claw is my favorite pattern.

Baits: Both natural baits and artificials are effective. Remember, though, blues prefer a moving lure to a still one, so get your bait or lure to the spot or depth where you suspect blues are feeding, then make it interesting by raising and lowering the rod tip or by reeling in erratically. Start to reel in the instant your bait hits the water. A slack line where blues are concerned can mean lost bait and/or lost fish.

Natural baits can be any baitfish (bunkers, butterfish, herring, smelts, etc.) cut into large slices or whole; squid, molting crab, or strips of fluke belly. Artificial lures include diamond jig, bucktail jig (3-ounce size with pork rind attached to animate it further), Scotch rig (the minnow-school look makes this particularly attractive to snappers), with or without squid or pork rind pieces attached, and rigged eel or eelskin lures for the biggies. Metal squids are especially effective when surf-casting. As a rule, however, natural baits are most successful early in the season, while artificial lures seem to be more effective as summer glows on.

FISHING METHODS: Gluttons by nature, blues will strike at practically anything that moves, so most fishing methods—bottom-fishing, drifting, trolling or surf-casting—can be effective. The first blues of the season are usually swimming deep, so look for them near or at the bottom. This is the one time of the year, however, that some fish, filled with milt or eggs, might be finicky diners. With spawning out of the way, however, appetites increase dramatically, as do catches.

Shore anglers should find the early morning or sunset hours the best time to hook bluefish. During the heat of the day, blues tend to follow baitfish into cooler, deeper waters. If you're boat-fishing you'll have to sample all depths, methods and speeds until luck starts fishing with you. Should you encounter a surfaced school, be sure to keep your boat to one edge or just ahead of the fish, or cast just in front or in back, rather than in the center of the school, so that you don't startle the fish and cause them to sound. When casting, vary the speed of retrieve and change your lure occasionally.

Once a bluefish takes your hook, you'll know it! There's nothing delicate about it, nothing prissy or tentative. As soon as he bites, he's off in a wild rush for freedom. Never allow him as much as an inch of slack! He may run with your line at first, but the minute he slows down or reverses direction, *reel in* to help set the hook and prevent your fish from tossing it or chewing his way up your line to bite it off.

Blues struggle mightily when landed and don't shy from directing their ferocious choppers at whatever's handiest—your fingers included. This is one fish that has no intention of cooperating in its own capture. Besides the danger of a nasty nip, it can easily be knocked off the hook while you're netting or gaffing. From start to finish, this is a scrappy, tricky, unpredictable fish.

SNAPPERS AND SNAPPER-BLUES

At our house we consider the perfect late-summer meal to be a bucket of snappers snapped from the bay only minutes prior to pan-frying, ears of corn pulled from their stalks only seconds before cooking, and tomatoes still tepid from the vine, all sprinkled with mincings of assorted fresh herbs from the flowerbox on our patio. Heaven! Although snappers are perfect without embellishments, in times of plenty some variety is pleasing.

(Allow 1 or 2 snappers per serving, depending on size.)

BACON-FRIED SNAPPERS WITH FRIED TOMATO SLICES

◆

6–12 Snappers, cleaned and scaled
Flour

6–12 Thin strips bacon
1 Recipe Fried Tomato Slices

Dust the fish lightly with flour. Use toothpicks to secure a bacon strip around each fish. Pan-fry as directed on page 26. The bacon gives the fish a delicious flavor that is complemented by the fried tomato slices.

OYSTER-STUFFED SNAPPERS

◆

6–12 Snappers, cleaned and
    scaled
Salt and pepper

Flour
6–12 Large shelled oysters
2 Tablespoons minced fresh thyme

Sprinkle the fish lightly with salt and pepper, inside and out. Dust lightly with flour. Roll oysters in thyme, place in the fish cavities and secure with toothpicks. Pan-fry as directed on page 26.

BAKED SNAPPER-BLUES WITH GARDEN STUFFING

◆

Yield: Enough to serve 6

There is a fine line between a large snapper and a small snapper-blue.

2 Cups garden-fresh lettuce, well
    washed
2 Cups spinach, well washed
3 Scallions, with 3 inches green tops
1 Tablespoon each minced fresh
    tarragon, thyme and parsley
2 Tablespoons butter
Salt and pepper

3–6 Whole lettuce leaves
¼ Cup Crème Fraîche
3–6 Snapper-blues, cleaned, scaled
    and butterflied, as directed on
    page 16
1¼ Cups dry white wine
Kneaded Butter

Cut the lettuce (reserve the whole leaves), the spinach and the scallions into ¼-inch strips. Sauté with the herbs in the butter until the vegetables wilt. Season to taste. Roll a bit of the wilted vegetables in each lettuce leaf with a spoonful of crème fraîche to form small, neat packages that can be slipped inside of the fish. Fasten with toothpicks.

Bake the fish as directed on page 26. Baste the fish frequently with the wine. Arrange the fish on a heated platter and keep them warm. Thicken the juices in the baking pan with kneaded butter. Adjust seasonings. Serve the fish with the hot sauce.

SNAPPERS IN PUMPERNICKEL CRUMBS

◆

These dark crusty crumbs contrast nicely with the pale, moist fish flesh.

6–12 Snappers
Dry pumpernickel crumbs, finely
    crushed

Rinse the fish but do not dry too thoroughly. Press the snappers into the crumbs and pan-fry as directed on page 26. Handle the fish with care so the crumbs do not fall off.

BAKED SNAPPER-BLUES WITH SHRIMP AND SCALLOP STUFFING

◆

Yield: Enough to serve 6

6 Small snapper-blues, cleaned, scaled
   and butterflied, as directed on
   page 16
Salt and pepper

1 Recipe Shrimp and Scallop Stuffing
1¼ Cups tomato juice
¾ Cup Crème Fraîche
1 Tablespoon minced fresh marjoram

Rub the fish lightly inside and out with salt and pepper, fill with the seafood stuffing and fasten with toothpicks. Bake as directed on page 26, basting the fish frequently with the tomato juice. Arrange the fish on a heated platter and keep them warm. Reduce the tomato-pan juices to ¾ cup and stir into the crème fraîche, along with the marjoram. Pass the tepid sauce with the fish.

SWEET AND TANGY BAKED BLUEFISH WITH FRESH-PICKED TOMATOES

◆

Yield: Enough to serve 6

Since bluefish is so highly perishable, it's best to eat it only when and where you can be assured of its freshness. Hamptons markets and restaurants have the advantage of close proximity to the sea, plus a tradition of bluefish cookery that dates back to Indian days. Tomatoes provide a nice counterpoint to the high fat content of this fish, and those vegetables ripened in gardens continuously sweetened by mists fresh off East End bays and inlets seem to develop a particularly high sugar content. Taste your tomatoes before you add them to this dish. If they seem to have an acid aftertaste, follow the advice of the nineteenth-century originator of this recipe and sprinkle them with a little *extra* sugar just before you pop them into the oven.

1 8-pound bluefish, cleaned
Flour
¼ Cup Clarified Butter
10 Medium-size tomatoes, peeled and
   seeded

1 Tablespoon each minced fresh basil,
   thyme and sugar
Salt and white pepper
Lemon slices

Wipe fish well and dust very lightly with flour. In a large, shallow ovenproof dish heat the butter in an oven preheated to 450 degrees F. Arrange the fish in the butter and place the tomatoes attractively around them. Sprinkle the tomatoes with the herbs, sugar and seasoning. Bake as directed on page 26, brushing the fish several times during cooking with the pan juices. Serve immediately, garnished with lemon slices.

BLUEFISH BAKED WITH FENNEL, REMSENBERG

◆

Allow ½ pound to 1 pound per serving

1 3–5-pound bluefish, cleaned and scaled
Salt and pepper
Branches of fennel, including some with seeds
1 Large leek, split, well washed and sliced

1 Cup dry white wine
¼ Cup melted butter
¾ Cup heavy cream beaten with 2 egg yolks
4 Thin lemon slices
2 Tablespoons chopped parsley

Rinse the fish, dry it well and rub it lightly inside and out with salt and pepper. Fill the cavity with fennel. (If fresh fennel is not available, crush 1½ tablespoons fennel seeds in a mortar or blender with one cup coarsely chopped parsley. Rub the cavity with half this mixture. Rub the outside of the fish with the rest.) Arrange remaining fennel branches and the sliced leek in the bottom of the baking pan. Place the fish on top of the herbs and vegetables, spoon a mixture of the wine and butter over it and bake as directed on page 26, basting frequently.

Place the fish on a heated serving platter and keep it warm. Purée the pan juices, herbs and vegetables and press through a strainer. Reduce the purée to 1 cup over medium heat, add the cream/egg-yolk mixture and stir until thickened over low heat. Do not let the sauce boil. Season to taste. Garnish the fish with lemon slices and parsley. Pass the sauce separately.

BAKED BLUEFISH WITH CARROT TWIGS, SAGG POND

◆

Allow ½ pound to 1 pound per serving

1 4–5-pound whole bluefish, cleaned
Salt and pepper
1 Large leek, split, well washed and sliced
½ Cup parsley, coarsely chopped
3 Tablespoons finely chopped fresh tarragon

1 Large clove garlic, minced
3 Tablespoons butter
1½ Cups white wine
1 Recipe Carrot Twigs
1 Cup Crème Fraîche
4 Lime slices

Rinse and dry the fish and sprinkle lightly, inside and out, with salt and pepper. Strew the leek, parsley, 2 tablespoons tarragon and the garlic over the bottom of a large baking pan. Arrange the fish on the vegetables and top with pats of butter. Add one cup wine to the pan and bake as directed on page 26, basting often. Meanwhile, prepare the carrot twigs.

Place the fish on a heated serving platter and keep warm.

Add the remaining half-cup wine to the baking pan and stir over medium heat until the liquid in the pan is reduced to ¼ cup. Purée in blender or food processor or press through a sieve. Stir this into the crème fraîche, along with the remaining tablespoon of tarragon. Adjust seasonings. Arrange the hot carrots around the fish. Decorate the fish with lime slices. Serve with the sauce.

BLUEFISH MARINATED IN CUMIN AND SOY

◆

Yield: Enough to serve 6

2 Whole cleaned bluefish, about
   2½–3 pounds each
2 Teaspoons powdered cumin
1 Tablespoon each fresh lime and
   lemon juice
2 Cloves garlic, peeled and crushed
1 Cup soy sauce
2 Tablespoons olive oil

Cut three ¼-inch-deep slashes in both sides of each bluefish.

   Arrange the fish in an ovenproof serving dish. Mix remaining ingredients and pour them over the fish, turning once so that both sides of the fish are well coated. Refrigerate 4 to 6 hours, turning once. Broil as directed on page 24, turning once. Serve hot with the strained pan juices.

BLUEFISH BAKED WITH YOGURT CHEESE

◆

Yield: Enough to serve 6

This fresh herb-cheese is wonderful cooked with fish. A house specialty, Chez Tarr.

3 1-pound bluefish fillets
Butter
1 Recipe Yogurt Cheese

Rinse and dry the fish and place in a well-buttered dish. Spread with the cheese and bake as directed on page 26. Serve immediately.

BLOWFISH

Sphoeroides maculatus

This quick-change artist is the local representative of the Puffer family (*Tetradontidae*). All puffers have the ability, when disturbed, to inflate with air or water to transform themselves from small, rather innocuous fish to ferocious-looking spiny globes capable of rebuffing the most determined predators. The common name here is Northern puffer, but the fish is also known as blowfish, swellfish, balloonfish, globefish, bottlefish and, as that high-priced delicacy sea squab.

BLOWFISH AS FOOD: An excellent table fish with delicate white meat that bears a surprising similarity to the moist, dense flesh of frog's legs, it lends itself to a multitude of culinary delectables from Sea Squab Diable to Bouillabaisse. The past slump in its popularity has been reversed, and blowfish is staging a strong comeback. Only the large strips of sweet, tender meat on either side of the backbone are considered safe to eat. All other parts, including the roe and viscera, should be discarded.

In Japan, where the fish is known as *fugu,* there are some 30 varieties to choose from, with 1500 *fugu* restaurants in Tokyo alone dedicated to serving them in season (October to March).

If possible, it's a good idea to let an expert either clean the fish or demonstrate before you attempt the cleaning job on your own. If no expert is available, here is the procedure: First get thick rubber gloves (for protection from the fish's prickly skin) and a very sharp knife. Place the fish, belly-side down, on a newspaper-covered surface. The fish's head should be to your right if you're right-handed, to your left if you're left-handed.

Holding the body with your free hand, make an incision behind the head, at right angles to the fish's long axis, until you've severed the backbone. Slip the end of the meaty spine out through this hole and pull it out, turning the skin inside-out, leaving only the clean, firm, white meat on the bone (something like a chicken drumstick in shape). Rinse this meaty piece well in salted water and pat dry. Refrigerate immediately. (Just to be on the safe side, wrap the remains in the newspaper and discard where pets won't nibble at them.)

◆ ◆

I've seen blowfish where there's no end to 'em. Bay was full of 'em. Now they're so scarce they go for five dollars somethin' a pound. People never eat 'em back then. Said they was poison. Well, inside they got a big gall in 'em, and that is poison. But if you get rid of that sack of gall on the liver, then they're not poison at all. Just put on gloves when you're cleanin' 'em or they'll tear your hands all t' pieces. They're sandy, you know. Sand-papery. Put on gloves and just cut 'em across the back, and turn 'em like that, inside out. Flip 'em over like you would an eel an' pull the skin right off over the tail. No trick to it at all.

◆ ◆

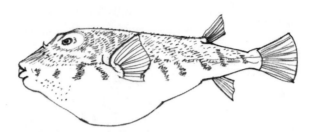

DESCRIPTION: A small inshore species averaging 8 to 10 inches in length, yellow-brown to green-brown on the dorsal area, fading to greenish-yellow sides, streaked with irregular crossbars and a white belly. Blowfish have single dorsal and anal fins, both set far back near the tail, and spiny, rough-textured skin.

HABITS, HABITAT AND SEASON: These are bottom-feeding fish that dine on small crustaceans, mollusks, marine worms and other small marine organisms. Blowfish seldom frequent waters more than 20 to 25 feet deep and are off-again, on-again visitors in quantity in East End waters. Once so plentiful locally that, according to one old-timer, "You could walk across the [Accabonac] Creek just steppin' on puffers from one shore t'other," they now are quite scarce and are an incidental catch.

BLOWFISH DIABLE

◆

Yield: Enough to serve 6

1½ Dozen cleaned blowfish
Flour
2 Eggs, lightly beaten
1 Tablespoon heavy cream
Fine bread crumbs
3 Tablespoons each butter and olive oil

2 Tablespoons minced parsley
3 Tablespoons Worcestershire sauce
¼ Teaspoon dry mustard
⅓ Cup bourbon
Parsley sprigs

Dust fish lightly in flour and shake to remove excess. Dip in eggs beaten with heavy cream and then in fine bread crumbs. Fry in 3 tablespoons butter and 3 tablespoons olive oil until golden on both sides. Arrange on a heated serving plate with tails pointing outward. Keep warm. Sprinkle parsley in oil remaining in the pan, add Worcestershire sauce, mustard and bourbon. Stir over low heat, until sauce is well integrated. Pour hot sauce over fried fish. Garnish center of platter with parsley sprigs and serve immediately.

BLOWFISH IN GARLIC BUTTER

◆

Yield: Enough to serve 6

1½ Dozen cleaned blowfish
1 Cup cold milk
Flour
8 Tablespoons butter
3 Tablespoons olive oil

Salt and pepper to taste
Lemon juice
1 Tablespoon peeled minced garlic
2 Tablespoons minced parsley

Soak fish in milk for 20 minutes, turning once. Dip in flour, shake off excess and sauté in 3 tablespoons butter and 3 tablespoons olive oil until golden brown on both sides. Arrange on platter with tails pointing outward, sprinkle with salt, freshly ground pepper and a few drops of lemon juice. Keep warm.

Lightly brown 5 tablespoons butter, add minced garlic and cook one minute longer. Pour hot garlic butter over fish, sprinkle with minced parsley and serve immediately.

BLOWFISH WITH VINE-RIPE TOMATOES: Follow directions for Blowfish in Garlic Butter, but add 2 peeled, seeded and chopped tomatoes, 2 teaspoons fresh thyme and ½ cup white wine to the garlic butter. Cook over medium-high heat until the sauce is slightly thickened.

BLOWFISH WITH GREEN TOMATOES: A nice variation of the above may be prepared with green tomatoes substituting for the red. In this case a generous pinch or two of sugar should be added. For a variation within a variation, a tablespoon of heavy cream stirred with the hot green tomato sauce mellows the flavor.

BLOWFISH WITH LEMON AND BROWNED BUTTER

◆

Yield: Enough to serve 6

1½ Dozen cleaned blowfish
1 Cup milk
Flour
6 Tablespoons butter
3 Tablespoons vegetable oil

Salt and pepper to taste
Lemon juice
18 Thin lemon slices
2 Tablespoons minced parsley

Soak fish in milk for 20 minutes, turning once. Dip each in flour, shake off excess and brown in 3 tablespoons butter and 3 tablespoons oil, turning once. Arrange fish on heated serving platter with tails pointing outward. Sprinkle with salt, freshly ground pepper and a few drops of lemon juice. Keep warm. Discard butter in pan. Heat remaining butter until it is a golden nut-brown and pour over fish. Garnish with thin overlapping slices of lemon, sprinkle with parsley and serve immediately.

BLOWFISH WITH TOASTED ALMONDS: Follow directions for Blowfish with Lemon and Browned Butter above, but to browned butter add 6 tablespoons blanched, slivered, toasted almonds.

BLOWFISH WITH SAUTEED POTATOES: Follow directions for Blowfish with Lemon and Browned Butter. While the fish is cooking, sauté in butter in a separate pan, until tender and golden brown, one peeled and finely diced medium-size potato for each person being served. Arrange fish over potatoes, pour the browned butter over all and serve immediately.

DEEP-FRIED BLOWFISH

◆

Yield: Enough to serve 6

1½ Dozen cleaned blowfish
1 Cup milk
3 Eggs, lightly beaten
1½ Tablespoons heavy cream

A pinch each of salt, white pepper
*   and nutmeg*
2 Cups fine white bread crumbs
Oil for deep-frying

Soak fish in milk for 20 minutes, turning once. Drain and dry thoroughly. Beat eggs with heavy cream, salt, pepper and nutmeg. Dip fish in egg mixture and then in bread crumbs. Fry in deep oil to golden brown. Drain on paper towels and serve immediately.

BUTTERFISH

Stromateidae

Two local representatives of the Harvestfish family (*Stromateidae*) are the butterfish (*Peprilus triacanthus*) and those occasional visitors their Southern cousins harvestfish (*P. alepidotus*). Neither of these small (6- to 9-inch average) finely-flavored look-alikes has much angling appeal, but both are eagerly sought after commercially and are usually marketed together.

The butterfish, also called dollarfish, is a silvery-blue, laterally-flattened oval fish with small, delicately overleafed silvery scales. Its dorsal and anal fins are of nearly equal length and the tail fin is deeply forked. Favorite foods include squid, shrimp, marine worms and small fishes.

Their marked preference for warm waters generally brings butterfish to the East End only during late spring and summer months, although the market season extends into fall. Nearly all of these are taken commercially by draggers and trawlers and in traps.

P. alepidotus is similar in dietary tastes and seasonal appearance but the body is deeper and more rounded in shape and the fins are longer and more pointed than those of butterfish.

BUTTERFISH AS FOOD: Butterfish, as the name implies, are high in fat content with dark-meated flesh of excellent flavor, especially when smoked. Scale and split, then broil or bake with skin intact as directed for any mackerel.

PAN-FRIED BUTTERFISH

◆

Yield: Enough to serve 6

Few fish pan-fry more successfully than butterfish.

6 Butterfish, cleaned and scaled
Salt and pepper
2 Beaten eggs
Bread crumbs or batter

1 Recipe Sauce Tartare or Tomato-Cream Sauce
Butter and/or oil for frying
Chopped parsley

Rinse the fish, dry them well and sprinkle lightly with salt and pepper, inside and out. Follow directions for pan-frying on page 26. Arrange on a hot platter, sprinkle with parsley and serve with Sauce Tartare or Tomato-Cream Sauce.

SMOKED BUTTERFISH

◆

Butterfish are particularly wonderful smoked because they are so flavorful and fatty and therefore do not dry out appreciably. Follow directions for smoking.

BROILED BUTTERFISH

These sweet, buttery little fellows are not only small but delicately fleshed, so it's important to broil them quickly and close to the source of heat, basting often and generously.

BROILED BUTTERFISH WITH SAUCE BÉARNAISE

◆

Yield: Enough to serve 6

6 Butterfish, cleaned and scaled
Salt and pepper
12 Good-sized mushroom caps

Butter
1 Recipe Sauce Béarnaise
Minced chives

Rinse the fish, wipe dry and sprinkle lightly, inside and out, with salt and pepper. Broil fish, as directed on page 24, along with the mushroom caps, brushing both generously with butter. Arrange the fish on heated plates, top each with 2 mushroom caps filled with hot Sauce Béarnaise. Sprinkle with chives and serve immediately.

BROILED BUTTERFISH WITH MUSTARD BUTTER: Follow directions for Butterfish with Sauce Béarnaise but fill the mushroom caps with Mustard Butter instead.

BROILED BUTTERFISH WITH TWO BUTTERS

◆

Nothing could be sweeter than discovering a cache of fat little butterfish at the fish market, lined up and just waiting to be bought and broiled either on an outdoor grill or indoors if the weather is bad. The two flavored butters provide both zest and subtle backup flavor.

6 Butterfish, cleaned
Salt and pepper
¼ Cup Anchovy Butter
½ Cup Green Butter

Parsley sprigs
Lemon wedges
2 Teaspoons grated lemon zest

Wipe the fish inside and out with a damp cloth and sprinkle with salt and pepper. Brush with Anchovy Butter and broil 5 or 6 minutes on each side (or until fish tests done), brushing with Anchovy Butter several times.

When fish are golden brown on both sides arrange on a heated platter, surround with parsley and lemon wedges and dollop with spoonfuls of chilled Green Butter and a sprinkling of lemon zest. Serve immediately.

FROSTED BUTTERFISH

♦

Yield: Enough to serve 6

A unique and attractive fish dish is this salt-frosted specialty.

6 Good-size butterfish
Kosher salt
⅓ Cup rice vinegar
3 Tablespoons Fish Stock

1½ Tablespoons Chinese soy sauce
1 Tablespoon oyster sauce
1 Scallion, with 3 inches green top, minced

Sprinkle the fish with salt inside and out and set aside for 25 minutes. Meanwhile mix vinegar, stock, soy, oyster sauce and scallion. Wipe the salt and liquid from the fish with paper towels. Skewer each fish from tail to head and then sprinkle with salt, coating the tails and fins heavily so that they will "frost up" on the grill. Broil or grill 2 to 3 minutes on each side, until the flesh flakes but is still juicy. Serve with small individual bowls of the vinegar dip.

THE CODFISH FAMILY

Gadidae

Codfish belong to a large and imposing family (twenty in all, in both Atlantic and Pacific waters) of elongated, soft-rayed, cold-water fishes. All are bottom-dwellers and all, except for whiting, sport a single barbel, a jaunty goatee-like appendage on the lower lip that functions as a sensory organ.

Local members of this outstanding family include not only the pearl-white Atlantic cod, but haddock, pollock, tomcod, squirrel hake and whiting (silver hake). The presence in this country's coastal waters of huge numbers of these cod and cod relatives was an important factor in the European colonization of both New England and Canada's maritime provinces. Beginning with John Cabot's first exploration of Newfoundland in 1497, glowing reports of offshore waters teeming with fish that literally leapt into weighted baskets lowered to catch them spurred thousands to seek their fortunes in the New World, not in fabled gold or exotic spices, but in fishing for the humble and ubiquitous cod.

What makes the waters off the eastern Atlantic seaboard so bounteous in codfish family members? The thermal conditions created by the juncture of the cold Labrador Current with the warmer Gulf Stream in the vicinity of the Grand Banks produce an ideal breeding ground for the chain of marine life upon which codfish directly or indirectly subsist. Commercial fishing vessels ply their trade all along the Continental Shelf, from the Grand Bank off Newfoundland to Georges Bank east of Massachusetts and southward, but some of the finest codfishing grounds in the world are located between Long Island's Montauk Point and Rhode Island's nearby Block Island. These waters supply most of the cod for the New York area (mainly from draggers and trawlers based on Long Island's eastern tip) as well as abundant table fare for hundreds of towns and villages up and down Long Island and into New England.

ATLANTIC COD

Gadus Morhau

Also known as codfish and rock cod, this is probably the most important food fish in the world, with an annual take by commercial fishing vessels of all nations exceeding 6 *billion* pounds.

CODFISH AS FOOD: Internationally prized for its delicate taste and beautiful texture, cod has the ability to graciously accept the flavors of foods whose gastronomical company it keeps. Its culinary applications are staggering . . . whether baked, broiled, fried, boiled, patted into fish cakes, served up with any one of an infinite variety of sauces or tucked into casseroles or chowders, its milky-white, rather firm flesh is really the star of the culinary show. This firmness depends not only on size of the fish (smaller fish are finer-grained than are large ones) but also on freshness. Some local authorities insist that refrigerating the fish overnight (or two) makes it more tender.

Commercially, cod is sold fresh or frozen as steaks or fillets, in cans or salted. Salt cod's popularity diminished as refrigeration became the rule rather than the exception in the American home, and this treat seems to me to be shamefully neglected in this country's cuisine. Internationally, however, salt cod is still highly prized.

Cod is also available smoked as *Finnan Haddie,* and as roe—fresh, frozen, salted, smoked or sold as caviar. Even tender cod cheeks are highly prized. Cod is also highly nutritious. Depression babies in particular will remember cod liver as the source of "mother's favorite" health food, cod liver oil, so rich in Vitamin D.

DESCRIPTION: Average fish size is about 2 to 3 feet in length and from 5 to 20 pounds in weight, although larger specimens are not uncommon. Deep-water granddaddy winter cods may measure 4 feet long and weigh in at 50 or more pounds. The catch record (dating back to 1895) is an incredible 6 feet and 211 pounds!

Color may also vary. Back and upper sides may range from gray-green to red-brown in some fishing grounds, but fish are generally gray-brown, spotted with reddish-brown with a rather pale lateral line. Belly color is light-gray or tan.

Other distinguishing characteristics are the slanting head; ample silhouette; large mouth and the *three* rounded soft-rayed dorsal fins of fairly equal size; two anal fins, of which the forward one is slightly larger; paired pectoral fins below and behind the gill covers; and an almost straight, very slightly concave tail fin.

HABITS, HABITAT AND SEASON: Atlantic cod roam in packs over sea bottoms at depths that range from a few feet to more than 1500; young cod (marketed as scrod) generally stay closer to shore in depths of less than 60 feet. Called "vacuum cleaners of the sea," cods' favorite food is herring, but their omnivorous tastes extend to clams, snails, mussels, lobsters and sea urchins (all still in their shells), starfish, fishes great and small, and, when the big fellows are really ravenous, legend has it that they'll swallow tin cans, bottles, nuts and bolts, ropes, light bulbs and even whole sea birds.

Cod love brisk temperatures and so are the main drawing card of winter anglers in local Long Island waters as well as up and down both sides of the North Atlantic. Smaller fish frequent shellfish beds as early as October, but the behemoths arrive in deeper waters in mid-November and generally remain well into April.

WHERE FOUND: Long Island's East End has been favored by nature since glacial times to provide us with our unique land and sea gardens. Although cod are migrators, they do, provided ideal circumstances, have the good sense to settle into a particularly satisfying location. Winter visitors elsewhere, cod can be caught nearly year-round in the waters between Long Island's Montauk and Rhode Island's Block Island, Cox's Ledge, southeast of Block Island, and around the ravaged remains of the *Andrea Doria*. Cod favor rocky or pebbled bottoms, but may also be found ranging over sand, mud or plant-laden bottoms or around underwater rocks and wrecks.

HOW TO CATCH: Although they cruise at different depths, cod are principally a deep-water species that prefer to do their own hunting at or near the ocean floor. Many are taken by anglers in charter or party boats, but fishing from piers or jetties or from small boats, weather obliging, can also be rewarding. Because most cod tend to be of appreciable size, the preferred tackle is a conventional fiberglass boat rod of medium weight or any sturdy rod of similar specification and a salt-water reel with star drag. Use a 30-pound monofilament line; it's rugged enough to handle fairly large cod and to withstand long immersion in icy waters. Tie on a bank-type or diamond sinker; weight can range from 6 to 12 ounces, depending on depth being fished and strength of tidal current. A special cod-catching favorite out our way is the Montauk Special—a 3-hook outfit with a high-low (bottom) rig with another hook midway for good measure.

Cod are singularly unchoosy about baits and will snap up strips of mackerel, herring, butterfish or squid, but the time-tested East End bait preference is skimmer clam on a standard codfish hook or other 5/0 to 9/0 pattern attached to a long 2-foot snell or leader. Even though cod rely a good deal on scent, it can't do any harm to do a bit of jigging. Be sure to have a gaff handy to help you in landing your catch.

TOMCOD
Microgadus tomcod

This delicious miniature version of Atlantic Cod is also known as Atlantic tomcod and frostfish and by its local Hamptons nickname—"Tommy cod."

TOMCOD AS FOOD: Commercial fishermen take only a few tomcod in traps and with bag-nets, so not many find their way to market. Most likely you will have to catch your own . . . and on a warm day in early spring this is a pleasant task well worth the effort. Dedicated tomcod fanciers, and there are a goodly number, consider the fish exceptional fare.

DESCRIPTION: In addition to size, which seldom exceeds one foot, the tomcod also differs from its larger relative in having prolonged ventral fins, a rounded rather than concave tail, and olive or brown-green dorsal coloring patterned with dark spots and blotches; belly color varies from white to yellow-white. Weight averages less than 2 pounds.

HABITS, HABITAT AND SEASON: An inshore fish that favors shoal waters of varying degrees of salinity, tomcod are rarely found in waters more than 20 feet deep, where they cruise the bottom in search of clams, squid, small fish, tiny shrimp, marine worms, and amphipods. Tomcod gets its local name "frostfish" from its early winter ascent of brackish coastal rivers (including the Hudson) to spawn. In winter and early spring, fish for these in harbors and bays and around breakwaters and piers; any bottom-fishing method, using any of their favorite foods, should net you some. During the spawning season, try estuaries.

POLLOCK

Pollachius virens

Also known as pollack, American pollock, Boston bluefish and sea salmon. This is another Atlantic cod look-alike, but lively pollock is prized by in-the-know anglers as a true gamefish. If you are looking for the perfect combination of angling pleasure and culinary treasure—this may be it.

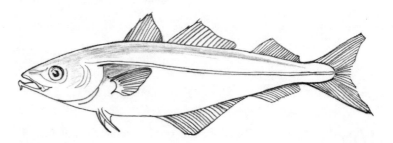

POLLOCK AS FOOD: Pollock is a relative of both Atlantic cod and haddock, with a flavor somewhere between the two but with a somewhat drier texture than either.

Very nearly as versatile as its more famous cousins, pollock is often less expensive and is delicious cut into steaks or fillets, then broiled, fried, barbecued or substituted for cod in any recipe (especially as cakes, creamed or boiled in a New England–style dinner).

Restaurants occasionally feature it as "Boston bluefish," and in retail markets, pollock is sold fresh, frozen and, occasionally, as smoked fillets.

DESCRIPTION: Pollock closely resembles and is often mistaken for Atlantic cod, but its color ranges from blue-green to gray-green to olive. Skin tones beneath the pale lateral line blend from light-green to yellowish-

or silvery-gray. The body is plumper, the head more pointed and the tail fin more deeply forked than the Atlantic cod's, but it has the common cod-family traits—3 dorsal fins, 2 anal fins and a fleshy chin whisker called a barbel. Pollock do occasionally grow as large as 4 feet and weigh up to 35 pounds, but the average fish runs from 4 to 12 pounds.

HABITS, HABITAT AND SEASON: Gluttonous bottom-feeders, pollock are found in shallower waters than either Atlantic cod or haddock. Feeding tastes run to herrings, sand eels, shrimp, squid and the like, but pollock are also voracious consumers of the young of their own codfish family clan. Bait-fish respect the pollocks' appetite and stay away from them in droves, causing the sea surface to boil with fish when pollock are feeding below. Look for this disturbance—or wheeling gulls—as a sign that pollock, or other worthy fish, are about. Pollock are not the flashy tricksters that bluefish are, but for tug-of-war determination pollock rate high. You'll know it when one of these babies hits, but later it may feel like you're reeling in a stubborn stone. Don't be fooled. Stay with it. . . . The feast you'll savor later will make it all worthwhile. In general, seasons are similar to those for Atlantic cod, but remember, pollock season peaks later in the spring—from April to mid-June.

WHERE FOUND: Pollock are taken on rod and reel by charter and party-boat anglers and commercially by trawls, hand-lines, gill nets, seines and traps in deeper offshore waters. They sometimes follow bait into shallow waters, giving anglers midspring opportunities.

HOW TO CATCH: Pollock is more of a true gamefish than the rest of the cod family tribe and its eyesight is better, so moving lures will be more intriguing. Trolling is the way to go here—either near the surface, at an intermediate depth or deep, as with cod. If trolling fails, try bottom-fishing with skimmer clams, strips or squid or sand eel; artificials most likely to work include large streamer flies, chrome spoons or diamond jigs. Surf-casters might do well with floating plugs or poppers.

HADDOCK

Melanogrammus aeglefinus

This cousin to the Atlantic cod runs its popular relative a close second in market value and, from a culinary standpoint, is rightly considered to be even more flavorful and finer-textured. Once abundant, in recent years its numbers have been declining in local waters.

HADDOCK AS FOOD: Few fish are more delicately flavored or more finely fleshed than this one. Its affinity for sauces is dazzling; its versatility, impressive. Fresh or frozen haddock steaks and fillets lend themselves to a wide variety of cooking methods: broiling, baking, frying and poaching.

Because haddock meat is softer than cod's, it is generally preserved by smoking rather than salting. Split into fillets and smoked, it comes forth as famed "Finnan Haddie," the Scottish vernacular for "Haddock from Findon," a small fishing hamlet near Aberdeen, where the delicacy originated more than a century ago.

The market term scrod usually refers to filleted young Atlantic cod but it is sometimes applied to haddock fillets as well.

THE HADDOCK FISHERS

Off the grand bank of Newfoundland
Amid the drifting fogs and rain
Now weltering in the drowsy calm
Now tossing in mad hurricane
Amid the sleety snows and hail
Wrestling with billow and with gale
The humble fishing schooner rides
The sport, the plaything of the tides.

DESCRIPTION: Haddock are similar in shape to Atlantic cod, but have a pointed forward dorsal fin, dark lateral line, silvery sides beneath a purple-gray dorsal area, and a distinctive dark blotch known as a "devil's mark" just above the pectoral fins. A much smaller fish than Atlantic cod, average weight is 3 to 4 pounds with lengths from 12 to 24 inches.

HABITS, HABITAT AND SEASON: A somewhat sluggish, cold-water fish, haddock feed similarly to Atlantic cod but in deeper waters. Commercially fished with gill nets or small-mesh trawl nets, a few are also hooked by nonprofessionals.

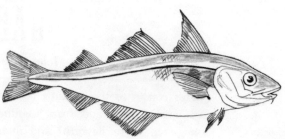

WHITING

Merluccius bilinearis

An unusual Hamptons happening is the appearance of whiting on the snow-dusted beaches. On a sooty-velvet winter night beached whiting may be harvested by "frost fishing," a method that's been a local Long Island tradition for generations. Only three conditions are required: a cold winter night, strong, cooperative seas and the stamina of a Samson. Fishermen drive their trucks along the sand until in the headlights' glow they locate the whiting, stunned into silvery frozen fish-icicles by the cold air. The fish are scooped up by hand or with small nets into plastic buckets. If you feel adventurous, try harvesting on foot with a large flashlight and a plastic garbage bag.

Also known as silver or New England hake or by their local nicknames, "frost fish" or "winter weakfish," this is one of a dozen or so hakes belonging to the codfish family.

WHITING AS FOOD: This soft-textured, moist, delicately flavored fish is highly perishable and rather temperamental when exposed to the heat of cooking. Keep your catch very cold and wrap it well if you must freeze it. Handle whiting with care when frying or poaching, or bake it with a sauce rather than broiling or sautéing it, to prevent the fish from falling apart. Whiting is a superb candidate for smoking, since this method not only adds flavor but removes some moisture, making the fish a bit easier to handle.

DESCRIPTION: Small, slender hakes differ from their larger, plump cod cousins in having only two dorsal fins and one anal fin, and also lack the characteristic cod-family chin barbel. A gleaming, silvery fish with a slightly darker upper back, shading to a pure-silver belly, whitings average 14 to 16 inches in length and weigh in between 1½ and 2½ pounds.

HABITS, HABITAT AND SEASON: Deep-water fish with large mouths, sharp teeth and ravenous appetites, whiting regularly charge into shallower waters in pursuit of squid, crabs, shrimp and baitfish, sometimes recklessly pursuing these into the treacherous surf, onto the beach and into East End skillets.

HOW TO CATCH: Regular bottom-fishing is fine here, with light tackle (or conventional if you're in cod/pollock waters), but remember, whiting's baitfish-chasing inshore dashes make surf-fishing profitable also. Use a medium-weight surf-spinning outfit, and bait 1/0 or 2/0 hooks with skimmer clams or pieces of squid or shrimp. Locals also fish for whiting at night, using kerosene or Coleman lanterns both as working lights and as a lure. Whiting are one of the few fish used as bait to catch their own kind, and are also excellent for hooking sharks, bluefin tuna and other large gamefish.

OTHER HAKES

In addition to whiting or silver hake, there are several hakes so abundant in Long Island waters that commercial fishermen regard them as nuisance fish because they have the bad manners to steal bait intended for the more lucrative cod. Although availability seems to have bred contempt, these are fine table fish, with white, mild-flavored meat.

RED HAKE (LING)

Urophycis chuss

Also known as squirrel hake and squirrel ling. Fishermen and fish buyers know this fish best by its simple, popular name—ling. It is not to be confused with the West Coast fish nicknamed "ling," nor is it any relative of the several European fish commonly called by the same name.

HAKE (LING) AS FOOD: The annual commercial take here runs into millions of pounds, much of which ends up in grocery store freezers as fish cakes, frozen fish sticks and the like. In addition to being a meaty fish, similar in taste and texture to whiting, ling has relatively few bones and is delicious in chowder, fish cakes, salad and stews.

DESCRIPTION: A slender, streamlined, rather dark fish that ranges in color from reddish-brown to greenish-brown, either uniform or covered with darker spots and blotches. The belly is a rather dirty white and the fins are mottled, with a tall, erect filament riding in front of the forward dorsal fin. The barbel, that cod-family chin whisker, here is barely a nub. Generally larger than whiting, ling can run over 5 pounds, and some of those taken commercially do, but recreational fishermen usually hook 2- to 3-pounders.

HABITS, HABITAT AND SEASON: A bottom fish that ranges from the shoreline to depths of 1800 feet, ling prefers soft rather than rocky bottoms. Although on occasion they do invade inshore waters, these are primarily ocean dwellers. Very young ling play a curious game of survival hide-and-seek, enjoying a commensal relationship inside the sea scallop shell— the fish neither eating the scallop nor being eaten by larger predator fish. (It is not known whether the scallop benefits from this partnership.)

As year-round bottom dwellers, ling may be caught by the same methods as those used to catch whiting, but ling are not as swift or challenging as whiting to rod-and-reelers.

SPOTTED HAKE

Urophycis regius

DESCRIPTION: Also called spotted ling. A small 18-inch fish with a dark-brown dorsal area lightening toward the belly. Elongated spots, like a series of dashes, punctuate the lateral line. The fish sports a barbel and filamentous ventral fins, but lacks the first-dorsal-fin filament usual in hakes. Feeds mainly on small fishes and is a winter breeder.

LONGFIN HAKE

Phycis chesteri

The smallest hake in our East End area, longfin hake is distinctive also for its long, trailing ray on the first dorsal fin and the extra-long ventral fins that reach back very nearly to the tail. The overall color, except for the white underbelly, is greenish-brown. The longfin prefers a deep-water habitat and has been taken from waters as deep as 500 fathoms (3000 feet).

BROILED SCROD AND SCALLIONS WITH EGG AND HERB SAUCE

◆

Yield: Enough to serve 6

. . . An old-time New England favorite.

3½ Pounds scrod fillets
Salt and pepper
1 Recipe Scallions in Fish Stock

1 Recipe Egg and Herb Sauce
2 Tablespoons minced thyme

Rinse the fillets, dry thoroughly and sprinkle with salt and pepper. Broil as directed on page 24. Transfer to a heated platter, arrange scallions on either end and serve with the hot sauce sprinkled with thyme.

SCROD FRITTATA

◆

Yield: Enough to serve 4

This may be prepared with small whole scrod fillets or cod fingers; however, the finished product is more attractive and succulent when the fillets are used. Serve as a luncheon or a light supper dish or as a cold hors d'oeuvre.

3 Small onions, peeled and thinly
  sliced
3 Small potatoes, peeled and thinly
  sliced
3 Tablespoons each vegetable oil and
  sweet butter
2 1½-pound skinned scrod fillets

2 Tablespoons flour
4 Large eggs, lightly beaten
½ Cup fine dry bread crumbs
¼ Teaspoon each salt and minced
  thyme leaves
1 Tablespoon minced fresh basil

In a large, nonstick skillet fry the onions and potatoes in the oil and butter until the potatoes are barely tender. Push these to the sides of the pan. Dip the fillets lightly in flour, then in egg and finally in bread crumbs.

Add the herbs and additional fat to the pan if necessary, and when it is hot, fry the fillets until golden brown, turning once. Arrange the potatoes and onions around the fish and pour the eggs around the edges. Cover tightly, turn heat to low and cook until the eggs are barely set. Turn out in one piece onto a heated large round platter. Serve at once.

VARIATION: Follow directions for Scrod Frittata but in addition to the potatoes and onions arrange around each fish 1 red and green sweet pepper charred over a flame, skinned and cut into ½-inch slices.

BROILED SCROD

To my mind only scrod—or slightly older fish, just barely too large to be classified as scrod—lend themselves to broiling. The older and larger fish become somewhat dry and grainy when prepared in this manner. There is no reason, however, that you need share my prejudice. Experiment and decide for yourself.

BROILED SCROD WITH GREEN BUTTER AND TURNIP TWIGS

◆

Yield: Enough to serve 6

3½ Pounds scrod fillets
Salt and pepper
1 Recipe Turnip Twigs

2 Scallions, green tops only, cut lengthwise into thin strips
1 Recipe Green Butter

Rinse the fish, dry thoroughly and sprinkle with salt and pepper. Broil according to directions. Arrange the fillets on a heated platter, surround with 6 bundles of barely cooked turnip twigs, each tied with slender ribbons of scallion top. Pour the hot butter over all and serve immediately.

NEW ENGLAND "TURKEY"

◆

Yield: Enough to serve 8

If you have access to a big fish rather than a big bird at Thanksgiving (or any other time) you might want to experiment with this unique old recipe. Stuff an 8- to 10-pound cod (or other large fish) with your favorite filling (or the one given here), serve forth with Mustard Gravy and you'll be surprised how similar in feeling it is to white-meat turkey. If you have a pan large enough to roast the whole fish, by all means do so; if not, remove the head. For ease in serving, the fish may be filleted and filled, but somehow this hasn't the appeal of spooning stuffing from the cavity of a grandaddy cod. Vegetarians may omit the salt pork and baste the fish more frequently.

8- to 10-pound cod, cleaned and scaled

STUFFING

1 Large onion, peeled and chopped
10 Medium-size mushrooms, sliced
2 Medium-size potatoes, boiled, peeled and diced

2 Ribs celery, chopped
2½ Tablespoons butter or cooking oil
½ Teaspoon each dried thyme, sage and marjoram

2 Cups soft bread crumbs

1 Cup fine bread crumbs

2 Tablespoons soy sauce

1–2 Eggs

4 Strips salt pork

¾ Cup Fish Stock or white wine

5 Thin lemon slices

Rinse the fish and dry it inside and out. Sauté the onion, mushrooms, potatoes and celery in butter and/or oil until the onion is transparent. Toss with the herbs, bread crumbs and soy sauce. Mix in the eggs, stuff the fish and cover it with strips of salt pork that have been simmered a few minutes in water. Sew the edges of the fish together. Wrap the whole fish in cheesecloth (make sure the ends of the cheesecloth are folded on top so you can lift the fish out easily). Arrange the fish in an S-shape in the roasting pan. Wet down with ¾ cup Fish Stock, water or wine.

Preheat oven to 400 degrees F. and bake about 8 to 10 minutes per pound, or roughly one hour, basting frequently with the pan juices. Unfold the ends of the cheesecloth and lift the fish gently from the pan onto a hot platter. Carefully remove the cheesecloth from underneath the fish. Scrape away and discard the fish skin between the head and the tail and decorate with lemon slices. Serve with Mustard Gravy.

MUSTARD GRAVY

2 Tablespoons flour

½–1 Teaspoon dry mustard (or to taste)

3 Cups Fish Stock, water or chicken broth

1 Cup heavy cream

Work the flour and dry mustard into the pan juices until well mixed. Add the stock, water or broth, mix well and bring to a boil, stirring constantly. When the sauce is thick and smooth, add the cream and simmer until nicely thickened. Serve hot over fish and stuffing.

COD IN PUMPERNICKEL CRUMBS

◆

Yield: Enough to serve 4

It may seem unusual to recommend frying fish in dark crumbs when most recipes call for the palest crumbs possible. This combination is, however, quite lovely. The crumbs fry up to a dense black crust with the purest of white fish flesh underneath. The salty crumbs also impart a unique flavor to the fillet, especially when served with fried onions, as in this dish.

4 Medium-size onions, peeled and thinly sliced

2 Tablespoons each vegetable oil and sweet butter

2 1½-pound cod fillets

¼ Cup heavy cream

1½ Cups very fine dry pumpernickel bread crumbs

Lemon slices

In a large pan fry the onions in the fat until they are limp and lightly browned. Push the onions to the edges of the pan (or remove them if the pan is not large enough). Dip both sides of the fish first in heavy cream and then, generously, in the crumbs. Add additional fat to the pan if necessary, then fry until the crust is black and crunchy and the fish flakes, turning once. Serve at once with the onions, which will now be quite crispy (if you've removed them from the pan, quickly fry them to this state), and a slice or two of lemon.

DANISH BOILED COD (OR HADDOCK)

◆

Yield: Enough to serve 6 to 8

This is an interesting way to entertain a small group of friends very nicely indeed. The meal is strictly informal, with much passing of garnishes and spearing of new boiled potatoes. An authentic Scandinavian import that particularly lends itself to the ease of Hampton living.

1 6–8-pound whole cod, cleaned and scaled
3 Tablespoons salt
Court Bouillon
Lemon slices
24 Small new potatoes, well washed and boiled
5 Hard-cooked eggs, shelled and chopped
12 Tablespoons hot melted butter
1 Recipe Dill Sauce

1 Recipe Sauce Hollandaise
¾ Cup chopped fresh parsley
1 Cup freshly grated horseradish
1 Cup grated apple tossed with 1 tablespoon lemon juice
10 Pickled beets, coarsely chopped
1 Cup chopped dill pickles
½ Cup capers
½ Cup coarse salt
Pepper

Rinse the fish, dry it thoroughly and sprinkle it inside and out with half the salt. Refrigerate for one hour. Rinse well and dry. Bring the Court Bouillon to a boil in a fish poacher with a rack. Wrap the fish in cheesecloth and lower it into the boiling Court Bouillon. Remove the pan from the heat. Let stand 20 to 30 minutes. If the fish does not flake at the end of this time, simmer it over a very low flame until it does.

Transfer the cod to a heated platter, remove the cheesecloth and drain the liquid from the platter. Remove the skin from the meaty part of the fish, leaving the head and tail intact. Garnish with lemon slices. Drain the platter again. Serve the fish surrounded by the potatoes. Pass small bowls of chopped eggs, hot butter, Dill Sauce, Hollandaise Sauce, parsley, horseradish, apples, beets, pickles, capers, salt and a pepper grinder.

COD (OR HADDOCK) STEAKS WITH SPINACH

◆

Yield: Enough to serve 6

6 Small cod steaks
Salt and pepper
4–5 Cups chopped spinach (fresh from the garden is best)

Nutmeg
1 Recipe Sauce Mornay
¼ Cup Parmesan cheese

Rinse the steaks, dry and sprinkle with salt and pepper. Poach as directed on page 28. Season the spinach with nutmeg, salt and pepper. Arrange the well-drained fish on the spinach in an ovenproof serving dish. Top with the sauce and sprinkle with cheese. Slide under broiler for a few seconds until lightly browned. Serve immediately.

FRESH COD "SOUNDS" AND TONGUES, MONTAUK LIGHTHOUSE

◆

Yield: Enough to serve 6

Fresh cod cheeks (sounds) are particularly tender and sweet, and the tongues provide an interesting contrast. This is a fisherman's straight-forward approach to what is generally treated as a delicacy.

1½ Pounds fresh cod "sounds" and
   tongues (If you use salted sounds
   and tongues they must be soaked
   overnight as directed.)
3 Tablespoons butter
2 Cloves garlic, peeled and crushed
4 Scallions, with 3 inches green tops,
   sliced

2 Tomatoes, peeled, seeded and
   chopped
⅛ Teaspoon dried thyme leaves
2 Eggs beaten with 1 teaspoon water
Salt and a lot of freshly ground black
   pepper

Lightly brown the sounds and tongues in the butter with the garlic and the scallions. Add the tomatoes and thyme and cook over high heat for 2 minutes until some of the juice from the tomatoes evaporates. Push the other ingredients aside and pour the egg into the center of the pan and stir until the egg thickens. At the last minute stir the egg into the other ingredients in one or two strokes. The egg should remain identifiable rather than mix with the other ingredients.

COD CAKES

◆

Yield: One dozen cakes

Golden-brown cod cakes, creamy in the middle and crunchy without. What could be more warming on a chilly winter's eve when the winds are whistling in from the bay?

1 Pound cooked, flaked cod, haddock,
   or ling
2 Eggs
½ Cup Enriched White Sauce
½ Teaspoon dry mustard
¼ Teaspoon powdered sage

Salt and pepper to taste
¼ Cup milk
Flour
¼ Cup dry bread crumbs
Oil for frying

Stir together fish, one egg, White Sauce and seasonings. Chill well. Shape into 12 cakes. Beat the remaining egg with the milk. Dip each cake first in flour, then in the egg-milk mixture and finally in the bread crumbs. Refrigerate 2 hours, or until ready to fry. Heat ¼ inch oil in a large skillet and fry to golden on both sides, turning once.

COD PISSALADE

◆

Serves 4 as a lunch or supper, 6 to 8 as an hors d'oeuvre

There are many variations on this adaptable dish and all seem quite tasty. This version is crustless, the specialty of a Spanish friend summering in Hampton Bays. I've given a few cod variations here—but you should mix and match as suits your palate.

1 Medium-size potato, peeled and thinly sliced

3 Tablespoons cooking oil

2 Small onions, peeled, sliced and separated into rings

¼ Teaspoon each dried thyme and marjoram

1 Pound fresh cod, cut into 2-inch strips

3 Scallions, with 3 inches green tops, sliced

4 Eggs, beaten

2 Tablespoons heavy cream

Salt and pepper to taste

12 Flat anchovy fillets

Cook the potato over low heat in 2 tablespoons oil until tender, turning once. Set the potato aside and heat the remaining tablespoon oil in the skillet. Sauté the onions with the herbs until onions are tender. Arrange the cod over the onions and top with the potatoes and scallions. Beat the eggs with the cream and pour them over the potatoes, tilting the pan so the eggs settle to the bottom. Cook over low heat until the eggs are not quite set. Add salt and pepper to taste. Criss-cross with anchovy fillets and place under broiler until top is just set. Loosen with a spatula and slide the whole omelet onto a platter. Cut into wedges and serve hot or at room temperature.

VARIATION I: Cut 1 each sweet red and green pepper into ¼-inch-thick slices. Follow directions given above, but sauté pepper rings with onions.

VARIATION II: Follow directions for Cod Pissalade, but add one medium-size tomato, peeled, seeded and sliced, to the sautéed onion and cook until the juice from the tomato has evaporated. Continue the recipe as given, adding ¾ cup cubed Swiss cheese with the eggs.

VARIATION III: Follow directions for Variation II, but add jalapeño or other hot peppers to taste and 8 pitted, sliced black olives along with the cheese.

PREPARING SALT COD FOR COOKING

Soak thick, white (not stringy or yellowish) salt cod in cold water to cover overnight, changing the water every few hours. At the end of this time, if the cod still tastes too salty, soak it an additional 15 minutes in warm water. Poach the cod in water to cover until it is slightly underdone. Remove the skin and bones.

Allow 5 to 7 ounces per serving, depending on the additional ingredients in the recipe.

SALT COD IN TOMATO SAUCE, OLD BETHPAGE

◆

Yield: Enough to serve 6

A turn-of-the-century favorite!

5 *Pounds salt cod*
3 *Medium-size onions, peeled and coarsely chopped*
5 *Cloves garlic, peeled and crushed*
1½ *Cups coarsely chopped leek (white and green)*
4 *Tablespoons oil*
8 *Medium-size tomatoes, peeled, seeded and coarsely chopped*
1 *Cup white wine*
¾ *Cup coarsely chopped pimento*
A pinch each of sugar, nutmeg and marjoram
Salt and pepper to taste
¼ *Cup grated Parmesan cheese (optional)*

Prepare the salt cod for cooking as directed. Poach and drain well. Meanwhile, sauté the onions, garlic and leek in the oil until the onion is transparent but not browned. Stir in the tomatoes, white wine and one cup of the water the cod was cooked in. Bring just to a boil, then lower the heat and simmer 15 minutes. Add the pimento and seasoning and simmer 15 minutes more or until the sauce is nicely thickened.

Preheat the oven to 350 degrees F.

Pour half the sauce in the bottom of a flat ovenproof serving dish. Flake the cod, arrange it over the sauce, then top with the remaining tomato mixture. Sprinkle with cheese and bake for 10 minutes. Slide under the broiler flame for a few seconds to lightly brown.

BRANDADE DE MORUE

◆

Yield: Enough to serve 6

This delectable dish, a purée of salt cod from southern France, is once more finding favor.

3 *Pounds salt cod*
2 *Large potatoes, baked, mashed and kept warm*
1 *Cup olive oil*
2 *Cloves garlic, peeled and minced*
1 *Cup heavy cream*
1 *Recipe Fried Toast Triangles*
Salt and pepper to taste

Follow directions for preparing salt cod for cooking. Cut the cod into 2-inch pieces and pound* in a mortar with about one pound warm mashed potatoes to produce a fine paste. Heat the oil with the garlic and pound it into the paste a little at a time, alternating with equal amounts of warm cream until the Brandade is white in color and light in texture. Season to taste and serve surrounded by toast triangles.

*This entire pounding process may be replaced by a few whirls in your food processor. Incorporate the olive oil and cream alternately a bit at a time as directed. The flavor will still be delicious but the texture will be heavier, more sticky. Many busy cooks are willing to accept this slight imperfection.

LENTEN BRANDADE DE MORUE

◆

In the South of France this dish is served cold as an hors d'oeuvre during Lent.

Prepare the salt cod purée as directed in Brandade de Morue, then chill and pass with small Fried Toast Triangles.

CRÊPES DE BRANDADE

◆

Yield: Enough to serve 6

A wonderful cold-weather luncheon dish or "go-with" for soup.

1 Recipe Brandade de Morue
1 Recipe Plain or Curry Crêpes
1 Recipe Enriched White Sauce

½ Cup Fish Stock, reduced to 2
tablespoons

Prepare Brandade de Morue as directed and use to fill the crêpes, rolling them up snugly. Serve with soup or, as a luncheon dish, pass with White Sauce thinned with the reduced stock.

KEDGEREE OF HADDOCK

◆

Yield: Enough to serve 4 to 6

This traditional English breakfast dish originated in India, most likely as a way to utilize leftover fish. I know several superb Hampton hostesses who serve variations of this as luncheon or light supper fare.

3 Tablespoons butter
¼ Cup finely chopped onion
1 Cup rice
2 Cups boiling water
Salt
1½ Pounds leftover fresh or smoked
haddock (or the same amount
freshly poached)

4 Cups Curry Sauce
4 Hard-cooked eggs
Freshly ground black pepper
2 Tablespoons chopped parsley

In a saucepan melt 2 tablespoons butter, add the onions and sauté until golden. Add the rice, boiling water and salt and stir once or twice, then cover and cook over low heat for 15 to 20 minutes or until the rice is just tender. Do not overcook. Stir in the remaining tablespoon of butter.

Mix the fish gently with the sauce and 2 whole hard-cooked eggs, chopped, and 2 additional chopped egg whites. Spread half the hot rice on a heated serving dish, top this with half the hot creamed fish and a generous sprinkle of black pepper. Repeat the layers. Garnish the border of the Kedgeree with chopped parsley and the center with the two remaining egg yolks, sieved. Serve immediately.

BOILED HADDOCK DINNER

◆

Many old New England recipes found their way to our nearby Hampton shores. In this one the herbs in the Egg and Herb Sauce are not traditional but are quite tasty. Omit them if you like. It's left to you to decide how many potatoes and beets your family or friends might consume.

1 4-pound haddock, cleaned and
  scaled
Salt and pepper
Boiling salted water

Boiled potatoes
Boiled beets
1 Recipe Egg and Herb Sauce
¾ Cup salt pork cubes

Rinse the fish, dry thoroughly and rub it inside and out with 2 table-spoons salt. Refrigerate the fish for half an hour, then rinse it again, dry it and rub it with pepper. Wrap the fish in cheesecloth and lower it into boiling salted water to cover. Remove from the heat, cover, and let stand for 20 minutes. If the fish is underdone at this point, replace the pan over a low flame and simmer until the fish flakes. Drain well. Arrange on a heated platter surrounded by boiled potatoes and beets. Serve with Egg and Herb Sauce and bits of hot, crisp fried salt pork.

FRIED HADDOCK FINGERS IN GOLDEN CREAM

◆

Yield: Enough to serve 6

2½ Pounds haddock fillets, cut into
  1½-inch-wide fingers
Flour
Ice water
Oil for deep-frying
2 Tablespoons Clarified Butter
1 Tablespoon minced parsley

2 Large cloves garlic, peeled and
  minced
1 Tablespoon flour
1 Cup Fish Stock or clam juice
2 Teaspoons vinegar
Salt and white pepper to taste
3 Egg yolks

Dredge the fish fingers heavily in flour, pressing the flour into the flesh. Shake lightly to discard excess flour. Dip very quickly in ice water, let drip for a second or two, then fry in ½-inch-deep hot oil until golden on all sides. Keep fish fingers warm. In a smaller frying pan heat 2 table-spoons each clarified butter and oil. Add parsley and garlic and *very lightly* brown them. Blend in the flour and let it take on the *slightest* bit of color. Add stock or clam juice and vinegar, salt and pepper, and stir until the sauce thickens. Beat the egg yolks with a few drops of oil and stir them into the sauce. Place an asbestos pad over low heat and stir the sauce over this until thick and creamy. Do not overcook or sauce will curdle. Pour over fish and serve immediately.

FINNAN HADDIE*

The split smoked haddock preparation that originated in the Scottish port of Findon is popular the world 'round . . . and deservedly so. This fine product lends itself to a variety of rich, mellow dishes satisfying at breakfast, lunch or supper. Cod is occasionally prepared in the same way and sold as "finnette," but this is coarser in grain and, to my mind, less

*Finnan Haddie recipes may be prepared with fresh haddock also.

exceptional. To differentiate when buying Finnan Haddie, look for a smaller fillet with or without the backbone still intact. Cod, being a larger fish, is usually sold in a bigger boneless chunk.

FINNAN HADDIE POACHED IN MILK

◆

Yield: Enough to serve 6

Milk (or half milk and half water) is by far the superior poaching medium for Finnan Haddie. Taste a bit of the fish, and if it is too salty, soak it in warm water for 20 to 30 minutes prior to poaching.

3 Pounds Finnan Haddie
1 Quart milk (or half milk and half water)

Rinse the fish and poach as directed on page 28, using milk or milk and water as the liquid. Reserve the liquid for use in sauces.

HAMPTON FINNAN HADDIE

◆

1 Recipe Finnan Haddie Poached in Milk
4 Onions, peeled and coarsely chopped
1 Cup each chopped sweet red and green pepper
¼ Cup butter

½ Cup flour
2½ Cups poaching liquid
1½ Cups heavy cream
3 Hard-cooked eggs, coarsely chopped
Bread crumbs
Butter

Soak the fish if necessary and poach as directed. Flake the fish and keep it warm. Sauté the onions and peppers in ¼ cup butter until the onions are transparent and the peppers are tender. Blend in the flour, then stir in the poaching liquid, pressing out any lumps with the back of a spoon. Add the cream and stir over medium heat until the sauce is thick and smooth. Gently stir in the flaked fish and eggs. Turn into a buttered baking dish, sprinkle with crumbs, dot with butter and bake in a hot 400 degree F. oven until the crumbs are brown. Serve immediately.

FINNAN HADDIE CAKES WITH BACON

◆

1 Recipe Finnan Haddie Poached in Milk
3 Cups mashed potatoes
10 Strips crisp bacon, crumbled

1 Egg, beaten
Salt and pepper
Butter

Follow directions for Finnan Haddie Poached in Milk. Flake the fish, mix with the potatoes, bacon and finally the egg. Season to taste. Form into ½-inch-thick cakes and brown in butter, turning once.

MILK-BAKED FINNAN HADDIE

◆

Arrange Finnan Haddie in a shallow, buttered, ovenproof baking dish. Dot fish with butter and pour enough warm milk over to cover the bottom of the dish. Bake as directed, basting frequently with the milk. Drain before serving hot.

VARIATION I: Prepare Milk-Baked Finnan Haddie, drain and serve with hot, boiled new potatoes and Green Butter.

VARIATION II: Prepare Milk-Baked Finnan Haddie, drain and serve with steamed asparagus and Hollandaise Sauce.

NOTE: I tested the following recipes using pollock, but cod or haddock could be substituted.

POLLOCK IN CURRY CUSTARD

◆

Yield: Enough to serve 4 to 6

5 Eggs
2 Cups light cream
1 Tablespoon minced chives
1 Tablespoon minced fresh thyme
Salt

½–1 Teaspoon curry powder (or to taste)
A dash each of cayenne and nutmeg
2 Cups flaked cooked pollock

Preheat oven to 350 degrees F.

Beat the eggs well, beat in the cream thoroughly and then the seasonings. Sprinkle the fish over the bottom of a well-buttered ovenproof dish and pour the egg mixture over. Place the dish in a pan in one inch hot water. Bake for 40 to 50 minutes or until still a little soft in the middle. Serve immediately.

POLLOCK LOAF, OLD HOOK MILL

◆

I came across this recipe in a nineteenth-century cookbook. Just across the page was an illustration of a mill that looked exactly like our beautiful Old Hook Mill in East Hampton. Hence the title. When I tested the recipe I served it with Sauce Nantua left over from the previous day's cooking, but any tomato-based sauce would be excellent.

3 Cups flaked cooked pollock
½ Cup finely crushed white bread crumbs
½ Cup ground almonds
3 Eggs, beaten
4 Tablespoons soft butter

4 Scallions with 2 inches green tops, finely minced
Salt, pepper and nutmeg
Hot cream
1 Recipe Sauce Nantua (or your favorite)

Preheat the oven to 375 degrees F.

Mix the fish, bread crumbs, almonds, eggs, butter, scallions and seasonings to taste. If the mixture is too stiff, moisten with a tablespoon or two of hot cream. Spoon into a well-buttered loaf pan and bake in a pan in one inch of hot water for 50 to 60 minutes, or until set in the middle. Cool slightly and turn out on a heated platter. Pass with the sauce.

WHITING QUEEN VICTORIA

Yield: Enough to serve 4 to 6

◆

This adaptation of a turn-of-the-century recipe presents both fish and vegetable at their peak. Choose a large baking dish so that the tomato wedges need not overlap too much. And don't skimp on the pepper—the combination of sweet and spice is important.

4–6 12-inch whole whiting, cleaned and with heads removed
2 Medium-size tomatoes for each fish
1½ Tablespoons sugar

3 Tablespoons sweet butter
Salt and coarsely-ground black pepper to taste

Arrange the fish backs up so that the tails are in the corners of the dish (a large round dish is best if you are serving six). Peel the tomatoes, cut them in eighths and gently squeeze out the seeds. Arrange the wedges attractively between the fish. Sprinkle the tomatoes with sugar and a little salt. Dot the fish with butter. Grind the pepper overall. Place about 8 inches beneath the flame and broil 10 to 15 minutes, or until fish are just ready to flake and tomatoes are speckled with brown.

BAKED WHITING FILLETS WITH CUCUMBER SPEARS

◆

Yield: Enough to serve 6

Whiting is most often served whole, pan-fried, broiled, etc., in the usual manner, but the delicate fillets are superb, provided they are handled with care so they don't crumble.

6 Whiting fillets
Salt and pepper
6 Cucumbers, peeled, seeded, and split lengthwise into eighths

Butter
¾ Cup heavy cream
1 Tablespoon minced tarragon

Rinse the fillets, dry and sprinkle with salt and pepper. Arrange with the cucumbers in a well-buttered shallow baking dish. Dot the fillets with butter and pour the cream over. Bake for 15 to 20 minutes (basting frequently with the cream) until the fish barely flakes and is flecked with brown. Serve immediately.

WINE-POACHED WHITING

◆

Yield: Enough to serve 6

6 Whiting fillets
Salt and pepper

White wine
Butter

Poach fillets in wine as directed on page 28. Drain well, transfer to a heated platter and keep the fish warm until serving. Serve with your favorite herb butter.

VARIATION I: Follow directions for Wine-Poached Whiting. Top with your favorite sauce. Sauce Aurore, Parsley Sauce and Egg and Herb Sauce are all excellent choices.

VARIATION II: Follow directions for Wine-Poached Whiting. Top with Sauce Mornay, sprinkle with grated Parmesan and slide under the broiler until the cheese is lightly browned.

MATTITUCK WHITING AND OYSTERS

Yield: Enough to serve 6

◆

1 Recipe Sauce Aurore
6 Whiting fillets
½ Cup dry white wine
18 Oysters, shucked and poached

Prepare the Sauce Aurore and keep it warm. Arrange the fillets in an ovenproof serving dish, pour the wine over and bake until the fish barely flakes, basting once or twice with the wine. Carefully (so as not to break the fish) pour the wine and juices into a small saucepan, reduce to 2 tablespoons and stir the liquid into the sauce. Surround the fillets with poached oysters, cover with the sauce and quickly brown under the broiler. Serve immediately.

LING AND LOBSTER SALAD

◆

3 Cups poached flaked ling
2 Cups boiled lobster, cut into ½-inch cubes
½ Cup minced tender white center celery ribs
¼ Cup ½-inch pimento squares
¼ Cup thinly sliced scallions, including some of the green tops
¾–1 Cup Green Goddess Dressing
6 Crisp lettuce leaves
3 Hard-cooked eggs, shelled and sliced
1 Tablespoon drained capers
Lobster claws (optional)
6 Lime wedges

Gently toss ling, lobster, celery, pimento, scallions and dressing. Arrange on lettuce, garnish with eggs, capers, lobster claws and lime wedges. Serve very cold.

EEL

AMERICAN EEL

Anguilla rostrata

Known variously as common eel, fresh-water eel, and as "elvers" when young.

EELS AS FOOD: Eels can be taken throughout most of the year, even when cold winds call across the Hampton bays like so many hungry gulls. Ice-fishing for eels provides hard-pressed Bonac fishermen with survival income during skimpy winter months when other fish have faded with the summer haze. Although eel is eaten and relished all over the world and was an important source of food for New England's early settlers, it now appeals chiefly to Americans with Old World ethnic origins.

Eels are sold live, dressed whole, cut into fillets, smoked, pickled, jellied or canned in oil. East End cooks seem to favor 2-inch pieces, dredged in flour batter or shake-and-bake, then fried or baked until brown, but eels are superb broiled, steamed or simmered in stews or soups such as the French specialties *bouillabaisse* and *matelote*, an eel stew flavored with cognac.

A skinned, cleaned eel from the fish store is easy to use, especially if it is filleted. Skinning and cleaning those you catch yourself or buy whole and alive is another matter . . . as is the business of killing them. The time-honored way to dispatch living eels is to put them in a container and cover them with coarse salt . . . a method that also de-slimes them. If you're planning to smoke your eels without skinning them, all that's necessary is to wipe off this slime.

Dispatch the eel with a blow to the back of the head, then nail its head to a board with a piece of heavy cord tied around its body just below the gills. Make an incision behind the head with a sharp knife or single-edge razor blade and cut three-quarters around the circumference. Loosen an inch-long flap of skin below this cut, then using a pair of pliers, peel off the skin. Cut off the head, then dress the eel by slitting its lower body to remove the entrails. Cut away the fins with scissors. The eel may then be cut into 2- or 3-inch chunks, or, to fillet, carefully cut away the flesh on both sides of the backbone.

Eel meat is firm and solid, so heat takes a little longer to penetrate it than with other fish. This presents no problem when pan-frying small eels weighing from 1 to 1½ pounds, but with larger specimens it's a good idea to simmer the pieces for 15 to 20 minutes in salted water to cover, to which a teaspoon or two of lemon juice has been added. Pan-fried eel meat has a tendency to burn before it is cooked through; poaching beforehand prevents this.

A Long Island specialty is the locally caught and smoked eel available at most area fish markets and stands. This meat is wonderful with a squeeze of fresh lemon, washed down with a shot of icy vodka.

DESCRIPTION: Eels are true fishes despite their unfishlike appearance. The dorsal, caudal and anal fins encircle the entire length of the elongated body in one continuous line, rather than in separate parts like the fins of other fishes. The head is small and conical, the mouth has true jaws and, although not noticeable, the fish does have almost microscopic scales and small pectoral fins just behind the head. Eels can grow to 3 or 4 feet in length and weigh up to 5 pounds (although one East End trap fisherman reports landing one of 9½ pounds, "biggest ever in a lifetime of trapping"), but most caught locally range from one to 2 pounds. The color is olive-brown to darker olive-brown along the back, with yellowish sides paling to yellow-brown or creamy white on the underside.

HABITS AND HABITAT: Many salt-water fish are anadromous, that is, they leave their usual ocean habitat to ascend fresh-water rivers in order to spawn. Eels reverse this procedure and are catadromous, which means they leave their fresh-water homes to spawn in the ocean. To the vast seaweed wasteland of the Sargasso Sea, obeying some mysterious instinct, each year come ripe females from both sides of the Atlantic to lay their eggs and die after a single spawning. The hatchlings, cigar-shaped, paper-thin and transparent, complete the round trip, unerringly making their way back to the same locale their parents came from, whether in

Europe or coastal North America. By the time they reach the parental home and begin to feed, they have covered thousands of perilous miles of open sea and have reached the "elver" stage, in which they resemble their parents but are transparent and colorless except for a row of black dots along their narrow bodies.

Male elvers remain in the tidal marshes and river mouths while the females proceed upstream, slithering sometimes through underground waterways, up dams, and even over damp rocks, to appear in inland ponds and streams, including some that have no visible connection to the sea. When fully grown, each generation of females backtracks by the same route to the sea from which, together with mature males, they set off to the spawning grounds to produce the next generation.

During the years between these two journeys these voracious scavengers live in fresh waters or in brackish marshes and salt ponds, hiding among stones and under muddy bottoms of these waters by day, to emerge at night to hunt. Growth proceeds slowly—males take about 8 years to reach full size, while females, who can grow twice as large, keep on growing for another 6 or 7 years.

SEASON AND HOW TO CATCH: During the annual fall migration, eels are netted or speared in great numbers. Even in December, catching eels for ethnic Christmas celebrations gives employment to many commercial fishermen. Eels are also caught in eel-pots, eel fykes (traps with funnel-shaped openings), and also by hook and line. The best places to find them are in brackish tidal streams, but they also are partial to wharves and docks.

Even in prosperous years local fishermen spear eels through the ice "to break the monotony" when cold weather prevents other kinds of fishing. East Enders feel that eel is tastiest in winter, firmer and less fishy-tasting, because the eels haven't been eating bait since fall.

◆ ◆

EEL-SPEARING BY TORCHLIGHT

The skies are dark; the moon is hid
Behind the dusky cloud of night;
A bank of drift-fog from the surge
Hangs heavy on the sea-shore height;
No hovering breeze uplifts its wing
Aside the misty gloom to fling.

But see! a star along the wave
Moves slow and devious, to and fro;
Now like a blazing camp-fire flares,

Now, flickering, trembles faint and low.
Anon it steady glows and burns,
As hither thro' the gloom it turns.

Tis the eel-spearer's pitchy torch
That like a lightship's lantern flings
Its ruddy, quivering bar of light
As in the rigging high it swings . . .
. . . With sudden plunge he thrusts the spear
Then draws it upward to the glow;
And see! the captives twist and coil,
Dark victims of his midnight toil.

◆ ◆

MARINATED ACCABONAC EEL

◆

Yield: Enough to serve 6

2 1½-pound eels, skinned, cleaned and cut into 3-inch pieces
½ Teaspoon each salt and pepper
¾ Cup white wine vinegar
⅓ Cup olive oil
3 Large garlic cloves, peeled and minced
2 Bay leaves
¼ Teaspoon each leaf thyme and powdered sage
⅛ Teaspoon cayenne pepper
2 Small onions, peeled, sliced and separated into rings

Rub eels with salt and pepper, pressing the seasonings into the flesh. Add wine vinegar, oil, garlic, herbs and cayenne to a skillet, heat and add eel pieces. Cover the pan and simmer 10 to 15 minutes, or until the fish is barely tender, turning the fish pieces several times. Transfer the eels to an ovenproof serving dish. Add the onions to the pan, cover and simmer 5 minutes. Pour the onions and the hot marinade over the eels, cool to room temperature and then chill overnight or up to 3 days, turning the pieces occasionally. Serve as an hors d'oeuvre.

FRESH EEL SOUP

◆

Yield: Enough to serve 6

¼ Pound dried mushrooms
3 Pounds fresh eel, skinned and cleaned
1 Teaspoon salt
2 Cups sour cream
¼ Teaspoon each freshly ground black pepper and paprika
2 Teaspoons rye flour
2 Tablespoons butter
3 Tablespoons finely chopped fresh dill

Rinse the mushrooms, cover with cold water and soak for 2 hours. Cut the eel into 2-inch pieces and place in a large saucepan. Drain the mushrooms, reserving the liquid; measure the mushroom liquid, add enough additional water to bring the total amount of liquid to 6 cups, and pour over the eel pieces. Add the salt and bring to a boil, then lower the heat and simmer, covered, until the eel is tender.*

Carefully remove the eel pieces from the soup and set aside. Stir the mushrooms into the soup and gradually add the sour cream, stirring all the while. Add the pepper and paprika. Knead the flour with 2 tablespoons butter, stir into hot soup a bit at a time and continue stirring until the soup comes to a boil. Return the eel pieces to the soup and cook just long enough to heat through. Serve piping hot, garnished with chopped dill.

EELS IN GARLIC-TOMATO SAUCE

◆

Yield: Enough to serve 6

When the eels are just a wiggle away from the cool waters of the bay, and the tomato purée is fresh or frozen from your garden, the resulting dish is especially sweet. If you are using canned tomatoes, a pinch of sugar might be required.

3 1-pound eels or 2 1½-pound ones, skinned, cleaned and cut into 2½-inch pieces
Flour
½ Cup olive oil
4 Large garlic cloves, peeled and minced
2 Large onions, peeled and finely chopped
2 Teaspoons each minced fresh rosemary and sage (or ¼ teaspoon powdered)

Zest from 1 small lemon (grated yellow top skin)
2 Cups thin tomato purée (or 2 cups tomato juice plus 2 tablespoons tomato paste)
2 Cups white wine
Salt and pepper to taste

Dredge the eel lightly in flour and sauté in the oil until light brown on all sides. Set the eel aside and sauté garlic, onion, herbs and lemon zest in the oil until onion is golden. Return eel to the skillet. Pour purée or tomato juice and wine over, cover the pan and simmer until the fish is tender.* Transfer fish to serving dish and keep it warm while the sauce boils and thickens slightly. Season to taste and serve hot with the fish, on toast points or pasta.

GREENPORT FARMS EEL IN MUSTARD SAUCE

◆

Yield: Enough to serve 6

3 Pounds eel, skinned, cleaned and cut into 3-inch pieces
Flour
2 Eggs lightly beaten with 1 teaspoon water
2 Cups fine cracker crumbs

3 Tablespoons each butter and oil
2 Cups light cream
2 Teaspoons onion juice
1½ Tablespoons Dijon mustard
Parsley sprigs

*Time will vary according to thickness of eel pieces.

Dust the eel pieces with flour, dip in egg and then in cracker crumbs. In the butter and oil, fry over medium heat until golden on all sides. Set the eel in an ovenproof serving dish. Add the cream, onion juice and mustard to the pan and stir until nicely thickened. Spoon the sauce over the eel pieces and bake for 10 minutes in an oven preheated to 350 degrees F. Serve immediately with parsley sprigs.

MRS. MILLER'S SHAKE 'N BAKE EEL

◆

A farmer's wife has her tricks for getting dinner to the table minutes after the chores are completed . . . no matter what time that may be.

Dip skinned and cleaned 3-inch eel pieces in vegetable oil and roll them in Shake 'N Bake. Bake in an oven preheated to 350 degrees F. until the eel is tender and nicely browned.

THE FLATFISH FAMILY

Right-handed flatfishes: *Soleidae*/**Left-handed flatfishes:** *Bothidae*

Long Island waters, particularly those bordering the South Shore and those stretching between Block Island and Montauk, furnish an almost perfect flounder habitat. A nonmigrating group of these fish is in permanent residence only a few miles from our windows . . . They are, like us, year-round inhabitants who recognize a good thing when they find it. What makes these flatfish-family residents unique (even in the Hamptons) are two rather strange physical characteristics: their bodies are flat, and both eyes are on the same side of their heads. Although the impression created is that of fish that have been passed over by a careless steam roller, every member of this wonderful family is simply a fish that swims as it pleases . . . on its side.

Flatfish begin life as hatchlings looking pretty much like any other fish, but as adulthood approaches one eye journeys around the head to join up with the other and their oval bodies begin to flatten out like crêpes. In such "right-handed" flounders as the Atlantic halibut, blackback (winter) flounder, and the yellowtail flounder, both eyes are located on the right when the fish is laid belly-side down. Conversely, fluke (summer flounder), fourspot flounder and windowpane flounder have eyes that lie to the left when the fish is laid on its white underside. Only a few of the more popular flatfish are mentioned here . . . no need to try to cover them all, considering that there are hundreds of relatives—a very respectable family indeed.

SOLE

Although this name is applied rather loosely by seafood retailers and restaurateurs alike, most fish sold and served as "sole" are not true soles. The true or common sole whose meat is so highly esteemed by gourmets is a gray-to-brown, oval-shaped, exclusively European flatfish (*Solea vulgaris*) enjoyed on both sides of the Atlantic as "Dover sole." Rightly regarded the prime member of the flatfish family, "Dover sole" has white, firm, delicate flesh that separates easily from the bone.

Though a flatfish by any other name may taste as sweet, it's generally a good idea to know exactly what it is you're buying and paying for, not to mention eating. Be aware that "lemon sole" is the common name for lemon dab, French sole and blackback flounder. Irish fishermen apply the name white sole to the witch flounder, while American seafood markets retail the same fish as grey sole. In addition, two types of flounder that make their homes in Pacific marine waters are routinely marketed as Dover sole and English sole, although any resemblance to the British original begins and ends with their names. The hogchoker, often encountered in Long Island waters, is, however, a true sole.

Sole, flounder, fluke—all adult flatfish, in fact, whether whole or filleted—lend themselves to a variety of ambrosial dishes, very nearly too vast to contemplate.

BLACKBACK FLOUNDER

Pseudopleuronectes americanus

Long Island's waters nourish many types of flounders, including delicious blackbacks, oversize members of which weigh in at up to 6 to 8 pounds and are called "snowshoes" by local anglers. Blackbacks are also known as winter flounder, blueback flounder, lemon sole, black flounder and grey sole.

BLACKBACKS AS FOOD: This is an excellent and very popular table fish, with firm, white, delicately flavored flesh—and perhaps a few too many bones. For this reason it's probably best to fillet larger fish and pan-fry smaller ones. Please do not neglect flounder roes. These are excellent!

Here's how to deal with your fresh-caught flatfish from hook (or fish market) to skillet. To fillet: Place your fish eye-side up on a cutting board and, with a sharp knife, first cut through to the spine at the point where the gill cover meets the long axis of the fish at right angles. Next, make a second cut from the tail to the head, angling close to and then away from the pectoral fin. Deepen this incision, working from head to tail, lifting and cutting the meat free as close as possible to the skin.

If left whole, as with fairly small specimens, or if the skin is to be left on fillets (some think this adds flavor), be sure to scale flounders. To prepare as a whole fish after scaling, cut off the head just behind the gills and pull all viscera out with it. Rinse out the inner cavity and pat dry.

DESCRIPTION: Expect lots of lively fishing action from this most plentiful of Long Island flounders. Most local specimens range from ½ to 3 pounds and measure from 12 to 15 inches, but the lucky angler may hook a rare 20-inch fish. The blackback's dorsal side is dark-brown, roughly-scaled and mottled to act as camouflage; the blind side is white and smooth. As in all members of the flatfish family, the fins run around the sides, rather than on top. The dorsal fin covers the dorsal side fairly evenly, but the pectoral fin is smaller. The tail is slightly concave.

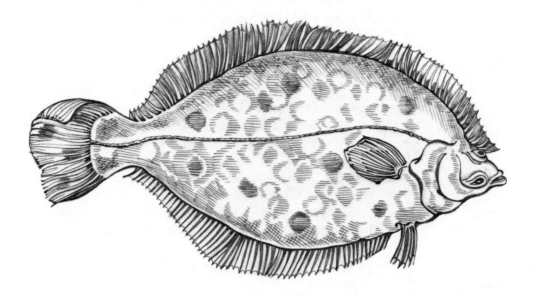

HABITS, HABITAT AND SEASON: Blackbacks favor bottoms of bays, inlets and channels lined with the soft mud that also pleases crustaceans and mollusks—prime morsels in the blackback diet. Sand, clay or fine-gravel bottoms are also preferred.

Blackbacks are also fussy about temperatures. Water colder than 40 degrees F. drives them to dig into the sand or mud bottoms they love so well. Water warmer than 50 degrees F., sends them swimming to deeper and cooler depths. What anglers wait for is that magic 10 degrees when water temperatures hit between 40 and 50 in early spring and again in fall.

Blackback season traditionally kicks off on St. Patrick's Day with a spring run that lasts through May, and diminishes until after the summer retreat to cooler waters—around Labor Day to (and sometimes through) October. Local charter boats don't usually start their runs until Good Friday, when blackbacks are hungrier—and huskier.

WHERE FOUND: Early in the season, the best hook-and-line action is found in channels and back bays (like Three Mile Harbor, Sag Harbor, Shinnecock and Southampton's back bays; Napeague Harbor and flats to the southeast, as well as Lake Montauk and the Shinnecock Canal). By mid-April, the action moves from channels to bays and into open waters. Blackbacks congregate in shallows ranging from 5 to 60 feet, with bottoms from 10 to 20 feet. Try any bottom-fishing technique . . . boat at anchor, dock, pier, bridge, or from shore. During the spring run, drift-fishing produces larger specimens. Begin your search in shallow waters and work out into deeper ones. And remember: shallows seem to be more productive when the tide is coming in; on the outgoing tide, try deeper holes and channels.

Blackbacks generally respond to chumming with crushed mussels or cut-up bunkerfish.

HOW TO CATCH: Light tackle is called for here, either standard fresh-water spinning-reel or a light salt-water model. Use a standard flounder rig, or simply equip your line with a snap-swivel to keep the snell and line from tangling.

Hooks: No one will snicker if you simply ask for flounder hooks—I've done it. But if you prefer to be more technical, ask for Chestertown-style hooks, popular because of their long-shank design. Flounder tend to gulp bait, so it lands in the back of the throat; and a long-shanked hook is easier to remove. No. 9 hooks are fine for smaller fish, No. 6 for larger. To snag two flounders for the price of one, try using a two-hook rig with a spreader.

Sinker: Attach to the lowest snap-swivel any bank-type sinker of just enough weight to hold the bottom. Because they lack front teeth flounder take bait rather delicately, without much jerk on the line. A heavy sinker will prevent you from feeling when your fish has taken bait and provide the fish with a nice free lunch. When you suspect a bite, raise your pole just a few inches, then once you feel the weight of the fish, jerk it a little bit more to set the hook. Don't be too muscular or your fish will get away.

Bait: Mussels seem to be all-time blackback favorites, but bloodworms and sandworms are also popular. Local legend has it that early in the season when blackbacks are just getting over spawning they prefer soft, succulent bait such as bank or horse mussels. Skimmer clams are another preferred bait, but blackbacks tend to be fussy—some days spurning clams, other days refusing to eat anything but. Your best bet is to take along several kinds of bait so that if one doesn't appeal, another will. And if you should run out of bait, don't worry—re-use the bait from the gullets of fish you've already caught.

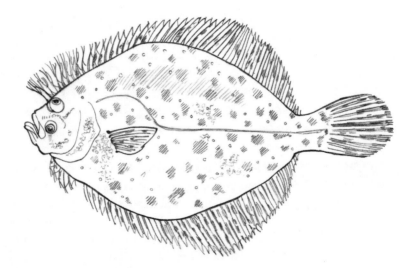

WINDOWPANE FLOUNDER

Scophthalmus aquosus

Also known as sand flounder, spotted flounder, sundials, seethroughs, and brill, these generally average up to one foot in length but can go to 1½ feet and 2 pounds. Whenever I'm bottom-fishing in the bays for just about anything, including snappers, I can usually count on hooking a windowpane or two. This delicate left-handed flounder, so thin-bodied it is practically transparent when held up to the light, has delectable sweet-tasting meat, but its small size and bony structure make it an unlikely candidate for elegant dining. However, if you don't mind eating with your fingers, these make a nice lunch when pan-fried as you would any small flounder.

Thanks to its friendly habit of interbreeding with other flounders, the windowpane may turn up in a wide variety of colors and shapes, but it is always distinguishable by the separated rays on the forward part of its dorsal fin. The skin is brownish with overtones of green, gray and/or rust, usually irregularly patterned with dark-brown spots. The tail is fully rounded.

Windowpanes frequent relatively shallow waters in search of the young tomcods, pollocks, striped bass, herring, smelts and sand shrimp that make up its diet.

FOURSPOT FLOUNDER

Paralichthys oblongus

Another flounder whose size relegates it to only incidental fishing and culinary importance, this left-handed small (seldom more than 15 inches) fish is recognizable by the four distinct, pink-edged spots paired off on the lower half of its dark-gray, slightly mottled side. Fourspots prefer shrimp, worms and small crustaceans and depths ranging from 50 to 100 feet.

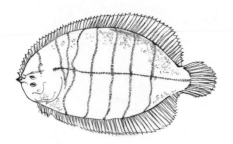

HOGCHOKER

Trinectes maculatus

Despite its small size (8 inches, ½ pound) and thick skin, the flavorful meat of this unusual fish makes it rate high with gourmets.

Also called American sole by virtue of being one of only four true soles (*Soleidae*) found in western Atlantic waters, this small, right-handed flatfish ranges from gray-brown to light-brown in color, sporting 7 or 8 dark-brown vertical stripes on its dorsal side, transected by a distinct dark-brown lateral line. Other identifying characteristics are its lack of pectoral fins, its circular shape and small snoutless mouth.

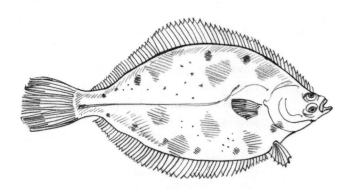

YELLOWTAIL FLOUNDER

Limanda ferruginea

This slim-bodied, right-handed flounder, so long a mainstay of the commercial fishing industry here in the Northeast, is now in danger of being overfished. Consequently, beginning in fall 1978, the National Marine Fisheries Service, despite continuing protests from Long Island commercial fishermen, severely reduced the number of yellowtails that may be taken.

This colorful fellow takes his name from the sunny markings on tail and other fins. Base color ranges from brown to olive-brown highlighted by large, irregularly-placed orange to red-orange spots that rapidly fade as soon as the fish is out of water. The blind side is white.

Average size is 15 to 18 inches, with some larger females reaching 22 inches and 2 pounds. Yellowtails prefer sandy and hard mud bottoms, depths from 30 to 300 feet, and shrimp, small crustaceans, and shellfish, as well as such small invertebrates as worms, amphipods and mysids.

YELLOWTAIL FLOUNDER AS FOOD: An excellent table fish with the fine texture and mild flavor expected in flounder. Use any flounder recipe.

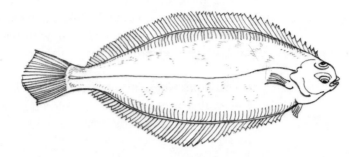

WITCH FLOUNDER

Glyptocephalus cynoglossus

Also known as grey sole and pole flounder. Practically a twin to its cousin the blackback flounder, the brown to brown-gray witch flounder can be recognized by its disproportionately small head and the dozen or so darkish spots scattered over its grayish-white blind side. More slender than the blackback, witch flounder ranges from 1 to 2 feet and weighs up to 4 pounds.

Rarely found at depths less than 60 feet, "the witch" prefers waters up to 150 fathoms (900 feet) deep and a diet that includes small shrimp and mollusks, marine worms and amphipods.

Commercially important only as an incidental catch, it is eagerly sought for its fine-flavored meat and usually caught with Danish seines and otter trawls.

WITCH FLOUNDER AS FOOD: The fish is absolutely first-rate, with qualities similar to those of the blackback flounder. The meat is marketed under the alternate name grey sole.

FLUKE

Paralichthys dentatus

Fluke is an excellent flatfish family member, so plentiful in summer and so similar in both taste and appearance to flounder that its nickname is summer flounder (which I suppose it technically is). Since both cooks and anglers frequently confuse flounder and fluke, a bit of clarification might be helpful. Besides the fact that fluke swim into our East End waters between the spring and fall appearances of blackback flounder (roughly from June to September) to provide us with flatfish all summer long, fluke can be distinguished by their greater size, their left-handed eye placement, their larger, toothy mouths and their slightly grayer flesh.

This superb table fish is the mainstay of summer sports fishery, an all-time popular adversary with commercial and part-time summer anglers and a particular favorite of mine.

FLUKE AS FOOD: Fluke has meat of superb quality, equal to or perhaps superior in flavor and texture to blackback flounder. Like other members of the flatfish family, fluke is a little bony, but this is certainly not a serious problem when the rewards are so great.

After gutting, dress and cook smaller fluke whole, and cut larger fish in fillets, with or without skin, as with flounder. Fluke will make better fillets since they provide larger slabs of exceptionally fine meat.

DESCRIPTION: Normally brown with darkish spots, this fish is chameleon-like in that it can assume the coloration of whatever bottom it happens to be frequenting at the moment, adding blues, greens, olive or gray to its skin tones as necessary to escape detection. The lateral line found on its dorsal side is slightly arched, and its tail is rounded.

Most fluke caught in the tender weeks of early Hamptons summer weigh in from one to 5 pounds, with 3 to 5 pounds being quite a respectable catch, but as summer sizzles on, size increases and larger, 13- to 15-pound flukes, known locally as "doormats," are not uncommon.

HABITS, HABITAT AND SEASON: Prime season is June through September into October, although commercial draggers begin picking up the spring run a bit earlier.

Fluke frequent depths ranging from 5 to 60 feet: bays, channels and inlets, anywhere up to a mile or two off the beaches. Medium-size specimens and doormats are usually taken offshore in the fall, but for the biggest fluke, drop your hook around sunken wrecks and submerged rocks.

Best fishing is in free-moving, fairly deep channels, from bridges and jetties, and from small boats. On an incoming tide, look for them in fairly shallow areas—on an outgoing tide, it's better to concentrate on those channels and holes where the tide washes food from surrounding flats as it retreats.

HOW TO CATCH: Light tackle is all you'll need to enjoy some really lively action, whether you're fishing from a boat or a stationary spot. If you're surf-fishing from the beach, use a light surf rod.

Try a standard fluke rig, or equip your line with a Carlisle hook, in any size from 1/0 to 6/0. Personally, I'd advise the larger, since fluke have larger mouths than blackbacks, for instance, and the 6/0 will give you a better chance with the biggies if you happen across one.

Sinker: Use a round one with just enough weight to hold bottom.

Bait: Fluke are most responsive to bait that either is alive or looks it. Live killifish are a stellar attraction, but since these are hard to find and harder still to keep alive and wriggling, other small baitfish such as spearing or sand eels should do the trick, especially when doubled up on the hook with strips of squid or fluke belly. For a flashy effect attach a couple of leaf spinners or a feather skirt alongside your bait. Or try using a 1- to 2-ounce bucktail jig, a silver spoon, or a plastic shrimp with a strip of baitfish or squid.

Chumming is a good teaser, too. Drop cracked mussels at regular intervals or use a chum pot with mussels, small chunks or bunkerfish, or even canned catfood.

Boat fishing? Try letting your boat drift so that your sinker and bait bounce along the bottom. That seductive movement brings fluke rushing to investigate. Try out different baits to see what fluke are sampling on any particular day. If you're using a two-hook rig, try a different bait on each hook until the day's preference is established.

Fluke fishing does require a bit of patience. These fish are occasionally coy, trying a nibble here, a nudge there, but once one strikes, you'll really know it! In contrast to the dainty bite of cousin blackback flounder, fluke are aggressive once they've made up their minds, and big ones will give you a nice fight. Tire your fish out before you try to land him and have a landing net ready for that plucky last-ditch attempt he'll make to gain his freedom. Hold the net just forward of your fish as you land him and slip it under him just as he clears the water.

ATLANTIC HALIBUT

Hippoglossus

By far the largest member of the flatfish family, halibut generally range from 20 to 300 pounds, with specimens on record of over 600 pounds. Quite an impressive fish fillet! Once of major commercial importance, their numbers have been steadily dwindling . . . it's only the lucky angler that encounters this formidable opponent in offshore waters these days.

Size alone makes this right-handed flatfish notable, but other distinguishing characteristics include a large mouth extending to the middle of the eyes, a lateral line broken only by the arch over the pectoral fin, and a concave tail. Color in adults is greenish-brown, with the familiar flatfish-family white underbelly; young halibut are slightly mottled.

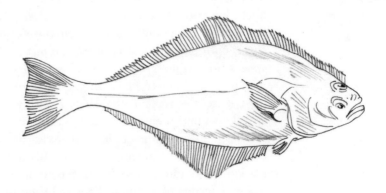

Halibut shun rocky or muddy bottoms, preferring sandy bottoms where water levels range from 30 to 500 fathoms (180 to 3000 feet). They are gluttonous feeders that dine voraciously on fellow bony fishes—other flounders, cod, haddock, perch, mackerel and herrings—as well as on lobsters, crabs, mussels, clams and skates.

Halibut taken nowadays are mainly caught by long-line bottom-fishing, although trawlers do take some.

HALIBUT AS FOOD: This is among the most delectable of fish, with its delicate, milky-white meat and paucity of bone. Sold as steaks or fillets, either fresh or frozen, halibut lends itself to an almost limitless variety of preparations. Halibut cheeks are considered a great delicacy, as are specimens of less than 20 pounds, which are sold as "chicken halibut." The meat is also sold in dried strips, and halibut liver yields a vitamin-rich oil.

FLOUNDER AND FLUKE: Flatfish are so finely textured, so delicately flavored, so gastronomically obliging in every way, that recipes seem almost superfluous. Given a flounder or fluke fillet, accurate basic-cooking instructions and a fistful of ideas, even the novice can produce culinary wonders.

There are, of course, more complex flatfish preparations too delicious to neglect. Many of these follow. Consider these, too, a mere starting point, then mix and match to suit your own tastes. So long as the fish is not overcooked, your flatfish creation will most likely be a triumph.

POACHED FLATFISH FILLETS

◆

Choose 6 fillets that average ½ pound each.

Bring white wine and/or Fish Stock to just *under* a boil, add the salted fillets, lower the heat to the lowest simmer possible (just enough to keep the liquid "trembling") and poach the skinless fillets in liquid just to cover, until they are pearly-white and just beginning to flake when tested with a fork. Fillets ½-inch thick should cook no longer than 4 to 5 minutes . . . thinner fillets should be cooked an appropriately shorter time. Carefully remove the fillets from the liquid with a long, slotted spatula, arrange them as directed in your recipe (on a heated platter, etc.) and keep them warm (unless otherwise instructed). Drain the platter, etc., again before saucing the fillets. Reduce the cooking liquid to half (or less) and add as directed to the accompanying sauce. Or serve with a simple wedge of lemon or lime and a bit of flavored butter.

FLATFISH FILLETS WITH NEW POTATOES AND GREEN BUTTER

◆

6 Poached flatfish fillets (see above)
1 Recipe Green Butter
2 Dozen boiled tiny peewee potatoes
 —like the ones left behind when
 our flat potato fields are harvested
 (or the smallest ones you can buy)

2 Tablespoons chopped fresh basil

Arrange the fillets on a hot platter, top each with a little Green Butter, surround with hot potatoes and sprinkle with basil. Serve with additional hot Green Butter.

FLATFISH FILLETS WITH FINGER-LENGTH ZUCCHINI

◆

Pour boiling water over 12 well-washed finger-length zucchini and let stand 5 minutes. The vegetables should still be quite crisp. Meanwhile poach 6 fillets, arrange side by side on a heated platter and sprinkle with 1 tablespoon chopped fresh dill. Pile the hot zucchini on either end of the platter. Garnish the fish with lemon slices and serve immediately with Crème Fraîche with Dill.

FLATFISH FILLETS WITH MUSHROOMS

◆

Add 12 whole mushroom caps, the chopped mushroom stems, 2 peeled and chopped shallots and 1 tablespoon lemon juice to the poaching liquid and reduce the liquid to ¼ cup. Arrange 6 hot poached flatfish fillets on an ovenproof serving dish and keep them warm. Place 2 drained mushroom caps on each fillet. Strain the reduced liquid, boil it briefly with 4 tablespoons butter and pour a little over each fillet. Brown quickly under the broiler. Serve immediately.

VARIATION I: Follow directions for Flatfish Fillets with Mushrooms, but instead of straining the reduced poaching liquid, bind it with one cup of Sauce Velouté before spreading over the fillets and lightly browning under the broiler.

VARIATION II: Follow directions for Flatfish Fillets with Mushrooms, but add one cup peeled, seeded and coarsely chopped tomatoes when you add the shallots.

FLATFISH FILLETS WITH ROE

◆

6 Flatfish fillets, poached as directed
Flatfish roe, poached in 2 tablespoons
 butter and ½ cup fillet poaching liquid

1 Recipe Sauce Aurore

Arrange the hot fillets on a heated platter, top with slices of poached roe; mask each with 2 tablespoons hot Sauce Aurore. Serve with additional hot sauce if desired.

FLATFISH FILLETS À L'AMÉRICAINE

◆

Arrange 6 poached hot fillets on a heated platter, mask with a little hot Sauce Américaine, surround with attractively placed hot shelled meat from 2 lobsters and 3 dozen sautéed button mushrooms. Decorate the platter with pieces of whole shelled claw-meat. Serve with hot Sauce Américaine.

FLATFISH FILLETS WITH ASPARAGUS TIPS, HOLLANDAISE

◆

Arrange 6 hot poached fillets on a heated platter, place 3 hot steamed asparagus tips on each and top each with a ribbon of hot Hollandaise Sauce. Sprinkle with chopped parsley.

FLATFISH FILLETS WITH ASPARAGUS TIPS, PARMESAN: Follow directions for Flatfish Fillets with Asparagus Tips, Hollandaise, but omit the Hollandaise Sauce and sprinkle each asparagus-topped fillet with an equal mixture of fine bread crumbs and Parmesan cheese and a little melted butter. Brown lightly in a hot oven. Serve immediately.

FLATFISH FILLETS, MARGUERY

◆

6 Flatfish fillets, poached in wine   3 Dozen mussels, scrubbed
2 Dozen shrimp, shelled and cleaned   1 Recipe Enriched White Sauce

Poach 6 flatfish fillets in white wine as directed on page 146, drain and keep warm. Poach 2 dozen shrimp in the liquid and arrange them around the fillets. Open 2 dozen scrubbed mussels as directed on page 257, using the poaching liquid from the fillets. Arrange half the mussels around the edge of the platter in their shells.* Remove the remainder of the mussels from their shells and arrange these over the fish. Reduce the poaching liquid and thin the sauce slightly with it. Cover the fillets with this sauce and glaze under the broiler. Serve immediately.

*The glossy blue-back shells improve the appearance of this dish and are especially appropriate when served informally near the bays where the mussels were nurtured.

FLATFISH FILLETS WITH ANCHOVIES AND OLIVES

◆

Open 1½ dozen mussels as directed on page 257. Place 6 hot poached fillets on a heated platter and keep them warm. Arrange the hot mussels around the edge of the platter. Add 3 tablespoons tomato paste to 2 cups of the poaching liquid and quickly reduce by half. Combine the hot sauce with 1 recipe Warm Crème Fraîche and pour over the fillets. Crisscross each with 2 anchovy fillets. Garnish with black olive slices and Anchovy Olives, sprinkle with basil and serve immediately.

SAUTÉED FLATFISH FILLETS

◆

Yield: Enough to serve 6

Flatfish are perhaps at their best when sautéed to a flaky, tawny brown. The classic preparation is one of elegant simplicity . . . 6 fillets or cleaned whole fish are dredged lightly in flour, seasoned with salt and pepper and quickly sautéed on both sides in hot Clarified Butter until white and tender on the inside, slightly crusty and golden on the outside. The fish are then arranged on a hot platter, sprinkled with lemon juice and chopped parsley and kept warm while 6 tablespoons of butter are heated until light-brown, with the aroma of toasted nuts. The still-foaming butter is poured over the fish, and the platter is immediately carried to the table.

FLATFISH FILLETS AMANDINE: Follow directions for sautéed Flatfish Fillets, but add 4 ounces of thinly sliced almonds to the final 6 tablespoons of butter and fry until golden. Pour the almonds and butter over the fish and serve while the butter is still foaming.

FLATFISH FILLETS BANNARO: Follow directions for Flatfish Fillets Amandine, but surround the platter with hot one-inch segments of firm banana fried in butter prior to pouring the almonds and butter over the fish.

SAUTÉED FLATFISH WITH EGGPLANT AND TOMATO: Prepare 6 flatfish fillets as directed in Sautéed Flatfish Fillets, but omit the brown butter. Top each fillet with one ½-inch-thick slice eggplant and 1 slice tomato, each dredged in flour and sautéed to a golden brown on both sides. Sprinkle each vegetable-topped fillet with one teaspoon grated Parmesan cheese. Slide under the broiler until the cheese browns lightly. Serve immediately.

SAUTÉED FLATFISH WITH SWEET PEPPERS AND THYME: Prepare 6 Sautéed Flatfish Fillets. Top each with a few strips Sweet Pepper Julienne and minced fresh thyme.

SAUTÉED FLATFISH FILLETS WITH ORANGE SLICES: Prepare 6 Sautéed Flatfish Fillets but omit the lemon juice. Garnish each fillet with one peeled orange slice and ½ teaspoon fresh tarragon before the browned butter is poured over.

FLATFISH FILLETS WITH ANCHOVIES: Prepare 6 Sautéed Flatfish Fillets, omit the lemon juice and parsley and top each fillet with two ½-inch-thick strips of pimento arranged on either side of an anchovy fillet. Slide under the broiler for an instant and serve immediately.

GRILLED FLATFISH

◆

Small, whole, cleaned flatfish are also superb grilled over hot coals. Dip the damp (not wet) fish in seasoned bread crumbs or dust with flour and brush with melted butter. Place 3 inches from the source of heat. Grill for several minutes, then turn and brush the top with butter. Repeat this process until the fish is golden and flakes when tested with a fork.

Serve with Sauce Tartare.

ROLLED, POACHED FLATFISH FILLETS

◆

The recipes for poached flatfish may all be prepared with rolled fillets instead of flat ones. Simply roll the fillets, milky skin-side in, and secure each with a few wraps of white thread (or a toothpick) and poach as directed on page 146. Drain well. Remove thread or toothpick.

POACHED FLATFISH TURBANS

◆

Flounder, fluke, sole, etc., have a natural perforation line that runs down the center of each fillet. After you poach the rolled fish, drain each and cool for a few seconds, then carefully cut apart at this line to form two small, pointy "turbans." This is a most attractive way to prepare any sauced flatfish dish.

BLACKBACK FLOUNDER LOUISIANE

◆

Yield: Enough to serve 6

An unusually compatible combination of ingredients: fish, bananas, sweet red peppers, hot nutty brown butter and creamy tomato sauce.

6 Flounder fillets
Flour
Salt and pepper to taste
3 Sweet red peppers, cut in ½-inch strips
6 Bananas, cut in 1-inch rounds

Clarified Butter
Brown Butter
1 Recipe Sauce Aurore
1 Tablespoon each fresh chervil and tarragon

Dust the fillets with flour, sprinkle with salt and pepper, and fry along with the peppers and bananas in Clarified Butter. Arrange on a platter and pour hot Brown Butter over all. Spoon Sauce Aurore attractively around the edge of the platter, sprinkle with chervil and tarragon and serve immediately.

PROMISED LAND BLACKBACK ROLL-UPS

◆

Yield: Enough to serve 6

Some of the best blackback fishing happens between our Accabonac Creek and Promised Land fish factory on the distant shore of Gardiner's Bay. This recipe cooks up into a perfect spring supper.

½ Cup each minced onion and chopped blanched almonds
3 Tablespoons butter
1 Cup cooked and finely chopped spinach
½ Cup fine bread crumbs

3–4 Tablespoons sour cream
A pinch each nutmeg and thyme
Salt and pepper to taste
6 Blackback fillets
¾ Cup dry white wine
1 Recipe Herb Hollandaise

Preheat oven to 350 degrees F.

Sauté the onion and nuts in the butter until the almonds are lightly browned. Mix with the spinach, bread crumbs, sour cream and seasonings. Place a generous spoonful of spinach stuffing on each fillet, roll up and secure with toothpicks. Arrange in an ovenproof dish just large enough to hold the fillets. Pour the wine over the fish. Baste and bake following directions on page 26. Drain well. Serve hot with warm Herb Hollandaise.

BAKED CORN AND CREAMED FLATFISH

◆

Yield: Enough to serve 6

This layering of creamed fish and fresh corn is a late-summer winner! The green pepper complements the corn and provides color but you may omit it if you prefer a more subtle flavor.

10 Ears fresh-picked and shucked corn on the cob
3 Tablespoons butter
½ Cup each chopped onion and green pepper
2 Tablespoons flour

1 Cup each light cream and milk
Salt, pepper and nutmeg to taste
1½ Pounds flatfish fillets, cut into 2-inch pieces
¼ Cup Parmesan cheese

Cut the kernels from the corn and scrape the cob to extract the cornmilk. Preheat oven to 375 degrees F.

Melt the butter in a skillet and sauté the vegetables until the onions are transparent. Sprinkle the vegetables with the flour, add the cream, milk and seasonings and stir over high heat until the sauce is thick. Drain off the cornmilk from the kernels and add it, with the fish, to this creamy sauce. Pour half the hot creamed fish into a buttered casserole, add the corn in one layer and top with the remaining hot creamed fish. Sprinkle with the cheese and bake for 30 minutes or until bubbling and lightly browned on top. Serve immediately.

VARIATION: Substitute one cup cooked baby lima beans for the ½ cup of green pepper.

MAGGIE YOUNG'S FLATFISH CROQUETTES

◆

Yield: Enough to serve 6

1½ Pounds poached flatfish fillets
1 Recipe Duchesse Potatoes
Enriched White Sauce
Salt to taste

2 Eggs, beaten
2 Cups fine white bread crumbs
Clarified Butter

Cut the fish into ¼-inch dice and thoroughly mix with the same weight of Duchesse Potatoes. Work in only enough thick Enriched White Sauce to bind (the mixture should not be runny). Salt to taste. Spread on a plate and chill well. Roll into 1½-inch cork-shaped lengths, dip each in egg and then in bread crumbs and fry in the butter to golden on all sides. Serve with a tomato sauce.

FLATFISH TURBANS WITH LOBSTER AND OYSTERS

◆

6 Flatfish fillets
Salt and pepper
1 Recipe Fish Forcemeat
1 Tablespoon each minced fresh
   rosemary and thyme
1 Recipe Sauce Nantua

1 Recipe Fish Quenelles for Soup
1 Lobster cooked and shelled
12 Medium-size mushroom caps,
   sautéed in butter
1 Recipe Fried Oysters

Rinse the fish, dry, sprinkle each fillet with salt and pepper, spread with forcemeat and sprinkle with herbs. Roll up and secure with thread or toothpicks. Poach as directed on page 146. Cool slightly, split the rolls into turbans and arrange these attractively in a shallow, ovenproof serving dish. Cover with hot Sauce Nantua thinned a little with a bit of reduced poaching liquid. Garnish with quenelles, slices of lobster, sautéed mushrooms and fried oysters. Serve immediately.

CHILLED FLATFISH TURBANS ON RICE SALAD

◆

Yield: Enough to serve 6

6 Flatfish fillets
Salt and pepper
1 Recipe Fish Forcemeat
1 Recipe Fish Jelly
1 Recipe Tarragon Mayonnaise

1 Recipe Basic Cold Rice for Salads
3 Hard-cooked Eggs, shelled and
   halved lengthwise
6 Rolled anchovy fillets
Chopped parsley

Rinse the fillets, dry, season with salt and pepper, spread with forcemeat, roll up and secure with thread or toothpicks. Poach as directed, on page 146, chill and split into turbans as directed above. Brush the fish turbans with ½ cup jelly mixed with ½ cup mayonnaise and chill until set. Arrange the jellied fish on a bed of rice salad alternately with the egg halves topped with rolled anchovies. Sprinkle with parsley. Serve very cold with the remaining mayonnaise in a small bowl set in the middle of the platter.

HALIBUT CROQUETTES SMITHTOWN MANOR

Yield: Enough to serve 6

1 Pound cooked halibut cut in
   ¼-inch dice
1 Pound mushrooms, minced
2 Teaspoons lemon juice
3 Tablespoons butter
Thick Sauce Velouté

⅛ Teaspoon powdered thyme
2 Eggs, beaten
1½ Cups fine white bread crumbs
Oil for deep-frying
1 Recipe Sauce Cardinal

Cut the fish into ¼-inch dice. Sauté the mushrooms and lemon juice in the butter until the moisture evaporates. Cool the mushrooms and mix with the fish and thyme. Work in only enough Sauce Velouté to bind (the mixture should not be runny). Chill well. Form into small finger shapes, dip each in egg and then in bread crumbs and fry to golden in hot oil to cover. Serve immediately with Sauce Cardinal.

POACHED HALIBUT WITH POTATO PUFFS AND CAVIAR BUTTER

Yield: Enough to serve 6

1 3-pound piece of halibut (or 2
   1½-pound steaks)
Court Bouillon

Chopped parsley
1 Recipe Duchesse Potato Puffs
1 Recipe Caviar Butter

Poach the halibut in Court Bouillon as directed on page 146. Arrange on a hot platter, sprinkle with parsley and surround with hot potato puffs. Serve Caviar Butter separately.

COLD POACHED HALIBUT WITH MINCED HERBS AND CRÈME FRAÎCHE

Yield: Enough to serve 6

1 3-pound piece of halibut
Court Bouillon
Salt and pepper
2 Large cucumbers, cut into 1½-inch
   thick rings with seeds removed

Dill fronds
1 Tablespoon each minced fresh dill,
   thyme and chives
1 Teaspoon lemon zest
1½–2 Cups Crème Fraîche

Poach the halibut in the Court Bouillon as directed. Add salt and pepper to taste. Remove any skin and chill the fish and the cucumber rings. Arrange the fish on a platter covered with fronds of dill. Mix the herbs and lemon zest with the Crème Fraîche; surround fish with cucumber filled with dollops of herbed Crème Fraîche. Pass remaining Crème Fraîche with the fish.

COLD POACHED HALIBUT WITH SAUCE RÉMOULADE

◆

1 3-pound piece of halibut (or 2 steaks)
Court Bouillon
1 Head buttercrunch lettuce
1 Recipe Carrot Twigs

1 Recipe Baby String Beans
1 Recipe Sauce Rémoulade
4 Large mushrooms, cut into thin, unbroken slices

Poach the halibut in the Court Bouillon as directed on page 146. Remove the skin, chill and drain the fish and place it on lettuce on a large platter. Arrange alternate bunches of chilled carrot twigs and string beans around the edge of the platter. Mask the fish with a little of the sauce and garnish with rows of mushroom slices. Serve additional sauce separately.

COVE HOLLOW HALIBUT STEAKS BAKED WITH TOMATOES

◆

Yield: Enough to serve 6

2–4 1-inch-thick halibut steaks (about 4 pounds in all)
5 Medium-size tomatoes, peeled and cut into ½-inch-thick slices
Flour
Salt and pepper

1 Tablespoon each chopped fresh oregano and basil
Sugar
Butter
1 Cup Fish Stock or clam broth
1 Recipe Garlic Butter

Preheat oven to 425 degrees F.

Rinse the fish and dry thoroughly. Dredge tomato slices generously in flour and arrange in a shallow, rectangular, ovenproof dish. Sprinkle with salt and pepper, herbs and a pinch of sugar. Dot with butter and pour the Fish Stock over all. Bake thirty minutes.

Arrange the fish over the tomatoes, brush with Garlic Butter and bake until fish flakes, brushing frequently with remaining Garlic Butter. Serve immediately.

HERRING

Clupeidae

True herrings, including shad, are among the most appetizing as well as the most commercially valuable of the world's major food fish. Once so numerous that they fairly blanketed vast sections of both the Atlantic and Pacific oceans, herrings (from the Latin *harengus*, a gray-white fish) are among the oldest fish consumed by humans. While still a very important catch, in the past they have been so in demand as a food source that their presence or absence in enormous numbers actually led to shifts in the balance of power among European countries. When the herring population in the Baltic Sea declined during the fifteenth century, the power of the Hanseatic League declined, too, and the Dutch herring fleet in the North Sea made the Netherlands preeminent. Dutch lust for the fish eventually led their fleet to North America's Atlantic coast and, inevitably, to their defeat by England during the Seven Years' War.

True herrings have one dorsal fin, set well back, a ventral fin directly opposite or just a bit back of the dorsal fin, and a deeply forked caudal fin. Most members of the family are small, with silvery scales that perfectly reflect the changing ocean depths, and are so similar in looks that all are dubbed simply "herring," with no further distinction made. But in Atlantic waters, two are preeminent—the sweet, sea-dwelling Atlantic herring, the mainstay of major food fishery, and another, East End's familiar bunkerfish (Atlantic menhaden), the most successfully harvested nonfood fish in the U.S., with over 8 million pounds caught each year.

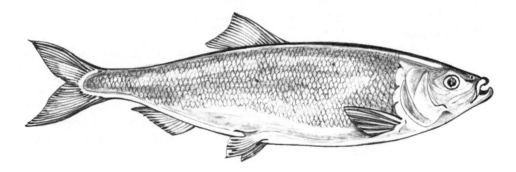

ATLANTIC HERRING

Clupea harengus

Also known as sea herring, common herring, Labrador sardine, sardine (when young), sperling and brit.

HERRING AS FOOD: This is one of the world's most important food fish, exceeding a 75,000-ton catch annually by U.S. commercial fishermen alone. Although delicious eaten fresh, the fish is more familiar to Americans in its preserved or semipreserved forms.

DESCRIPTION: The average size here is usually less than 12 inches, but the fish can reach as much as 1½ feet and 1½ pounds. Color ranges from steel-blue to green-blue, with silvery sides and belly. The dorsal fin is located about midway along the laterally flattened body, and the scales are large and loose. Most herring lack teeth, but the Atlantic herring does have a set in the roof of his mouth.

HABITS, HABITAT AND SEASON: Atlantic herring prefer colder waters, with a temperature range from 38 to 40 degrees F., and so are rarely found south of Nantucket, except in fall and winter, when they migrate to our

Long Island waters. Spawning takes place in the open ocean in the fall, when the males release so much milt the sea water at times turns milky. Fry can reach a length of 5 inches within a year, subsisting on such planktonic sea life as copepods, small shrimp, and crustacean larvae, although adults occasionally dine on other small fishes as well.

SHAD

AMERICAN SHAD

Alosa sapidissima

Also called common shad, although this fish is anything but, since it is equally esteemed by sports fishermen for its fighting qualities as it is by gourmets for its palate-pleasing flesh and roe. Range is along the Atlantic coast from Nova Scotia to Florida and also on the Pacific coast.

SHAD AS FOOD: *Sapidissima* means "most delicious," and that is a perfect description for both the flesh and roe of this exquisite fish. At your market shad is available from January to May but locally spring is the season to hook them. Female (roe) shad, being larger, are the preferred catch, since boning is tricky—each fish has 360 (count 'em) bones—and as long as you are going to the trouble, you might as well end up with an adequate fillet. The buck shad are just as tasty as the females but, being smaller, are more difficult to successfully bone. These are the gifts your sports-fishing friends are most likely to leave on your doorstep—hopefully on ice—along with females from which they've extracted the roe. The flesh is so delectable that it's worth a little extra effort.

Getting at bones buried inside shad meat has been described as 1) very simple or 2) requiring a surgeon's skill. It is closer to the truth to say that boning shad is difficult but gets somewhat easier with practice. If you have only one shad before you and you are a bit uneasy about filleting it, I suggest that you stuff and bake it and pick out the bones as you eat it. However if you are feeling particularly adept and happen to have a regular shad "connection," here is the filleting procedure to follow:

The important thing to know before tackling shad with a boning knife is that the "extra" bones in *each* fillet lie in two rows that parallel the backbone. You can feel them by running your fingers about one inch above and one inch below the center line.

Before you can get at these bones, however, there's a bit of preliminary work. First, carefully make a very shallow slit from anal canal forward to avoid puncturing the roe. Remove the roe *very* gently, gut the fish, scale, skin it and cut off its head. Prepare the fillets by cutting the fish lengthwise into halves and removing the backbone. Place one fillet skin-side-down on your work surface, with its tail toward you; locate the bones on one side of the fillet's center line, then make a lengthwise cut without cutting through the skin, from nape to tail, about ½ inch from the center line. Now move your knife to the other side of this line of bones, and make a similar cut running the full length of the fillet. Insert the knife point in one side of either of the lengthwise cuts and work it underneath the bone, loosening it so that you can get a good hold, then pull the bone up gently and work the entire length of it out of the fillet. Don't forget to repeat this same procedure with the second set of bones lower down in the fillet—remember: *each* fillet does have *two* rows of bones.

Roes purchased from your fish dealer will no doubt be pan-ready, but roes from your own catch will need prior preparation before cooking. To prepare roe, separate from the viscera and rinse thoroughly under running water to remove all blood, veins, slime, and exterior membrane, but be very careful to leave the thin inner membrane intact. Soak in salted ice water for a few minutes before using. If baking or broiling roe, no further preparation is necessary. For frying or sautéing, you may parboil briefly beforehand to make roe easier to handle without breaking the membrane, but I generally omit this step.

Note: New York State has closed the Hudson River to commercial food fishing. The only exceptions to this rule are Atlantic sturgeon under four feet and shad, which are taken from the river each year in gill nets set by commercial fishermen. The rationale behind these exceptions is that adult shad only spend about 2 weeks per year in the river, during spawning runs, and sturgeon are also not full-time residents. These visits are not considered long enough for the fish to ingest the large quantities of PCBs found in other Hudson-dwelling fish. Hopefully as Hudson River water becomes less dangerous these bans will be lifted.

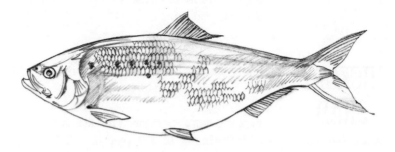

DESCRIPTION: This is the largest member of the herring family, averaging 1½ feet in length but often running up to 2½. Weight ranges between 1½ and 8 pounds, but a whopping 10- to 12-pounder is occasionally taken. Males generally run to about 4 pounds, a little over half the size of the females. The dorsal area here can be dark-blue, blue-green, or green with silvery sides and belly. A row of dark spots extends on a line from the eyes, just behind the gills to the back edge of the dorsal fin. A shad's most distinctive feature, however, is its toothless lower jaw, which closes entirely within its upper (also toothless). In other herrings, the reverse of this is true.

HABITS, HABITAT AND SEASON: A truly remarkable anadromous fish that ascends rivers such as the Delaware, Hudson and Connecticut every spring to spawn. The parent fish return to the sea after depositing their eggs, leaving when autumn touches the trees with color. Hatchlings find their way to the salt sea uninstructed. From 2 to 5 years later, these now-adult fish return to spawn in the very stream where they were born.

Spring is the season when great numbers of shad ascend rivers to spawn. It is also the time of year when shad—and their roe—are sought. These are usually thought of as the commercial fishermen's province—since most fish that appear in the market are netted as they swim up-river—but shad may also be taken with rod and reel, particularly in such shad-spawning waters as the Pocono reaches of the Delaware River, where shallow waters (as opposed to deeper waters of the Hudson and lower Connecticut) are the rule.

HOW TO CATCH: The shad's strike has been favorably compared to that of the bluefish . . . fast, hard and exciting. Standard equipment is a fairly stiff-backed spinning outfit and an ample supply of shad darts—those tiny lead jigs with bucktails attached. Casting and jigging are standard boat-fishing techniques here, but you may have just as much—if not better—luck, if you simply allow your dart to follow the current downstream. But remember, shad has a tender mouth, so a hook can easily tear loose, or your lure may get hung up on moss-covered rocks, so carry a good supply of darts. A long-handled net for lifting your catch from the water is also a must.

HICKORY SHAD

Alosa mediocris

Other names by which this more southerly-ranging shad is known are fall herring and shad herring.

HICKORY SHAD AS FOOD: This fish is smaller than American shad and not as tasty but it is still very popular with anglers and commercial fishermen. It may be purchased fresh, smoked and pickled. Roes of high quality are also sold.

DESCRIPTION: Among herrings, hickory shad are second in size only to American shad. The fish can reach 2 feet in length and usually ranges from one to 3 pounds in weight, but it can go as high as 6 pounds. The hickory is similar to most herrings in color—gray-green, with silvery sides and belly—but topside these fish may show faint longitudinal markings resembling stripes, and adults have a row of dark spots on shoulders from gills to dorsal fin. Unlike American shad, the hickory shad's lower jaw extends beyond its upper jaw.

HABITS, HABITAT AND SEASON: Like most herrings, this is an anadromous fish that seeks fresh water for spawning, but prefers offshore waters rather than the open sea at other times. Hickory shad may be taken on a variety of lures . . . live or cut-up baitfish, small spoons or streamer flies.

Hickory shad generally favor more southerly waters than do American shad, but since these last have diminished in such rivers as the Potomac, the hickory seems to be filling the gap.

ALEWIFE

Alosa pseudoharengus

Other names are graywife, fresh-water herring, wall-eyed herring, spring herring, sawbelly and branch herring.

ALEWIFE AS FOOD: For 300 years netted in great numbers during spring "runs," alewives in the past were salted, sun-dried, smoked and strung through the eyes on willow sticks. From that day to this, the fish have been sold for a few cents each "by the stick"—a chewy, smoky delicacy when and if you can find them. From a culinary point of view the main drawback here is the number of bones. For this reason most of the alewife catch is now sold for pet food or bait rather than for human consumption. Alewife roe, however, is excellent. If you find yourself where these fish are available fresh (in Maine, for example, in April and May), press their bellies on either side with thumb and forefinger. If there is a slight discharge of roe, these are the fish to buy. Clean and prepare the roe as you would shad roe. Alewives also "run" in the early spring in the Hamptons.

HABITS, HABITAT AND SEASON: The annual spring "run" of alewives from the salt-sea depths into the tidal estuaries, up the ladders of inland streams to fresh-water ponds to spawn is mystifying and deeply moving to experience. Driven by some ancient instinct to return by the billions to their sweet-water places of birth, the big-eyed alewives run the gauntlet of slashing gull beaks and man-made nets. Once they reach the spawning ponds the females each release as many as 100,000 eggs, which hatch into fry. These eventually wend their way to the seas to again return to spawn in the very ponds in which they were born. At times alewife populations become landlocked, as did those which entered the Great Lakes through the Welland Canal. These fresh-water alewives are more fragile than their sea-returning kin (averaging only 3 to 6 inches in length) and have a high mortality rate when waters warm rapidly.

◆ ◆

THE HERRING AND PILCHARD

Countless your squadrons, numberless as the stars
That sow with light the spaces of the skies
Countless as sands that pave the ocean beach
Ye migratory wanderers of the seas!
. . . So thick they move the ocean seems alive
And black with their exhaustless multitudes

◆ ◆

BLUEBACK HERRING

Alosa aestivalis

Other names for this fish are glut herring, summer herring, and kyack.

BLUEBACK HERRING AS FOOD: These are popular as baitfish, but commercially they are only an incidental catch. Sometimes called English blue herring by local fishermen, they are mostly caught in spring in gill nets set out for other species. Delicious pickled!

DESCRIPTION: The dorsal side here is blue to blue-gray, with silver flanks and belly. The fish averages one foot or so, with spotted top scales that give a striped appearance. The blueback differs from the alewife in that it has black rather than pink or gray interior lining.

HABITS, HABITAT AND SEASON: Bluebacks are common all along the Eastern Seaboard from Nova Scotia to Florida. Except for a brief dash in the spring up small tributaries of fresh-water streams to spawn, they spend all their lives in the salt seas. Probably because their spawning run is later in season than that of alewives, bluebacks are also called summer herrings.

BUNKERFISH

Brevoortia tyrannus

The formal name of this fish is Atlantic menhaden; it is also known as mossbunker, pogy or fatback. Across the bays (Accabonac and Gardiner's) from my garden, where I kneel burying bunkers deep in the soil beneath my tomato seedlings, I can see the lonely ruins of the old Smith Meal Company shrouded in the mists of Promised Land. The fish factory fell victim to several years' decline in the local stocks of bunkerfish, and of generally changing times in the menhaden fishery of the Northeastern seacoast. During that past bunker cycle of about three to five years the industry at Promised Land supported upward of about 500 local families. Its passing, along with diminished menhaden catches, made for difficult times here on Long Island's East End. Although it's unlikely that this oily, rather unpleasant-tasting fish will ever be welcome as table fare, it was the center of the largest industry in this area until a few years ago.

Indians and colonial farmers alike dug the silvery bunker into the soil for fertilizer, and now it is commercially important for that use, as well as a basis for many manufactured products . . . lipsticks, pet foods, paints, oils, etc.

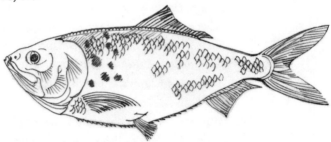

BUNKERS AS FOOD: Try as I might, I have been unable to find a way to elevate bunkers to palatability. I have baked, broiled, grilled, fried, smoked, salted, pickled, oiled and boiled them. I have soaked them in everything from wine, vinegar, cider, vodka, sherry and brandy to milk, yogurt, sour cream, buttermilk and whey. All with singularly unspectacular results. Bunkers still taste distastefully oily and bristle with hair-thin bones. That is not to say that you could not eat them in a pinch, particularly after soaking them in milk overnight, rinsing them well and pickling them with onions. But why bother? There are far too many other fish in the sea!

DESCRIPTION: The bunker is recognizable by its large scaleless head, straight-sided scales (as opposed to more rounded scales of other herrings), small ventral fin and toothless mouth. Its color is basically dark-blue or blue-brown topside, with silvery sides and belly, but the overall effect is an ethereal, transparent silver ranging to gold. Look for the distinguishing single large dark spot on each shoulder, surrounded by a number of lighter spots.

HABITS, HABITAT AND SEASON: Bunkerfish are visitors to East End waters from midspring through mid-October. Their presence is a key to movements of many valuable food fishes (bluefish, striped bass, various tunas and the like) for which bunkerfish are an important food source.

Like sand eels and other baitfish, menhaden are direct converters of plankton into the food chain. Smaller bunkers are used live and whole as bait; larger fish are ground up for chum.

New York State law forbids purse seining for any food fish except menhaden, within a 3-mile territorial limit.

◆◆◆◆◆◆◆◆◆◆◆◆◆◆◆◆◆◆◆◆◆◆◆◆◆◆◆◆◆◆◆◆

BUNKER-FISHING

On ocean waters, sound, and bay
The twinkling Maytime sunbeams play
And white with foam the billows shine
Where the moss-bunkers lash the brine
Above them flocks of seagulls swing
Beneath, the hungry bluefish spring
And, deadlier still, the surf-men strain
The oar, and run the meshing seine

Where sweeps the broad and breezy bay
Engirt by shores with woodlands gay
In shoals innumerable as sands
That sparkle in the wrinkled strands
The bunkers gather on the flood
Roaming the ocean-paths for food
And here the fish-er-boats invade
Deep with the shining burden weighed

Off by the low New Jersey shore,
Off where Long Island surges roar
Off where the Narragansett Bay

Its tribute to the sea doth pay
Off Massachusett's Bay profound
Off Maine shores with pine woods crown'd
Off where the billows chafe and fret
O'er rocks along New Brunswick set
The fish innumerable pass
O'er tumbling seas, or seas of glass

The watchman's eye from sandy mound
Or eyrie in some tall tree found
Surveys the broad extended main
Views of the fishy shoal to gain
And when the welcome prize draws near
In acres, o'er the waters clear
He hoists his signal to the breeze
That all may hasten to the seas

Then rush the crews from shop and field
Leave plough in glebe the oar to wield
The surf-boat down the beach is drawn
The oar is seiz'd with arm of brawn
The boat is launch'd where breakers pour
While guides the helmsman with the oar

Then hard and emulous the toil
Rivals all anxious for the spoil
The ablest boat, the manliest crew
Tug hard with muscle and with thew
And victor in the race surrounds
The leaping fish with snaring bounds
Then laden is the boat, till more
May not be added to the store

They pull for shore, and soon the soil
Is opulent with scaly spoil
In glittering heaps the shiny hoard
O'er all the yellow sand is pour'd

GRILLED FRESH HERRING

◆

Whole or split herring are excellent brushed with garlic butter and quickly grilled 3 inches above open coals. Allow two small fish per serving. For an extra fillip of flavor, salt or pickle the fish briefly first.

PAN-FRIED FRESH HERRING

◆

12 Small cleaned whole or split and boned herrings
Salt and pepper
Flour

Butter and/or oil
Garlic butter
Lemon wedges

Sprinkle the fish inside and out with salt and pepper and follow directions for pan-frying on page 26. Serve with additional butter or garlic butter and lemon wedges.

CRISPY FRESH HERRING WITH TOMATO SAUCE

◆

6 Medium-size tomatoes, peeled, seeded and coarsely chopped
2 Large cloves garlic, peeled and crushed
Sugar to taste
1 Tablespoon minced fresh marjoram
Butter

12 Small, cleaned, split and boned herrings
Salt and pepper
Milk
Cornmeal
Butter and/or oil
Sour cream

Sauté the tomatoes, garlic and seasonings in butter and simmer until nicely thickened. Sprinkle the fish inside and out with salt and pepper, dip them in milk and then in corn meal and pan-fry as directed on page 26. Serve the fish with the hot sauce and a dollop of sour cream.

FRESH HERRING AND ANCHOVY PUDDING, OLD COVE MILL

◆

Yield: Enough to serve 6

Butter
1 Cup fine bread crumbs
3 Large potatoes, peeled and thinly sliced
2 Pounds fresh herring fillets (cut in 1-inch-thick strips if the fish are large)

12 Flat anchovies
2 Large onions, peeled and thinly sliced
Pepper, thyme and sage
3 Eggs, beaten with 2 cups hot milk
1 Recipe Lemon Butter

Preheat oven to 350 degrees F.

Butter a baking dish and sprinkle the entire inner surface with bread crumbs. Arrange layers of potato slices, herring pieces, anchovy fillets, onion slices and a sprinkling of pepper, thyme and sage in the order given. Repeat the layering until all ingredients are in the dish. Top with 4 anchovy fillets. Pour the egg-milk mixture over the pudding and bake 35 to 45 minutes, or until the potatoes are tender. Serve hot with Lemon Butter passed separately.

PICKLED, SALTED AND SMOKED HERRING

◆

Herrings are top-notch fresh, but they are absolutely gorgeous pickled and/or salted.

Since the directions for these two processes are fully described in the sections on Pickling and Salting, that's where I've tucked my favorite herring recipes. Please look for them there, as well as for directions for Smoking these small treasures.

SHAD ROE POACHED IN BUTTER

◆

Yield: Enough to serve 6

You may interpret 6 "shad roes" to mean either 6 single or 6 double lobes, depending upon the size of the roes and/or the appetites of those you intend to serve. I am quite satisfied with one medium-size lobe. My husband, however, easily consumes at least two.

6 Shad roes
Flour
½ Cup butter

2 Tablespoons finely chopped parsley
Salt and pepper to taste
Lemon wedges

Dust roes lightly with flour. Melt the butter in a large skillet. Dip both sides of the roes completely in the butter, then arrange them in the skillet and poach over *very* low heat for 8 to 10 minutes. Turn the roes and poach 8 to 10 minutes longer, or until cooked through but still a little soft in the centers. Sprinkle with salt and pepper and serve immediately with lemon wedges.

BROILED SHAD ROE

◆

Yield: Enough to serve 6

6 Shad roes
Salt and pepper to taste

¼ Cup melted butter
Lemon wedges

Salt and pepper the roes, brush a rack with butter and broil the roes 5 inches from the flame until light brown, brushing several times with butter. Turn the roes and broil until golden brown, basting with butter. Serve immediately with lemon wedges.

VARIATION: Follow directions for Broiled Shad Roe; serve with hot Black Butter.

SHAD AND ROE IN DEVIL'S BUTTER

◆

Yield: Enough to serve 6

Although both shad and roe are excellent served simply with sweet or black butter, both also lend themselves to a little spicing up.

3 Shad fillets
2 Large cloves garlic, peeled and
    crushed
½ Cup butter
¼ Cup soy sauce

3 Tablespoons lime juice
A generous sprinkling of cayenne
    pepper
3 Shad roes, poached as directed on
    page 28

Rub the shad fillets with one clove garlic mixed with 2 tablespoons butter. Heat the remaining butter and garlic with the soy sauce, lime juice and cayenne. This sauce should be quite fiery.

Bake the fish fillets at 400 degrees F. in an ovenproof dish for 15 minutes, basting several times with the sauce.

Arrange the roe around the fish and broil for 5 minutes, basting with a little of the remaining sauce. Serve immediately.

SHAD AND ROE, ORIENTAL

◆

Yield: Enough to serve 4 to 6

Shad roe and shad fillets, stir-fried in cornstarch and hot oil Chinese-style, combine with vegetables and rice to produce an interesting and unusual spring supper.

2 Shad (or other) roes, poached and chilled
4 Shad or sea robin fillets
Cornstarch
Oil for frying
8 Scallions, each with 3 inches green tops
8 Fresh water chestnuts, peeled (or 3 Jerusalem artichokes, scraped)
10 Mushrooms
4 Slices fresh peeled ginger, minced
½ Teaspoon Szechwan peppercorns
1 Cup Fish Stock (or chicken stock)
¼ Cup soy sauce
1 Tablespoon sugar
3 Tablespoons sherry
½ Pound fresh spinach, well washed
Salt to taste
2½ Cups hot cooked rice

Cut the roe and fish into one-inch diagonal slices, roll in cornstarch and quickly fry in 3 tablespoons hot oil in pan or wok until lightly browned. Remove from the pan with a slotted spoon. Heat 2 additional tablespoons oil in pan or wok. Cut scallions into one-inch diagonal slices. Slice water chestnuts (or artichokes) and mushrooms and stir-fry these vegetables with the ginger and pepper until the vegetables are tender but still crisp. Remove with slotted spoon and add to fish and roe.

Stir one tablespoon cornstarch into the stock and add to pan or wok with soy sauce, sugar and sherry. Bring to a boil, stirring constantly until sauce is clear and slightly thickened. Add roe, fish and vegetables and stir one minute, or until hot. Season with salt if necessary and serve over hot rice.

KINGFISH

Menticirrhus saxatilis

Perhaps a kingfish by any other name would taste as sweet, but when several fish are given the same monicker, confusion is bound to follow. The kingfish we're talking about here is a scrappy Drum family member alternately called Northern or king whiting—*not* the cod-family member called whiting. Because of the kingfish's small size (about one foot in length and one pound in weight, although some run larger) they are not generally available in Long Island seafood shops, although they are commercially taken in the Chesapeake Bay area and are available there.

KINGFISH AS FOOD: The kingfish has that rare combination of fighting spirit and fine flavor that particularly appeals to the angler-chef. Tops as a table fish, with lean, white, fine-flavored meat, their small size makes them great candidates for pan-frying. If you're lucky enough to come upon a larger specimen, do fillet it and try the recipes that follow.

Be cognizant, though, that as a member of the Drum family (*Sciaenidae*) and related to weakfish, croakers and drums, kingfish are susceptible to and may harbor trematode parasites. These are rendered harmless with normal cooking, but no member of the Drum family, including kingfish, should be eaten raw, as in Seviche or Sashimi.

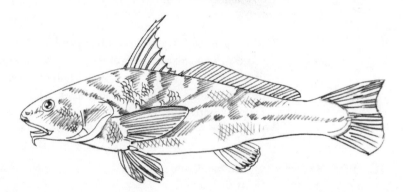

HABITS, HABITAT AND SEASON: Kingfish are fair-weather fish that swim into Long Island inshore waters along about May to take up residence for the summer. The young are rapid growers, achieving nearly 6 inches in size by the time they vacate local waters in early September for their winter homes. Kingfish have a decided preference for shallow waters with sandy bottoms, where they feed on crabs, shrimps and all available mollusks.

HOW TO CATCH: Look for kingfish in shallow, sand-bottomed flats or in any sandy bottom whose shallow waters (5 to 40 feet) are kept warm by the summer sun. For an exciting skirmish, all you will need are small bits of squid, shrimp, clam or bloodworm on small hooks. Remember that kings are bottom-feeders, so be sure your sinker is just heavy enough to hold bottom. Set your hook immediately if you feel a series of sharp tugs—kingfish are great bait-stealers and will eat and run if you're not alert. Not easy to find, but a treat when they do show up.

PAN-FRIED KINGFISH WITH SWEET PEPPERS AND DEVILED BUTTER

◆

Yield: Enough to serve 6

6 Small kingfish or 3 larger fillets
Salt and pepper
Butter

3 Each red and green peppers, with
    pith and seeds removed
1 Recipe Deviled Butter

Rinse the fish, dry thoroughly and sprinkle with salt and pepper. Pan-fry in butter as directed on page 26. Slice the peppers into ¼-inch-thick rings and fry until just tender in the butter left in the pan. Arrange the fish on a hot platter and garnish with the pepper rings. Serve immediately with hot Deviled Butter.

SESAME-FRIED KINGFISH

◆

Yield: Enough to serve 4 to 6

2½–3 Pounds kingfish fillets, cut into
    1½-inch-thick strips
Salt and pepper
2 Eggs, thoroughly beaten with
    1 tablespoon cornstarch and 1
    teaspoon water

1 Cup sesame seeds
Oil for frying
Soy sauce
Sherry
Finely grated fresh ginger

Rinse the fish, dry thoroughly, sprinkle with salt and pepper. Dip each piece in egg mixture, sprinkle with sesame seeds and deep-fry in hot oil until golden brown. Serve immediately with small individual bowls of dipping sauce made by combining equal parts soy sauce and sherry flavored with ginger.

KINGFISH WITH SPINACH AND HOLLANDAISE

◆

Yield: Enough to serve 4 to 6

2½–3 Pounds kingfish fillets
Court Bouillon
2 Cups cooked, drained and chopped
    spinach

3 Hard-cooked eggs, shelled and
    sliced
1 Recipe Sauce Hollandaise

Poach the fillets as directed on page 28 and keep them warm. Drain well and arrange on a hot platter. Spread each fillet with spinach, top with several egg slices and cover with a spoonful of Hollandaise. Serve immediately with additional warm Hollandaise.

Note: You may substitute kingfish for scrod.

MACKEREL

ATLANTIC MACKEREL

Scomber scombrus

Known locally as just plain mackerel, other common names are Northern or Boston mackerel (from the nineteenth-century salt-mackerel caught off New England and sold in Boston). Of world-wide commercial importance, the Atlantic mackerel is a member of the huge family that also includes such other mackerels as Spanish, sierra, cero, chub, king and their more distant relatives, tunas, albacores, bonitos and wahoo. The fish's name actually derives from the French word *maquereau,* meaning "pimp" or "procurer," which no doubt seemed appropriate to the practical French, since mackerel are often found accompanying schools of herrings, and are believed to escort young "virgin" shad to their males.

Our annual mackerel visitation on Long Island erupts when the temperature of local waters reaches just the right degree of warmth, enticing schools of fish moving north from their winter homes. I've hooked these brilliant beauties in the dusk of a late-spring twilight and wondered at their restless world-wide wanderings and how they came to my bay, to my hook, to my sizzling skillet.

MACKEREL AS FOOD: A family relation of the tuna, this excellent fish has in common with its cousin an oily outer band of red muscle with lighter interior meat. I've found that soaking the raw fish a few minutes in a lime-juice bath or broiling and basting them with tomato or wine-based sauces solves this problem. Freshness is another key to peak flavor. When hooking your own macks, be sure to pop your catch into an ice chest as soon as you remove them from the water to prevent the fish from losing their characteristic mackerel flavor. Mackerel are also wonderful marinated as Seviche or as mackerel gravlax, a variation on the traditional Scandinavian dill-cured salmon theme.

To prepare larger mackerel for cooking, scale, gut and remove the head and fins, then dip briefly in cold, salted tap water and pat dry. To fillet, you must work around the extra set of bones that flare out along the middle of the ribs. Cut vertically straight down to these, then slide your knife along them where they end at the skin. Cut back under these. Make another vertical cut toward the anal fin. If you like, to lessen the strong taste, remove the dark strip of meat that runs under the skin along the midline (as you would with bluefish) by making V-cuts along the entire length of the body on both sides with a flexible, sharp knife.

SPANISH MACKEREL

When fields are green and woods of June
Are vocal with the song-bird's tune
When willows lithe, a lovely group
Full foliaged o'er the meadows droop
When hazels their soft catkins ope
By rivulet edge and grassy slope,
Then swift those rovers of the deep
O'er all the Northern surges leap
Far off the billows of Montauk
Above them hovering gull and hawk
Far off the isles of Orient
Where the Sound's billowy waves are spent
And by the rough New England shore
Where the vex'd tides incessant roar
Their gleaming schools flash far and wide
Disporting in the flowing tide
The yellow-tinted pickerel
Lie hidden, motionless and still
The dorsal fin, the forket tail
Scarce stir the waters, clear as air
But jaws are open to assail
And glassy eyes all murderous stare
But when the small fry of the lake
The minnow and the shiner bright
Across the limpid surface break
Shooting like pearly sparks of light
Then, as an Indian tiger grim
Rends antler'd stag in jungles dim
So doth the water-tyrant slay
The helpless, unresisting prey.
The crab, the shrimp, the mussel-shell
The sea-egg with its thorny cell
The moss to slippery rock that clings
The dulse, the sea-weed with its rings
Its emerald garlands drifting wide
Rising and falling with the tide—
All these, the wealth of waters blue
Are ever wondrous, ever new.

DESCRIPTION: Schooling mackerel travel in packs reaching incredible proportions . . . their slender, elliptical bodies flashing through the water in continuous motion to prevent the death that would come if they paused for so much as a moment and cut off oxygen to their gills. Macks have beautiful, boldly-patterned blue to blue-green bodies (fading to silvery-white on the belly), vertically striped with dark, wavy bars. The average fish runs from about a foot to a foot and a half in length and weighs in at about 1 to 2 pounds, although specimens ranging up to 4 pounds are fairly common. You'll be able to recognize mackerel (and tunas too—all of the same family) by the series of small pointy finlets between the tail and second dorsal fin, and tail and anal fin.

Macks travel vast distances across the Atlantic in pursuit of a wide variety of marine foods: smaller fish, worms, shrimp, crabs and planktonic organisms. They in turn are highly relished as eggs, young and adults, by the larger sharks, tunas, whales, porpoises, cod, bluefish and striped bass, as well as by sea birds.

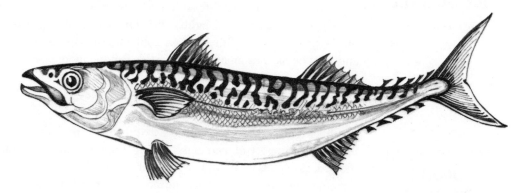

HABITS, HABITAT AND SEASON: Water temperature seems to be the key to when these fish arrive, or whether they show up at all. The last several years have been particularly abundant with deeply packed schools.

What brings macks toward shore in droves in the late spring is that old reproductive urge. Once they find water temperatures (60 degrees F. and over) to their liking, both milt and eggs are automatically released. By fall the young, called tinkers (and absolutely delicious eating), grow to 8 or 10 inches and account for most mackerel catches, particularly in bays and mouths of rivers.

Mackerel season usually lasts from 4 to 6 weeks, although some stragglers do hang on until early fall.

HOW TO CATCH: Major mackerel fishing is done from party boats, which in good years, barely leave port before hooking up with massive schools of macks that provide fast and dramatic action for their anglers. But since these fish often enter bays, harbors and other inland waters where they are more accessible, they may often be caught with ease using light tackle.

Tackle: Chumming with ground-up bunker is a good idea here. Mackerel are not excessively choosy about lures, but it's wise to keep a variety in your tackle box. Use a lightweight diamond jig when fish are close to the surface of the water. At times, a multicolor spoon may do the trick where the diamond jig fails. When macks are attacking in quantity even unbaited lures are sufficient; at slower times try baiting with squid or a bit of mackerel belly.

Slices of mackerel are unparalleled as bluefish or striped bass bait.

CHUB MACKEREL

Scomber japonicus

Also called hardhead and tinker. This long, slender mackerel is a traveling companion of its larger cousin the Atlantic mackerel and is usually an incidental catch when you're out for Atlantics.

Markings here are slightly different: the steely-blue or greenish dorsal markings are thinner and lighter in color, with mottling extending below the lateral line. The fish is often sold and served as Atlantic mackerel and may be used as an alternate for this fish in any recipe.

SPRING MACKEREL IN TOMATO-PIMENTO SAUCE

◆

Yield: Enough to serve 6

Fresh-caught spring mackerel are exquisite—especially when simmered in tomato sauce. Unfortunately, spring tomatoes leave something to be desired. You may, if you wish, substitute your own frozen garden tomatoes or one cup tomato purée (or canned Italian tomatoes) for half the fresh ones.

6 Mackerel fillets
3 Medium-size onions, peeled and coarsely chopped
1½ Cups coarsely chopped leek (white and green)
3 Cloves garlic, peeled and crushed
4 Tablespoons oil

8 Medium-size tomatoes, peeled, seeded and coarsely chopped
¾ Cup coarsely chopped pimento
1 Cup white wine
¾ Cup Fish Stock
1 Pinch each of sugar, thyme and sage

Rinse and drain the fillets. Sauté the onions, leek and garlic in oil until the onions are transparent. Add the tomatoes and cook 5 minutes over medium heat, stirring occasionally. Stir in the pimento, wine, stock and seasonings and simmer 15 to 20 minutes, or until the sauce is fairly thick.

Preheat the oven to 350 degrees F.

Pour half the sauce in the bottom of a flat ovenproof serving dish, arrange the fillets on top and cover with the remaining sauce. Bake for 15 minutes or until the fish flakes. Serve hot or cold.

GRILLED MACKEREL, ACCABONAC BAY

◆

Yield: Enough to serve 6

Early-arriving spring mackerel are wonderful as the main ingredient in the first cookout of the season.

*6 Small mackerel or 3 larger ones,
  cleaned and dressed*

Oil or butter

1 Recipe Parsley Sauce

Follow directions for grilling given on page 25. Serve with Parsley Sauce.

MACKEREL WITH NEW POTATOES AND GREEN BUTTER

◆

Yield: Enough to serve 6

*3 Good-size mackerel, cleaned and
  dressed*

Salt and pepper

White wine

*3–3½ Dozen tiny new potatoes,
  boiled in their jackets*

1 Recipe Green Butter

Rinse the fish, dry thoroughly and sprinkle with salt and pepper. Poach in white wine as directed on page 28. Skin the fish and arrange on a hot platter with the hot potatoes. Serve with Green Butter.

SOUTH SHORE MACKEREL WITH CLAMS AND ROE

◆

Yield: Enough to serve 6

When springtime offers fish heavy with roe, prepare this superior dish.

*2 Dozen cherrystone clams, well
  scrubbed*

*6 Small mackerel, cleaned and filleted
  with their roe*

Court Bouillon with Vinegar

*3 Cups broccoli florets, steamed
  until barely tender*

1 Recipe Sauce Velouté

4 Tablespoons butter

3 Tablespoons grated Parmesan cheese

1 Egg, beaten

Bread crumbs

Open the clams by heating them briefly in a little of the Court Bouillon.

Poach the fillets in Court Bouillon as directed on page 28 just until they flake. Drain well and arrange in an oblong ovenproof baking dish.

Arrange the broccoli and the clams in their shells around the fillets. Thin the Sauce Velouté with a few tablespoons of the poaching liquid, then stir in one tablespoon butter. Spoon the sauce over the fish, broccoli and the clam meats. Sprinkle with cheese. Place under the broiler until cheese is brown.

Meanwhile, sauté the roe in the remaining butter over low heat for 5 minutes on each side. Carefully cut the roe into ½-inch-thick slices, dip each in beaten egg and then in bread crumbs and fry until golden brown on both sides in the butter in the pan. Arrange the hot roe in a line down the center of the dish. Serve immediately.

CURRIED MACKEREL WITH MUSSELS AND ROE

◆

Yield: Enough to serve 6

6 Small mackerel, cleaned and filleted
    with their roe
Salt and pepper
White Wine Court Bouillon
Cooked rice
2 Dozen mussels, well scrubbed

2 Mackerel roes
1 Egg, beaten
Bread crumbs
Butter
1 Recipe Curry Sauce

Rinse the fish, dry thoroughly and sprinkle with salt and pepper. Poach in the Court Bouillon as directed on page 28. Arrange the pieces on a bed of hot rice on a heated platter and keep warm. Open the mussels by cooking briefly in a little poaching liquid. Cut the roe into inch-thick slices, dip in egg and then in bread crumbs and quickly sauté in butter until golden on all sides. Arrange the mussels in the half-shell and the roe around the edges of the platter. Pour over all the hot Curry Sauce (prepared with a bit of reduced poaching liquid).

POACHED MACKEREL, OLD ENGLISH STYLE

◆

Yield: Enough to serve 6

3 Cleaned and dressed mackerel, each
    cut into 3 pieces
Salt and pepper
White Wine Court Bouillon
12 Small hot boiled potatoes

1 Tablespoon each chopped fresh
    parsley and tarragon
Lemon wedges
1 Recipe Sauce Poulette

Rinse the fish, dry thoroughly and sprinkle with salt and pepper. Poach in White Wine Court Bouillon as directed on page 28. Arrange the fish on a heated platter, surrounded with potatoes, sprinkle with the herbs and garnish with lemon wedges. Serve Sauce Poulette separately.

MONTAUK MACKEREL WITH YOGURT CHEESE

◆

Yield: Enough to serve 6

6 Mackerel fillets
1 Recipe Yogurt Cheese
Melted butter

Spread the fillets with Yogurt Cheese softened to spreading consistency with a little melted butter (the cheese should still be stiff enough to hold its shape). Broil as directed on page 24. Serve immediately.

MONKFISH

Lophius americanus

A bizarre fish with an oversize head that makes up the largest part of its body—to know one is definitely not to love one, unless the encounter takes place at table. Better known locally as bellyfish (other names include goosefish and anglerfish), its meat is as lovely as the beast is forbidding. The only edible part of a monkfish is the tail section, which is solid white meat of rich flavor, somewhat similar in texture to dogfish but not as moist.

MONKFISH AS FOOD: Most monkfish that finds its way to market as bellyfish is landed as an incidental catch by trawlers out for cod or other game. Americans in general disdain this fish, but Europeans value it highly.

I would never tackle a big, ugly, whole monkfish, dead or alive, unless I found one in my refrigerator (as I did one gloomy day) glowering at me, demanding attention (the sort of Hamptons happening to take in stride). Any cook so blessed by friend or foe should arm him or herself with a roll of paper towels, a very sharp knife and an indomitable spirit, and proceed as follows:

Cut away and dispose of the ungainly head (the paper towels are to help you hold the slippery thing). Rinse the fish tail well under running cold water and, again using paper towels to prevent slipping, slit the skin on the underside of the tail all the way to the tail fin. Cut and pull away the skin and discard it. Remove the pinkish-tan membrane between skin and flesh. Fillet the meat and use uncut or slice into cutlets or fingers. The most successful cooking methods are poaching, braising or stewing, but the firm, white flesh may also be broiled, fried or sautéed if properly handled.

DESCRIPTION: An inshore representative of that highly specialized deep-water family known as anglerfish (*Lophiidae*), monkfish, along with their deep-sea relatives, have a first dorsal fin with a modified spine complete with small fleshy tip—a built-in fishing rod to attract prey, just as a human angler would jig bait. Other unusual monkfish features are a huge head and cavernous, tooth-filled mouth, and fleshy, footlike pectoral fins. The fish has scaleless, slippery dark-brown skin peppered with darker and lighter brown spots fading to a dingy white underbelly. Monkfish can reach lengths of 4 feet and weigh up to 50 pounds, but most are much smaller.

HABITS, HABITAT AND SEASON: Common along the Atlantic coast from New-foundland to North Carolina, and from the low-tide line all the way out to the Continental Shelf, monkfish hug the coastline in winter, then meander out to deeper depths as summer warms the blue waters. Blessed, or cursed, with an omnivorous and insatiable appetite, just about every type of fish and marine invertebrate living or visiting in local waters is fair game to this unattractive fellow. Even sea birds may be taken while busily searching the shallows for food of their own.

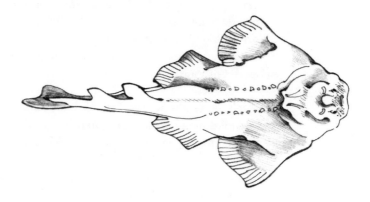

SEA CAPTAIN'S MONKFISH STEW

◆

Yield: Enough to serve 4 to 6

The nicely chewy, lobster-like texture of monkfish, the still-crunchy cooked onion and tomato-wine sauce combine here to produce an unusually delicious stew.

3 Pounds monkfish, trimmed and cut into 1-inch cubes
Flour
2½ Tablespoons cooking oil
2 Large onions, peeled
2 Cloves garlic, peeled and minced
4 Large tomatoes, peeled, seeded and coarsely chopped
2 Tablespoons chopped parsley

1½ Cups white wine
1 Teaspoon sugar (optional)
1 Tablespoon butter
⅛ Teaspoon each leaf thyme and black pepper
Cayenne pepper to taste
Salt to taste
Cooked rice or sautéed croutons

Dredge the fish lightly in flour and sauté in hot oil until tender and golden brown on all sides. Add a little more oil if necessary to keep the flour from burning. Remove the fish and drain on a paper plate. Cut the onions in half, place each half flat side down and slice at ¼-inch intervals. Add to pan with garlic and sauté 3 minutes. Stir in tomatoes and parsley and sauté for 5 minutes more. Add wine, sugar and the butter kneaded with one teaspoon flour. Stir in thyme, the two peppers and the salt. Stir until boiling. The onion should still be crunchy. Add the sautéed fish, stir for one minute or until hot and serve immediately in flat bowls with a spoonful or two of hot rice or croutons.

SAUCEY MONKFISH CUTLETS

◆

Yield: Enough to serve 6

Monkfish has wonderfully sweet meat, but it does contain areas of tough, chewy membrane. The objectionable material is mostly light tannish-pink in color and should be cut away and discarded.

3½ Pounds 3 x 5 inch monkfish fillets	*1 Tablespoon water*
Flour	*Bread crumbs*
Oil	*Sauce Aurore (optional)*
2 Large eggs	

Cut the fillets into ½-inch-thick cutlets. Press a very *light* dusting of flour into the flesh. In a large skillet heat ⅛ inch oil until a sprinkle of flour bubbles rapidly. Add fish 3 or 4 pieces at a time; cook on both sides in oil just hot enough to sizzle until the flesh takes on the texture of tender lobster meat. The object here is to cook the fish pieces through, not necessarily to brown them. Taste a corner of one fillet. If it still tastes somewhat gelatinous it needs more cooking.

Remove the cutlets, cool them to room temperature and press them lightly between paper towels to rid them of excess moisture and oil. Dust each fish piece lightly in flour again if necessary to make them hold the beaten egg, as they must for the final step.

Beat the eggs with the water. Dip the cutlets first in the egg mixture then in bread crumbs. Fry to golden brown on both sides in hot oil. Serve with the sauce of your choice.

MONKFISH CUTLETS WITH OLIVE SAUCE

◆

Yield: Enough to serve 6

If you have one, you may use a food processor to make the herb paste.

3 Pounds monkfish fillets, cut into ¾*-inch-thick slices*	*2 Eggs, beaten*
	Bread crumbs
5 Large garlic cloves, peeled and minced	*Oil for frying*
	2 Tomatoes, peeled, seeded and chopped
1 Teaspoon each salt and ground cumin	¾ *Cup sliced pimento-stuffed olives*
2 Tablespoons each rosemary and parsley, minced	*A pinch of sugar*
Flour	*1 Cup Crème Fraîche*

Rinse the fish and cut off any ragged edges. Process, blend or use a mortar and pestle to crush the garlic, salt, cumin, rosemary and parsley into a paste. Rub half of this into the fish and reserve the other half. Dust the fish cutlets lightly with flour, dip each in egg and finally in bread crumbs and fry in ¼ inch of hot oil until golden, turning once. Arrange the cutlets on a heated platter and keep them warm.

Quickly cook the tomatoes and the remaining herb paste until most of the moisture has evaporated. Stir in the olives, sugar and crème fraîche and heat but do not boil the sauce. Serve with the fish.

MOCK LOBSTER TAILS, WITH LOBSTER BUTTER

◆

Yield: Enough to serve 6

The point of this recipe is to amuse and to please, not to deceive. Since monkfish has a texture similar to that of lobster plus a not-dissimilar flavor, the illusion may be enhanced by cutting monkfish flesh into triangular "tails" and drenching these in Lobster Butter.

3–3½ *Pounds monkfish fillet cut*
   1-inch-thick and as illustrated below
Flour
Clarified Butter

1 *Recipe Lobster Butter**
Paprika
Lemon wedges

Work a *light* dusting of flour into the monkfish flesh. Sauté in Clarified Butter until the meat is firm. If it tastes gelatinous it needs more cooking. A few minutes before the fish is firm add 3 tablespoons of the Lobster Butter and baste the fish pieces with it as they finish cooking. Sprinkle lightly with paprika. Serve hot, garnished with lemon wedges. Pass additional hot Lobster Butter separately.

*If he has one your fish-store owner will probably be happy to contribute the shell of a cooked lobster to use in preparing the butter.

MONKFISH AND POTATO PIE

◆

Yield: One 9-inch pie

8 *Slices bacon*
3–4 *Medium-size potatoes, peeled and*
   thinly sliced
2 *Medium-size onions, peeled and*
   thinly sliced
Salt and pepper
1 *Tablespoon each minced fresh*
   thyme and marjoram

2 *Pounds monkfish fillets, cut into*
   ½-*inch slices*
Flour
¾ *Cup heavy cream*
1 *Recipe Basic Pie Pastry*

Preheat the oven to 400 degrees F.

Arrange a layer of 4 bacon slices in the bottom of a 9-inch pie plate, top with a layer each of potato and onion slices, sprinkle with salt, pepper and one teaspoon each thyme and marjoram. Dredge the fish slices generously in flour and arrange them over the herbs. Top with a layer each of potatoes and onions, 4 bacon slices, salt and pepper and the remaining thyme and marjoram. Pour the cream over all and top with pie crust slashed in several places to allow steam to escape. Bake 10 minutes, then lower heat to 350 degrees F. and continue to bake 35 to 45 minutes, or until crust is nicely browned.

SALT-WATER GEFILTE FISH

◆

Yield: Enough to serve 6

This version is far from traditional, but it is delicious. Your food processor makes it easy.

1½ Pounds monkfish, bass or
    weakfish, cleaned and skinned*
2 Pounds flounder, cleaned and
    skinned
4 Large onions, peeled
¼ Cup matzo meal
1 Teaspoon salt
Freshly ground black pepper

2 Eggs
Cold water
1 Large carrot, scraped and sliced
1 Large rib celery
3 Sprigs parsley
Bottled horseradish

Cut the flesh away from the bones and finely chop or grind it with 2 of the onions. Mix in the matzo meal, salt, pepper, eggs and enough cold water to bind the ingredients lightly together. Wet your hands and shape the fish into patties.

Sever the skin from the bones and put the bones and heads, the remaining onions, thickly sliced, the carrot, the celery and parsley in cold water to cover in a small roasting pan with a rack and bring to a boil.

Arrange the fish patties inside the fish skin and lower carefully into the water on the rack. Lower the heat and simmer, covered until the patties feel firm in the center. Set patties and carrot slices aside. Reduce liquid to 1½ cups and strain it. Replace patties in the liquid and allow to cool for 30 minutes. Chill and serve jellied liquid with the horseradish and cold fish. Garnish with carrot slices.

*Reserve 2 large pieces of fish skin (not from monkfish).

MONKFISH SEAFOOD SALAD WITH CRÈME FRAÎCHE

◆

*Yield: Enough to
serve 6 to 8*

A foolproof way to "fill out" a seafood salad, when more guests are expected than you originally planned, is to tuck cooked and chilled monkfish pieces in among the authentic shellfish.

2 Pounds monkfish fillets cut into
    strips ¾ inch by 1½ inches
2 Cups water mixed with 1 cup
    white wine
2 Dozen mussels
½ Pint bay scallops
1 Lobster
¾ Cup finely minced celery

4 Scallions, with 2 inches green tops,
    thinly sliced
1 Recipe Crème Fraîche with Dill
Sauce Mayonnaise
Salt, black pepper and cayenne
    pepper to taste
Lime slices

Poach the monkfish in water and wine, turning once, until the meat is firm and has lost its gelatinous quality. Chill thoroughly. Open the mussels and scallops in the poaching liquid. Steam the lobster. Shell and chill the shellfish thoroughly, then slice the lobster. Mix the fish and shellfish with the celery, scallions and Crème Fraîche. Stir in as much mayonnaise as is necessary to moisten the salad. Season to taste with salt and the two peppers. Serve cold garnished with lime slices and the meat from the lobster claws.

MONKFISH AND SEAFOOD SALAD WITH GREEN BEANS, VINAIGRETTE: Follow directions for Monkfish and Seafood Salad with Crème Fraîche, but substitute one recipe Baby Green Beans for the celery and Vinaigrette à la Moutarde for the Crème Fraîche and the mayonnaise. Garnish with 2 tablespoons capers.

MONKFISH AND SEAFOOD SALAD IN AVOCADO SHELLS: Follow directions for Monkfish and Seafood Salad with Crème Fraîche, but stir 2 chilled and chopped hard-cooked eggs into the salad with the mayonnaise. Heap the salad onto very ripe seeded, halved avocado shells. Yields enough to serve 10 to 12.

MULLET

STRIPED MULLET

Mugil cephalus

This rich, nutty, rather fat but fine-tasting fish, known also as grey mullet or common mullet, is a member of the large and very popular mullet clan of which there are upwards of 100 members flipping their fins up and down both American coasts, along English shores, into the Mediterranean and around the world to Hawaii. As if that were not confusing enough, our own striped mullet is often confused with the red mullet so popular in Mediterranean cuisine, which is not a mullet at all but rather a member of the goatfish family.

MULLET AS FOOD: Mullet is high in iodine content and rich in minerals and protein. Two thirds of the flesh is sweet and white; the remaining third is dark and oily, with very poor keeping qualities. Cut away and discard this fatty lateral band of meat, particularly if you intend to freeze the fish. The white meat by itself may be safely stored at zero degrees or below for up to 6 months.

Mullet, popular in Bayou country, can be prepared in many ways: baking, pan-frying, salting, smoking with apple or hickory chips or broiling (especially over charcoal). The delicious large roes are also deservedly popular.

Prepare whole mullet for cooking by scaling and dressing the fish, or scale and cut into fillets with skin intact. One shortcoming of mullets caught on hook and line in fresh water is their "muddy" taste, which may sometimes be eliminated by skinning the fish after filleting.

DESCRIPTION: Dark-blue or green on the dorsal area, fading to silver on the belly, with two small fan-shaped dorsal fins and a fairly deeply notched tail. Large, round silvery scales have darker centers that form dark, horizontal stripes. Size ranges to 20 inches, but most are smaller.

HABITS, HABITAT AND SEASON: Mullets are basically marine vegetarians, though they may on occasion nibble an hors d'oeuvre of fish eggs and/or snails. These fish have the strange eating habits shared by other basic converters of plankton into the food chain . . . they scoop up both food and mud in their mouths and then filter out all but the edible portions. This is mainly a marine fish, but it does frequently venture into brackish and even into fresh water. You'll recognize its characteristic leaps high out of water, ending in a distinctly ungraceful backward fall.

HOW TO CATCH: Being vegetarian by nature, mullet are a rare catch on hook and line, since bait is likely to be animal. Those fish taken by anglers are the few that will accept bits of bait worm while swimming in fresh-water areas. Most mullet are caught by gill nets, haul seines and other nets. The best-tasting are those caught in the surf or other clear waters with sandy rather than muddy bottoms. Those netted in muddy tidal flats are usually used for bait.

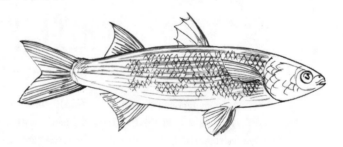

GRILLED MULLET WITH MUSTARD BUTTER

◆

Yield: Enough to serve 6

Grilling over hot coals best brings out the flavor here.

6 Small whole mullets, cleaned and
   scaled
Salt and pepper
Dijon mustard

Flour
1 Recipe Mustard Butter
Lemon wedges

Rinse the fish, dry thoroughly and sprinkle inside and out with salt and pepper. Brush the inside of the fish with mustard, dust lightly with flour and grill as directed, brushing frequently with Mustard Butter. Arrange on a hot platter and serve with additional hot Mustard Butter.

Note: Mullet may be prepared using any snapper blues recipe; the roe is excellent in any roe recipe, and the fish smokes wonderfully too (see appropriate directions).

ROE-STUFFED BAKED MULLET WITH TARRAGON BUTTER

◆

Yield: Enough to serve 6

6 *Small whole mullets, cleaned and*
  scaled
Salt and pepper

1 *Recipe Vegetable-Roe Stuffing*
1 *Recipe Tarragon Butter*
Chopped parsley

Rinse and dry the fish and lightly sprinkle with salt and pepper, inside and out. Fill the fish with the stuffing and secure with toothpicks. Bake as directed on page 26, basting frequently with Tarragon Butter. Arrange on a heated platter, sprinkle with parsley and serve immediately with additional Tarragon Butter.

FRIED MULLET AND OYSTERS WITH TOMATO CREAM

◆

Yield: Enough to serve 6

6 *Small mullet fillets*
Salt and pepper
Milk
Cracker crumbs

Oil and butter for frying
12 *Oysters, shucked*
1 *Recipe Tomato-Cream Sauce*

Rinse the fish, dry thoroughly and sprinkle with salt and pepper. Dip both fillets and oysters first in milk and then in cracker crumbs and pan-fry as directed on page 26. Arrange the mullet and the oysters on a heated platter with the bowl of Tomato Cream in the center.

WHITE PERCH

Morone americana

Also called sea perch. This small, temperate bass (family *Percichthyidae*) is closely related to striped bass. Being year-round Hamptons residents in restricted, inshore areas (Georgica and Mecox Ponds, for example), white perch can be taken locally most of the year. East End bay-men particularly favor them during February and March, when scallops are scarce. White perch also frequent brackish and salt water. They are excellent table fish.

WHITE PERCH AS FOOD: The firm, moist flesh and delicate flavor of white perch make it a superb candidate for all cooking methods and a perfect vehicle for a dazzling variety of sauces. To prepare for pan-frying, simply scale, then cut off the head and slit the belly to remove the entrails. Another delicious way to prepare the firm white meat is to fillet the fish, dip in tempura batter and crisp-fry.

Note: Hudson-dwelling or spawning white perch are every bit as subject to PCB contamination as their striped bass cousins. New York State has banned commercial fishing for white perch in this river.

DESCRIPTION: A small pan-fish that averages 8 to 10 inches in length and one pound in weight, white perch can run as large as 15 inches and 2½ pounds. Dorsally it is olive to dark-green, paling to silvery green on the sides and fading to white on the belly. Coloration, however, is likely to change according to habitat, with fish taken in brackish or salt water tending to be more golden than their fresh-water brothers. The juveniles resemble striped bass but have less pronounced stripes that fade as they mature to disappear in adults. Other distinguishing characteristics are a narrow, deep body that is flattened sideways, first and second dorsal fins separated only by a notch and loose scales that make cleaning easy.

HABITS, HABITAT AND SEASON: Although some white perch do frequent salt-water areas to depths of 100 feet, large ponds connected to the sea and brackish estuaries and bays are their favored habitats. Resident populations of white perch are found all along the Atlantic Coast from Nova Scotia to North Carolina, and inland as far as the Great Lakes.

Salt-water-inhabiting white perch gather during the winter in the deeper parts of bays and creeks to hibernate, then, come spring or early summer, migrate into tributary rivers to spawn. White perch seem to eat whatever is seasonally available and abundant: I make a habit of checking my catch to see what it has been feeding on aside from the bait on my hook. According to my notes, year-round batches I caught had gobbled the following: midge larvae in winter, mayfly nymphs and minuscule shrimp in spring, and insects, crustaceans and tiny fish in summer and fall. Commercial landings of these beauties are small, but white perch is a very popular gamefish.

HOW TO CATCH: In areas where white perch abound, you'll get peak action once you locate a school. Lightweight tackle is all you'll need—a fly or spinning rod is ideal. The tried-and-true method is bottom-fishing at anchor, but you might also try trolling until you locate a school, then drop anchor and still-fish. White perch can be found at all cruising levels, from 30-foot-deep mud bottoms where midge larvae and mayflies hide, to surface levels where insects are abundant in the early evening hours. Since salt-water white perch also feed on small fish of all kinds, an artificial lure such as a small spinner or streamer fly might prove as irresistible as such natural baits as pieces of squid or small crustaceans. For a pan-size fish, white perch will give a good, if short-lived, fight.

POACHED WHOLE WHITE PERCH, GEORGICA POND

◆

Yield: Enough to serve 6

6 Small, whole perch, cleaned and
   scaled
Roe
Salt and pepper

1 Recipe Fish Forcemeat
1 Recipe Mousseline Sauce
2 Tablespoons finely chopped dill

Rinse the fish, dry thoroughly and season inside and out with salt and pepper. Mix the forcemeat and any roe from the fish and spoon equal amounts into the fish cavities. Sew or secure with toothpicks. Poach the fish as directed on page 28 until the stuffing is set. Skin the fish, drain well and arrange on a heated platter. Drain once more before serving if necessary. Mask the fish with a little Mousseline Sauce, sprinkle with dill and pass additional sauce separately.

POACHED WHITE PERCH FILLETS WITH OYSTERS, THE CREEKS

◆

Yield: Enough to serve 6

12 Oysters, shucked
Court Bouillon
6 Medium-size white perch fillets
   (6 to 8 ounces each)

Salt and pepper
24 Medium-size mushrooms sautéed
   in butter
1 Recipe Sauce Nantua

Cook the oysters in their own juices as directed on page 262 and keep them warm. Add enough Court Bouillon to the oyster juices to poach the fillets as directed on page 28. Season to taste. Arrange the well-drained fillets on a heated platter, surround with oysters and sautéed mushrooms and pour the hot sauce over all. Serve immediately.

FISHERMAN'S ONION-FRIED WHITE PERCH FILLETS

◆

Yield: Enough to serve 6

6 Medium-size white perch fillets
   (6 to 8 ounces each)
Salt and pepper
Melted butter

1 Cup finely chopped onion
Chopped parsley
Lemon wedges
1 Recipe Sauce Tartare

Rinse the fish, dry and sprinkle with salt and pepper. Dip each fillet in melted butter and then in onion and fry to golden on both sides, turning once. Handle carefully so as not to break the onion crust. Arrange on a hot platter, sprinkle with parsley, garnish with lemon wedges and serve with Sauce Tartare.

WHITE PERCH WITH PARSLEY BOUQUETS

◆

Yield: Enough to serve 6

The clean, clear, taste of fresh parsley contrasts nicely with mellow Hollandaise and potatoes.

6 Medium-size potatoes, peeled and quartered, or 12 new potatoes
6 Medium-size white perch fillets (6–8 ounces each)
Court Bouillon with Vinegar

1½ Recipes Herb Hollandaise
A nice-size bunch of parsley, well washed and with coarsest stems removed
4 Scallions

Boil the potatoes in salted water until they are tender. Poach the fish in Court Bouillon until they flake, then skin them (leaving on the heads and tails) and drain them well. Keep them warm while you prepare the Hollandaise. Arrange the perch attractively on a platter and surround with the potatoes alternated with small bunches of parsley tied with strips of scallion tops. Mask each fish with a spoonful of Hollandaise, sprinkle with minced scallion, and serve immediately with additional sauce on the side.

WHITE PERCH WITH ANCHOVIES AND OLIVES

◆

Yield: Enough to serve 6

6 Small perch, cleaned and scaled
Salt and pepper
Flour
Butter and oil

12 Flat anchovy fillets, split lengthwise
10 Large pimento-stuffed olives, sliced
1 Recipe Green Butter

Rinse the fish, dry them and sprinkle inside and out with salt and pepper. Dust lightly with flour and pan-fry as directed on page 26. Criss-cross 4 split anchovies in a grid pattern on each of the fish, place an olive slice in the center of each square and arrange the fish on an ovenproof serving platter. Slide under the broiler for a second or two, then serve immediately with Green Butter passed separately.

SAGG POND WHITE PERCH WITH SEAFOOD CROQUETTES

◆

Yield: Enough to serve 6

1 Recipe Seafood Croquettes
6 Small perch, cleaned and scaled
Salt and pepper
Flour
2 Eggs, beaten

Bread crumbs
Oil and butter
Lemon slices
1 Recipe Sauce Aurore

Prepare the Seafood Croquettes and keep them warm.

Rinse the fish, wipe dry and sprinkle with salt and pepper inside and out. Dust with flour, dip in egg, then in bread crumbs and pan-fry as directed on page 26. Place the fish in a radial pattern (tails in, heads pointing out) on a heated platter. Arrange the croquettes in-between and garnish with lemon. Pass the sauce separately.

Note: White perch may also be substituted for snappers in any recipe and are excellent smoked.

PORGY

Stenotomus chrysops

Many children growing up along the Atlantic seacoast are introduced to the mysteries of inshore waters and the excitement of sports fishing by pin-hooking for porgies. Important catches for both amateur and commercial anglers, more than 15 million pounds of porgies were purchased last year on the Atlantic coast alone. Also called scup and Northern porgy, this is only one of a number of porgy varieties found in Atlantic coastal waters. All belong to a family of fishes (*Sparidae*) popular worldwide, known and highly appreciated as sea bream. The name porgy is derived from the Narrangansett Indian word for the fish, *mishcuppauog*. *Pauog* or *pogy* were the Indian names for fertilizer, for which the fish were used.

PORGEE

In all the tides that sweep the coast
By Labrador's remotest shores,
Far down to where the Chesapeake
Its affluent flood to ocean pours
The porgees, bright with silvery scales
In numberless great schools abound
At river-mouth, in open bay
In estuary and in sound

Where foams the flood-tide swift and clear
O'er sands and shoals of ocean's bed
Their flashing, shifting multitudes
Quick darting to and fro, are spread
Where whirls and wheeling eddies spin
O'er weedy rock and hidden ledge
Their pearly legions mustering fill
With swarming life the channel-edge

Rough ocean coasts and open seas,
Where cruise piratic blue-fish foes
They soon forsake for cove and bay
And where the shallow river flows
Yet there the fisher still pursues
And anchor'd yacht and dory boat
And pier and wharf with anglers lined
Thin out their schools where-er they float.

◆—◆

PORGIES AS FOOD: Known as "pan-fish of the sea," the porgy has a sweet, rather rough-textured flesh that responds best to simple preparation. From a culinary point of view there are two drawbacks to overcome before the white flesh and delicate flavor can be enjoyed . . . the many bones and the difficult-to-bridge scales. To deal with the first problem, cut large fish into fillets, skin them and use your fingers to feel out and discard as many remaining bones as is possible without tearing the flesh. It's best to scale porgies, if at all, as soon as possible after catching them or, better yet, to fillet the fish carefully without cleaning it, then cut away and discard the skin, scales and all, really quite an easy job once you get the hang of it. To serve small porgies whole, cut off the head, remove entrails and skin by sliding the knife underneath the tough skin and cutting outward. Remove fins. For best results pan-fry, grill or sauté.

DESCRIPTION: An oval, laterally flattened fish with silver, iridescent skin tones blotched or barred with darker shades of gray or blue. The fish has big eyes, a small mouth and thick scales. Large "humpback" porgies can reach as much as 5 pounds and 12 to 14 inches in length, but inshore specimens are much smaller, averaging a pound or so to much smaller. The dorsal fin runs from the top of the rounded back almost to the forked tail in one continuous line. The pectoral fins are sharply pointed and the anal fin is fairly large.

HABITS, HABITAT AND SEASON: Porgies are bottom-feeders, preferring smooth underwater terrain. In a good year, from late May to September porgies can be found just about everywhere in Long Island, in waters ranging from 5 to 60 feet deep. Even in a bad year a mother load of porgies is often just around the corner. Humpbacks lead off the run in early May, then the species as a whole defers to those voracious porgy gluttons, the bluefish, until these diminish at the end of June. Porgies then return in full force to stay to September.

HOW TO CATCH: Take the kids with you to bottom-fish from some stationary spot—shore, dock, bridge or anchored boat. They'll enjoy the scrappy fighting and fast action as these cooperative fish jump onto their hooks.

Tackle: Light tackle is all that's needed here—porgies will clean your line of bait time after time if your tackle is too heavy. Start with one-ounce bank-type sinker, adding just enough additional weight to hold the bottom. Use porgy or regular pan-fish hooks, No. 1/0 for humpbacks, No. 2/0 for smaller fish. Because porgies are school fish and not fussy feeders, almost any bait will entice them when they are around in numbers. Bloodworms, shrimp, skimmer clams, seaworms or squid are all good, but clams seem to be the favorite delicacy. Lower chum pots or drop cracked clams into the water to attract the fish.

OTHER PORGIES

What Long Islanders call porgy and Rhode Islanders refer to as scup is only one of numerous fishes of the *Sparidae* or sea bream family living in Atlantic waters. Most confine their swimming range to more southerly latitudes, but one species whose range occasionally reaches as far north as Cape Cod is the Sheepshead (*Archosargus probatocephalus*), once so abundant in the New York area that Brooklyn's Sheepshead Bay was named in its honor.

DESCRIPTION: The sheepshead is similar in appearance to but larger than the porgy, reaching 2 feet in length. Color is darkish silver, with 5 to 7 dark vertical bars on the sides. The tail is rounded rather than forked. The teeth are strong enough to scrape barnacles from pilings and crush crabs and mollusks.

SHEEPSHEAD AS FOOD: This is a fine foodfish, but the skin is tough and must be removed from fillets before cooking.

SEASIDE PORGIES GRILLED WITH BACON

◆

Yield: Enough to serve 6

6 Small to medium porgies, cleaned
   and skinned
Pepper
Milk

1½ Cups finely chopped onions
12 Strips bacon cut in half
2 Tablespoons chopped basil
1 Recipe Lemon Butter

Rinse the fish; dry and sprinkle generously with pepper. Dip in milk and then in onions. Criss-cross each side of the fish with 2 half-slices of bacon, sprinkle with basil and wrap each in a double thickness of aluminum foil, making tight double-folds along the edges. Handle gently so as not to disarrange the onion and bacon. Grill over hot coals (see page 25), turning once until the bacon is done. Cooking times will vary according to the temperature of the coals. Cut a small hole in one foil package to test the bacon. To serve, fold back the corners and serve with a little Lemon Butter poured into each packet. Eat the fish with your fingers.

PAN-FRIED PORGIES WITH LATE-SUMMER VEGETABLES

◆

Yield: Enough to serve 6

6 ½-inch-thick eggplant slices
6 ½-inch-thick green tomato slices
6 ¼-inch-thick onion slices
Flour
Oil and butter
6 Small, whole porgies, cleaned and
   skinned

Salt, pepper and powdered thyme
Lemon wedges
1 Recipe Sauce Rémoulade (optional)

Dip the vegetable slices in flour, then fry until tender in oil and butter. Set aside to keep warm.

Rinse the fish, dry thoroughly and season inside and out with salt, pepper and thyme. Dust with flour and pan-fry in oil and butter as directed on page 26. Arrange the fish on a hot platter with the vegetables and serve with lemon wedges and Sauce Rémoulade if desired.

COLONIAL PORGY AND POTATO PUDDING

◆

Yield: Enough to serve 6

6 Medium-size porgy fillets
Salt and pepper
4 Large potatoes, peeled and thinly sliced
2 Large onions, finely chopped
1 Cup shelled peas

Flour
Finely chopped fresh thyme and sage
Butter
2–3 Cups hot milk or light cream (or a combination of both)
½ Cup grated Swiss cheese

Preheat oven to 350 degrees F.

Rinse the fish, pat dry and season with salt and pepper. Place a ½-inch layer of potatoes in the bottom of a fairly deep well-buttered baking dish. Sprinkle with onions, peas, one tablespoon flour, salt, pepper, thyme and sage. Arrange a layer of fish over all and dot with butter. Repeat the layerings, beginning again with the potatoes and continuing with onions, peas, flour, seasonings, fish and butter. Pour the milk or cream over the fish (it should just reach the top layer), and dot with butter. If your dish is too large, additional liquid and cheese may be needed. Arrange a final layer of potato slices attractively over the top. Bake 30 minutes, sprinkle with cheese and continue baking until potatoes are tender.

MONTAUK PORGIES IN SPICY OLIVE SAUCE

◆

Yield: Enough to serve 6

6 Small porgies
Salt
Flour
5–6 Tablespoons olive oil
4 Cloves garlic, peeled and halved
3 Medium-size onions, peeled and thinly sliced
10 Large mushrooms, thinly sliced
1 Dried chili pepper with seeds removed

18 Large pimento-stuffed olives, sliced
1 6-ounce can tomato paste
1 Cup each white wine and tomato juice
2 Teaspoons each sugar and lemon juice
½ Teaspoon each ground cumin and cinnamon

Rinse, dry and lightly salt the fish and dredge in flour. In 5 tablespoons hot oil, fry the garlic and fish until the fish are very light golden brown on both sides. Do not overcook. Remove the fish and arrange them, overlapping slightly, in a rectangular ovenproof dish.

Preheat the oven to 350 degrees F.

Discard the garlic and fry the onion slices and mushrooms in the remaining garlic oil (adding more oil if necessary) until onions are tender but not browned. Remove and arrange over the fish. Finely chop the pepper and add all remaining ingredients except 10 olive slices to the pan. Mix well and simmer until the sauce is fairly thick. Pour over the fish and vegetables and bake in preheated oven for 20 minutes. Serve immediately garnished with a center line of the remaining olive slices.

SALMON

ATLANTIC SALMON

Salmo salar

This is one of the world's best-known and most highly prized food and game fishes. Its pale rosy, succulent meat—rich yet delicate—is incomparable. In colonial times, salmon were so abundant along our North Atlantic coastal rivers that they were used as fertilizer. Today their numbers have been so depleted that unless protective action is soon taken on an international scale, Atlantic salmon may be doomed. There is a ray of hope in this otherwise gloomy outlook. The fish have been returning in some numbers to Maine's Penobscot River, and in Canada the number of grilse (small salmon that return to spawn in one year rather than 2 or 3) has increased tremendously.*

SALMON AS FOOD: Prized by both local Indian tribes and early colonists, Atlantic salmon has been a North American favorite for centuries. Whereas these salmon were once plentiful in every river along the Atlantic shore from the Delaware north (with the exception of the Hudson, which lacks the gravel-bottomed tributaries salmon find so appealing), these may now be found in only a few streams in Maine and in Canada's Maritime Provinces.

Nearly all the fresh salmon found in East Coast markets today is Pacific salmon air-freighted from the West Coast, (which may be used in any of the recipes that follow). The small amount of fresh Atlantic salmon available in our markets is Canadian-caught except for the occasional passing Atlantic hooked in local waters. These are absolutely spectacular prepared in any number of recipes both plain and fancy. Poaching, baking, broiling, spit-smoking and pickling can all be recommended. What cannot be recommended is hooking the fish in the first place. Any Atlantic salmon left safely in our waters means a chance at survival for future generations of the fish.

*In addition, in Reykjavík, Iceland, in the winter of 1982, nations engaged in the production and/or harvesting of Atlantic salmon agreed to a treaty aimed at conservation of the species.

DESCRIPTION: Average weight runs about 12 pounds, but specimens between 15 and 20 pounds are not uncommon, and fish as large as 70 pounds have been taken. Salmon belong to the same family (*Salmonidae*) of soft-rayed fishes as trout and resemble these closely when young. Most adult salmon are blue-black topside (peppered with small X-shaped spots), fading to silver over the rest of the body. Males, as they mature, develop a strongly hooked lower jaw known as a kype.

HABITS, HABITAT AND SEASON: Although Atlantic salmon is basically an anadromous, migratory species, landlocked fresh-water varieties also exist in the Great Lakes and a few lakes and rivers in Maine and Eastern Canada. Those in the Great Lakes feed mostly on alewives and are pale and rather unpleasant-tasting, but landlocked salmon from New England and Canada have a more palatable diet of small, sweet smelt and have, as a result, more delicately flavored and textured flesh.

Each spring, fish from Atlantic waters enter clear, cold coastal rivers and tributary streams, overcoming seemingly insurmountable barriers . . . dams, rocks, waterfalls and rapids . . . to journey to spawning grounds far inland. Fat, large and handsome at the beginning of the trip, they eat nothing along the way and ultimately arrive thin and exhausted. Unlike the Pacific salmon, however, which die soon after their journeys up Pacific coastal rivers, some Atlantic salmon do survive to repeat the spawning trip once or twice more.

After hatching, the young salmon, or "parr," slip down to the sea in easy stages, growing all the while. They enter the ocean ravenously hungry for the shrimp, capelin and other forage fishes that quickly fatten them from 6-inch silvery "smolt" into 4-pound "grilse." Once they reach the necessary size and maturity, they leave the sea once more and, obeying some mysterious instinct, return to repeat the cycle in the very river or stream that nurtured them.

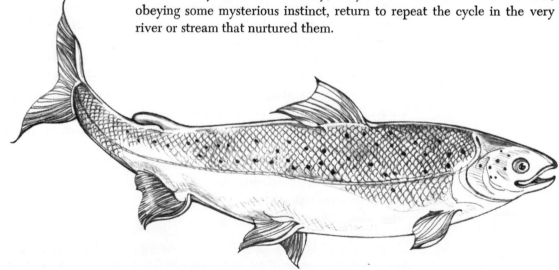

POACHED SALMON

If there is a more perfect fish dish than this one, I cannot think of it at the moment. Succulent pink salmon, wonderful in its own right, is also the perfect vehicle for spoonfuls of silken sauce. Whether the fish is to be served hot or cold, it should be slightly underdone to preserve its exquisite texture and flavor.

NORTH SHORE FISH PUDDING

◆

Yield: Enough to serve 6

Just-picked peas from your garden are spectacular in this hot fish ring. Try small cherry tomatoes in the center if you plan to serve the dish cold.

1½ Pounds salmon, flounder or haddock, or a combination of these, boned and skinned
3 Eggs
2 Tablespoons finely chopped fresh dill

½ Teaspoon salt
⅛ Teaspoon white pepper
1 Cup heavy cream
¼ Cup fine white bread crumbs
Sauce Aurore or Tomato-Cream Sauce

Preheat the oven to 300 degrees F.

Cut the fish into one-inch cubes, pick over carefully and discard any bones. Using a food processor or blender, whirl the fish pieces until coarsely ground; then, with the motor still running, add the eggs, dill, salt and white pepper through the spout or top. Shut off the machine and use a spatula to scrape down the sides of the container.

Turn on the motor once more and pour in the cream in a thin, steady stream, stopping the motor once or twice during the process to stir the mixture with the spatula. Whirl 5 seconds after the last of the cream has been added; the pudding should now have the consistency of soft whipped cream. Butter a one-quart ring mold and dust with bread crumbs, shaking out the excess; spoon in the pudding and cover with aluminum foil. Set the mold in a large pan and pour water into the pan around the mold to a depth of one inch. Bake 1½ hours, or until a knife inserted into the thickest part of the pudding comes out clean. Unmold and serve hot with Sauce Aurore, or cold with chilled Tomato-Cream Sauce.

WHOLE POACHED SALMON WITH ASPARAGUS AND POTATOES

◆

A large poached salmon is classically served with steamed potatoes and at least two sauces, Hollandaise and one or two others. I can never resist adding fresh asparagus, since it is also a perfect go-with for Hollandaise Sauce. The size of the fish available will determine the number of people to be fed . . . and the amounts of vegetables and sauce needed.

1 Medium-to-large salmon
Poaching liquid
Steamed or boiled potatoes
Steamed asparagus

Easy Hollandaise Sauce
Sauce Nantua
Thin lemon slices
Olive slices

Poach the fish as directed on page 28. Under-poaching and allowing the fish to cool somewhat and cook a bit further too off the heat is probably the safest. Drain the fish well, remove the skin from the body only and carefully transfer to a heated platter. Let stand for 5 minutes (or while you prepare the Hollandaise), then drain again. Garnish the body of the fish with overlapping lemon slices. Make a collar of olive slices and cover the eye with one as well. Serve with the hot vegetables and the hot sauces passed separately.

WHOLE CHILLED SALMON WITH VEGETABLES AND CRÈME FRAÎCHE

◆

1 Whole, poached, chilled salmon
Cold Carrot Twigs
Cold Baby String Beans
Cold Scallions in Fish Stock
Thin orange slices
Pitted black olive slices

Minced chives
Minced fresh tarragon
Grated orange zest
Crème Fraîche (mixed with mayonnaise if you like)

Place the skinned salmon on a chilled platter with bunches of carrots and string beans arranged attractively around the top of the platter and the scallions along the bottom. Arrange orange slices over the body of the fish, olive slices in a semicircular collar behind the back of the head and one slice of olive over the eye. Mix the herbs and orange zest with crème fraîche and pass separately.

SAUCED SALMON IN SHELLS

◆

Yield: Enough to serve 6

If you happen to be fortunate enough to have some leftover poached salmon, serve it in sea scallop shells in any of the following ways.

I. Line each of 6 shells with 2 tablespoons cooked minced mushroom or spinach, top with boned and flaked salmon, mask with Sauce Verte and garnish with a border of finely chopped hard-cooked egg. Serve chilled.

II. Line each of 6 shells with 2 tablespoons very finely shredded lettuce, top with boned and flaked salmon, cover with Sauce Russe and garnish with a border of minced fresh dill. Serve chilled.

III. Place a spoonful each of Curry Sauce and cooked rice in each of 6 shells, top with flaked salmon, cover with more Curry Sauce, sprinkle with fine bread crumbs and melted butter and brown quickly in a very hot oven.

OLD SAYBROOK SALMON STEAKS WITH SPINACH AND EGG SAUCE

◆

6 *Small salmon steaks*
White Wine Court Bouillon
3 *Cups cooked spinach*
Nutmeg

Salt and pepper
Butter
1 *Recipe Egg and Herb Sauce*
Minced chives

Cut the steaks into ovals and poach in the Court Bouillon as directed on page 28. Drain the fish, arrange on a heated platter and keep warm. Press into a custard cup ½ cup hot cooked spinach seasoned with nutmeg, salt, pepper and butter. Place the mound of spinach on one salmon steak. Repeat the process until each steak has its own crown of spinach. Spoon hot Egg and Herb Sauce over each and sprinkle with chives. Serve immediately.

SUMMER SUNDAY SALMON STEAKS

◆

Yield: Enough to serve 6

6 *Small salmon steaks*
White Wine Court Bouillon
1 *Head buttercrunch or Boston lettuce*
3 *Hard-cooked eggs, shelled and chilled*

12 *Flat anchovy fillets*
1 *Recipe Tarragon Mayonnaise*
Capers
1 *Radish rose*

Poach the salmon in the Court Bouillon as directed on page 28. Chill and arrange attractively on a bed of lettuce on a chilled platter (save the heart of the lettuce to decorate the center of the plate). Cut the eggs in half lengthwise and arrange in-between the fish steaks. Criss-cross each egg with 2 anchovies and mask the fish with half the mayonnaise. Sprinkle with capers and place the radish in the center of the lettuce heart. Serve cold with remaining sauce.

SARDINES

Fresh sardines, if you are able to obtain them, are delicious cleaned and boned, then sautéed, deep-fried or baked and served hot or cold. Canned sardines bear little resemblance taste-wise to fresh ones, but they are excellent in their own right when used for canapés or appetizers, as salads or sandwich fillings, or for a hurry-up meal when the larder is otherwise bare. Follow any recipe for young herrings or alewives.

ANCHOVY-STUFFED SARDINES WITH SUMMER SAVORY

◆

Yield: Enough to serve 6

2 Dozen whole fresh sardines, cleaned, boned and scaled
Pepper
2 Dozen flat anchovies
Flour
2 Eggs, well beaten
Bread crumbs
Oil for frying
Summer savory, minced

Wipe the fish inside and out with a damp cloth and season generously with pepper. Place one anchovy fillet neatly in each sardine, dust lightly with flour, then dip in egg and bread crumbs and deep-fry as directed on page 27. Sprinkle with summer savory.

SARDINES STUFFED WITH ANCHOVY AND CHEESE: Follow directions for Anchovy-Stuffed Sardines with Summer Savory, but roll the anchovies in grated Swiss cheese before inserting them in the sardines.

SARDE A BECCAPICO

◆

Yield: Enough to serve 6

2 Dozen whole fresh sardines, cleaned, boned and scaled
¾ Cup each bread crumbs and pine nuts
½ Cup each raisins and finely chopped onion
¼ Cup minced anchovies
Salt and pepper to taste
2 Tablespoons each minced parsley and oregano
1 Egg, well beaten
1½ Cups Ripe Tomato Purée
¼ Cup white wine
1 Teaspoon sugar
⅛ Teaspoon each allspice and nutmeg
2 Tablespoons olive oil

Wipe the fish with a damp cloth, inside and out. Mix the bread crumbs, pine nuts, raisins, onion, anchovies, parsley, oregano and salt and pepper to taste. Mix in the egg and stuff the fish. If there is stuffing left over, roll it into ½-inch balls. Boil the tomato sauce, wine, sugar, spices and one tablespoon of the oil for 3 minutes. Pour half the tomato sauce into a shallow baking dish. Arrange the fish and stuffing balls over it and top with the sauce and the remaining oil. Bake as directed on page 26.

BAY-SIDE SARDINE AND ORANGE SALAD

◆

Yield: Enough to serve 6

2 Dozen whole, fresh sardines, cleaned, boned and scaled
Oil for frying
3 Small white onions, peeled and sliced
2 Cups orange segments free from skin, membranes and seeds
2 Tablespoons each pine nuts, golden raisins and capers
1 Recipe Vinaigrette à la Moutarde

Fry the fish to a golden brown on both sides in the oil. Remove from the pan and fry the onions over high heat until just beginning to brown (they should still be crisp). Arrange the fish neatly on a shallow oblong dish (glass is best), garnish with the onions, orange sections, nuts, raisins and capers. Pour the sauce over and let stand for 15 minutes prior to serving.

SEA ROBIN

Triglidae

First acquaintance with this rather bizarre Hamptons underwater resident admittedly does give something of a shock. The head is wedge-shaped, hard and bony, covered with rough scaly skin. The eyes are slanted, with a look that ranges somewhere between baleful and shifty. The oversize pale-orange pectoral fins resemble birds' wings but, in addition to swimming, are used for walking along the bottom of inland waters, stirring up sand as the fish search for tiny crustaceans, mollusks and other small marine animals to lunch upon. When danger threatens, these same pectorals help the fish dig quickly into the bottom, leaving only their eyes glaring up from the sand. Pull them wriggling from the water and they're apt to express their indignation by grunting or what local fishermen call barking. No doubt about it. A unique fish.

There are two family representatives of the sea robin clan common to Long Island waters: the Northern sea robin (*Prionotus carolinus*) and the striped sea robin (*P. evolans*). These are similar in appearance, both displaying traditional raspberry-brown to gray-brown body color fading to a delicate white. The striped sea robin, however, has a distinct stripe on each side of its body and is longer on average (up to 18 inches) than its cousin *P. carolinus* (which rarely exceeds 12 inches) and all its fins, especially the pectorals, are larger.

No special angling tips are necessary here. Both fish are notorious bait-stealers and will practically leap onto your hook if you're fishing in their neighborhood.

SEA ROBINS AS FOOD: Vast numbers of these superb fish are regularly pulled from Hamptons waters by surf- and bottom-anglers and just as regularly tossed back in. A mistake. These make wonderful eating and are, in fact, the same fish the French know as *grondin* and pop into bouillabaisse. Thousands of pounds of sea robins are anonymously marketed annually as fresh or frozen fillets; still, this fish is difficult to find in fish markets and remains an untapped source of inexpensive fresh fish. I'm sure that haul seiners and trap fishermen, who catch more sea robins than they know what to do with, would be delighted to sell them to seafood markets if there were a demand. Fish stores would be happy to stock sea robins if they were sure that you wanted and would buy them. If you're interested in sampling them, why not make your desires known at your local fish market?

Sea robins have a rather unusual design and therefore these few special cleaning instructions might be helpful:

Make a shallow slit from the anal vent forward to the V-shaped breastbone. Run your knife alongside this bone on both sides. Now make a sharp cut downward behind the bony head, behind the pectoral fins to the belly. Snap the head back to break the backbone—the entrails should pull out automatically. The sea robin is one of the few fish with skin that will actually pull off with ease. Slit the skin down the backbone on each side of the dorsal fin and pull it downward and off over the tail. Fillet as directed on page 19.

Sea robins are excellent broiled with butter, fried, sautéed, poached or smoked. Serve up in any of the recipes that follow.

ACCABONAC SEA ROBIN BAKED IN CREAM

◆

Yield: Enough to serve 6

Simple, down-home fare.

2½ Pounds sea robin fillets	4 Tablespoons butter
Salt and pepper	4 Tablespoons flour
Heavy cream	½ Lemon
1 Bay leaf	¾ Cup sliced pimento-stuffed olives
1 Medium onion, peeled and sliced	2 Tablespoons chopped parsley
¼ Teaspoon leaf thyme	
3 Hot hard-cooked eggs, shelled and split lengthwise	

Butterfly each fillet by splitting nearly but not quite through. Rinse the fish, dry thoroughly and sprinkle with salt and pepper. Flatten each fillet slightly and arrange in a shallow ovenproof dish. Pour cream about ¾ of the way up the fish, add the bay leaf, the onion and the thyme and bake as directed on page 26, basting often. Drain the fillets well and arrange attractively with the hot egg halves on a heated platter. Keep warm.

Melt the butter in a saucepan, add the flour, gradually stir in 2 cups of the cream in which the fish was cooked and stir constantly until the sauce boils. Squeeze in the juice of the lemon, add the olive slices and stir. Spoon the sauce over the fish and eggs, sprinkle with parsley and serve immediately.

SEA ROBIN IN SNOWPEA SAUCE

◆

Yield: Enough to serve 6

6 Small sea robin fillets
Salt and pepper
Flour

Butter
1 Recipe Snowpea Sauce

Rinse the fillets, dry and sprinkle with salt and pepper. Dust with flour and poach in butter until fish flakes. Serve immediately with Snowpea Sauce.

SEA ROBIN, AUTUMN GARDEN

◆

Yield: Enough to serve 6

6 Sea robin fillets, split lengthwise
Flour
⅓ Cup olive oil
2 Cloves garlic, peeled and crushed
1 Tablespoon each minced fresh dill, parsley and thyme

2 Cups young white corn, cut from the cob
4 Large tomatoes, peeled, seeded and chopped
Salt and pepper
1 Tablespoon minced fresh chives

Rinse the fillets, dry well and dust with flour. Fry in the hot oil and garlic until golden, then set fillets aside. Add to the pan the dill, parsley, thyme and the corn, sauté 2 minutes, then add the tomatoes and salt and pepper to taste. Bring to a boil. Boil 3 to 5 minutes, or until the sauce is slightly thickened, then add the fish and simmer a few minutes more, until the fish flakes. Arrange the fish on a heated platter, top with the sauce, sprinkle with chives and serve immediately.

DEEP-FRIED SEA ROBIN WITH LICHEES AND SWEET PEPPERS

◆

Yield: Enough to serve 6

6 Sea robin fillets, cut into ½-inch-thick slices
Salt and pepper
2 Eggs, well beaten
1 Tablespoon cornstarch
1 Teaspoon water
Oil for deep-frying

2 Each red and green sweet peppers, cut into 1-inch squares
1 Can lichees
1 Tablespoon each cornstarch, honey, vinegar and soy sauce
½ Teaspoon finely grated fresh ginger
Hot cooked rice

Sprinkle the fish pieces with salt and pepper. Beat the eggs and cornstarch together, mixing until the cornstarch is smooth and well incorporated. Thin the batter with the water. Dip the fish pieces in the batter and deep-fry in oil as directed on page 27. Keep the fish warm. Dip the pepper slices in the batter, deep-fry and keep warm. Mix the juice from the lichees with the cornstarch, honey, vinegar, soy sauce and ginger. Bring to a boil, stirring constantly, until sauce is thick and clear. Stir in the lichees, fish and pepper slices and serve over rice.

SEA ROBIN, PROMISED LAND

◆

Yield: Enough to serve 6

Sea robins abound between my kitchen and the old fish factory across Gardiner's Bay in Promised Land. Many of our summer dinners are caught right off the shore within earshot of the winds that whistle around the factory ruins.

3 Tablespoons butter
3 Shallots, peeled and finely chopped
6 Sea robin fillets
4 Tomatoes, peeled, seeded and chopped
2 Cloves garlic, peeled and split

½ Cup tomato juice
2 Tablespoons Kneaded Butter
Salt and pepper
1 Tablespoon sweet butter
2 Tablespoons chopped parsley

Melt 3 tablespoons butter in a shallow ovenproof baking dish and sprinkle with shallots. Arrange the fillets in the dish, top with the tomatoes, garlic and tomato juice and bake as directed on page 26. Remove the fillets to a heated platter and keep them warm. Transfer the pan juices and tomatoes to a small pan and reduce the sauce slightly over high heat. Thicken with Kneaded Butter, season to taste, stir in the sweet butter and spoon the sauce over the fillets. Sprinkle with parsley and serve immediately.

SEA ROBIN WITH MUSHROOMS AND OLIVES: Follow directions for Sea Robin, Promised Land, but add 12 each sliced mushrooms and large pimento-stuffed olives at the same time that you add the tomatoes. Thicken with one cup white sauce rather than with Kneaded Butter.

SUNDAY LUNCH SEAFOOD CROQUETTES

◆

Yield: Enough to serve 6

Sunday is a nice, lazy day for lunching with friends and enjoying the view, particularly when you prepare these croquettes in advance and deep-fry them at the last minute.

1 Recipe Sauce Villeroi
6 Fresh mushrooms
1 Tablespoon butter
2 Cups cooked flaked sea robin or other firm-fleshed fish and/ or finely chopped shellfish

Vegetable oil for deep frying
2 Eggs
1 Tablespoon water
Flour
1½ Cups bread crumbs
Sauce Nantua or Sauce Aurore

Prepare Sauce Villeroi and cool to room temperature. Meanwhile, finely chop the mushrooms and sauté in the butter until just golden. Stir the mushrooms and flaked fish into the sauce, spread the mixture on a plate, and refrigerate until well chilled. Form the mixture into desired croquette shape and refrigerate again until well chilled.

Heat the vegetable oil in your skillet or deep-fryer to 375 degrees F. Beat together the eggs with the water. Dip each croquette first in flour, then in the eggs, and then in bread crumbs; fry in the hot oil until crisp and golden. Drain briefly on paper towels before serving hot with Sauce Nantua or Sauce Aurore.

SHARKS, SKATES AND RAYS

Selachii

I call these the "unholy three" and list them together not only because they are related but because each has something of an evil reputation. While it's true that some members of this family are rather intimidating (the 22-foot, 2-ton devil ray and/or film stars Jaws I and II, for example), many are rather benign. With all the bad press these amazing creatures have had, it's pleasant to be able to point out something positive . . . Many varieties are not only wonderful to eat but are also available for next to nothing from Long Island haul seiners or trap fishermen.

Sharks, skates and rays belong to the class of fishes (*Selachii*) whose skeletal structures are cartilaginous, that is, they lack the true bone of the "true" fishes (*Pisces*). Other characteristics they share include narrower gill openings, internal fertilization and, among some varieties, the bearing of live young.

SHARKS

The East End shark season really gets off to a good start around about mid-May when the porbeagle and blue sharks sail into our Northeastern waters to stay through the summer and on through September, along with the mako and those occasional visitors, the threshers and the magnificent whites.

Mako is the best of the game sharks, a fighter with real flash and style. It is also the best eating shark (best for us to eat, that is), with the porbeagle and/or the thresher running it a close second. For complex

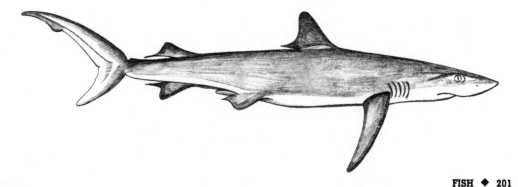

reasons having to do with enzyme action, shark meat does occasionally have a slight ammonia taste or odor that may be dissipated by soaking the meat in lightly salted water (or milk), covering it for several hours in a little lemon juice mixed with water or by placing it under cold running water for half an hour or so.

The thresher shark is sold in fish markets along California's coast and is quite tasty. The blue shark is perhaps the least palatable of all our East Coast sharks, but it too can be enjoyed if it is placed under cold running water for 30 to 45 minutes and then pounded as one would pound veal scallopine.

If you don't intend to eat your shark, follow the example of many concerned anglers who tag and release their catch so that these superb specimens may be studied and also live to fight another day.

HOW TO CATCH: Both smooth and spiny dogfish (sand sharks) can be caught from the beach, but to hook their larger cousins you'll have to own, rent, borrow or be invited aboard a boat. Chumming from a drifting or an anchored boat is probably the best way to find these impressive fish anywhere from a half-mile or so from the beach to the deepest waters offshore.

To begin, you'll need a medium outfit that can handle a 50-pound test* (after you get the hang of the thing you can move to a lighter test for faster action) unless you decide to take on the real behemoths that weigh in anywhere from 1,500 to 2,000 some-odd pounds. You'll need a heavy rig for these biggies, but then you'll miss a lot of action if smaller fish is all you encounter.

No matter what your rig, be sure to have a long (12- to 18-foot) leader able to take the abuse of sandpaper skin that can rough its way through ordinary line with ease.

Sharks aren't too fussy about their meals, but it doesn't hurt to have along their favorite bait—bluefish, whiting, mackerel and menhaden (bunkers). Live is best but they'll go for just-killed or frozen bait, too. Just to hedge your bets, try dangling a couple of different baits at different depths.

DOGFISH

There are actually two varieties of sharks swimming in local waters under the name of dogfish: the smooth dogfish (*Mustelus canis*), known also as gray dogfish, grayfish or smooth hound, the only Atlantic representative of its family (*Triakidae*); and the spiny dogfish (*Squalus acanthias*), also called spined dogfish, piked dogfish, or grayfish, which belongs to a different family (*Squalidae*).

* Test refers to the tensile strength of a fishing line, that is, how many pounds of fighting fish you can keep at the end of your fishing line before the line snaps.

SMOOTH DOGFISH

DESCRIPTION: The average length of this sleek slate-gray fish runs 3½ to 4 feet, but those specimens most frequently caught average not much more than 2 feet. The underbelly is white or cream-colored, the two dorsal fins are almost equal in size, and the tail fin, like those of other sharks, has lobes of unequal size. The small teeth are the flat, grinding variety.

HABITS, HABITAT AND SEASON: These are bottom-dwellers that favor waters of bays and estuaries less than 60 feet deep, although they are often found in deeper waters offshore. Their preferred prey includes crustaceans, squid, bunkerfish and blackfish. The young, born live after a 10-month gestation period, are one foot long at birth and begin foraging for food almost at once. Smooth dogfish winter offshore in southern waters, moving north with the spring as local waters warm.

One of the most abundant varieties found in Eastern Long Island waters, these are generally considered "trash fish" by both anglers and commercial fishermen. Thanks to their indiscriminate bait-snatching, large numbers of these delicious fish are caught by various methods all summer long but most, unfortunately, are wastefully killed or abandoned to suffocate on the sands of our beaches.

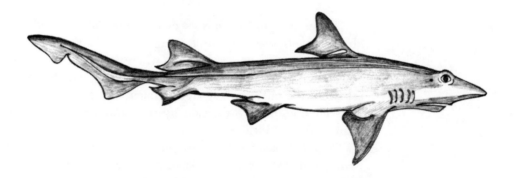

SPINY DOGFISH

DESCRIPTION: Similar to the smooth dogfish in both size and color, the chief difference is that the spiny dogfish lacks an anal fin, has almost equal-sized dorsal fins armed in front with sharp spines, and gives birth to juveniles likely to have white-spotted sides.

HABITS, HABITAT AND SEASON: This is essentially a cold-water species, found well offshore except during winter, when schools move inshore to waters from 600 feet deep to surf-shallow. They are voracious eaters that will devour any fish, shellfish or marine invertebrate they can sink their single row of knifelike teeth into.

Females carry one to 4 eggs for a gestation period that lasts from 18 to 22 mouths. The young are born live.

DOGFISH AS FOOD: Of all the fish I prepared while testing this book (and I tested extensively every variety mentioned herein), dogfish ranked with my family's all-time favorites . . . blowfish, shad and its roe, flounder, whiting, perch and striped bass. A four-star recommendation. The meat is sweet, firm, rich and just a bit gelatinous—slightly reminiscent of lobster—and hot or cold it's delicious.

Dogfish, like other sharks, should be dressed as soon as possible after being caught; the meat deteriorates quickly in the sun. If an expert (a charter-boat crew member or trap fisherman) will clean and fillet these for you, all the better, since the shark's sandpaper skin will make short shrift of your fingernails and rasp your fingers to a frosted finish any safe-cracker would envy. If you must do it yourself, keep the following essential points in mind.

The edible portion consists of two long fillets found along the fish's back, on either side of the cartilaginous skeleton. To remove this meat, begin by cutting under the fins (where the skin is weakest) up to the dorsal fin. Cut off the dorsal fin, then make a cut the full length of the shark to the tail. Working from semicircular cuts made at either end of this incision, remove the skin by slicing and pulling it free as you go. Cut off the solid white fillets.

Dogfish fillets can be prepared any number of wonderful ways . . . broiled, baked, smoked, pickled, poached in a tomato-based sauce, stir-fried Chinese style, or deep-friend in batter and served up with fried potatoes as that British national passion, Fish and Chips, the authentic version of which utilizes spiny dogfish, porbeagle, haddock or cod.

MACKEREL SHARKS

The bad press accorded this family of sharks (*Lamnidae*) is mainly due to the reputation of its larger members—particularly the great white shark—as people-eaters. Despite this, in other parts of the world meat of the two mackerel sharks has long been prized. Even in the United States these varieties are now becoming more popular commercially.

The shared characteristics of mackerel sharks include a mouthful of very sharp, highly visible teeth, large (for sharks) gill openings, anal fin, and tail fins whose lobes are nearly equal in size.

MAKO SHARK

Isurus oxyrinchus

DESCRIPTION: This streamlined shark is nearly a dead-ringer for the white shark of *Jaws* fame, but is somewhat smaller, averaging around 8 feet in length from its pointed snout with slightly protruding teeth to the tip of its nearly symmetrical tail. From a safe vantage point looking down into the water, the mako appears deep-blue above and white beneath, but once the fish is landed, its skin takes on gray to gray-blue tones above, light-gray below.

HABITS, HABITAT AND SEASON: The mako is one of the most popular deep-sea gamefish, whose fearlessness is legendary—not only in fighting for its freedom but in attacking sharks twice its size. One of the speediest fish around, this flashy-dasher often leaps several feet out of water in play or in pursuit of prey. The mako seldom ranges inshore, preferring open ocean waters where tunas, mackerel and herring tribe members can be taken.

MAKO AS FOOD: Similar in taste and texture to swordfish (in fact, sometimes retailed as a substitute for this high-priced and scarcer fish), mako meat differs in being slightly softer, less dry; the small tail pieces are even more delicious. Brine and/or marinate as directed on page 202 if any trace of ammonia is present.

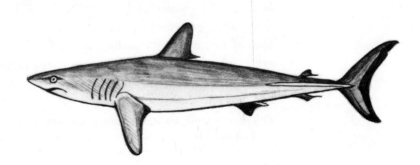

PORBEAGLE

Lamma nasus

Also known as blue mako, blue dog shark and mackerel shark.

DESCRIPTION: A heavy-bodied shark of average length (runs 5 to 7 feet and around 200 pounds) the back and upper sides of the fins are a dark steel-blue, while the belly is white. The porbeagle differs from mako and white sharks in having a more asymmetrical tail fin, a first dorsal fin almost directly over the pectoral fin, and a second dorsal fin directly over the anal fin.

PORBEAGLE AS FOOD: Like its near-relative the mako, the porbeagle is often marketed as swordfish. Brine and/or marinate as directed on page 202 if the fish has an ammonia odor.

HABITS, HABITAT AND SEASON: These are open ocean dwellers (on both sides of the Atlantic) that frequent deeper waters than the other mackerel sharks, preying on bottom-dwelling fishes like codfish and flounder family members, as well as on such schooling fishes as mackerel and herring.

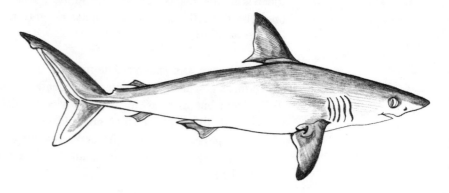

Once in a while you get a surprise in the trap. A salmon or some southern fish comes up . . . I guess he gets lost. Then sometimes we get skates and rays. Most we get 'round in through here is sand skate, we call 'em. Not too big. We dress 'em off, just cut the head and tail off and leave the wings and back stickin' together. We ship 'em to market that way. Don't get much money for 'em. Most time they're not worth the time of dressin' 'em. Usually not much meat on 'em. But in the stinger ray's case—they're the big, black dark-colored ones—they're nice an' fat an' thick, about four, five inches in the wing. They have a big long tail on t'em, and a spike that's poisonous. Won't bother you, though, unless you walk on it, an' who'd be fool enough to do that?

SKATES AND RAYS

Close relatives of the shark as well as of each other, skates and rays belong to an order of cartilaginous fishes known as *Rajiformes*. All are characterized by large winglike pectoral fins, with which they "fly" over the ocean floor, and slender, whiplike tails. Of the two, skates are the more likely to be used as food, but the names are used interchangeably (*raie*, for instance, persists in French cookery).

SKATES

All members of this family (*Rajidae*) are bottom-feeding fish of rather sluggish temperament. In appearance, the several Atlantic seaboard varieties resemble one another so closely that it's difficult to tell them apart. Most plentiful in the Hamptons is the 18-inch shoal-water species known as little skate (other names: common skate, sand skate and summer skate), the bane of surf anglers hoping to hook stripers. The next time you find one of these at the end of your line, save it. While skate meat is less plentiful and a little more difficult to get at than bass fillets, the final product is at least as tasty and exquisitely white and delicately flavored.

HABITS, HABITAT AND SEASON: Depending on the variety, skates can be found on cool-water bottoms from the tide line to depths of over 100 fathoms (600 feet). They are not as active as their ray cousins and not as likely to travel in schools, but they have the advantage of having their powerful jaws conveniently located underside, where they can easily scoop up clams, snails, small crustaceans and other such bottom-dwellers.

Skates reproduce by laying eggs, then affixing each in its individual pouch to seaweed or submerged rocks for its year-long incubation. Once the baby skates emerge, these rectangular black "mermaids' purses" with their pincerlike "handles" drift onto East End beaches.

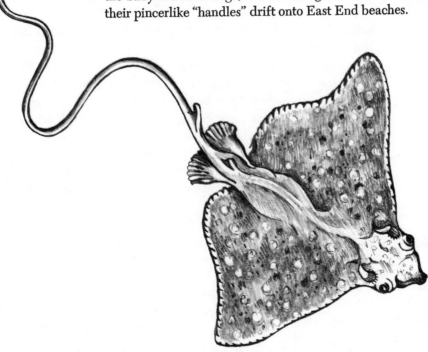

RAYS

Rays differ from skates in that most varieties have a barbed spine or spines on top of the base (not at the end of) the tail. Some of these, stingrays for example, can inflict a painful and poisonous wound if accidentally trod upon. Otherwise, ray in general differ from skates in being bigger (the wingspread of the manta ray can reach 22 feet), and in being much more active, using their "wings" to stir up bottoms in search of mollusks and crustaceans.

SKATES AND RAYS AS FOOD: Although the meat from these fish is popular in cuisines around the world, in the United States it is primarily appreciated by those of French, Italian or Oriental ancestry. The sweet taste and texture of the wing meat, which is the only edible part, is so similar to that of sea scallops that two varieties, winter skate (*Raja ocellata*) and the smooth butterfly ray (*Gymnura micrura*) have in the past been cut into rounds and passed off as the real thing.

Skates and Rays are sold whole and gutted (if young and small), or cut into wing pieces if fairly large. If these are unskinned, the thick viscous coating must be rinsed and scraped away before cooking.

The easiest way to remove the skin is to poach the animal in water to cover for a minute or two, or until the skin loosens. Do not overcook. When pieces are cool enough to handle, scrape away and discard the skin from both sides of each wing, along with the red streaks on either side. Be careful when handling these bizarre creatures—there are spines along the wing edges that face "in" rather than out as you might expect them to do, and these can give a nasty gouge. Chop off or trim away the bones along the edges of the wings. Keep the meat refrigerated until you are ready to use it.

In France many cooks feel that meat from large skates should be refrigerated for a day or two to tenderize it. This wait might result in an ammoniac aroma, which can be counteracted by adding a few tablespoons of vinegar to the poaching liquid, then serving with black butter (*Raie au Beurre Noir*). Aside from adding flavor, the butter when it browns forms acrolein, known to neutralize ammonia and render it odorless. Small wings are usually quite tender and sweet-tasting to begin with; however, if there is any ammonia odor, brine as with shark.

SKATE WINGS, SAUCE GRIBICHE

◆

Yield: Enough to serve 6

Unusually delicious.

6 Small skate "wings" (or 3 medium ones cut in half)
Salt
Vinegar
Water
18 Thin lemon slices
⅙ Cup coarsely chopped parsley
1 Recipe Sauce Gribiche

Prepare wings as directed above. Chill in a little of the cooking liquid. Drain well, arrange on individual plates, then garnish each with 3 lemon slices and a sprinkle of parsley. Serve cold with Sauce Gribiche on the side.

FRIED SKATE WINGS

◆

Prepare wings as directed above. Dredge lightly in flour, then dip in egg beaten with a teaspoon of water and finally roll in fine bread crumbs. Fry in Clarified Butter. Serve with Sauce Tartare.

RAIE AU BEURRE NOIR

◆

Prepare wings as directed above and keep them warm. Heat butter until it bubbles and is nicely browned. Add 2 tablespoons well-drained capers. Pour the butter over the wings and serve immediately.

ENGLISH FISH AND CHIPS

◆

Three secrets to frying fish and potatoes the English way were whispered to me by a London friend enjoying summer in our Hamptons. The first is dogfish fillets; the second is to parboil the potato strips before deep-frying them; the third is to fold a beaten egg white into the batter.

1 Cup flour
¼ Cup beer
1 Egg, separated
¼ Teaspoon salt
⅓ Cup each milk and cold water, mixed
2 Pounds baking potatoes, peeled and cut lengthwise into ½-inch strips

Oil for deep-frying
2½ Pounds dogfish fillets cut in 3-inch pieces
Malt vinegar
Salt

Place the flour in a mixing bowl and make a well in the center. Add the beer, the egg *yolk* and the salt and mix these ingredients well, gradually incorporating the surrounding flour. By hand beat half the milk and water mixture into the batter until it is smooth, then beat in enough of the remaining liquid to make a batter that is not too thick, yet not so thin that it will run off the fish. Let stand 30 to 40 minutes. Just before you are ready to serve the fish, beat the egg white until it holds stiff points and fold it into the batter.

Put the potatoes in a pot of cold water and bring quickly *just* to the boil. Immediately remove the pot from the heat, drain the potatoes well and spread them on paper towels to dry thoroughly. Deep-fry in hot (375 degree F.) oil until crispy golden brown on the outside and creamy on the inside.

Dip each fish piece in the batter until well-coated and deep-fry as directed on page 27.

Serve the fish on a large heated platter surrounded by potatoes. Pass vinegar and salt, to be sprinkled over the fish and chips as they are eaten.

MOCK TEMPURA

◆

Dogfish has a texture and sweetness similar to that of shrimp. Cut the flesh into butterflied pieces, dip in batter and deep-fry—and the resemblance is enhanced. Serve with a sauce flavored with the real shellfish and the illusion is complete. No one will actually be fooled (nor are they meant to be) but this does provide something of a "conversation piece" when served as an hors d'oeuvre.

1 Pound dogfish
1 Recipe Tempura Batter
Oil for frying

½ Cup each soy sauce and mirin
(or sherry), mixed

Cut the dogfish into pieces 2 inches long by one inch thick. Butterfly the top of these "fingers," open, dip in batter and deep-fry in hot oil until golden brown on all sides. Dip in the soy sauce and mirin.

SKEWERED SHARK WITH BASIL

◆

Yield: Enough to serve 6

36 1-inch cubes of shark steak
1 Lime, juiced
1 Lemon, juiced
Salt and pepper
Oil
10 Slices bacon, cut into 1½-inch
    pieces

2 Each red and green sweet peppers,
    cut into 1½-inch squares
3 Tablespoons chopped basil
Melted butter

Marinate the shark pieces in the citrus juices for 15 minutes, then drain well, season with salt and pepper and brush with oil. Thread on skewers in this order: a cube of shark, a bacon piece, a red pepper square, a green pepper square, a cube of shark, a bacon piece, etc. until all the shark has been skewered. The pieces should be touching. Grill without turning until the bacon pieces adhere to the shark, then rotate, brushing once or twice with oil until the shark just begins to flake. Do not overcook. Serve hot sprinkled with basil. Pass the melted butter separately.

SKEWERED SHARK WITH ANCHOVY BUTTER: Follow directions for Skewered Shark with Basil, but substitute mushroom caps for the green pepper and melted Anchovy Butter for the melted plain butter.

DOGFISH PROVENÇALE

◆

Yield: Enough to serve 6

3 Pounds dogfish fillets
Flour
¼ Cup olive oil
1 Green pepper
1 Large onion, peeled and coarsely
    chopped
¼ Pound sliced mushrooms
2 Large cloves garlic, peeled and
    minced
4 Tomatoes, peeled, seeded and
    coarsely chopped
1 Cup each white wine and Fish
    Stock

2 Tablespoons each minced parsley
    and fresh basil
2 Teaspoons minced fresh thyme
1 Tablespoon flour kneaded with
    2 tablespoons Kneaded Butter
Salt and pepper
¼ Cup pimento, cut into ½-inch
    squares
1 Tablespoon drained capers
1½ Tablespoons minced chives

Rinse and dry the fish well, dust lightly with flour and brown on all sides in olive oil. Remove fish carefully and set it aside. Char the green pepper over an open flame, scrape away and discard the skin, remove the seeds and cut the flesh into one-inch squares. Sauté the green pepper, onion, mushrooms and garlic in the oil remaining in the pan until the onion is transparent. Add the tomatoes and simmer for 5 minutes. Pour in the wine and Fish Stock and add the herbs. When hot, add the Kneaded Butter and stir until the sauce boils. Cook at a low boil for 8 minutes or until nicely thickened. Add the fish and cook until it flakes when tested with a fork. Carefully remove fish to a hot platter, season the sauce to taste and spoon it over the fish. Garnish with pimento squares, capers and chives. Serve immediately.

SEA CAPTAIN'S DOGFISH TERIYAKI

◆

Yield: Enough to serve 6

Very nearly any firm-fleshed fish (salmon, mackerel, tuna, etc.) is delicious when marinated and then grilled this way.

2½ Pounds dogfish, cut into 1-inch cubes

12 Very small white onions, peeled and parboiled 3 minutes

½ Cup each soy sauce and mirin (sweetened sake) or use sake or sherry with a generous pinch of sugar

2 Green peppers, with pith and seeds removed

1 Tablespoon light brown sugar

3 Scallions, with 3 inches green tops, chopped

Marinate the fish and onions for one hour in ¼ cup each soy sauce and mirin, sake or sherry, turning twice. Cut the peppers into one-inch squares and add them to the fish.

In a small saucepan boil the remaining mirin, sake or sherry, soy sauce and brown sugar until the sauce is syrupy. Thread the fish, onions and green peppers on 6 small skewers, brush with the hot sauce and broil or grill, turning twice and basting each time with additional sauce. The fish should be glossy and dark.

Add the liquid in which the fish marinated to the boiled sauce and cook until syrupy. Arrange each skewer on a plate and spoon the remaining hot sauce over. Serve at once sprinkled with scallion.

DEVILED DOGFISH, PROMISED LAND

◆

Yield: Enough to serve 6

A first course or light lunch dish.

2 Medium-size onions, peeled and coarsely chopped

3 Dozen small mushroom caps (or 18 medium-size caps, halved)

1 Cup bay scallops well rinsed and dried

3 Tablespoons butter

2 Teaspoons each dry mustard and chili powder

½ Cup pimento, cut into ½-inch squares

1 Teaspoon flour

2 Tablespoons tomato paste

1½ Cups heavy cream

1½ Pounds dogfish fillets

2 Tablespoons sherry

A pinch each of allspice, nutmeg and cayenne pepper

½ Teaspoon Szechwan peppercorns, crushed

2 Tablespoons grated Parmesan cheese

Preheat oven to 400 degrees F.

Sauté the onions, mushrooms and the scallops in the butter until the onions are transparent. Stir in the dry mustard, chili powder, pimento, flour and tomato paste until well mixed. Add the cream and stir over low heat until the sauce is smooth and fairly thick.

Cut the fish into ½-inch cubes and stir into the sauce along with the sherry and spices. Divide among 6 scallop shells or ramekins and sprinkle each with a teaspoon of cheese. Bake for 8 to 10 minutes, or until fish is tender. Serve immediately.

MAKO WITH PEPPERS

◆

Yield: Enough to serve 4 to 6

2 Pounds shark steaks

Salt and pepper

Olive oil

1 Large onion, peeled and chopped

1 Green pepper, with pith and seeds removed, diced

1 Clove garlic, crushed

5 Tomatoes, peeled, seeded and chopped

1 Bay leaf

A sprinkle each of celery salt and thyme

1 Quart Court Bouillon

1 Lemon

Kneaded Butter

2 Tablespoons diced pimentos

½ Cup pimento-stuffed olives, sliced

1 Tablespoon capers

Rinse the fish, pat dry and season with salt and pepper. Brown on both sides in the hot olive oil, then remove from the pan. Add the onion, green pepper and garlic and sauté 2 minutes. Add the tomatoes, bay leaf, celery salt, thyme, Court Bouillon and juice of the lemon and boil over high heat for 5 minutes.

Arrange the fish in an oiled ovenproof dish, and pour the boiling tomato and bouillon over it. Braise as directed on page 27, basting frequently. Transfer the fish to a heated platter and keep it warm. Reduce the sauce slightly, thicken with Kneaded Butter if necessary and stir in the pimentos and olives. Pour the hot sauce over the fish and serve immediately sprinkled with capers.

SMELT

Osmeridae

Smelt, those tiny relatives of salmon and trout and distant cousins of herring, are sweet-fleshed and delicious to eat. Best of all, whether sold fresh or frozen, they're inexpensive. North American waters are home to 9 varieties of fish belonging to the *Osmeridae* family, but by far the best-known is rainbow smelt (*Osmerus mordax*), one of the world's major food fishes. This is an anadromous marine fish, but it does also occur in many landlocked waters in the northeastern United States and southeastern Canada.

RAINBOW SMELT

Also called American smelt, Atlantic smelt, salt-water smelt and Arctic smelt.

SMELT AS FOOD: Whether you catch smelt yourself, or buy them fresh or frozen from your local fish dealer, freshness is the key to peak flavor, because the fish is so high in oil content. Store the smelt you hook yourself in an ice chest from the moment you pull them from the water. If you've caught more than you can use at one time, place the cleaned fish in suitably sized plastic containers, fill with lightly salted water to within one inch of the top (be sure fish is completely submerged), and freeze at 0 degrees F. or below. Smelt frozen this way will keep six months.

Fish stores usually sell smelts whole and gutted, but occasionally they are also sold pan-dressed and frozen. Larger fresh fish may be broiled, but pan-frying is far and away the most popular method of cooking this delicacy. Scale small smelt and cut off their heads, then gut and fry them as you would whitebait. The meat may be picked from the bones, but real addicts eat head, tail, bones and all—everything but the wiggle. Smelt roe is delicious, as are the male gonads. Leave these delicacies in the body cavity and cook them with the fish.

About ten or twelve smelt make a pound.

DESCRIPTION: Depending on their habitat, rainbow smelt can be pale- to dark-green, with silvery sides and belly, but generally sea-dwelling specimens are a good deal darker than their landlocked cousins. Fresh-water smelt may also have a distinct silvery lateral band that runs at eye level from shoulder to tail.

Smelt can grow to a length of 14 inches, but most average 8 to 10 and can be easily distinguished from young salmon and trout by their pointed snouts and slender, flattened bodies. Smelt also differ from herring in that they have a fleshy adipose fin (characteristic of salmon and trout) along the back between the dorsal and caudal fins.

HABITS AND HABITAT: Salt-water rainbow smelt are found along the Atlantic seaboard from Nova Scotia to New Jersey. They stick close to coastal areas and are rarely seen more than one mile from shore or in waters deeper than twenty feet. Spring is their spawning season, when as anadromous fish, the rainbow smelt seeks fresh-water in which to lay eggs. Many landlocked populations of this species also exist, with millions of pounds harvested each April in Lake Superior alone. One hundred years ago, rainbow smelt appeared to be an almost unlimited food resource, and today's commercial take is still huge, but the fish's former abundance has declined, and some states have enacted strict laws to control smelt fishing.

Smelt are partial to small shrimp, clam worms, and other small fishes.

SEASON AND HOW TO CATCH: Smelt are most in demand as game and commercial foodfish during their ten-day spawning season in late April. During this time they are taken in harbors, bays and estuaries as they make their way into fresh-water rivers to spawn. Winter is another prime fishing time, when the fish are taken in great quantities by anglers "shanty fishing" through the ice in inland water areas.

BAKED SMELT HORS D'OEUVRE

◆

3 Dozen smelt, cleaned
2 Dozen small mushrooms, halved
2 Dozen tiny pearl onions, peeled
2 Dozen Greek olives
1 Recipe Ripe Tomato Purée
½ Cup white wine
3 Cloves garlic, peeled and minced

2 Bay leaves
10 Peppercorns
½ Cup each olive oil and vinegar
2 Tablespoons sugar
1 Teaspoon each allspice, cinnamon and cloves

Arrange the fish, mushrooms, onions and olives attractively in a large, flat, ovenproof dish. Bring the purée, wine, garlic, bay leaves, peppercorns, oil, vinegar, sugar and spices to a boil, then lower the heat and simmer for 10 to 15 minutes. Meanwhile preheat the oven to 400 degrees F. Pour the hot sauce over the fish and bake for 10 to 15 minutes. Cool and then chill overnight.

SKEWERED SMELT

◆

2 Pounds smelt, cleaned
Flour
2 Eggs, well beaten

Bread crumbs
Lemon wedges
Salt and pepper

Thread the fish on skewers in an S-shape by first piercing them through the head, then the body and finally the tail. Dust with flour, brush generously with beaten egg and cover with bread crumbs. Grill over hot coals until golden on both sides. Sprinkle with lemon, salt and pepper.

CORN-FRIED SMELT

◆

2 Pounds smelt, cleaned
Salt and pepper
Flour

2 Beaten eggs
Corn meal
1 Recipe Sauce Tartare

Sprinkle the fish with salt and pepper inside and out. Dust with flour, dip in egg and then in corn meal and pan-fry as directed on page 28. Serve with Sauce Tartare.

SMELT WITH SLIVERED ALMONDS

◆

2 Pounds smelt, cleaned and boned
Salt, pepper and powdered thyme
Flour
2 Beaten eggs

Bread crumbs
¾ Cup each Clarified Butter and
    thinly sliced almonds
Lemon wedges

Season each fish, inside and out, with salt, pepper and a pinch of thyme. Dust with flour, dip in egg and then in bread crumbs and sauté in half the butter until nicely browned on both sides. Arrange the fish on a heated platter and keep them warm. Melt the remaining butter, add the almonds and stir until golden. Sprinkle over the fish and garnish with lemon wedges. Serve immediately.

STURGEON

ATLANTIC STURGEON

Acipenser oxyrhynchus

This primitive, bony-plated fish was a neglected but abundant food source until 1873, when it began to be exploited for caviar. Within three decades, the Atlantic sturgeon was practically extinct. Today, although some fish are still taken from the Hudson by anglers and commercial fishermen, and occasionally a few stray into our waters, most smoked Atlantic sturgeon in area markets comes from South Carolina and Georgia.

STURGEON AS FOOD: Very little fresh sturgeon makes its way to the retail market. Most of the commercial catch (which includes, along with the Atlantic sturgeon, the even more difficult to find shortnose sturgeon (*Acipenser brevirostrum*) of Atlantic waters, the white sturgeon of the Pacific northwest, the lake sturgeon from the Great Lakes and various other sturgeons from other areas of the country) ends up as that expensive but irresistible delicacy, smoked sturgeon. Small amounts of sturgeon are also pickled and sold in jars, or smoked and canned in oil.

If you should catch your own, sturgeon, especially when small, have firm, delicately flavored meat that can be prepared in a variety of ways. Whole or in large pieces, it can be braised or poached. Cut into steaks, it can be baked, broiled, or barbecued. Fingers or cubes may be pan- or deep-fried.

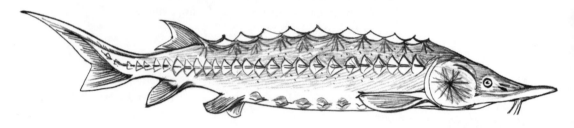

DESCRIPTION: Atlantic sturgeon once grew to 18 feet, but its size today is apt to be much smaller. This is a long, slender fish with five rows of bony plates stretching from head to tail. It has a flattened, pointed snout, with 4 barbels on the underside, and a toothless mouth. The dorsal, ventral and anal fins sit well back on the fish's body, and its tail is similar to that of a shark. Color is olive- or blue-gray, fading out on the sides to a white underbelly.

HABITS, HABITAT AND SEASON: Atlantic sturgeon is an anadromous fish, ocean-dwelling for most of the year but ascending fresh-water rivers in late spring to spawn. Some of the brood remain at the mouth of the river for several years after swimming downstream; others, known as "sperlets," will go directly to sea when less than a year old and a few inches long.

The fish matures very slowly, but is long-lived . . . up to 75 years. For food, Atlantic sturgeon prefer marine worms and clams, but will often condescend to dine on small fishes.

Despite its relative scarcity, Atlantic sturgeon is still being taken from the Hudson River during late spring, by both anglers and commercial fishermen. The fish is one of two species (the other is the American shad) that New York State still permits to be taken from the PCB-contaminated waters of the Hudson for commercial and foodfishing purposes. The rationale here is that like the shad (and unlike Hudson-dwelling striped bass and white perch) the Atlantic sturgeon is a transient in the river. Be aware, though, that this ruling applies only to sturgeon under 4 feet; larger fish from these waters may not be used for food.

SUMMER SUNDAY STURGEON AND CHAMPAGNE SOUP

◆

Yield: Enough to serve 6

3 *Pounds fish heads, bones and trimmings, preferably from firm, white-fleshed fish (cod, haddock, etc.)*
8 *Cups water*
2 *Large onions, peeled and chopped*
1 *Large rib celery, including leaves, finely chopped*
6 *White peppercorns, cracked*
1 *Bay leaf*
1½ *Pounds fresh sturgeon*
3 *Cups dry champagne (or fine dry white wine)*
8 *Scallions, with 3 inches green tops, finely chopped*
1 *Lemon, cut into eighths*

To make a stock, bring the fish trimmings to a boil with the water. Skim off any surface scum, lower the heat to medium and cook for 15 minutes, then skim the surface once again and add the onions, celery, peppercorns and bay leaf. Allow the stock to simmer, partially covered, for one hour. Skim the stock a third time and strain it through a fine sieve lined with several layers of cheesecloth. Reduce to 6 cups over high heat.

Lower the heat to simmering; add the sturgeon and poach until the pieces are just cooked through. Meanwhile, heat the champagne over low heat in a separate saucepan. To serve, stir the champagne into the soup. Salt to taste. Remove from the heat and put a piece of sturgeon into each soup bowl. Ladle the broth over, sprinkle with scallions, and serve immediately with lemon wedges.

MATILDE MILLER'S STURGEON WITH ANCHOVIES

◆

Yield: Enough to serve 4 to 6

2–3 *Pounds sturgeon fillets, cut into flat, thin slices*
Salt and pepper
Flour
2 *Eggs, well beaten*
Bread crumbs
2 *Tablespoons each oil and butter*
16 *Flat anchovies*
6 *Pitted black olives, sliced*
1 *Recipe Mustard Butter or Sauce Aurore*

Preheat broiler.

Season the fish slices with salt and pepper, dust with flour, dip in egg and finally in bread crumbs. Pan-fry in a mixture of oil and butter until golden, turning once. Criss-cross each escalope with 2 anchovy fillets, place a slice of olive between the ends of the anchovies (4 for each escalope) and slide under the broiler for 2 seconds to melt the anchovies slightly and heat the olive slices. Serve immediately with hot Mustard Butter or Sauce Aurore.

ESCALOPES OF STURGEON, MARSALA

◆

Yield: Enough to serve 4 to 6

2–3 Pounds sturgeon fillets, cut into flat, thin slices
Salt and pepper
Flour
2 Eggs, well beaten
Fine white bread crumbs
2 Tablespoons each oil and Clarified Butter
18 Medium-size mushrooms, thinly sliced
1 Lemon
¾ Cup Marsala
Chopped parsley

Season the fish slices with salt and pepper, dust them very lightly with flour, dip in egg and finally in bread crumbs. Fry in oil and Clarified Butter until golden on both sides, then transfer the slices to a heated platter and keep warm. Quickly cook the mushrooms until they begin to brown, squeeze in the juice from the lemon and add the Marsala. Simmer for 5 minutes and pour the sauce over the fish. Serve immediately, sprinkled with parsley.

ESCALOPES OF STURGEON IN CREAM: Follow directions for Escalopes of Sturgeon, Marsala, but instead of the lemon juice sprinkle 3 tablespoons warm cognac over the lightly browned mushrooms and set aflame. Substitute for the Marsala 1½ cups heavy cream. Continue as directed.

CHILLED STURGEON WITH RED AND BLACK CAVIAR IN MUSHROOM CAPS

◆

Yield: Enough to serve 6

1 3-pound piece fresh sturgeon
Salt and pepper
White wine and Fish Stock
24 Large mushroom caps
18 Tiny white pearl onions
1 Cup Fish Jelly
1 Recipe Tarragon Mayonnaise
Red and black caviar
18 Sliced cold Carrot Flowers
12 Pimento-stuffed olives

Season the fish with salt and pepper and braise in a mixture of wine and Fish Stock as directed. Poach the mushroom caps and onions in the same liquid. Chill fish and vegetables well. Cut the fish into thin slices, trim to uniform shapes and arrange attractively on a chilled platter. Arrange 12 mushrooms and the onions in-between. Mask with Fish Jelly mixed with ½ cup mayonnaise. Chill well. Fill half the remaining mushrooms with red caviar and half with black. Garnish the platter with these filled mushrooms, carrot flowers and stuffed olives. Serve chilled with additional Tarragon Mayonnaise passed separately.

SWORDFISH

Xiphias gladius

Also called broadbill and broadbill swordfish. A very popular food fish, highly prized both by anglers and commercial fishermen.

SWORDFISH AS FOOD: Swordfish's firm, rich flesh makes it highly sought after. Not even its removal a few years back from the commercial market because of high mercury content diminished the fervor of swordfish aficionados. In fact, swordfish meat is unique in texture and flavor. Its only true taste-alike is mako shark, which occasionally passes for swordfish at restaurants and retail markets during periods of scarcity and high prices.

The most usual cooking method for swordfish steaks (the meat is always streaked) is oven-broiling. Arrange on a greased broiling pan and cook in an oven preheated to 375 degrees F. for 12 to 14 minutes, basting frequently with seasoned butter (Garlic, Herbed, Lemon and/or Anchovy), turning once. Swordfish steaks also respond beautifully to charcoal-broiling. Marinate beforehand in Herbed Salad Oil or Soy Marinade and broil several inches from the coals for 10 to 12 minutes, turning once and basting with the marinade several times. Swordfish recipes are easy to come by, so I've included only a few of my favorites.

DESCRIPTION: Unmistakable because of the long, flattened, swordlike prolongation of its upper jaw that gives the fish its name (*gladius* being the short sword once carried by Roman soldiers), the fish has other distinctive features—an unusually large gaping mouth; a high, sharklike dorsal fin; two anal fins, one large and one small; and a deeply-forked caudal fin. The overall length can run to 16 feet. Swordfish are quite variable in color, ranging in topside tones from blue to dark-gray or brown, and underside from white to silvery. Adult fish can weigh in at as much as 1000 pounds or more, but average around 250 pounds.

HABITS, HABITAT AND SEASON: Of world-wide distribution in warm and temperate waters, swordfish range in Atlantic waters from Newfoundland south. During winter, those in more northerly areas travel south, reversing their early summer migration patterns.

These behemoths will take on almost anything edible: mackerel, bunkerfish (menhaden), bluefish, herring and other small fishes, as well as squid. Swordfish feed either by downing a fish in one gulp or by slashing into schooling fish and then consuming victims at their leisure.

Offshore waters of the East End generally attract swordfish from early summer through fall, and sometimes to December. Swordfish spend a good deal of their time basking near or on the surface, with the dorsal fin and upper fork of the tail displayed above water, and both anglers and commercial fishermen take advantage of this habit when stalking this illusive but aggressive fighting fish. Sports anglers, who consider swordfish the number-one big-game prize, cruise likely waters until a swordfish is spotted, then troll lines baited with squid or bonito (with stainless steel cable leader) or still-fish with live bait.

GRILLED SWORDFISH STEAKS WITH ONIONS AND HERBS

◆

Yield: Enough to serve 6

6 Individual swordfish steaks, 1-inch thick
Salt and pepper
½ Cup olive oil

2 Teaspoons each fresh oregano, basil, thyme and marjoram
6 Medium-size onions, peeled, sliced and separated into rings

Season the fish with salt and pepper. Mix ¼ cup oil and the herbs and marinate the fish in this for one hour, turning once. Meanwhile fry the onions in the remaining oil until they begin to brown but are still crunchy. Grill the fish over hot coals as directed on page 25. Arrange the steaks on a heated platter with a few onion rings on each, the remainder around the edge of the platter.

GRILLED SWORDFISH STEAKS WITH LEMON BUTTER: Proceed as directed for Grilled Swordfish Steaks with Onions and Herbs. Serve with Lemon Butter that includes ¼ teaspoon grated lemon zest.

GRILLED SWORDFISH STEAKS WITH ANCHOVIES: Proceed as directed for Grilled Swordfish Steaks with Onions and Herbs, but arrange the fish on an ovenproof platter with the onions around the edge. Just before serving, criss-cross each steak with 2 anchovy fillets centered with halved black olives and slide under the broiler for a few seconds.

HATTIE KING'S DEVILED SWORDFISH WITH OLIVES

◆

Yield: Enough to serve 6

6 Individual slices swordfish, each
    about 1-inch thick
Salt, pepper and paprika
Soft Mustard Butter

3 Tablespoons butter
12 Pimento-stuffed green olives,
    chopped
Cayenne pepper to taste

Season the fish with salt, pepper and paprika. Cover with half the Mustard Butter and broil the top side as directed on page 24. Turn the steaks, cover the uncooked side with Mustard Butter and continue broiling as directed. Arrange on a heated serving platter while you melt 3 tablespoons butter with the olives and cayenne. Spread the foaming olive-butter over the fish and serve immediately.

SPANISH SAFFRON SWORDFISH

◆

Yield: Enough to serve 6

These baked swordfish steaks have a lovely golden color—appropriate, since you need the Midas touch just to afford the saffron.

6 Individual swordfish steaks, each
    1-inch thick
Salt and pepper
4 Cloves garlic, peeled and crushed
1 Slice fine white bread, crumbled
1 Bay leaf, crumbled

1 Tablespoon parsley, minced
¼ Cup olive oil
¼ Teaspoon ground saffron
Water
White wine

Preheat oven to 350 degrees F.

    Season the fish with salt and pepper and place in a shallow ovenproof serving dish. Sauté the garlic, bread, bay leaf and parsley in the olive oil until golden. Mash or blend with the saffron and add enough water to form a smooth thin sauce. Spoon over the fish and bake as directed on page 26, basting with wine until the fish flakes. Serve immediately with the pan juices.

SOUTHOLD SWORDFISH SALAD

◆

Prepare Spanish Saffron Swordfish, cool to room temperature and coarsely flake the fish, sauce, pan juices and all. Add just enough Sauce Mayonnaise to moisten. Garnish with ripe tomato wedges and hard-cooked egg quarters. Serve at room temperature or chill.

TILEFISH

Lopholatilus chamaeleonticeps

A pink-fleshed fish with delicious moist, firm-textured meat reminiscent of lobster or scallops. This is a rising star of the retail fish trade, with upwards of 10 million pounds taken each year.

TILEFISH AS FOOD: Excellent and relatively inexpensive, tile may be served in a great variety of ways . . . broiled, baked, deep-fried, poached, braised, smoked—or raw, as in the traditional Japanese delicacy Sashimi. Cooked and chilled tilefish can substitute for shrimp, lobster or scallops in cold fish salads, dips and hors d'oeuvre. This is a fish you will surely want to experiment with if you are fortunate enough to find it on ice at your fish market or (more unlikely) at the end of your fishing line. If your fish store doesn't carry it . . . ask!

DESCRIPTION: These stout-bodied fish can grow as large as 50 pounds, but most average less than 30 pounds and measure about 3 feet in length. Distinctive features are rather fleshy protuberances in front of the first dorsal fin and on the sides of the lower jaw; a second dorsal fin that covers most of the fish's back; and bright, multicolored skin, with back and upper sides ranging from green to blue and fading on the flanks to yellow and dusty-pink to white on the belly. The body is sprinkled with bright-yellow dots. Colors tend to fade after the fish leaves its protective underwater environment, so be prepared to encounter a somewhat less colorful specimen in your fish store. The yellow dots, however, usually persist, and these are the most common identifying marks.

HABITS, HABITAT AND SEASON: Tilefish are deep-water fish, rarely found at depths of less than 200 feet. They are bottom-feeders that dine on squid, sea anemones, mollusks and marine worms, as well as crabs and shrimp, which probably give the fish its distinctive shellfish flavor.

Tilefish support a large commercial fishing industry. Because of the depth at which these fish swim, most East End catches are made by long-line boats working the grounds from the Vetches to the Baltimore Canyon throughout most of the year. In addition, some charter and party boats switch over from other gamefish to tile in the late fall and winter.

According to local fishermen, tile run in definite cycles and have disappeared at least four times in the past . . . once in 1882, when 4000 square miles of the Atlantic were blanketed with dead tilefish said to have fallen victim to extreme fluctuations in water temperature. Not a single tile was seen the following few years, after which the fish made a gradual comeback.

TILEFISH VERONIQUE

◆

Yield: Enough to serve 6

Fresh, delicate . . . and different. My family loves it.

2½–3 Pounds tilefish fillets, cut into
¾-inch cubes
2 Tablespoons butter
1½ Cups heavy cream
¾ Cup Crème Fraîche
2 Cups seedless white grapes, halved
1 Tablespoon minced fresh tarragon
leaves

Salt and white pepper
3 Oranges, peeled and cut into thin
slices
Scallion tops slit into curled green
threads
Rice

Simmer the tilefish cubes in the butter and 1½ cups cream until the fish is barely tender. Remove with a slotted spoon. Reduce the cream to a thick sauce and stir in the Crème Fraîche, fish, half the grapes and the tarragon. Season with salt and pepper to taste. Do not cook the sauce—merely heat it. Arrange 3 to 4 overlapping orange slices on each plate, top with the creamed fish and garnish with curled slivers of scallion tops and the remainder of the uncooked grapes. Serve with hot cooked rice.

PAN-FRIED TILEFISH FINGERS AND GREEN TOMATO SLICES

◆

Yield: Enough to serve 6

6 Medium-size green tomatoes, sliced
2½–3 Pounds tilefish fillets, cut into
    fingers ½ by ½ by 3 inches
Salt and pepper
Flour

2–3 Beaten eggs
Bread crumbs
Oil and butter
1 Recipe Sauce Choron

Season the tomato slices and fish fingers with salt and pepper, dust with flour, dip in egg and then bread crumbs and pan-fry as directed on page 26. Transfer to a heated platter and serve with Sauce Choron.

DILLED TILEFISH SALAD

◆

Yield: Enough to serve 6

2½–3 Pounds tilefish fillet, poached as
    directed on page 28
½ Sweet onion, peeled, quartered
    and sliced
½ Cup minced dill
1 Recipe Baby String Beans

6 Mushrooms, sliced
3 Tablespoons olive oil
2 Tablespoons white wine vinegar
Salt, pepper and cayenne to taste
Lettuce leaves

Chill the fish and cut it into ½-inch cubes. Toss with the onion, dill, beans, mushrooms, oil and vinegar. Season with salt, pepper and cayenne. Serve spooned into lettuce cups.

VARIATIONS: Follow directions for Dilled Tilefish Salad, but substitute for the oil and vinegar, one recipe Vinaigrette à la Moutarde. Surround the platter with shelled hard-cooked eggs and plum tomatoes, cut in quarters.

AUNT ELLIE'S TILEFISH IN CREAM WITH ANCHOVY TOASTS

◆

Yield: Enough to serve 6

My aunt's favorite crabmeat recipe also sets off tilefish to advantage.

2½ Pounds tilefish, poached as
    directed on page 28
Salt and pepper
½ Cup sherry
2 Tablespoons melted butter
2 Cups sliced mushrooms
1 Tablespoon each chopped chives
    and fresh thyme

1½ Cups heavy cream
1 Teaspoon flour
3 Drops Tabasco sauce
2 Egg yolks, lightly beaten
1 Recipe Anchovy Toasts
Chopped parsley

Flake the fish, sprinkle with salt and pepper, and toss with the sherry. Sauté in the butter the mushrooms, chives and thyme until the mushrooms are tender. Add the cream, blended into the flour. Cook until thickened. Immediately stir in the fish, Tabasco and egg yolks. Let stand 5 minutes. Serve on toasts with a sprinkle of parsley.

TILEFISH IN SCALLOP SHELLS: Follow directions for Aunt Ellie's Tilefish in Cream with Anchovy Toasts, but substitute one cup coarsely chopped green pepper and ¼ cup diced pimento for one cup of the mushrooms.

Continue as directed in the recipe but omit the toasts and spoon the creamed fish into scallop shells. Sprinkle generously with equal amounts of fine bread crumbs and Parmesan cheese. Arrange the shells on a baking sheet and slide under the broiler until lightly browned. Serve immediately as a first course or a light lunch.

TILEFISH IN TOMATO SHELLS: Follow directions for Tilefish in Scallop Shells, but spoon the creamed fish into hollowed-out, firm tomato shells instead of scallop shells. Top with crumbs and cheese and brown lightly under the broiler. (Don't overcook or the tomatoes will collapse.)

WEEKEND SPECIAL TILEFISH SALAD

◆

Yield: Enough to serve 6

This salad is attractive and easy to prepare, especially if you cook the fish and eggs before guests arrive.

3 Pounds tilefish fillets, poached as directed on page 28

2 Heads Boston lettuce

4 Medium-size tomatoes, peeled, sliced, seeded and chilled

2 Large, soft but not mushy avocados, peeled and pitted

2 Tablespoons each white wine and olive oil

1 Recipe cold Sauce Russe

3 Hard-cooked eggs, finely chopped

3 Tablespoons chopped fresh parsley

2 Tablespoons capers

Chill and flake the fish. Arrange the lettuce as flat as possible on a chilled platter. Arrange the drained tomato slices over the lettuce. Cut the avocados into ½-inch thick lengthwise slices and marinate with the wine and olive oil. Spread the tomato slices with a generous layer of Sauce Russe. Top with the fish. Arrange a ring of avocado around the edge of the fish, sprinkle a border of egg around the edge of the avocado and a circle of parsley inside the egg. Sprinkle the center of the salad with capers. Serve immediately.

TUNA

Tunas journey northward to waters off Montauk Lighthouse just as summer is winding down—somewhere around the blistering last days of August to the beginning of September—then return to the warm waters of the Gulf Stream as winter approaches. Despite their abundance during this short season when these tackle-smashers bring the charter boats out in force, fresh tuna has never been a big consumer attraction. Americans, it seems, prefer their tuna canned.

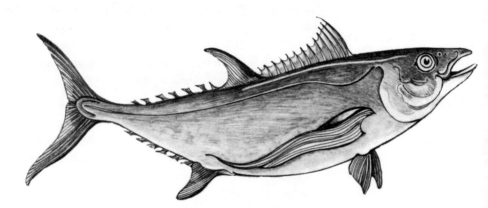

Mainly, these close relatives of the mackerels (family *Scombridae*) are noted for their fighting fury and the challenge they present to sports anglers. Like mackerel, the several species of tunas are all speedy, streamlined fishes in a wide range of sizes, but all have such distinctive family features as: two dorsal fins, one spiny and one soft; a series of small finlets lined up from tail to second dorsal fin and also along underside from tail to anal fin; and a tail that is either deeply forked or crescent-shaped. Tunas that make the round trip from warmer waters are described below.

BLUEFIN TUNA
Thunnus thynnus

This is the premier fighting fish of the clan and the one most eagerly sought by anglers. Local specimens can reach 1000 pounds (the record is 1,235 pounds), but most taken in local waters are medium-size—between 80 and 250 pounds.

Although not in favor in the United States, bluefin is highly prized in other cultures. As soon as it hits dockside, most of the Montauk catch is sold for export to Japan to be used as Sashimi. The bluefins taken off Hamptons shores are much in demand both here and abroad because they are considerably fattened by the time they reach these waters, and fat bluefins taste best raw.

Fresh bluefin does well in any fresh tuna recipe, particularly if it is first brined briefly in salted water, then cooked, refrigerated overnight and served—either cold or reheated—the following day.

Since bluefin tuna stocks have been in decline in recent years, the National Marine Fisheries Service has set stringent catch limits for both sports and commercial fishermen. Persons buying and selling, as well as fishing for the species, must obtain licenses, and individual anglers may take a total of only four school or medium-size bluefin in any one season.

ALBACORE
Thunnus alalunga

This is the most commercially valuable of tunas and the only one permitted to bear the label "white-meat tuna" when canned. Also known as longfin tuna, the albacore is steel-blue topside and silvery-white below, but it can easily be distinguished from its kinsmen by its long pectoral fins and the narrow white band along its tail. It runs much smaller in size than the bluefin—top weight on record is only 88 pounds.

Albacore is an offshore fish not as common in northern Atlantic waters as the yellowfin tuna (see below), but anglers consider it a good gamefish and ship out in charter boats in hot pursuit.

Don't let albacore's preeminence as canned tuna deter you from trying it fresh. It is especially good poached, and leftovers make canned albacore pale in comparison. For a nice change of pace, cut it into steaks and barbecue or pan-fry it. Fresh albacore is not as strong-tasting as bluefin and therefore does not need prior brining.

YELLOWFIN TUNA
Thunnus albacares

The most colorful of all tunas and the most abundant in Long Island waters, yellowfin is prized for its sweet "light meat." Its back is a deep blue-gray fading to silver along the lower flanks and belly, but its sides and fins are edged with yellow. The belly in adults is marked with white spots and vertical streaks, while younger yellowfin are more apt to have white vertical lines. Other distinguishing features are longish second dorsal and anal fins. Yellowfins grow to moderate size, about 3 to 5 feet long.

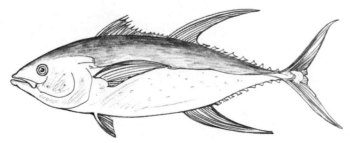

These are good gamefish and also valuable market fish, with pale meat ranging somewhere between dark bluefin and white albacore. Excellent poached or broiled without brining.

STRIPED BONITO

Euthynnus pelamis

This Tuna . . . also known as skipjack tuna, striped tuna, and oceanic bonito, among others . . . averages about 20 pounds and 2½ feet but it will put up quite a fight for its weight on light tackle. Colors are the traditional deep-blue above and white below, with distinguishing dusky stripes that begin on its sides just below the lateral line.

Bake, broil or pan-fry after brining.

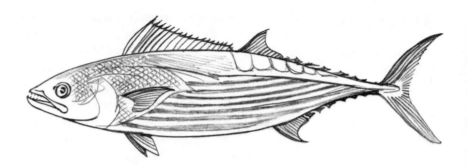

LITTLE TUNNY

Euthynnus alletteratus

This small (up to about 15 pounds and 2½ feet) tuna is also called false albacore or bonito. It is a popular sports fish because it frequents inshore areas, but its dark, strongly flavored meat is not too popular. Dark-blue above and silver or cream below, little tunny can be distinguished from the young of other species by the wavy lines along its back and the black spots that punctuate its sides just below the pectoral fins.

For best results, if you do decide to cook little tunny, bleed it immediately after catching by slashing it above the tail, then soak the deep red-orange flesh in brine or vinegar and brine, and grill or hot smoke it.

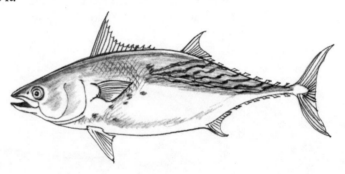

ATLANTIC BONITO

Sarda sarda

Other names for this fish are horse mackerel and common bonito. Although Atlantic bonito can reach a length of 3 feet and is a real fighter, its dark-red meat has a strong flavor and little commercial value in the United States. It's imperative to bleed and brine the meat first if you do decide to cook it. Distinctive markings are the series of oblique stripes that fan out over its back and a first dorsal fin bristling with spines.

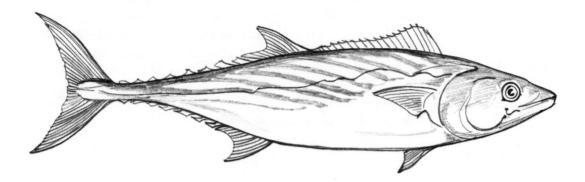

HOW TO CATCH: A medium-weight boat or all-purpose outfit should handle all but the largest schooling tunas. For lures, try artificials, especially feathers or cedar plugs. Hook size doesn't matter much as long as hooks, like the rest of the gear, are rugged—when a school tuna hits, you'll really know it!

Finding the fish is another matter. If they're hungry enough you may sight them feeding at the surface. At other times, trolling blind may work . . . Tuna are often lured by the wake of a fast-moving boat. But probably your best bet is to work the same territory as the commercial draggers, where tuna feed off the spillage from the commercial nets.

TUNA AS FOOD: Raw fresh tuna varies in quality among different species. The white meat of the albacore is considered the finest, and a small part of this meat does make its way to fish markets, but most local tuna winds up in canneries or as air freight to the Far East.

If you catch and want your tuna, be sure to bleed it as soon as possible after it's landed by cutting into it a few inches above the tail. Cut the fish into fillets or steaks and discard the strip of dark, strong-flavored, oily meat that runs along the midline section of flesh. Rinse well under running water and immediately ice. These fish have an extra set of bones, as do their cousins, the mackerels. Follow filleting directions on page 169. Except for albacore and yellowfins, all fillets and steaks of tunas and bonitos should be brined to reduce their strong flavor and leach out blood.

Tuna steaks and fillets can be broiled or pan-fried, but one of the best uses is in your own tuna salad. Simmer in water to cover until the meat flakes into separate chunks, then cool and use at once or put into serving-size containers, cover with cooking juices to within ½ inch of the top, seal and freeze.

Canned tuna (the commercial variety) has many uses, not all of them pedestrian. Best of the lot is the albacore, otherwise known as all-white meat solid pack. But depending on the use intended, many canned tuna products are highly satisfactory. With a little imagination, canned tuna can be turned into tasty salads, including, of course, the delectable *salade niçoise*. Beaten into a smooth paste along with olive oil, egg yolks and lemon juice and enhanced with anchovies and capers, canned tuna will flavor the delightful cold veal dish known as *vitello tonnato*. Still in the Italian vein, canned tuna can serve as the basis for a fine pasta sauce. The following recipes should get you started:

TUNA-CAPER DIP WITH GARDEN VEGETABLES

◆

Yield: Enough to serve 8

3 4-Ounce tuna fillets
3 Tablespoons vegetable oil
1 Large onion, peeled and sliced
1 Small onion, peeled and chopped
2 Cloves garlic, peeled
2 Tablespoons mild vinegar
2 Tablespoons each heavy cream, mayonnaise and capers
½ Cup Crème Fraîche
Salt and pepper to taste
Carrot sticks
Scallions
Radish roses
Cherry tomatoes

Sauté the tuna in the oil for 3 minutes, add the sliced onion and continue cooking until the fish flakes. Purée the tuna, cooked onion slices, raw chopped onion, garlic, vinegar, heavy cream, mayonnaise and capers in a blender or food processor. Stir in the crème fraîche by hand. Season and refrigerate until serving time. Serve with chilled vegetables.

GRILLED TUNA AND EGGPLANT

◆

Yield: Enough to serve 6

4 Garlic cloves, peeled and crushed
¾ Cup olive oil
1 Tablespoon each fresh thyme, oregano and basil (or 1 teaspoon each dried)
½ Cup lemon juice
1 Teaspoon anchovy paste
Tuna steaks, 1 inch thick
3 Eggplants, cut into ¾-inch-thick slices

Mix the garlic, oil, herbs, lemon juice and anchovy paste. Soak the steaks and eggplant in the marinade for one hour, turning several times. Grill fish and vegetables over hot coals as directed on page 25.

TUNA WITH PASTA

◆

Yield: Enough to serve 6

1 Box linguini
3 Cups flaked tuna, cooked as directed opposite
4 Cloves garlic, peeled and minced
1 Cup ½-inch green pepper squares

⅓ Cup olive oil
½ Cup ½-inch pimento squares
Salt and pepper to taste
1 Tablespoon each minced fresh oregano, basil and parsley

Cook linguini as directed on the package.

Sauté the garlic and green pepper in the olive oil until the green pepper is tender. Toss linguini with all ingredients. Serve immediately.

◆━━━━━━━━━━━━━━━━━━━━━━━━━━━━━━━━━━◆

WEAKFISH

Cynoscion regalis

◆━━━━━━━━━━━━━━━━━━━━━━━━━━━━━━━━━━◆

Also known as sea trout, gray trout, gray weakfish, yellow fin, tide runner and occasionally by its Narragansett Indian name—*sequeateague* or *squeteague.*

WEAKFISH AS FOOD: Fraunces Tavern menus listed *squeteague* as a house specialty when George Washington steered the fledgling U.S. government from New York City, but there have been times since when weakfish have disappeared completely and mysteriously from the Eastern seaboard. Between 1800 and 1870 so few weaks were hooked that even seasoned New England fishermen forgot how to identify the fish. Then in 1880, unpredictably, a huge school of weaks inundated the Atlantic coastline, and this fine fish has been with us in greater or lesser numbers ever since.

This is a top-notch and versatile foodfish. Its sweet white meat—lean, flaky and fine in texture—is suitable to every cooking method.
Note: Weakfish is a member of the Drum family (*Sciaenidae*); all members of this family, which includes kingfish and various croakers and drums, are susceptible to and may harbor trematode parasites. Therefore, it's best to cook the flesh thoroughly before eating and never use raw, as in Seviche or Sashimi. If you are smoking weaks, hot-smoke to an internal temperature of at least 140 degrees F.

DESCRIPTION: A slim, beautifully proportioned fish with dorsal colors that vary from olive-green to brown-green, and sides burnished with tones of violet, lavender, blue, green or coppery-red, overlaid with tinges of copper or gold. Black, green or coppery blotches form irregular lines over the back and upper sides, the dusky tail fins are occasionally margined with yellow, the ventral and anal fins are creamy, and the underbelly is white. The forward dorsal fin is spiny and stands higher than the soft-rayed one behind it, the tail is slightly curved, and the ventral and pectoral fins are pointed and nearly identical in size.

Peconic bays once regularly yielded weaks weighing as much as 15 pounds, but fish taken from these same waters today are not as hefty, generally ranging in the 4- to 11-pound class and measuring from one to 2 feet in length.

This otherwise handsome species was tagged with its popular name because of the fragile mouth parts, which give it something of a hangdog look.

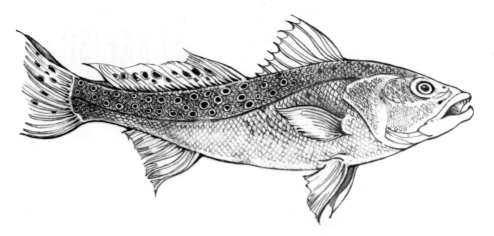

HABITS, HABITAT AND SEASON: Long Island is prime weakfish territory, since our waters abound in the silversides, butterfish, killifish, bunkerfish, sand eels, sea worms, squid, crabs and bivalves weaks favor. These fish incline naturally toward shallow waters with sandy bottoms, but almost any bottom, with depths ranging from 8 to 80 feet, will please them.

Large schools are regular visitors to the Peconic bays, especially on the south side of Little Peconic, but they are likely to show up in salt-water creeks, channels, tide rips, sloughs and other shallow bays—anywhere their favorite inshore fishes are apt to be foraging. Weaks can also be taken in the surf and during twilight and night hours from docks, piers and bridges.

Season extends from early May to about mid-September, with prime fishing time extending from mid-May to the beginning of July.

HOW TO CATCH: A highly adaptable species, weaks are temperamentally suited to cruise at any water level in their quest for food. Just about any angling method—top- or bottom-fishing at anchor, drift-fishing, trolling or surf-angling—can be productive.

Tackle: Use a strong but flexible rod. Any light- to medium-weight outfit should perform nicely. When bottom-fishing, use a light rod and a high-hook, low-hook rig; snap weakfish hooks with leaders attached (Carlisle or Sproat Nos. 3/0 to 5/0) to the swivels. Tie on a bank-type sinker just heavy enough to hold bottom, and you're in business.

Bait: When either top- or bottom-fishing, try shrimp, skinned strips of squid, bloodworms or sandworms, alone or in tandem and jig the rig occasionally to induce weaks to overcome their shyness.

When drifting, or casting from shore, try strips of baitfish, squid, crab or shrimp or artificials such as metal squids, small surface plugs, or small, flashy chrome spoons with a bit of feather, bucktail or pork rind for added appeal. When you're bottom-fishing, bounce your lure along to imitate baitfish movements. When trolling, spinners baited with sandworms, both surface and diving plugs, spoons, bucktails, or small metal squids can all be effective.

Chumming with ground-up baitfish helps if you're fishing at anchor. Patience is the key here. Weakfish approach bait in a leisurely, offhand manner with delicate, tentative nibbling followed by a "thunk" or steady pull when the bait has been taken. Raise the rod tip firmly but gently to set the hook. Be prepared for some swift maneuvering . . . a hooked weakfish is an unpredictable weakfish. Tire him out a bit before you reel in in earnest . . . and be sure to use a net. Any attempt to land a weak directly from the water could result in an empty hook that has slipped right out of its fragile mouth. Weakfish flesh is fine-textured and very fragile. Unless your catch is iced within minutes of catching, quality and flavor quickly deteriorate, even on days when the sun is in seclusion.

WEAKFISH WITH KIWI AND TARRAGON
◆

Fish cooked and then marinated in lime has a texture that is temptingly tender but still retains a little of the bounce, or tremble, of the raw fish. For peak effect arrange the salad at one end of the plate, bracket with avocado slices and decorate the rest of the plate with thin scrolls of scallion tops.

2 Pounds weakfish fillets cut into ½-inch cubes
Fish Stock or Court Bouillon
4 Limes, juiced
4 Small white onions, sliced
10 Small, very fresh mushrooms, thinly sliced

The lightest, fruitiest olive oil available
Tarragon vinegar
3 Kiwi fruit peeled and sliced
3 Tablespoons fresh tarragon leaves
Salt and Szechwan pepper to taste

Plunge fish into simmering stock or bouillon for 3 minutes and immediately drain. Marinate the fish and onions in the lime juice overnight. Toss with mushrooms, oil and vinegar and chill well. Just prior to serving, toss with the kiwi, tarragon leaves, salt and freshly ground Szechwan pepper.

WEAKFISH IN CRACKER CRUMBS WITH DEVILED BUTTER

◆

Yield: Enough to serve 6

6 Small weakfish, cleaned and scaled
Salt and pepper
Flour
2 Eggs, beaten

Cracker crumbs
Oil and butter
1 Recipe Deviled Butter
Lemon wedges

Rinse the fish, dry well, season with salt and pepper, dust with flour, dip in egg, then in cracker crumbs. Pan-fry in hot oil and butter. Serve immediately with Deviled Butter and lemon wedges.

CRISPY PAN-FRIED WEAKFISH

◆

Yield: Enough to serve 6

Foot-long weaks are marvelous pan-fried until the skin is crisp and the flesh is moist and flaky.

6 Small weakfish, cleaned and scaled
Salt and pepper
Cornstarch
Oil for frying

¼ Cup each soy sauce and sherry
1 Teaspoon grated fresh ginger
1 Teaspoon chopped chives

Rinse the fish, dry thoroughly and season with salt and pepper. Rub cornstarch into the skin and fry in hot oil until crispy and brown. Serve with small dishes of mixed soy sauce, sherry, ginger and chives.

EGG-BAKED WEAKFISH, NORTH SHORE

◆

Yield: Enough to serve 4 to 6

East End fish fillets with an Oriental touch.

2–3 Weakfish fillets
Salt
4 Egg yolks
2 Teaspoons each sugar and prepared
   yellow mustard

1 Recipe Sweet and Sour Sauce
   (optional)

Sprinkle the fillets with a little salt, let them stand 25 minutes, then pat dry with paper towels. Beat together the egg yolks, sugar and mustard. Spoon the egg mixture over the fish. Bake for 8 minutes in a 350-degree oven, then coat again. Bake 3 or 4 minutes longer, or until the fish is done and the coating is flecked with brown. Serve immediately with Sweet and Sour Sauce on the side.

POTATO-STUFFED WEAKFISH, OLD HOOK MILL

◆

Yield: Enough to serve 4 to 6

When I pass East Hampton's Old Hook Mill on my way to Montauk and the deep-sea fishing boats, I always wish I could have been living here in the Hamptons way back when the mill was still grinding grain. This recipe is reminiscent of the sustaining cold-weather suppers my grandmother served in those days.

2 1½-pound weakfish fillets
Salt and pepper
1 Recipe Old-Fashioned Potato
   Stuffing

1 Recipe Lemon Butter

Rinse the fish, dry, season with salt and pepper and arrange one fillet in a well-buttered, oblong, shallow ovenproof dish. Spread the fillet with potato stuffing and top with the second fillet. Bake as directed on page 26, basting frequently with Lemon Butter. Serve hot with additional Lemon Butter if desired.

WEAKFISH NIÇOISE

◆

Yield: Enough to serve 4 to 6

2 1-to-2-pound weakfish fillets
Salt and pepper
4 Large tomatoes, peeled, seeded
   and chopped
8 Flat anchovies, quartered
2 Tablespoons olive oil
10 Pitted black olives, sliced

10 Pimento-stuffed olives, sliced
12 Tiny pearl onions, peeled and
   blanched in boiling water
½ Teaspoon each sugar, dried thyme
   and oregano
Salt and pepper to taste

Rinse the fish, dry, season with salt and pepper and arrange in a shallow, oblong ovenproof dish. Cover with tomatoes, anchovies, olive oil, olive slices, onions, sugar, herbs, salt and pepper. Bake as directed on page 26.

WEAKFISH WITH GARDEN SPINACH AND ALMONDS

◆

Yield: Enough to serve 4 to 6

2 1–1½-pound weakfish fillets
   (of equal size)
Salt, pepper and nutmeg
1 Recipe Sauce Mornay

2 Cups steamed spinach, coarsely
   chopped
Melted butter
¼ Cup finely sliced almonds

Rinse and dry the fish and season them with salt, pepper and a sprinkle of nutmeg. Place one fillet in a well-buttered shallow ovenproof serving dish. Spread a layer of Sauce Mornay over it and then the well-drained spinach. Top with the second fillet and bake as directed on page 26, basting frequently with melted butter. When the fish is a few minutes away from being done, spread it with the remaining Mornay and top with the almonds. Slide under the broiler until the nuts are lightly browned. Drain well and serve immediately.

WEAKFISH AND MUSSEL SALAD WITH CUCUMBER CRÈME FRAÎCHE

◆

Yield: Enough to serve 6 to 8

1 1½-pound weakfish fillet
Salt and pepper
White Wine Court Bouillon
1 Recipe Mussels Vinaigrette
2 Zucchini, 1 inch in diameter, thinly sliced
1 Recipe steamed Carrot Flowers
3 Scallions, with 3 inches green tops, sliced

2 Tablespoons raspberry vinegar
2 Tablespoons light olive oil
1 Cucumber, peeled and grated
1½ Cups Crème Fraîche
Salt and freshly ground pepper
Cayenne pepper

Rinse and dry the fish and season it with salt and pepper. Poach as directed on page 28. Drain and chill the fish, flake it and gently toss it with the mussels, zucchini, carrots, scallions, vinegar and oil. Squeeze the liquid from the grated cucumber, mix in the Crème Fraîche and a generous amount of salt, freshly ground pepper and cayenne. Serve separately along with the chilled fish salad.

WHITEBAIT

There is, to my mind, no method of harvesting our inlets and bays that is so pleasurable to perform, so beautiful to observe . . . as the netting of whitebait. Given a calm morning when the tide is low, a 30-foot billow of fine mesh net attached at either end to a long bamboo pole, *and* a bit of patience, one of the finest of all the fruits of the sea is yours for the taking.

The seiners move slowly in the thigh-high currents, straining the weight of the water through the lacy openings in the net. One pole is jabbed into the pebble bottom, the other is walked around it in a radial arc that barely skims the floor of the bay. The steps of the seiners are measured, graceful, forced into exaggerated Kabuki dance movements by the water's resistance. Around their legs a silvery underwater stream of spearing and sand eel flash into and out of the pouch of the net, first tantalizingly close, then distant, until for one instant they hesitate. The netters recognize that split-second turning point and turn toward the beach. The second the net touches the sand, fish explode into the air. They flip and somersault like tiny silver-clad acrobats. Only those from 2 to 4 inches are scooped up into ice chests; the rest are returned to the bay to hightail it for waters unknown.

This delicacy is no more than a collection of whole tiny fishes, all species that would otherwise be ignored as unworthy of culinary notice or banished to the tackle shop to be sold as bait. But deep-fried in hot oil (either unadorned, dusted with flour or dipped in blistery, transparent batter) until crispy, and served up by the plateful, these minuscule fish provide an incomparable hors d'oeuvre.

First to see the culinary possibilities in a netful of minnows was an English fisherman named Robert Cannon, who introduced the idea in the late 1700s. The original English version of whitebait combined tiny young herring, sand eel, smelt, sprat, stickleback and pipefish. Spearing and sand eel are both available in copious quantities in Long Island waters for East End whitebait fanciers.

SPEARING
Menidia menidia

DESCRIPTION: A slender, silvery fish, no more than 6 inches long and usually smaller, present in large numbers all along the Eastern seaboard, from Nova Scotia to Florida. It is also known as silverside, Atlantic silverside, whitebait, sand smelt, shiner and green smelt. Its basic color is blue-green to olive-green peppered with brown speckles, with white beneath. A distinct silver streak runs from the pectoral fin to the tail. This small fry can be differentiated from smelt, which it resembles, by its two dorsal fins, one spiny and one soft-rayed (smelt has only one), and by the lack of a fleshy adipose fin on the dorsal side near the tail.

HABITS AND HABITAT: Spearing frequent our inshore waters, often in large schools, seeking their own favorite seafoods—shrimp, marine worms, copepods, mysids and immature mollusks. The silversides are themselves prime fare to many species of fish, which makes them important Hamptons visitors since their presence draws fish in abundance, including such valuable gamefish as striped bass and bluefish.

OTHER SILVERSIDES

Spearing is only one of a group of fishes known as silversides. Another common to our Atlantic waters is the tidewater silverside (*Menidia beryllina*), which is practically identical to spearing. There is absolutely no reason why you should bother to differentiate. Just eat and enjoy.

SAND EEL
Ammodytes americanus

DESCRIPTION: A particularly abundant Hamptons resident, this small eel-like fish, with its slender, tapering body and needle-like snout, averages 4 inches but can grow to 7. Color here is metallic-brown to brown-green above, silvery-white below, with occasional faint-blue stripes on the sides. It does resemble the elver (immature eel) but can be distinguished by the distinctly forked tail and separate dorsal and anal fins. It is also known as the sand launce or lance.

HABITS AND HABITAT: Sand eel are shore fish that congregate in vast schools in shallow waters in pursuit of small marine animals—sea worms, copepods and the like. When trapped close to shore by retreating tides, sand eels will use their pointed noses to speedily dig themselves into the sand to escape predators and await the swelling of the tide. Clammers often inadvertently expose these hiding places and harvest two delicacies instead of one.

Sand eels are valuable to Long Island waters. Their presence lures hordes of striped bass, bluefish, cod, mackerel, pollock, tuna, marlin, swordfish, porpoises and sharks, and these in turn provide livelihood for our fishermen.

Because gamefish find sand eels so toothsome, the small fish are available for bait in tackle stores, and tackle manufacturers are making artificials that resemble them.

SPEARING AND SAND EEL AS FOOD: Collectively or separately, these tiny baitfish, along with young herrings, anchovies, smelts and mackerel, are marketed as whitebait. Because of their abundance in Long Island waters, spearing and sand eel are the combination most frequently available locally. When the fish are small enough (2 to 3 inches) they are cooked and eaten whole, without any cleaning. But these must be consumed within hours of gleaning—they deteriorate rapidly. To prepare, chill the fish, rinse under cold running water, then pat dry. Sprinkle to taste with salt and pepper, and if you like, dip them lightly in flour or thin batter and fry for a few minutes in hot oil, a handful at a time, turning once or twice to brown and crisp evenly. Drain briefly on paper towels and serve with lemon wedges or your favorite sauce. Slender slivers of onion, the same length as the fish, are an excellent accompaniment, dipped in flour or batter, fried and served with the sizzling whitebait.

WHITEBAIT WITH ANCHOVIES, SOUTH SHORE

◆

These are wonderful passed with cocktails or served as a patio first course. In either case, provide stacks of napkins.

Whitebait (3- to 4-inch specimens are best), cleaned
Canned flat anchovies
Flour
Beaten egg

Fine bread crumbs
Oil for frying
Fried Parsley
Lemon wedges

Clean, wash and dry whitebait. Fill each cavity with half a canned anchovy fillet, press stomach together and dip each fish in flour, beaten egg and then in bread crumbs. Deep-fry in hot oil until golden brown. Drain briefly on paper towels and serve hot on platters garnished with fried parsley and lemon wedges.

FRITTO MISTO MARE
◆

In seaside areas the world around there exist variations on this marvelous Mediterranean theme—literally "fried mixed (food) of the sea." Fish that are too small to fillet but are otherwise sublime are dipped in a feathery, almost transparent batter and deep-fried until crunchy and golden. Odd bits of larger fish fillets, shelled shrimp, slices of zucchini, yellow squash, parsley, etc., all lend their unique textures and flavors to the feast. If you are fortunate enough to count among your friends a trap fisherman (or have a fish trap of your own), enough sundry aquatic inhabitants will be available to keep your table groaning.

Baby mackerel, sand eels, herrings, etc. that are 5 inches or over should have their heads removed and their small gut sack pushed out (with your thumb). Whitebait may be fried as they are; small whiting should be cleaned and cut in half. Strips of sea robin, sand shark, blackfish, etc. are all excellent served this way. Shrimp must be shelled. Vegetables should be fried last. Prepare the batter first so it may rest while you deal with the fish.

INGREDIENTS FOR BATTER

½ Cup flour

⅛ Teaspoon salt

1 Cup tepid water plus 1 tablespoon

4 Teaspoons vegetable oil

1 Egg white

Sift flour and salt. Mix water and oil and stir into the flour mixture. Beat the batter until smooth, then set aside. When you're ready to fry the fish, fold the egg white, stiffly beaten, into the batter.

INGREDIENTS FOR FRITTO MISTO

About ½ pound of a combination of the above-mentioned fish

4–5 Slices of vegetable per person, drained between paper towels

8 Sprigs parsley

Oil for deep-frying

Lemon wedges

Sauce Tartare

Prepare fish as described above. Heat the oil in a deep-fryer (or heavy deep skillet) to 375 degrees F. Use tongs to dip fish in batter, letting the excess drop back into the bowl. Fry 5 to 6 minutes or until crisp and golden on both sides. Drain on paper towels or paper plates. Keep warm. Deep-fry vegetables in similar manner. Serve fish garnished with fried vegetables and parsley and lemon wedges, with Sauce Tartare on the side.

WHITEBAIT FORTE DEI MARMI

♦

Yield: Enough to serve 6 to 8

Larger whitebait specimens caught with the smaller fish deserve special handling. This dish is a particularly pleasing one when meatier fish are involved.

3 Pounds cleaned whitebait
   (specimens over 4 inches)
Flour
ice water
Oil for frying
3 Cloves garlic, peeled and minced
2 Tablespoons each finely chopped
   fresh parsley and basil

¾ Cup white wine
4 Medium-size tomatoes, peeled,
   seeded and chopped
¼ Teaspoon each red pepper flakes
   and sugar
Salt and pepper to taste

Dredge the damp (not wet) fish in ample flour. Dip *very quickly* in ice water, let drip a second or two, then fry in ½ inch hot oil until golden brown on all sides.

Preheat oven to 400 degrees F.

In another pan lightly brown garlic in 2 tablespoons oil. Stir in one tablespoon each parsley and basil, add the wine and simmer for 2 minutes. Add tomatoes, red pepper and sugar and simmer for 20 minutes, or until sauce is nicely thickened. Arrange fish in an ovenproof serving dish, pour the tomato sauce over and heat 2 minutes in oven (larger fish, 4 minutes). Sprinkle with remaining parsley and basil and serve immediately.

WOLFFISH

Anarhichas lupus

Also called Atlantic wolffish. The tasty meat of this odd-looking, little-known fish has some following in the United States but is far more popular in Europe.

WOLFFISH AS FOOD: About 1½ million pounds of wolffish are taken annually in the United States, with some marketed here under the alternate names of ocean whitefish or ocean catfish. Europeans—the Scandinavians, Spanish and French in particular—value this fish highly . . . in Denmark as *Havkat*; in Iceland as *Steinbitur*; in Norway as *Steinbit*; in Holland as *Zeewolf*; in Germany as *Katfische* and *Wasserkatze*; in France, as *Loup*; in Spain as *Lobo*; in Italy as *Bavosa Lupa*; and in Portugal as *Gata*.

The wolffish's passion for mollusks of all kinds results in white meat that is unusually firm and good-tasting. Use in recipes that call for tilefish, dogfish and monkfish.

DESCRIPTION: What sets the wolffish distinctively apart from its fellow deep-water fish are its large, rounded, walruslike head and oversized tusklike teeth. Average size is 2 to 3 feet, although it can attain 5 feet and 40 pounds. A long, high dorsal fin caps its dark-colored body from the back of the head to the tail. The lack of ventral fins also gives the body an unfishlike outline. The fish's sides are streaked with 10 or so dark bars, while the belly and throat are off-white.

HABITS, HABITAT AND SEASON: Prefers cold, fairly deep waters (60 to 500 feet) over hard bottoms; rarely strays farther south than Long Island. Being neither a schooling nor migratory fish, wolffish are found in the same areas all year round. Preferred foods are clams, mussels, whelks and other mollusks, which, with their large canines and molars, wolffish crunch in the shell.

SHELLFISH

At seven o'clock on a late spring evening, a sudden line of fog shrouds Napeague and Amagansett. It nibbles across Gardiner's Bay, then eats at the sand spit of Louse Point. The budding trees on Tick Island reach briefly for the sky, then disappear. The pointy rock halfway from there to here appears and reappears and then gives up the ghost. The fog gobbles up four flapping Canada geese in residence in our field and three horses nuzzling in the mist. Our fenceposts vanish.

The fog licks at my lettuce, red and green, then, fingering, reaches my window, its gray palm against the glass. Far off somewhere down Montauk way, a horn moans to ships caught unawares. For an instant a gust of wind tunnels the haze. I catch a glimpse of a tiny boat in Accabonac Creek, its captain at the bow, imperturbably scratching the grassy bottom for clams, using the same rake his grandfather did before him—harvesting the bay the way I harvest my garden.

CLAMS

The Indians called Long Island *Si-wan-aki*, "The Island of Shells," and it is this rich abundance of mollusks—clams, oysters, mussels and the like—that has made our island a fishing paradise. These tasty bivalves, flapping away seductively beneath our local waters, lure the multitudes of fishes which in turn attract recreational and commercial fishermen to seek them out.

Clams begin life accidentally from the chancy union of eggs and sperm discharged into warm waters each summer by their stationary parents. Each fertilized egg joins that soup of microscopic creatures on the water's surface until, at the age of 2 weeks, it follows its parents' semi-mobile lifestyle, drops to the bottom, and attaches itself to a handy grain of sand or bit of seaweed by means of a shaggy byssus, or thin thread. From time to time the adolescent clam may throw off one byssus and move off to other sandier or grassier pastures to spin another, but at the age of 2 years, the adult finds a spot to its liking under the sand and digs down to live happy as a clam, for as long as 12 years. The living mantle extracts lime from the water to build its shell (the inner surface of which records this growth with curved rings that represent its age in annual growth lines . . . narrow in winter, wider in summer). Clams are a group of bottom-dwelling, double-shelled mollusks with soft, mantle-covered bodies, double-barreled siphons and the hatchet-shaped foot that further differentiates them as *Pelecypods*.

Pressure is continuously exerted on two adductor muscles that control the opening and closing of the shells in live clams (expired bivalves gape because these adductor muscles are no longer operative).

The clam resides in its sandy home at water's edge with siphon or "neck" up and foot down—a vertical posture that enables it to extend or retract its siphon to fit the passing tides.

On any clam-digging expedition, avoid all areas where the coliform bacteria count is likely to be high—near marinas or waterways through which boats pass, or where outfall pipes deposit raw sewage. Clams taken commercially are tightly regulated and subject to rigid inspection.

Fresh clams come to market in the shell or already shucked. Make sure those you buy in the shells are live ones with their valves tightly closed. Live *soft* clams, whose shells never close, will draw back their long necks into their shells when you touch them. Shucked clams, sold in pints or quarts with their juices, should be free of pieces of shell.

Clams are also sold shucked and frozen, canned, minced or whole, and smoked, then canned in oil.

HARDSHELL CLAMS

Venus mercenaria

There are clams, and there are clams . . . and all of them are delicious. Littlenecks, cherrystones, quahogs . . . by any name they taste as sweet. Clam fanciers have long found the various names given *V. mercenaria* confusing, so New York State's Department of Environmental Conservation has attempted to unravel the muddle, making size the criterion by naming

- any hardshell clam whose shell is less than 1″ thick a "seed clam";
- any clam whose shell ranges between 1″ and 1 7/16″ thick a "neck" or littleneck;
- any clam whose shell ranges from 1 7/16″ to 1 ⅝″ in thickness a "cherry" or cherrystone;
- any clam larger than 1 ⅝″ "chowder."

Long Island natives have their own designations—"littleneck" is seldom used, but any hardshell at least 1″ thick and up to three inches in diameter is a "cherry" or cherrystone (after Cherrystone Creek in Virginia). Those beyond this size are "quahogs," a corruption of *quahaug*, the Algonquin Indian name for the hardshell (also the name New Englanders use). Quahogs tend to toughness and are best ground or minced and reserved for chowders and other cooked dishes, but half-grown littlenecks and cherrystones, those young and tender adolescents, are wonderful without a touch of flame—served raw on the half-shell.

HARDSHELL CLAMS AS FOOD: Whoever coined the phrase "to clam up" must have had the stubborn hardshell in mind, but with a little muscle and a lot of patience even the most recalcitrant shell will surrender.

Sprinkle a handful of corn meal into your bucket of clams and let them stand in cool, fresh (not sea) water for up to three hours while they feast on the meal and void their sand. Scrub the shells under cold running water with a stiff vegetable brush (discard any with broken or gaping shells), then refrigerate the clams again for several hours to relax them and make opening easier.

To open, hold a clam cupped in your left hand, hinged end alongside your thumb. With your right hand (reverse hands if you're left-handed) insert a clam knife or other thin strong knife between the shells, cutting around the entire edge, then move the knife blade around to sever the adductor muscles and separate the clam from its shells.

To serve fresh in the half-shell, leave the clam in the bottom, more curvaceous shell and remove any broken bits of shell from the meat before serving.

If the clams are to be cooked, opening them is simplified if you pop them onto a rack in a kettle with a small amount of rapidly boiling water and allow them to steam for a few minutes, or until the shells begin to open. Placing clams in their shells briefly over hot coals or an outdoor barbecue will also relax the adductor muscles. With either method, be sure to discard any clams that refuse to open after a significant amount of cooking time.

DESCRIPTION: These have a rather dowdy chalky-gray exterior in contrast to the lovely glossy purple-and-white inside shell walls, from which the Indians fashioned their ceremonial necklaces and "wampum" belts.

HABITS, HABITAT AND SEASON: Shallow, mud and/or sand-bottomed bays, where salt and fresh waters meet, are favorite hardshell haunts. Look for them near low-tide marks, between tides, or at the edges of tidal flats. Commercial fishermen also dredge for hardshells in deeper waters.

Hardshell clams are always in season, but some towns have local regulations requiring a permit. All localities set limits on your daily take, and New York State law prohibits taking any that are less than one inch thick. To measure, hold the clam so that the beaks, or shell edges, point away and the hinged end faces you at eye level. If the thickness between top and bottom measures one inch or more, the clam is yours . . . if not, return it to the water and look for it next year.

HOW TO DIG FOR CLAMS: Hardshells have short, stubby siphons that make living close to the surface a must, so you'll find these easy to snare. Dig your clammer's scratch rake (a small-scale version of a garden rake) into the sand or mud, pull it along a few feet, then lift it and gather your treasure. Hard work, but worth it. If you don't mind the feel of mud between your toes, your foot is the best clam detector of all. Walk along the beach at low tide and dig your toes in about an inch, wherever you see small bubbling holes. When you find one clam, its likely your whole meal is nearby, since clams tend to be friendly. If your luck is poor on the beach, take a plastic bucket (or a metal one with an inner tube around it), wade out into the water and use your feet to "feel out" the smooth, round shells. Reach down with your hand, a strainer or a pair of oyster tongs, snatch the clam from its home and put it in the bucket.

SOFTSHELL CLAMS

Mya arenaria

Living in peaceful coexistence with their hardshell relatives—in the soft tidal mud and sand flats of serene bays, inland harbors and creeks—are the delicately flavored softshell clams. Also called the soft or steamer clam (and ingloriously nicknamed "piss clam" because it squirts water skyward), it differs physically from the hardshell in two important ways —its tough, leathery siphon cannot be completely retracted, making the softshell one of the few clams that cannot "clam up," and its shell is thin, brittle and chalky.

The shell size and thickness of softshell clams varies according to age; large specimens can reach 3½ inches in length and 2 inches in thickness.

SOFTSHELL CLAMS AS FOOD: Softshells may be served raw on the half-shell, or substituted for other clams (or even for mussels) in your favorite recipes, but by far the most popular method of preparation is steaming.

To prepare . . . rinse the softshells thoroughly under running water, then scrub the shells well. If the clams are those you've collected yourself, soak them beforehand for several hours in sea water (*not* fresh water) to allow them to void their sand. Place the clams in a large kettle, with one inch of boiling water, half a bay leaf, a sprinkling of thyme and a rib of celery, then cover and steam until the shells open. Discard any unopened clams.

To eat the clams with your fingers, pull them from the shell one by one by the leathery black siphon and dip them first in hot clam broth and then in melted butter. Eat the tender, plump clam and discard the siphon and the thin dark "veil."

To eat the softshells with a fork, first discard the siphon and "veil," then use your fork to dip the clam in broth and then in butter.

HABITS, HABITAT AND SEASON: In recent years, populations of softshell clams have been declining, due in large part to run-off of DDT and other dangerous pesticides into local waters. Since softshells spawn only in shoal waters, which catch this runoff, they are particularly vulnerable. East Hampton (and other areas) began banning the use of more dangerous pesticides a few years back, and softshells seem to be staging a comeback locally.

Softshells may be taken year-round, but check local ordinances regarding permits, size, etc. New York State Fish and Wildlife Law prohibits you from taking softshells less than 1½ inches in length, but some towns . . . Southold and Shelter Island, for instance . . . forbid the taking of any soft clams less than 2 inches long.

Most ordinances do allow a daily take for your own table use (non-commercial) of up to one peck.

HOW TO DIG: Softshell clams burrow deep, so you'll need a pronged clam hook or pitchfork . . . and a mighty strong back.

Begin your search when the tide is just beginning to fall, and you'll have about 2 hours before it returns to locate the clam holes that indicate a colony of softshells have just withdrawn their siphons and disappeared at your approach. Dig carefully . . . these delicate clams crush easily. To determine whether a clam is still alive, squeeze it gently between thumb and forefinger . . . a live clam will squirt water. If it doesn't squirt, throw it back.

RAZOR CLAM

Ensis directus

This slender bivalve gets its name from its resemblance, in both shape and sharpness of shell, to the old-fashioned, straight-edge razor. The graceful, nearly transparent shells are slightly curved and average 6 to 7 inches, but many specimens grow to 10 inches. The thin, brownish-green or olive periostracum gives the otherwise almost transparent shell its color.

RAZOR CLAMS AS FOOD: Fish and seafood stores do not carry razors despite their delicious meat, because these mollusks refuse to clam up. The thin, fragile shells gape slightly at both ends, making keeping qualities poor. After removing them from their clammy beds, keep them in sea water and use the same day before they have a chance to dry out.

Wash the clams and soak for several hours, changing the water at least twice to allow them to void their sand. Small razors are wonderful served raw on the half-shell. To open, insert a thin knife between the shells opposite the hinge end. Slide the knife all the way down the shell to sever the adductor muscles. Carefully force the shell open and cut away any remaining tendons anchoring the clam to its shell. Larger razors are best used in cooking, in which case they may be steamed just until they open.

There are two schools of thought concerning the use of the dark interior meat. Some think this is the sweetest, most flavorful part, others insist this darkish mass near the hinge should be discarded, and only the tender, white meat be served.

I generally grind the dark meats to flavor and thicken chowders and stews, then float the soft, rather bulbous oyster-like centers in the hot liquid or dip them in cracker crumbs and fry them.

HABITS, HABITAT AND SEASON: The razor clam has a short siphon, which requires it to live close to the surface of the sand. When threatened, it disappears in seconds straight down into the sand, and the tip of its pointed, muscular foot swells to hold on in a tenacious grip. In a test of wills to see whether you or the razor yields first, you may well come out second-best.

Razors shun river mouths, where salinity is apt to be low, or any area where water temperatures are too high. Their favorite turf is fine clean sand without gravel or clay, through which they glide as easily as a fish swims through water.

HOW TO FIND AND DIG FOR RAZOR CLAMS: To locate razors, look for a group of squarish holes in the sand near the water's edge. Capturing these delicious but elusive creatures requires some finesse. Shovel under them to cut off retreat, then use a pair of tongs to gingerly extract your catch from the sand. Don't try to dig with your fingers—razor shells are sharp enough to warrant the name. The trick is to figure out just how deep to shovel to keep from cutting these speedy mollusks in half. As soon as you get a grip with your tongs, dig away the sand with a garden trowel held in the other hand. Razors are sometimes so stubborn they would rather yield their shells than their grip. Collecting them calls for a double portion of patience. After each success, you'll have to wait until neighboring clams gain enough courage to surface again.

SKIMMER CLAM
Mactra solidissima

Skimmer clam is the East End name for the surf or sea clam used both in cooking and as live bait.

SKIMMERS AS FOOD: The soft, meaty skimmer is ideal bait for hooking a host of local gamefish, but is often disdained for cooking because, in comparison to other clams, the meat is quite tough. Nevertheless, skimmers have served as cheap, abundant and nutritious food as far back as colonial times, when thrifty housewives not only chopped these clams up for clam pies and other hot dishes, but converted their shells into "skim-alls" used for ladling soup, skimming fat, and the like.

Despite their toughness, skimmer meat can be delectable stewed in chowders, fried into fritters and sauced for spaghetti. This is, in fact, the same meat that commercial canners process and sell as "chopped clams."

The skimmer clam's two adductor muscles can be served as tender, flavorful substitutes for scallops in any recipe, and are as tender raw as the meat of any cherrystone. To harvest adductor muscles, collect only skimmers 5 inches or more in length—smaller specimens won't yield muscles worth the trouble of opening the clams. Grind and freeze the clam bodies.

Shucking skimmers is similar to the hardshell technique. Use the same thin, round-edge knife and push the blade into the narrow opening between the shells on the edge where the siphon protrudes. Tip the knife down so the blade hugs the bottom of the shell, then push under and sever the forward adductor muscle; this forces the clam to relax just enough to allow you to slide the knife all around the shells' edges and sever the second adductor. Once freed from the shells, adductors are easy to separate from the remaining meat. To clean adductors, dip them into the collected clam juices.

DESCRIPTION: Skimmers are the largest clams in the East End area, growing to 7 inches in length. The elliptical shells range in color from brown to straw-colored or perhaps a little lighter in rough waters. (Those white shells you find washed up on the beach are generally bleached by the sun.)

Since the skimmer's siphon is short, it lives in the sand just beyond the low-water mark. Its tongue-shaped foot is marvelously adapted to this perilous shore-bound existence because it is strong enough to anchor the clam to the sand against most waves and storms.

HABITS, HABITAT AND SEASON: In any surf environment at the margin of the sea you'll likely find the skimmer burrowed just below the surface of the sand or skimming along for short distances on the water's surface. These clams are always in season. Look for them while the tide is out on sandbars, spits or peninsulas or in areas uncovered only by unusually low tides (during the period of full or new moon). Gulls overhead in any area is a good indication that skimmers are plentiful.

Note: Clams may be used interchangeably unless otherwise noted.

FOXEY BOGUE MINCED CLAM APPETIZER

◆

Yield: Enough to serve 6

2 Cups clams, shucked, minced and
  drained
1 Cup minced green pepper
1 Cup minced sweet onion
2 Cups peeled, seeded and minced
  tomatoes

1 Small hot red pepper, minced
  (optional)
1 Cup minced avocado
2 Tablespoons each olive oil,
  Worcestershire and lemon juice
Salt and black pepper to taste

Mix all ingredients and refrigerate 2 hours. Serve cold.

FIERY MINCED CLAM SLAW

◆

Follow directions for Foxey Bogue Minced Clam Appetizer but add ½ small cabbage minced, one to 2 tablespoons sugar and enough additional oil and lemon juice to moisten.

CLAM BROTH BISQUE

◆

Yield: Enough to serve 6

This is the least complicated soup to prepare from my collection of cold soup recipes—and possibly the most unusual. The clam liquid must be *very* fresh and icy cold. The cups or bowls and spoons must be well chilled also.

1½–2 Cups fresh, cold clam liquid
1 Cup very cold light cream or
  half-and-half

1½ Teaspoons Pernod
White pepper

Mix the cold clam liquid and cold cream in a cocktail shaker and place in the freezer 5 minutes prior to serving. Add the Pernod and shake once. Pour into very small white chilled cups or bowls. Top with a sprinkle of pepper and serve *immediately.*

CLAM NECTAR

◆

Follow directions for Clam Broth Bisque above, but substitute ½ cup fresh, cold coconut milk for half the light cream. Omit the Pernod, but shake one drop Tabasco sauce onto the surface of each cup of soup. Serve as above.

CLAM NECTAR WITH SCALLOPS

◆

Yield: Enough to serve 6

Unbelievably simple to prepare. Unbelievably delicious. Just fresh, uncooked ingredients at their natural best.

1 Cup bay scallops, each cut crosswise to make 2 thin slices
2 Limes, juiced
1–1½ Cups fresh, cold clam liquid

1 Cup very cold light cream or half-and-half
Cayenne pepper

Refrigerate scallop slices in lime juice overnight, stirring occasionally. Drain well, rinse lightly, and drain again.

Just prior to serving mix the cold clam liquid and cream. Divide into small, cold cups or bowls. Add two spoonfuls of marinated scallops to each.

Sprinkle with cayenne and serve immediately in cold bowls with cold spoons.

COLD STUFFED CLAMS, GRECIAN STYLE

◆

Yield: Enough to serve 6

2 Dozen cherrystone clams, well scrubbed and opened
½ Recipe Basic Cold Rice for Salads, made with the clam juices

¼ Cup each pine nuts and currants
¼ Teaspoon each allspice, sugar and dried oregano
3 Pimento-stuffed olives, sliced

Leave the clams in their deep bottom shells but drain well. Mix the rice, pine nuts, currants, allspice, sugar and oregano. Mound the rice over the clams, top with olive slices and chill one hour. Serve cold.

HOT STUFFED CLAMS, GRECIAN STYLE

◆

Follow directions for Cold Stuffed Clams, Grecian Style above, but stir ¼ cup tomato purée into rice. Top rice-covered clams with a little feta cheese, arrange the shells in hot rock salt and bake in a preheated 400-degree F. oven for 15 minutes.

DEVILED CLAMS, SAGG POND

◆

Yield: Enough to serve 6

1 Cup each finely chopped celery and onion
3 Tablespoons butter
1 Cup heavy cream
3 Beaten egg yolks
2 Cups finely minced or ground clams
1 Tablespoon each minced fresh thyme, marjoram and chives

1½ Cups soft bread crumbs
Salt, pepper and cayenne pepper to taste
Grated Parmesan cheese
Melted butter

Preheat oven to 400 degrees F.

Sauté the vegetables in the butter until the onion is transparent. Add the cream and reduce to half. Beat in the egg yolks, then add the clams, herbs, bread crumbs and seasonings. Spoon into six empty sea scallop shells. Sprinkle with cheese and melted butter and bake 15 to 20 minutes or until hot clear through and nicely browned on top.

CLAMS LINGUINI

◆

Yield: Enough to serve 4 to 6

1 Pound linguini, or thin spaghetti
2 Large cloves garlic, peeled and minced
6 Tablespoons butter
1 Cup coarsely chopped cherrystone clams (about 1½ dozen)
1 Tablespoon each finely chopped basil and minced thyme

1¼ Cups heavy cream
⅔ Cup freshly grated Parmesan cheese
Salt to taste
Black pepper
3 Tablespoons finely chopped parsley

Cook the linguini according to package directions for *al dente*. Meanwhile sauté the garlic in half the butter until pale yellow. Add the herbs and cream and simmer for 4 minutes. Add clams and simmer 2 minutes more.

Drain the linguini well and immediately toss it with the clam sauce, the remaining butter, the Parmesan, the salt and generous quantities of freshly ground black pepper. Sprinkle with parsley. Serve immediately.

CLAM HASH, BRIDGE LANE

◆

Yield: Enough to serve 4 to 6

After an afternoon of ice-boating, when the wind has a bite of both snow and sand, this hearty clam hash is most satisfying.

3 Large potatoes peeled and cut into ⅓-inch cubes
Salted water
2 Medium-size onions, peeled and finely chopped
6 Tablespoons butter
Salt and pepper to taste

¼ Teaspoon each powdered marjoram and thyme
3 Cups chopped clams
½ Cup heavy cream
Lemon wedges
Chopped parsley

Boil the potatoes in salted water to cover until they are just tender. Drain. In a large nonstick skillet, sauté the onion in 2 tablespoons of the butter until it is transparent. Add 2 more tablespoons butter and then the potatoes and seasonings. Lower the heat and cook 10 minutes. Spread the drained clams over the potatoes, pour the cream over and continue to cook until the hash is crusty and brown on the bottom. Slide the hash onto a large plate in one piece. Melt the remaining 2 tablespoons butter, slide the hash back into the pan and cook until the bottom is brown. Slide the hash onto a heated serving plate, sprinkle with parsley and surround with lemon wedges.

OLD-TIME NORTH SHORE CLAM FRITTERS

◆

Yield: Enough to serve 6

2½ Cups minced fresh clams
3 Eggs, separated
1½ Cups cracker crumbs
1 Tablespoon minced chives

1 Tablespoon crisp, cooked crumbled bacon
Salt and pepper to taste
Oil for deep-frying

Drain the clams well and reserve the juices. Mix together the egg yolks, cracker crumbs, chives and bacon. Stir in the clams and enough clam juice to make a stiff batter. Beat the egg whites until stiff and fold them into the batter. Drop by spoonfuls into deep hot oil and fry until golden brown on both sides, turning once.

LONG-LINER'S CLAMS IN BEER

◆

Clams are also marvelous when simmered in beer . . . and less expensive than when prepared in wine.

6 Dozen clams
1 12-ounce can light beer
1 Bay leaf
¼ Teaspoon leaf thyme
3 Tablespoons butter

2 Tablespoons flour
A pinch of cayenne pepper
1 Cup cream
Crusty bread

Scrub the clams, then place in a large kettle and add the beer and herbs; cover and bring to a boil and cook until the shells open. Discard any clams that do not open.

Strain the cooking liquid. Knead the butter with the flour and cayenne and stir into the hot liquid. Bring to a boil, stirring constantly. Add the cream and reheat without boiling. If this sauce tastes too strong, add more cream. Heap the clams in the shells in shallow bowls with a bit of the sauce. Serve with crusty bread to sop up the sauce.

GRANDMA MILLER'S HURRY-UP CLAMS

◆

1 Quart softshell clams, shucked and well drained
2 Cups pancake mix
Oil for deep-frying

Salt and pepper to taste
Lemon wedges
1 Recipe Sauce Tartare

Blot clams in paper towels. Place dry pancake mix in a small paper bag. Shake the clams a few at a time in the mix, then deep-fry in hot oil a minute or two, or until golden brown. Do not over-brown. Sprinkle with salt and pepper and drain briefly on paper plates. Serve immediately with lemon wedges and Sauce Tartare.

SLICED POTATO AND CLAM PIE
◆

1 Recipe Basic Pie Pastry
2 Quarts cherrystone clams, well
    scrubbed
2 Cups white wine
1 Bay leaf
1 Onion, peeled and sliced
Salt and pepper

2 Baking potatoes, peeled and sliced
3 Scallions, with 3 inches green tops,
    sliced
3 Tablespoons Madeira
1 Recipe Sauce Velouté, made with
    the clam liquor

Prepare the pie pastry and refrigerate. Open the clams by steaming in the white wine, bay leaf, onion, salt and pepper as directed on page 244. Reserve the clam meats, discard the shells and use the broth to make the sauce. Cook the potato slices until barely tender. Roll out the crust and line a pie plate. Arrange the cooled potato slices over the bottom. Sprinkle with salt and pepper and half the scallions. Arrange the clams on top, sprinkle with salt, pepper and the remainder of the scallions. Stir the Madeira into the cool velouté and pour 1 to 1½ cups over all.

Preheat oven to 450 degrees F. Top with crust, nicely crimped and slashed in several places to allow the steam to escape. Brush with egg yolk and bake 15 minutes. Lower heat to 350 degrees F. and bake until well browned.

CLAM PIE, FIREPLACE ROAD: Follow directions for the above but substitute cubed potatoes for the sliced ones and minced quahogs for the cherry-stones. Instead of the Madeira stir ½ cup chopped and fried bacon into the sauce.

HAMPTON FRIED CLAMS
◆

1 Quart softshell clams, shucked and
    well drained
2 Eggs
1 Tablespoon heavy cream
1 Cup each fine bread crumbs and
    flour mixed with 1 teaspoon salt and
    ½ teaspoon pepper

1 Tablespoon butter
1 Cup vegetable oil
Lemon wedges
1 Recipe Sauce Tartare

Blot clams in paper towels. Beat the eggs with the cream. Dip the clams in the bread crumbs and flour, mixed with seasonings, then in the egg mixture and finally in the crumbs again. Fry in sizzling butter and oil until golden brown on both sides. Drain briefly on paper plates. Serve immediately with lemon wedges and Sauce Tartare.

CLAMS IN CREAM ON SHRIMP TOASTS

◆

Yield: Enough to serve 4

2 Tablespoons butter
2 Shallots, peeled and finely chopped
1½ Cups heavy cream
2 Cups shucked clams
⅛ Teaspoon grated lemon zest

1 Tablespoon minced fresh thyme
Salt, white pepper and cayenne
    pepper to taste
1 Recipe Shrimp Toasts

Melt the butter in a chafing dish and sauté the shallots until they are transparent. Add the cream and simmer until reduced by half. Add the clams, lemon zest, thyme, salt and pepper and barely heat. The clams should not cook. Arrange 3 or 4 toast points attractively on each plate. Spoon the clams in the center of each.

Serve immediately with a sprinkle of cayenne.

MUSSELS

On the first really warm day of early spring, when the winds soften and the water gives up its look of melted lead and turns to a pale-blue jell, I wait for low tide and sneak out to my *sub rosa** mussel larder to harvest a clandestine bucket or two to welcome in the vernal equinox. (*Hamptonites are a friendly lot and willing to share with their neighbors their last crust of bread, their last glass of wine, perhaps even last year's spouse, but never would they ever share the location of their secret garden of shellfish.)

The water is cold and nibbles at my ankles above my soggy tennis shoes. My plastic gloves drip brine onto the raggedy cuffs of my musseling sweater. At the shore the mussels grow in clumps, their steel-blue wings frozen in place like swarms of migrating armor-clad moths. Their pointy beaks are attached by rough black threads that drip from their lower lips like the dark beards of untidy uncles. The shells are, as I remember them from last fall, "three-inchers" and very nearly perfect, with crisp, sharp edges and bodies as sleek as satin. My feet are beyond aching, numb from the cold. My finger is throbbing from a slice-wound from a ragged shell. Pain flashes between my shoulder blades from too much bending and tugging too early in the season. But the gulls call over my head as they drop their favorite tidbits on the rocks to crack the shells, and the waves whisper at the shore "Hush . . . hush." So I count my mussels—and my blessings.

At home I scrub the adult blues, and field or bank mussels (including the seedlings that clung to their parents' skirts) and serve them forth in their shells in a peppery saffron broth similar to one I once sampled in

Toledo, Spain. Each plate of golden broth holds at least a dozen small open blue-black mussels. We spear the shellfish with toothpicks, then gulp the steaming soup. Later, we wash down buttery Moules Marinière with chilled glasses of an exceptionally dry, home-pressed wine. We dip crusts of just-baked bread and wonder if anyone could be deserving of such wonderfully simple pleasures.

BLUE MUSSEL

Mytilus edulis

Mussels may not yet be the favorite seafood of the Eastern Coast but their popularity is rocketing. The plump and tender mussel has long been looked down on, if not blatantly ignored, by residents of the United States—a strange prejudice, since these mollusks abound from Canada to North Carolina. Europeans have long considered the mussel a delicacy and, for myself, I prefer its sweetness and delicate flavor to that of the clam. This double-shelled beauty provides an abundant and inexpensive source of vital nourishment, yielding as much protein per pound as your average steak.

BLUE MUSSELS AS FOOD: Natives of almost every European country savor the blue mussel in such great quantities and with such passion that this shellfish supports a widespread and highly profitable aquaculture industry. Since its primitive beginnings in France some 700 years ago, aquaculture of mussels has become a large and mechanized sea-bottom venture. Spain—with its thousands of large rafts, each supporting hundreds of ropes on which grow tons of mussels—is the leader in this fascinating field, with Holland also deeply involved. Off-bottom growing techniques seem to be most promising for our Long Island area, and many local fishermen are at least considering muscling in on this adventure. The off-bottom specimens produced are cleaner; have more attractive, sharper edges; grow larger and faster; are protected from bottom-dwelling predators like crabs and starfish; have smaller, easy-to-remove beards; less sand or mud in their shells and fewer problems with the troublesome *Gymnophallus* parasites that cause the irritated bivalves to create those tiny gray pearls.

Mussels are easy and fun to gather and simple to prepare. If you are harvesting your own, look for large 3-inch specimens still firmly attached. (While beds polluted by harmful organisms do exist, these are closely monitored and are closed to fishing if dangers are present.) Be sure to discard any mussels whose shells do not remain tightly closed when you are ready to cook them. Occasionally, adductor muscles of even fresh, live mussels will loosen if they are soaked or scrubbed under tepid water. In this case, press the mussel between your thumb and forefinger as though you were sliding the top shell across the bottom one. Shells of live mussels will not move. Discard any whose shells yield under this pressure. Another way to determine whether the mussels you gather or buy are alive-and-well is to try to pull the shells apart. If the shell resists, or slides right back into place, you can be assured of its freshness.

Scrub the mussels with a stiff brush or a soapless copper scouring pad. Discard any unusually heavy mussels, which may be filled with sand or mud. The little beard of dark fibers that dangles from the tip may be removed or not as you prefer. Many enthusiasts insist the beard adds flavor to the cooking broth and serves as a handle for "dunking" in butter. The usual way to serve mussels is in their shells. There are about one dozen large, or 15 medium-size, mussels to the pound. Better figure 1½ to 2 pounds per person for any main-course cooked-in-the-shell mussel dish. Mussels are always served cooked, eliminating the danger of hepatitis, but be sure to discard any suspicious mollusks whose shells refuse to open after 6 or 7 minutes over high heat.

DESCRIPTION: This sleek mollusk is easily identified by its elongated blue-black shell that terminates in a beak and by its lovely pale-violet inner shell and black silky beard (byssus). The blue mussel, like its close relatives the clam and oyster, has a hatchet-shaped foot, but one much smaller in size; this handicap, however, is compensated for by its well-developed byssogenous gland, which spins threads in all directions, assuring the shellfish a firm foothold even in pounding seas. Although mussels are thought of as stationary animals, the byssus actually allows them limited freedom of movement in a narrowly circumscribed area. Like the clam and oyster, the blue mussel has a powerful adductor muscle to regulate the opening and closing of its shell.

HABITS, HABITAT AND SEASON: These most abundant and easily gathered of shellfish live in large colonies on the ocean's edge, anchored beak-down to large rocks or pilings or, under some circumstances, to one another.

Mussels are always in season. In our town you may take up to one bushel a day at any time of the year (check your local ordinances). It's best to avoid any mussel not firmly secured to some kind of mooring and also to spurn mussel beds regularly exposed for prolonged periods of time by low tides, especially during the heat of summer.

MUSSELS IN SAFFRON CREAM

◆

Yield: 8 to 10 servings

4 Tablespoons butter
½ Cup peeled shallots, finely chopped
1 Large clove garlic, peeled and
   minced
1½ Teaspoons saffron threads (or
   double this quantity, if you can
   afford it)

3 Quarts scrubbed mussels
2 Cups dry white wine
Tabasco sauce
½ Cup finely chopped parsley
4 Cups heavy cream
Salt and pepper

In a kettle melt the butter, add the shallots, garlic and saffron. Stir over low heat for 3 minutes. Add the mussels, wine, Tabasco and parsley, cover and cook for 5 minutes, or until the mussels open. Add the cream and bring to a boil. Season with salt and pepper to taste. Discard any mussels that have not opened. Serve the soup hot with the mussels in their shells.

MUSSELS MARINIÈRE, GORDON'S AMAGANSETT

◆

Yield: Enough to serve 20

George, the amiable chef at Gordon's Restaurant on the Montauk Highway in Amagansett, every year turns out bushels of plump mussels in creamy white wine sauce to please his hundreds of devoted customers. His recipe, while not quite classic, *is* delicious and practically foolproof.

If you're planning to serve twenty guests (or ten guests on two consecutive evenings) George's trade secrets will guarantee a successful party every time.

First, gather or order your mussels a day in advance and hold them overnight in fresh, cool, salted water to permit them to void their sand and/or any strong or off flavors. Change the water several times.

Second, prepare the white wine cream sauce as directed and refrigerate until needed.

Third, scrub the mussels.

Fourth, stir the sauce and mussels over a medium-hot flame until the shells open and the mussel liquid thins and mellows the broth. Serve immediately in shallow bowls with hot rolls or French bread for dipping.

½ Bushel mussels, well scrubbed
   and bearded
½ Pound butter
1½ Pounds peeled and finely chopped
   onions
¼ Pound peeled and finely chopped
   shallots

¼ Pound peeled and minced garlic
4 Bay leaves
4 Tablespoons leaf thyme
2 Quarts white wine
2 Quarts Enriched White Sauce

Let the mussels stand in cool, salted water for 3 hours or overnight. Melt the butter in a kettle, add the onions, shallots, garlic, bay leaves and thyme and sauté until the onions are transparent. Pour in the wine, bring to a low boil, and continue cooking for 15 minutes. Blend in the white sauce and simmer for 20 minutes. The sauce will be thick. Refrigerate until you are ready to prepare the mussels. Divide the mussels between 2 kettles, pour half the sauce over each, and stir over medium-high flame until the shells open. Discard any mussels that do not open. Serve immediately.

SKEWERED MUSSELS, TWO MILE HOLLOW

◆

Yield: Enough to serve 6

6 Dozen mussels
White wine
½ Cup chopped shallots or onion
Thyme and ½ bay leaf

2–3 Beaten eggs
Bread crumbs
12 Thin bacon slices
1 Recipe Sauce Aurore

Open the mussels by steaming in white wine, shallots or onion, thyme and bay leaf as directed on page 257. Shell. Dip each mussel first in egg and then in bread crumbs. Pierce a bacon slice through one end of a skewer and let it hang while you slip a dozen breaded mussels on the skewer. Pierce the end of another bacon slice on the top of the skewer and wrap it down around the mussels. Similarly wrap the bottom slice up around the mussels until the two bacon strips meet. Fasten them with a toothpick. Repeat this process with 6 skewers. Grill, turning the skewers until the bacon is done. Serve immediately with Sauce Aurore.

FRITTERED MUSSELS

◆

Yield: Enough to serve 6

6 Dozen large plump mussels
White wine
½ Cup chopped shallots and/or onion
Thyme and ½ bay leaf

1 Recipe Sauce Velouté
1 Recipe Fritter Batter with Beer
Oil for deep-frying

Open the mussels by steaming in white wine, shallots and/or onion, thyme and half bay leaf as directed on page 257. Reduce to half the cooking liquid in which the mussels were opened and stir ½ cup of this into the Sauce Velouté. Shell the mussels, wipe them dry, dip each in batter and fry to golden in deep hot oil. Serve the fried mussels with sauce on the side.

DEEP-FRIED MUSSELS, MECOX BAY

◆

Yield: Enough to serve 6

6 Dozen large mussels
White wine
½ Cup chopped shallots and/or onion
Thyme and ½ bay leaf
3 Eggs, beaten

2 Tablespoons cornstarch
1–2 Teaspoons cold water
Oil for deep-frying
Fried Parsley
1 Recipe Sauce Andalouse

Open mussels by steaming in white wine, shallots and/or onion, thyme and bay leaf as directed on page 257. Shell and blot dry. Mix thoroughly the eggs and cornstarch, pressing out any lumps with the back of a spoon. Add just enough cold water to make dipping possible. Dip each mussel in batter and deep-fry as directed on page 27. Serve immediately with Fried Parsley and Sauce Andalouse.

MUSSELS DEEP-FRIED IN THE SHELL
◆

Steam open the mussels as directed, remove the top shells, drain and dry well the mussels in the bottom shells. Keeping the mussels in their shells, dip them into the batter given in Deep-Fried Mussels, Mecox Bay, above. Drain a bit and deep-fry until golden brown. Serve with Sauce Verte.

MUSSELS IN THE SHELL WITH GARLIC BUTTER
◆

Yield: Enough to serve 6

6 Dozen mussels
White wine
½ Cup chopped shallots or onions
Thyme and ½ bay leaf

1 Recipe Garlic Butter
Bread crumbs
Well-washed watercress

Steam open the mussels as directed on page 257. Remove the top shells, drain and dry well the mussels in the bottom shells. Sprinkle with Garlic Butter and bread crumbs and brown under the broiler. Serve attractively on a bed of watercress.

BASIC CHILLED MUSSELS
◆

Yield: 3 dozen mussels

An unusually pleasing and appropriate seaside hors d'oeuvre. Serve an assortment with chilled white wine.

Scrub the mussel shells and rinse in fresh water several times.

3 Dozen medium-size mussels—plus
    a few*
1 Medium-size onion, peeled and
    chopped
2 Shallots, peeled and chopped

6 Sprigs parsley, well washed
2 Sprigs fresh thyme
A grind of fresh pepper
1 Cup white wine

Place all the ingredients in a large skillet or shallow pan. Cover and set over high heat for 2 minutes. Shake the pan and return it to the heat for 2 minutes. Shake the pan and cook 2 minutes more. Remove the cover. The mussels should all be open. If many of them are not, return the pan to the heat and repeat the process until they are. If only one or two remain closed, discard these, then drain, chill and use the open ones. Reduce any liquid to 2 to 3 tablespoons and refrigerate for use in sauces, stews, etc.

Most recipes call for one shell of the mussel (the one to which the meat is *not attached*) to be discarded. Serve on the remaining shell.

*Always add a few mussels for good measure, in case one or two choose not to open.

MUSSELS IN CURRY MAYONNAISE

◆

Yield: 3 dozen

Drain any liquid from 3 dozen Basic Chilled Mussels. Leave them in the shell to which the meat is attached. Pipe about half a teaspoon Curry Mayonnaise around each. Sprinkle each end with parsley. Chill until ready to serve.

VARIATION: Follow directions for Mussels in Curry Mayonnaise but substitute Tarragon Mayonnaise for Curry Mayonnaise. Sprinkle each lightly with minced fresh thyme. Chill until ready to serve.

MUSSELS VINAIGRETTE

◆

Yield: Enough to serve 6

6 Dozen Basic Chilled Mussels
2 Cups Sauce Vinaigrette
Cupped leaves of buttercrunch lettuce

Remove mussels from their shells. Toss the mussels with the sauce and refrigerate several hours or overnight. Arrange in lettuce cups and serve cold.

VARIATION I: Follow directions for Mussels Vinaigrette, but substitute Sauce Ravigote for the Sauce Vinaigrette.

VARIATION II: Follow directions for Mussels Vinaigrette, but substitute Sauce Rémoulade for Sauce Vinaigrette and garnish with sieved hard-cooked egg yolk.

MUSSELS VINAIGRETTE IN THE SHELL

◆

Yield: 3 dozen mussels

3 Dozen Basic Chilled Mussels
1½ Cups Sauce Vinaigrette

Remove the meats from the shells and refrigerate overnight in the sauce. Retain and refrigerate half of the shells as well. Return the mussels to their shells, along with a little of the sauce. Chill until ready to serve.

VARIATION: Follow directions for Mussels Vinaigrette, but substitute Sauce Vinaigrette à la Moutarde for the plain Vinaigrette.

SEASIDE MUSSEL AND AVOCADO SALAD WITH RICE

◆

Yield: Enough to serve 6

1 Avocado, peeled and pitted
1 Recipe Basic Cold Rice for Salads
½ Recipe (3 dozen) Mussels
  Vinaigrette

½ Cup pimento, drained and cut
  into ½-inch squares
Freshly ground black pepper
Salt to taste

Cut the avocado into ½-inch cubes. Toss together all ingredients. Let stand 10 minutes at room temperature before serving.

OYSTERS

Crassotrea virginica

C. virginica, known also as blue point, Cape Cod, Chincoteague, and Apalachicola (among others), is the most common of the four oyster varieties found on Atlantic shores. Extensive natural beds, once so thick with oysters and shells that they blocked harbors, are now fast disappearing, due to overharvesting and pollution. . . .

FROM JASPER DANCKAERTS' JOURNAL, 1679

. . . We proceeded on to Gouannes, a place so called, where we arrived in the evening at one of the best friends of Gerrit, named Symon. He took us into the house, and entertained us exceedingly well. We found a good fire, half-way up the chimney, of clear oak and hickory. There had been already thrown upon it, to be roasted, a pail-full of Gouanes oysters, which are the best in the country. They are fully as good as those of England and better than those we ate at Falmouth. I had to try some of them raw. They are large and full, some of them not less than a foot long, and they grow sometimes ten, twelve and sixteen together, and are then like a piece of rock. Others are young and small. In consequence of the great quantities of them, everybody keeps the shells for the purpose of burning them into lime. They pickle the oysters in small casks, and send them to Barbados and the other islands.

DESCRIPTION: The familiar rough, shaggy, rather unlovely shell is easily recognized. The animal itself has a mantle like other mollusks, but no foot to speak of (oysters are stationary throughout all but the first 2 or 3 weeks of life), no siphon which would allow it to burrow under the sand like its clam cousins, no byssus with which to spin attaching threads like the mussel. It lives out its immobile life by cementing itself to other oysters, to brush or to rocks, or when cultivated, to materials especially geared to help it grow.

OYSTERS AS FOOD: The United States leads the world in oyster production with *C. virginica*, only one of four species found along North American coasts. Most Long Island oysters that go to market are raised by two Long

Island companies. Long Island Oyster Farms, Inc., East Marion, North Fork; and Frank M. Flower & Son, Bayville, Oyster Bay. Some also come from the Shinnecock Indian reservation, but these are somewhat less uniform than those from commercial oyster farms and more like natural-growth specimens.

Oysters are at their peak and in season in the late fall, winter and early spring. Healthy live specimens keep their shells tightly closed, and are heavy with juices. When buying shucked oysters be sure the surrounding juices are not cloudy or milky.

The best shucking tool is a specifically-designed oyster knife about 6½ inches long, with a fairly rigid, blunt, even-sided blade and blunt, round-nosed tip. Hold the oyster in a pot holder in your hand, with the hinge end against your palm, the rounded shell down and the flat one up. Holding the oyster knife securely in your other hand, push the blade between the shells halfway between the hinge and the lip about 1/16 inch from the outside edge of the top shell. When you hit the right spot a little liquid will bubble out. Work the knife back and forth until you can easily slide it back against the flat side of the shell and sever the adductor muscles. Once these muscles are cut, the oyster will relax its grip and the top shell should come off easily. Now slide the knife under the oyster and lift it from its bottom shell.

If you find shucking too difficult, and the oysters are ultimately to be cooked, steam the bivalves for a *few seconds* or place them in a large skillet over a hot burner until the shells separate slightly. When the shells are cool enough to handle, carefully shuck the oysters, collect the juices and proceed as with raw oysters.

Oysters are classically eaten raw on the (bottom) half-shell steadied in crushed ice or rock salt to keep them from tipping and spilling their juices. (The salt is also used when cooking.) If the occasion is informal, serve a large platter of the bivalves surrounded by lemon wedges accompanied by a chilled Pouilly Fuissé or Fumé as an elegant *al fresco* first course. More formal occasions call for special oyster plates with indentations to hold oysters. Eat the oysters with small oyster forks, then drink the juices from the shells.

Oyster aficionados, and they are legion, generally prefer these treats *au naturel* or with just a squeeze of lemon juice. However, a grind of fresh black or Szechwan pepper does provide a nice change of pace.

When cooking oysters, the rule is . . . gently does it. Cook in the juices just long enough for the edges to curl, then remove immediately from the heat. A classic oyster stew is a very simple brew.

To prepare: Plan on 6 to 8 shucked oysters per person. Drain the meat in a colander, reserving the juices. Discard any bits of shell and place the oysters in a pot. Strain the juice, leaving any grit behind, pour the juice over the oysters and bring *just* to a boil. Remove from the heat and add milk or cream in amounts equal to the quantity of meat and juices. Return the pot to the flame and cook just long enough to reheat . . . never boil! Add a chunk of butter and salt and pepper to taste to each bowl. Ambrosia!

HABITS, HABITAT AND SEASON: Oysters prefer fairly brackish waters . . . those bays, estuaries and tidal creeks where fresh water dilutes the saltiness. The free-swimming "spat," about the size of a grain of sand, abandons its vagabond life after two or three weeks, drops to the bottom, cements its bottom shell to some clean, hard object and settles down for life.

All oysters start life as males, then switch, once they reach middle age, to being females. It is as older females and younger males that oysters release, respectively, eggs and sperm. Only if an oyster lives to ripe old age does it revert to its original sex.

"Natural-growth" oysters are fast disappearing, although there are still a few to be found. Commercial replenishment through oyster farming is perhaps the only way to ensure a continuing supply, but even this is barely enough to keep up with the demand.

There are still a few places in the Peconics and on the eastern tip of Long Island where water quality is such that some natural-growth oysters can be taken. The season extends from September 1 to April 30, and the best way to find these treasures is to get out there and search, particularly along the shorelines where mouths of creeks and tributary streams flow into the sea. Look for the smooth, pearly spats on stones or the empty shells that betray the presence of oyster colonies. Choose a beautiful day for a seaside outing, and don't be disappointed if you get nothing for your trouble but a polish on your suntan. Even if you should locate them, most oysters live in deep beds under several feet of icy water, and the only tools permitted for gathering them are long-handled oyster tongs and scratch rakes . . . a cold, muscle-straining, generally fruitless venture. If you *are* lucky enough to find a hidden few natural-growth oysters (wonderfully tasty—even when opened and consumed *in situ*), be prepared to work for your feast. These oysters cling in clusters and consequently have misshapen shells that may require a direct attack with a wooden pole or length of pipe to separate them. Before you gather, be sure you have a permit and that the waters are pollution-free.

All local ordinances in the East End specify that a permit is required before anyone may gather oysters.

Southampton allows ½ bushel (2 pecks) per day for noncommercial purposes, to be gathered only between sunrise and sunset. No dredges or mechanical devices are permitted. In Mecox Bay, only hand-operated tongs, eagle-claw or scratch rakes not to exceed 24 inches in width are permitted.

Southold allows 2 pecks (noncommercial) daily between sunrise and sunset, as long as oysters measure 2 inches or more from hinge to bill.

East Hampton makes an exception in the permit rule and allows anyone without a digger's permit to harvest one peck of oysters daily. Otherwise, between sunrise and sunset, diggers with permits can take one bushel (4 pecks) daily for noncommercial purposes. Seed oysters (less than 3 inches long) cannot be taken.

Shelter Island also allows diggers without permits to take one peck of oysters.

OYSTERS BAKED IN THEIR SHELLS

◆

Yield: Enough to serve 6

1 Egg
1 Tablespoon water
2–3 Dozen large oysters in their
   well-scrubbed bottom shells

Fine dry bread crumbs
Butter

Preheat oven to 450 degrees F.

Beat the egg and water together. Dip each oyster in this mixture, roll each in bread crumbs and arrange on their shells. Dot generously with butter, arrange in rock salt and bake until golden brown. Serve 4 oysters to each person if served before dinner or with drinks—at least 6 each if served as an entree.

COLONIAL ESCALLOPED OYSTERS

◆

Yield: Enough to serve 6

1½ Quarts shelled oysters, with
  ½ cup liquid
4 Cups cracker crumbs
¼ Pound butter

Salt and pepper
Powdered mace
½ Cup light cream

Preheat oven to 350 degrees F.

Sprinkle a thin layer of cracker crumbs in a well-buttered 6-cup casserole. Add a layer of drained oysters and a dash each of salt, pepper, and mace. Cover with a layer of crumbs and dot with some of the butter. Continue the layerings, reserving several tablespoons of crumbs and a tablespoon of butter. Pour the cream and ½ cup oyster liquid over, sprinkle with reserved crumbs and dot with remaining butter. Bake 35 minutes.

SAVOURY ESCALLOPED OYSTERS: Follow directions for Colonial Escalloped Oysters, but substitute a sprinkling of Worcestershire sauce for that of the mace.

ANGELS ON HORSEBACK

◆

Yield: Enough to serve 6

30 Oysters, shucked
Thinly sliced bacon

1 Recipe Anchovy Toasts
Chopped Parsley

Wrap each oyster in a piece of bacon long enough to completely surround it and slip them 5 each on 6 small skewers. Grill until bacon is cooked, turning frequently. Arrange on Anchovy Toasts. Sprinkle with parsley and serve immediately.

EAST END OYSTER CHOWDER

◆

Yield: Enough to serve 6

3 Tablespoons butter
1 Large onion, peeled and coarsely chopped
1 Rib celery, finely chopped
1 Cup clam juice
2 Cups water
3 Large potatoes, peeled and cut into ½-inch cubes
1 Cup finely chopped fresh parsley
½ Teaspoon salt

¼ Teaspoon freshly ground black pepper
5 Ears corn cut from the cob (scrape the cobs to extract corn milk)
¼ Cup pimentos, drained and cut in ½-inch squares
3 Cups milk
3 Cups fresh oysters with their liquor
Cayenne pepper

Melt the butter and sauté the onion and celery until the onion turns golden. Add the clam juice, water, potatoes, parsley and seasonings; bring to a boil, cover and cook over low heat for 15 minutes. Add the corn and corn milk and simmer for 5 minutes, then add the remaining ingredients. Bring the soup to just under a boil; lower the heat and simmer one minute or until the oysters plump up and their edges curl. Take care not to overcook, or the oysters will toughen. Serve at once with a sprinkle of cayenne.

AUNT SUE'S OYSTER LOAF

◆

Yield: Enough to serve 6

1 Long French bread, split lengthwise
8 Tablespoons butter
1 Large clove garlic, peeled and crushed
1 Recipe Deep-fried Oysters
1 Cup ketchup

2 Tablespoons grated horseradish
1 Tablespoon lemon juice
1 Teaspoon Worcestershire sauce
1 Tablespoon minced parsley
Tabasco sauce

Pull the soft insides from the two French bread halves so that the sides are about ½ inch thick. Melt the butter, add the garlic and brush the bread shells liberally. Place on a baking sheet and bake for 10 minutes, or until lightly browned, in a preheated 400-degree oven. Arrange the fried oysters on the bottom half of the bread shell. Mix the ketchup, horseradish, lemon juice and Worcestershire, spoon over the oysters, sprinkle with parsley and Tabasco to taste. Cover with top half of bread shell and serve immediately, cut into individual servings.

DEEP-FRIED OYSTERS

◆

Yield: 1½ dozen

18 Oysters, shucked and drained
1 Cup yellow corn meal

Salt and pepper to taste
Oil for frying

Dredge the oysters in corn meal, season to taste and deep-fry in hot oil 1 minute, or until golden.

LONDON PUB GRILLED OYSTERS

◆

Yield: Enough to serve 6

3 Dozen oysters, well scrubbed and
  opened

8 Tablespoons butter
1 Tablespoon Worcestershire sauce

Discard the top shells. Melt the butter, add the Worcestershire and spoon about one teaspoonful of this mixture over each drained oyster. Arrange the shells in heated rock salt and slide under the broiler just until the edges begin to curl.

FRIED OYSTERS, VILLEROI

◆

Yield: Enough to serve 6

18 Oysters, shucked and poached as
  directed on page 262
1 Recipe Sauce Villeroi

Beaten eggs
Bread crumbs
Oil for deep-frying

Dry the oysters and dip them in cool, thick Sauce Villeroi so that they are thickly covered. Arrange them on a chilled plate and refrigerate for 2 hours, or until quite cold. Just prior to serving, dip the oysters in egg, and then in bread crumbs and deep-fry as directed on page 27. Serve 3 each on small folded napkins or cut-glass plates.

ROAST OYSTERS WITH SMOKED SALMON BUTTER

◆

Yield: Enough to serve 6

3 Dozen oysters, well scrubbed
1 Recipe Smoked Salmon Butter

Preheat oven to 450 degrees F.
    Roast unopened oysters on a baking sheet until the shells open (10 to 15 minutes). Serve on the half-shell dotted with hot Smoked Salmon Butter.

OYSTERS NANTUA

◆

Yield: Enough to serve 6

18 Oysters, shucked (reserve the
   bottom shells)
1 Recipe Fish Forcement (made with
   ½ cup each cooked shrimp and
   crabmeat)

1 Recipe Sauce Nantua

Scrub the 18 bottom shells. Poach the oysters as directed on page 262. Place the forcemeat in each shell, top with an oyster, cover with Sauce Nantua and lightly brown under the broiler. Serve immediately.

OYSTERS FLORENTINE

◆

Yield: Enough to serve 6

Butter
6 Scallop shells
1 Recipe Steamed Spinach
6 Plump oysters, poached as directed
   on page 262

1 Recipe Sauce Mornay
Grated Parmesan cheese

Place a dot of butter in each of 6 scallop shells, top with a spoonful of well-drained hot spinach, an oyster, a masking of Mornay and a sprinkle of cheese. Slide under the broiler for a few seconds, or until lightly browned.

COLONIAL BLUEPOINT OYSTER CAKE

◆

*Yield: Enough to
serve 6 to 8*

A hearty meal for a cook with an oyster "connection."

24 Oysters, shucked and with liquid
   reserved
Clam juice
4 Tablespoons flour

Old-Fashioned Potato Stuffing
Salt and black pepper
¼ Cup coarse dry bread crumbs
2 Tablespoons butter

Simmer oysters a minute or two in their juices to barely cover until edges curl. Do not overcook. Remove the oysters with a slotted spoon. Measure oyster juices and add enough clam juice to make 2 cups liquid. Blend in flour and mix thoroughly. Heat until boiling, stirring constantly.

Preheat oven to 350 degrees F.

Spread a layer of Potato Stuffing on the bottom of a well-greased casserole. Arrange a layer of oysters over the stuffing. Spoon half the thickened oyster juices over the oysters and season with a little salt and pepper. Repeat the layerings, ending with stuffing. Sprinkle with bread crumbs and dot with butter. Bake 30 to 40 minutes until bread crumbs are golden brown. Serve hot.

There is a ritual we go through at our house come autumn. Along about the end of August we begin to look longingly at Accabonac Creek, beyond the vegetable garden. We know that soon "bugs"—the young scallops—will be nipping at the surface of the waves, squirting up bay water like inverted rain drops. If you row out in a boat you can comb the tops of the ripples with your fingers and catch perfect purple and orange and white scalloped shells. But, being law-abiding, you don't. You return them to the bay to propel themselves merrily along under the warm fall sun. "Bugs" never appear when it would be legal to consume them. Mother Nature and the powers that be, are not daft after all, and those babies must live on if the species is to continue.

So we wait. Through the last steaming days of August. Through the glorious golden days of September. Then, along about the time the winds have strengthened a bit and the days are too cool to be bathing-suit weather, we know we haven't long to curb our appetites. The first day of scallop season, when I blink my eyes open at 6 A.M., Accabonac Bay—my bay—is bobbing with boats. They ply systematically back and forth, not one crossing the direct path of another, looking like illustrations in a child's grade-one arithmetic book. If two boats plus two boats are multiplied by four boats plus four boats . . . it's sure to equal scallops in the pan.

No one who gives a damn about East Hampton or about food eats steak that night (save perhaps a few fishermen's families who might by now be sick of it all). As the sun sets in a copper haze, as the mist sweeps in and the dust swirls up against the wind . . . I imagine that the mists and swirls are steam rising from hundreds of skillets of hour-old scallops, from hundreds of kettles of sweet scallop stew. I walk to my garden for two handfuls of fresh herbs. I swear the air itself smells of scallops, and butter and thyme.

On the first day of scallop season we eat sautéed scallops. On the second day they're fried. On the third day of scallop season we slurp up scallops with avocado in saffron cream. On the fourth day it's Coquilles St. Jacques. On the fifth day . . .

SCALLOPS

Pectenidae

This large family of graceful bivalve mollusks (four-hundred-odd world-wide members) all flaunt the familiar fluted fan-shaped shells prominent for centuries in mythology, architecture, religion and art . . . Venus rising full-blown from her scallop shell, medieval Crusaders displaying this, the personal emblem of St. James, etc. Gastronomically, it's almost impossible to think of this mollusk without a mental cross-reference to Coquille St. Jacques or "St. James's shell," a term applied by the French both to the scallop and to the traditional dish.

Long Island waters are abundant in both the small, sweet bay scallop (*Pecten irradians*) and the larger ocean variety (*P. magellanicus*).

BAY SCALLOPS

Pecten irradians

Diminutive by comparison with the deep-sea variety, the shell diameter of the adult bay scallop reaches only two to three inches from hinge end to rounded "bill" or top. Shell colors vary from black through blue-gray to light purple-gray. "Ears," the winglike projections on either side, are equal in size. Shell interior is shiny, with the inside rib grooves corresponding to the outer ones. Unique to this species is the orange- or scarlet-edged mantle, which protrudes beyond the shell (because this bivalve does not "clam up") and on which thirty to forty bright-blue "eyes" sparkle.

BAY SCALLOPS AS FOOD: Even fish loathers usually love these firm tender, protein-rich nuggets. Scallops differ from some other bivalves in that they have only one oversize adductor muscle (clams, for instance, have two smaller ones), and this "eye" is the only part consumed by most people, although the entire bay scallop is edible. An ideal way to feast on this treat is live, direct from the eelgrass, opened on the spot, the pearl-white adductor muscles removed, sprinkled with lemon juice and popped into the mouth like peanuts.

For the less adventurous, bay scallops "cooked" in lime juice make superb Sashimi and are one of two seafoods used in the classic Seviche of Peru.

To prepare bay scallops for frying or sautéing, pat dry, then add to well-heated butter or oil to seal in the natural juices and prevent them from escaping into the pan. For any method of preparation, it's best to underdo rather than overdo this delicate shellfish . . . too-high heat or prolonged cooking will cause the meat to shrink, ridge and dry out.

Scallops, either bay or sea, can be frozen, but don't expect quite the tender, juicy flavor of the fresh mollusks . . . defrosting causes some loss of natural liquid.

HABITS, HABITAT AND SEASON: The bay scallop has no siphon tube, so it cannot burrow under sand as clams do, but it does have a foot of sorts, in keeping with its family name pelecypod. Swimming not only backward and forward but sideways, it achieves a kind of jet propulsion by opening its valves to draw in water, then forcing a jet stream of water out of the bill end to propel itself forward hinge end first (its eyes facing backward).

Scallops favor sheltered bays and inlets with an abundance of the eelgrasses that provide food, protection from strong currents and a place to spin an anchoring byssal thread and get a bit of rest.

If you examine an empty bay scallop shell, you will see its life records, growth lines for each year of life distinctly etched on both the exterior and interior.

HOW TO FIND: Shellfish ordinances in local areas vary a bit, but most are very definite about when scallops may be taken from local waters and how large those taken must be (see below). Scallops can be found in waters over a variety of bottoms, particularly where eelgrass grows. Look for them wherever you see bunches of empty scallop shells decorating the shore. Scallops are pretty speedy, but if you're quick with a long-handled net you might be able to scoop them off the bottom.

Southampton: Scallops may only be taken from town waters during the period from the third Monday in September to March 31, inclusive. Only bay scallops having an annual growth line or measuring not less than 2¼ inches from the middle of the hinge to the middle of the bill may be taken.

Shelter Island prohibits taking of scallops which do not show an annual growth ring; also, scallops may not be taken between April and September 15, inclusive.

Southold prohibits taking of scallops that do not have an annual growth line or measure less than 2¼ inches. Season begins on the first Monday after the third Sunday in September (for those who hand-pick or use scalp net for scallops; any dredging for scallops must wait until October 10) and lasts until March 31, inclusive.

East Hampton allows scallops to be taken only from October 1 through March 31, inclusive (commercial pickers must wait until the day after the third Monday in October). Scallops taken must only be those showing an annual growth ring.

All towns are more liberal in amounts of scallops they allow to be taken in contrast to other shellfish, but all require permits.

All towns also conform to New York State law, which specifies that bay scallops may be taken during the period from the third Monday in September to March 31, inclusive. Only bay scallops having an annual growth line or measuring not less than 2¼ inches from the middle of the hinge to middle of the bill may be taken; any smaller ones must be returned to the water. State law also requires that bay scallops be culled (removed from their shells) when taken, which is probably good practice, since bay scallops do not keep their shells firmly closed, and lose body moisture quickly once out of the water.

SEA SCALLOPS

Pecten magellanicus

This largest (up to 5½ inches) of the East Coast scallops is the mainstay of the commercial market, since it is so much more abundant than the vanishing bay scallop. Size aside, distinguishing characteristics are rounded rather than fluted shells of unequal lengths, one valve being larger and more rounded than its partner and also lighter in color. Shell colors range from red to brown to an ash-gray.

Most sea scallops are taken by commercial dredgers, sometimes in waters as deep as 900 feet. New York State law allows sea scallops of any size to be taken in any manner at any time of the year, so these are available at most retail fish markets all year long.

SEA SCALLOPS AS FOOD: The adductor muscle or "eye" of meat here is naturally larger, but sea scallops may be prepared in any manner suitable for bay scallops . . . either whole, if small, or cut into halves or quarters. If prepared whole, allow a little extra cooking time, but the same rule about undercooking rather than overcooking holds true.

Legend has it that unscrupulous retailers will sell you sea scallops that have been cut from some other less expensive fish, skate, for example, but I have never experienced this treachery.

SEA SCALLOPS WITH FLAMING FENNEL

◆

Yield: Enough to serve 4 to 6

1 Quart sea scallops
Thinly sliced bacon

Melted butter
Dried fennel branches

Rinse the scallops and blot them dry. Pierce the ends of 4 strips of bacon with a 10-inch skewer, thread on 6 or 7 scallops, then arrange the bacon strips up over the sides of the scallops, piercing the ends of the bacon at the top to secure them. Repeat the process until all the scallops have been skewered and surrounded by bacon. Brush generously with melted butter. Grill over open coals, setting fennel aflame under the shellfish as they cook. Turn the skewers frequently. Grill only until the bacon is done. Do not overcook. Serve immediately with melted butter (flavored with fennel if you prefer).

LINGUINI WITH BAY SCALLOPS AND ARUGULA

◆

Yield: Enough to serve 4 to 6

If arugula is not available, substitute fresh spinach. In this case add a generous pinch of dry mustard to the olive oil.

1½–2 Pints bay scallops
3–4 Limes, juiced
2 Cloves garlic, peeled and minced
⅓ Cup fine, light olive oil
2 Tablespoons minced chives
2 Cups coarsely chopped arugula

1 Pound linguini, cooked al dente and kept hot
A generous amount of salt and freshly ground black pepper
Lemon wedges

Rinse the scallops, cover with the lime juice and refrigerate overnight, stirring occasionally. Mix the garlic and oil and let stand overnight. When ready to serve, drain the scallops, strain the olive oil and toss them over low heat for 2 minutes with chives, arugula, linguini, salt and pepper. Serve immediately with lemon wedges.

BAY SCALLOPS WITH AVOCADO IN SAFFRON CREAM

◆

Yield: Enough to serve 6

2½–3 Pounds bay scallops
5 Tablespoons butter
1 Teaspoon flour
A generous pinch or two of powdered saffron

2 Cups heavy cream
2 Avocados, one cut in ½-inch cubes, one sliced
Cayenne pepper
Rice ring

Sauté scallops for a minute or two in 3 tablespoons hot butter. Remove and drain over a bowl. Add 2 tablespoons butter to pan, blend in flour and saffron. Add the cream all at once, and bring to a boil over medium heat, stirring constantly. Add drippings from scallops. Reduce over low heat if necessary to bring sauce to a nice thickness. Add cubed avocado and the scallops to the sauce just long enough to heat them through. Serve in a ring of rice. Sprinkle lightly with cayenne pepper and garnish the edge of the rice ring with thin slices of avocado. Serve immediately.

BAY SCALLOPS IN PERNOD CREAM

◆

Yield: Enough to serve 4 to 6

1 Quart bay scallops
Flour
6 Tablespoons Clarified Butter
3 Tablespoons Pernod
2 Tablespoons each minced fresh
  chervil and tarragon

2 Cups heavy cream
Salt and white pepper to taste
4–6 Artichoke bottoms, cooked
4–6 Trimmed, buttered toast squares

Rinse the scallops, blot them dry and dust very lightly with flour. Sauté in hot butter for 2 to 3 minutes—enough to firm the flesh somewhat, but not to brown. Remove the scallops from the pan with a slotted spoon and set aside. Add the Pernod, warm slightly and set aflame. Stir in the herbs and cream and simmer until the cream is about the consistency of a thin white sauce. Add the scallops, season to taste and stir over low heat for one minute. Serve on hot artichoke bottoms set on toast squares.

PINEAPPLE, LIVER, LEEK AND SEA SCALLOP KEBABS

◆

Yield: Enough to serve 6

8 Tablespoons butter (1 stick)
2 Large cloves garlic, peeled and
  crushed
18 Small to medium-size sea scallops
4 Leeks, ¾ inch thick, with 2 inches
  green tops

12 Mushroom caps
2 Tablespoons each soy sauce and
  honey
8 Chicken livers, cut in half
12 Pineapple chunks

Melt 6 tablespoons butter, mix in the garlic and the scallops and let stand 10 minutes. Meanwhile wash the leeks well, cut them into one-inch lengths and carefully rinse these pieces again to make sure no grit remains. Do *not* handle carelessly or the lengths will break apart. Drain leek pieces well and add them, with the mushroom caps, to the garlic butter.

Mix the soy sauce and honey and mix with the livers and pineapple. Thread on skewers a pineapple chunk, a half liver, a mushroom, a leek section, a scallop and a pineapple chunk (in that order). Repeat on each skewer. Broil about 5 minutes on each side. Turn once and brush with garlic butter.

COQUILLES ST. JACQUES

◆

Yield: Enough to serve 6

1½ Pounds bay scallops
4 Tablespoons butter
5 Shallots, peeled and finely chopped
10 Mushrooms, finely chopped
1½ Cups white wine
3 Tablespoons Kneaded Butter

1 Lemon, juiced
4 Egg yolks, beaten
1 Cup heavy cream
Equal amounts grated Parmesan
  cheese and bread crumbs

Rinse the scallops and cut into ¼-inch slices. Melt the butter and sauté the shallots and mushrooms until tender. Add the wine and scallops and simmer 3 minutes. Pour off the liquid into another pan and stir it with Kneaded Butter over medium heat until thick and smooth. Add the lemon juice, eggs and cream and simmer over very low heat until thick, without letting the sauce come to a boil. Stir in the scallops and mushrooms, spoon into scallop shells, sprinkle with Parmesan and bread crumbs and brown lightly under the broiler. Serve immediately.

BROILED SCALLOPS WITH BLUE CHEESE

◆

Yield: Enough to serve 6

2½–3 Pints bay or sea scallops
8 Tablespoons butter
¼ Pound blue cheese

1 Tablespoon lemon juice
Rice ring (optional)

Rinse the scallops and press between paper towels to remove excess moisture. Dot a flat ovenproof baking dish with 2 tablespoons butter, melt under the broiler, stir in the scallops and broil for 2 minutes. Remove from the heat and pour off liquid. Simmer the blue cheese with the remaining butter, add the lemon juice and scallop liquid and reduce until fairly thick. Spoon over the scallops. Broil until cheese is flecked with brown. Serve hot in a rice ring or directly from the baking dish.

CASSEROLE OF SCALLOPS AND CORN, OLD MONTAUK

◆

Yield: Enough to serve 4 to 6

10 Ears fresh-picked and shucked corn on the cob
4 Tablespoons butter
1½ Pints scallops
3 Shallots, peeled and chopped
2 Tablespoons flour

1 Cup each light cream and milk
A pinch each of nutmeg, thyme and cayenne pepper
Salt and white pepper to taste
¼ Cup grated Swiss cheese

Cut the kernels from the corn and scrape the cob to extract the corn milk.

Preheat oven to 375 degrees F.

Melt the butter in a skillet and sauté shallots until transparent. Stir the flour into the butter remaining in the pan, pour in the cream, milk and seasonings, and stir until thick and bubbling. Stir in the corn milk and the scallops and immediately pour half into a buttered casserole. Add the corn in one layer and top with the remaining creamed scallops and, finally, the cheese. Bake 15 or 20 minutes, or until the sauce is just beginning to bubble and is flecked with brown. Serve immediately.

BAY SCALLOPS AND MUSSELS VINAIGRETTE

◆

Yield: Enough to serve 6

1 Pint bay scallops
3 Limes, juiced
3 Small white onions, peeled and
  thinly sliced

Salt, pepper and cayenne pepper
  to taste
1 Recipe Mussels Vinaigrette

Mix the scallops, lime juice, onion rings and seasonings and refrigerate for 4 hours or overnight, stirring frequently. Drain the liquid from the scallops and onions and toss them with the Mussels Vinaigrette, adding more vinaigrette if needed. Sprinkle with coarsely ground black pepper and cayenne.

BAY SCALLOPS AND MUSSELS, RÉMOULADE

◆

Scallops and mussels are also delicious when tossed with Sauce Rémoulade. Proceed exactly as in Bay Scallops and Mussels Vinaigrette but substitute Sauce Rémoulade for Sauce Vinaigrette.

◆――――――――――――――――――――◆

SQUID

Loligo pealei

◆――――――――――――――――――――◆

Their free-swimming lifestyle notwithstanding, squid are mollusks and as such do have a shell of sorts—a narrow, horny plate deep within their bodies. Squids, however, are cephalopods, a marvelously apt term meaning "foot-in-the-head." Each squid has a foot which is literally fused in part to its head, just above the eyes and around the mouth, a physical feature they share with other cephalopods . . . the larger squids, octopuses, and the Chambered Nautilus of poetic fame.

SQUID AS FOOD: Delicately flavored squid is considered by Mediterranean and Asian peoples every bit as desirable as the clams and oysters Long Islanders prize so highly. From a nutrition standpoint, lean squid meat contains about 18 percent protein (of a kind that is nutritionally perfect), and there is little waste—about 80 percent of the shellfish is edible, which makes it a very economical buy weight-wise in comparison to bonier finfish.

In the Hamptons, spring is the season when squid is at its tastiest and is most tenderly sweet. When you're buying fresh squid, look for pure, milky-white color. Just-caught squid should be cleaned and held in the refrigerator for one or 2 days prior to using to allow the muscular flesh to relax and release flavor. Squid you buy over the counter is most likely ready to use at once.

Here's how to clean the squid you bring home: holding the body in one hand and head and tentacles in the other, firmly but gently separate the two so that the inner sac (mantle) comes away with the head and tentacles. Cut the tentacles free from the head and mantle and set aside. Discard head and mantle. Remove the quill-like pen, then thoroughly wash the body and tentacles under cold running water, rubbing both with your fingers while you peel off the pinkish-brown skin. Rinse the squid in several changes of water until the water runs clear. Pat the pieces thoroughly dry before using.

DESCRIPTION: Sprightliest and most highly organized of all the mollusks (and most intelligent, too) squid have small, cylindrical bodies tapering to quill-like tails and two long, finlike tentacles extending from the head which are used to seize prey. The fused foot is highly differentiated, with the upper side divided into eight armlike appendages, each lined with a series of suckers for holding prey while the parrotlike beak tears it into bite-size pieces. The under part of the foot is a siphon which the squid uses to locomote (by shooting water through it) and for ejecting ink which not only clouds the water but takes on a squidlike shape, confusing any predator and allowing the squid to escape.

The eyes are prominent and well-developed, enabling the animals to spot danger, and the red and purple dots which ordinarily fleck its outer covering can be protectively contracted and expanded or changed in color for camouflage.

HABITS, HABITAT AND SEASON: Speediest of all the invertebrate swimmers, squid propel themselves through the water with amazing rapidity, backward, forward . . . in any direction. They are voracious and not at all fussy feeders that will take on any fish, large or small, and will even devour fellow squid.

Squid are surface-dwellers in depths ranging from quite shallow waters to those about a mile. Smaller squid travel in schools (although their giant counterparts prefer a solitary life), surfacing at night to feed. Schools in hot pursuit of prey are often beached on bright nights . . . victims of swimming too fast, too close to shore, in the glimmering moonlight.

The annual run of squid in East End waters usually begin in mid-spring. Local lore has it this run should be simultaneous with the blossoming of the dogwood trees but in recent years squid have been seen as early as late April. Squid are a commercial catch, usually taken by seines, traps, trawls and the like. The commercial value in the past was almost exclusively as bait, but acceptance is growing for this underutilized and abundant food source.

Last week in April last year we had a good last week. First week in May we got a lot of squid. Seventy-five cents a pound. Sixty cents, then down to fifty cents. That makes the money come in pretty fast when you get a ton, ton and a half, two tons a day. Yeah, last year first two weeks was good. Don't know what it's goin' to be this year. They sold that squid somewhere over in Korea somewhere. These squid we caught last year, I don't know how many thousand pound, they had orders for't go over t' Korea, Japan or somewhere. Father and Grandfather just used squid for bait. They ate some, I guess, in New York, but the most thing they caught 'em for was bait. I've seen 'em have the trap right full of squid an' they jest let 'em go. Wasn't worth nothin'. . . . Save what they had orders for for bait an' let the rest go. They're just like the blowfish. Years they come along by the ton and years they don't come at all.

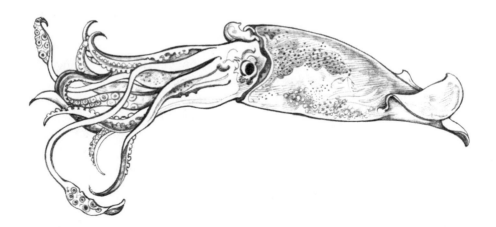

Unless otherwise indicated in your recipe clean the squid as directed in Squid as Food, cut it into ¼-inch thick circles or strips and blanch it in boiling water for 1 minute. Drain immediately. If it is to be baked or fried, omit the blanching and instead soak the squid in milk for 1 to 2 hours.

BATTER-FRIED SQUID

◆

Yield: Enough to serve 6

Squid is excellent dipped in flour, beaten egg and bread crumbs and deep-fried, but this batter-fried version is even more tasty.

6 Small cleaned squid cut in ¼-inch slices	*Oil for frying*
1 Recipe Fritter Batter with Beer	*Salt and pepper to taste*
	Sauce Tartare or Sauce Rémoulade

Clean the squid as directed but do not blanch it. Dry squid well, dip it in batter and deep-fry just until golden. Drain on paper towels. Season to taste and serve immediately with the sauce of your choice.

SPRINGS SQUID SALAD

◆

Yield: Enough to serve 6

6 Small squid cleaned, cut into
 ¼-inch circles and blanched
2 Small pearl onions, peeled and thinly
 cut into ¼-inch-thick slices
3 Tablespoons olive oil
Juice of one lemon
1 Large garlic clove, peeled and
 minced

½ Cup each *petite peas, cooked and
 chilled; pitted black-olive slices;
 and cooked, chilled and thinly
 sliced shrimp*
2 Teaspoons each minced Italian
 parsley, tarragon and chives
Salt and pepper to taste
Buttercrunch lettuce

Dry squid well and toss with onions, oil, lemon and garlic. Refrigerate 2 to 4 hours or overnight. Toss with remaining ingredients. Serve cold on lettuce leaves.

SQUID SALAD AIOLI: Follow directions for Springs Squid Salad but substitute for the oil and lemon juice ½ recipe Quick Aioli thinned with 2 tablespoons olive oil. Substitute for the peas, 1 cup cooked and chilled green beans cut into 1-inch pieces.

BAKED SQUID WITH TOMATO-NUT STUFFING

◆

Yield: Enough to serve 6

6 Small whole cleaned squid, soaked
 in milk
Double recipe Crunchy Tomato-Nut
 Topping
½ Cup fine white bread crumbs

3 Tablespoons white wine or tomato
 juice
¼ Cup melted butter
Fine bread crumbs
1 Recipe Garlic Butter

Preheat oven to 500 degrees F.

Dry squid inside and out and fill with double recipe of topping mixed with ½ cup bread crumbs and enough wine or tomato juice to moisten slightly. Brush filled squid with butter, roll in bread crumbs and arrange in an ovenproof glass baking dish. Dot with Garlic Butter and bake 10 to 15 minutes or until golden. Serve immediately with additional Garlic Butter.

SAUTEED SQUID ITALIENNE

◆

Yield: Enough to serve 6

6 *Small squid cleaned, cut into* ¼*-inch slices and soaked in milk*

¼ *Cup olive oil*

½ *Bermuda onion, peeled and cut into* ½*-inch dice*

2 *Garlic cloves, peeled and minced*

¼ *Teaspoon each powdered sage, thyme and fennel*

½ *Teaspoon sugar*

1 *Cup Fresh Tomato Purée*

½ *Cup white wine*

While still moist (not wet) dust squid with flour. Sauté until golden in hot oil and set aside with a slotted spoon. In the same pan sauté onion until tender (add more oil if necessary). Add garlic, herbs and sugar and sauté 1 minute more. Stir in tomato purée, white wine and squid and simmer until squid is tender and sauce is nicely thickened.

EDIBLE SEA SNAILS

In that vast underwater larder of oceans, bays and inlets from which seaside residents may garner their fill, Mother Nature has stocked a few surprises. These fascinating free groceries come intricately packaged and in a dazzling variety of textures and flavors.

Among the less familiar mollusks, gastronomically speaking, are the edible snails that belong to the gastropod branch of the huge mollusk clan. These have in common a soft, mantle-clad body capped by a graceful one-piece spiral shell and a flat, horny operculum or trap door on the back side of a large, muscular foot that neatly closes for protection whenever the animal withdraws into its snug shell. Although gastropod does translate "stomach-footed," the internal organs of these snails are protected well up within the shells. The animals only look as if they are traveling on their stomachs; actually, they move along on their joined head and foot.

On Long Island's shores are abundant edible snails, large and small, an intriguing bounty to be had just for the picking. While our early East Coast Indians savored them, as their excavated kitchen middens clearly indicate, and our European cousins still do, Americans—except for those of Italian descent who use the whelk for making *scungilli*—have almost totally by-passed this source of delicious seafood. Only in the tropics, where conch (pronounced "conk") lends its subtle goodness to chowders, salads and stews, and on the West Coast, where abalone, another gastropod relative, is relished, do edible snails come into their own.

PERIWINKLES

Littorina littorea

I was first introduced to periwinkles by a young Cockney woman, homesick both for her London home and her favorite English food, "winkles" —by her definition a "'andsome dish." Our camping trip that year was along the New England seacoast, and one of my most exciting discoveries was a strip of shore teeming with those very same spiral-shelled delicacies. I had had no experience with periwinkles, but, following my instincts and my limited knowledge of shellfish lore, I imprisoned my captives in a bucket of sea water, then scrubbed them and tried to dislodge the little snails from their shells with crochet hook and safety pin . . . to no avail. In desperation I plunged them into fresh sea water and warmed them for a few minutes to see what, if anything, would happen. Inadvertently I made an important discovery: the heat and the salt in the sea water firmed up the winkles slightly and made them easy to remove from their shells with the very same pin.

That evening we had a feast of Periwinkles in Garlic Butter, washed down by cold Chablis that seemed almost silver in contrast with the golden garlic sauce. We mopped up our plates and scrubbed out the tiny shells with thumbnail-size pieces of crusty, freshly baked, coarse peasant bread. Then we dipped ripe raspberries in gritty raw sugar and sipped black-velvet espresso. Even Patricia Draper, born within the sound of Bow Bells, agreed—it was indeed a "'andsome meal."

PERIWINKLES AS FOOD: Roasted or fresh, popular periwinkles are sold in great quantities all over Great Britain and Northern Europe, but are available only on a limited basis in American seafood markets. However, if you live or vacation near the shore these are so plentiful that they are remarkably easy for anyone so inclined to gather. Look in unpolluted waters for specimens at least ¾ inch high and ¾ inch wide or slightly larger—smaller winkles are not apt to be worth the bother . . . and be sure these are alive and moving when picked, and kept alive in a bucket of sea water until ready for use.

Removing the meats from the shells is simply a matter of bringing the shells just to a boil in sea water or salted water to cover, just long enough for the meat to shrink slightly so that the operculum, or trap door by which the animal secures itself inside the shell, drops off. A pin or nutpick will help dislodge the meat once the shell cools enough to handle. Serve swimming in melted garlic butter, in seafood stews, or dipped in fritter batter and fried. If you intend to serve the periwinkles in the shells, be sure to scrub these first.

DESCRIPTION: These small univalve mollusks are the most abundant snail of the Atlantic coast. Adult size is about one inch high and approximately one inch wide. The shells vary in color, most being olive or gray, but some have shells that are banded with a rich dark-red or reddish-brown.

HABITS, HABITAT AND SEASON: Vast colonies of periwinkles may be found along the coastline, clinging to rocks and pilings. They tend to be unfussy about their environment, and can be found in fresh or brackish as well as in salt water. In more northern waters look for them on rocks washed by the surf; further south you'll find them in marshy areas only lightly surf-washed.

Although *L. littorea* is the familiar "winkle" so dear to English hearts, it is a relative newcomer to western Atlantic shores. Whether it spread here from northern Europe by way of the Arctic or was accidentally introduced over a hundred years ago when its presence was first noted here is anyone's guess. What is known is that its absence during colonial times caused a break in the tradition of eating winkles that unfortunately persists to this day.

Remember, edible periwinkles are *sea snails* that release eggs and sperm into the water, just like other mollusks (oysters, clams, etc.) and as such the young go through a free-swimming stage before settling down on or near shore. Escargots are *land snails* that are born live and intact with their shells. They are, however, so similar in taste and texture that they may be used interchangeably.

PERIWINKLES "BOURGUIG-NONNE"

◆

Yield: Enough to serve 6 to 8

60–80 Periwinkles, with well-scrubbed shells, simmered in white wine to open

1 Recipe Snail Butter

Chill the periwinkles and remove them from their shells. Put a little snail butter in each shell, insert a cooled, cooked periwinkle, cap with more snail butter and chill for several hours. Preheat oven to 450 degree F. Place snails on snail plates (or a baking sheet) and bake for 10 to 15 minutes. Serve immediately with crusty bread.

PERIWINKLES IN MUSHROOMS WITH WALNUTS AND CHUTNEY

◆

Yield: Enough to serve 6

36 Periwinkles, removed from well-scrubbed shells
18 Large mushroom caps
6 Tablespoons butter
½ Cup walnut halves, broken in pieces
¾ Cup chutney, coarsely chopped
Watercress, well washed

Sauté mushroom caps in butter until barely tender. Set the caps aside and keep them warm. Add the periwinkles, nuts and chutney to the pan and sauté for 3 to 5 minutes, or until the sauce thickens somewhat. Fill the mushrooms with the mixture, making sure there are 2 snails in each cap. Broil for 1 minute. Arrange three caps on a bed of watercress on each of 6 plates. Serve hot.

PERIWINKLES IN CREAM

◆

Yield: Enough to serve 6

4 Shallots, peeled and finely chopped
6 Tablespoons butter
3½ Tablespoons flour
2 Cups heavy cream
4 Egg yolks, beaten
96 Periwinkles, cooked and removed from their shells
Salt and white pepper to taste
18 Fried Garlic Toast Triangles
Cayenne pepper
Chopped fresh parsley

Sauté the shallots in butter until transparent, stir in the flour and then the cream and continue stirring until the sauce boils and thickens. Beat in the egg yolks, then stir in the periwinkles, salt and pepper. Transfer to the top of a double boiler and stir over hot water until sauce thickens further. Do not boil. Arrange 3 toast points on each of 6 plates. Spoon the creamed periwinkles in the center, sprinkle with cayenne and edge with parsley.

SEAFOOD SALAD, HAMPTON BAYS

◆

Yield: Enough to serve 8

1½ Cups each cooked and chilled periwinkles, cubed lobster meat, steamed and chilled mussels, and cooked, shelled shrimp, split lengthwise
½ Cup each finely chopped celery and whole scallions
1 Tablespoon each minced fresh thyme and marjoram
1½ Cups Sauce Mayonnaise
Juice of half a lemon
Salt, pepper and Tabasco to taste
Tomato wedges and hard-cooked egg quarters

Toss shellfish, celery, scallions, herbs, mayonnaise, lemon juice and seasonings together. Spoon into a mound on a serving dish, chill lightly and serve garnished with tomato and egg.

PERIWINKLES VINAIGRETTE

◆

Yield: Enough to serve 6

96 Periwinkles, removed from their shells

1 Recipe Sauce Vinaigrette

3 Scallions, with 2 inches green tops, sliced

1 Avocado, peeled and pitted and cut into ⅓-inch cubes

¼ Cup pimento, cut into ½-inch squares

1 Tablespoon minced fresh tarragon leaves

Lettuce cups

Mix all the ingredients but the lettuce in a glass bowl and refrigerate for several hours. Serve cold in lettuce cups.

WHELKS

There are three kinds of whelks residing in Long Island's waters . . . the waved whelk, the knobbed whelk and the channeled whelk.

WAVED WHELK

Buccinum undatum

This 3- to 4-inch snail is the most common whelk of the Atlantic coast, distributed most abundantly from Maine to Massachusetts but also occurring in large numbers as far south as New Jersey. A lovely shell, the spire of the velvety, yellowish-brown exterior is sculpted with wavy longitudinal ridges, smoothed with a white or yellow porcelainlike interior.

KNOBBED WHELK

Busycon carica

The largest mollusk in Atlantic waters north of Cape Hatteras, the knobbed whelk, which averages 9 inches in length but occasionally reaches 12, has a large, fleshy body with a broad muscular foot. The gray pear-shaped shell has a low, twisted spire and a ring of blunted, knobby spines encircling the top of its wide body whorl. The opening is a dull or a polished shiny brick-red, depending on whether the ocean bottom the particular whelk frequents is stony or sandy.

Carnivorous sea snails like these whelks feed by first breaking oyster, clam and mussel shells with repeated blows from their own knobby shells, then by extending their long flexible snouts (the ends of which have rasp-like tongues with sharp teeth) into these victims and systematically sawing them into bite-size tidbits. The knobbed whelk's fondness for bivalves, incidentally, is what gives its own meat a special succulence.

CHANNELED WHELK

Busycon canaliculatum

Although it averages only 6 to 9 inches, the channeled whelk has the same pear shape and low spire of the knobbed whelk, but here the whorls of the spire are flattened and the big body whorl makes up almost the total length of the shell. The living animal's external gray shell is covered with a thick brown periostracum etched with revolving lines. The shell interior is yellow.

WHELKS AS FOOD: Whelks are available chiefly at specialty or Italian fish markets, where the shelled and cleaned meat is sold as *scungilli*. Whelk meat is also often incorrectly called conch (conk), a name given to a group of sea snails common to tropical waters.

To prepare the whelks you have gathered for cooking, wash the shells thoroughly, place them in a large kettle (or two), add enough water to barely cover, and bring to a boil. Cook one hour and drain well. Remove the whelk from each shell, then remove and discard the soft, flabby viscera that clings to the bottom and inside of the body, leaving only the firm, fleshy foot. Split the foot open with your fingers or a knife and remove and discard the operculum.

Scrub the meat all over inside and out with a terry-cloth dishcloth or small towel under running water to eliminate all sand and foreign matter. Return the meat to the kettle, cover with water to a height of 5 inches above the surface of the meat, and bring to a boil. Cook 3 to 4 hours, or until tender. Large pieces may require longer cooking.

Cut into ¼-inch slices and cook as directed in recipes or freeze in serving-size portions in lightly salted water.

HOW TO CATCH: Folding nets similar to those used in crabbing baited with fish heads or skimmer clam pieces should lure some waved whelks, but the channeled and knobbed varieties are not so easily caught. It's best to skin-dive for these in waters from 12 to 20 feet. If you prefer to do

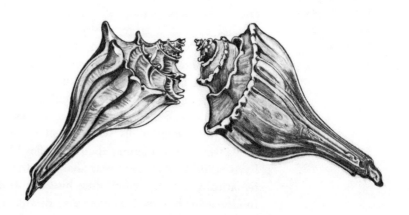

your hunting on dry land, check out local beaches right after rough-and-tumble storms. Areas where empty shells litter shores are good places to look.

Shelter Island's Shellfish Ordinance prohibits returning any whelk to town waters. Along with starfish, whelks do much damage to clam beds.

SCUNGILLI MARINARA

◆

Yield: Enough to serve 6

2½ Pounds precooked whelk meat, thinly sliced
3 Cloves garlic, crushed
2 Medium-size onions, sliced
¼ Cup olive oil
1 Recipe Ripe Tomato Purée

2 Cups Fish Stock
½ Teaspoon each salt, black pepper, dried oregano, basil and fennel seed
1 Bay leaf
Cayenne pepper to taste
Pasta (optional)

In a heavy pot, sauté the whelk, garlic and onions in the oil until the onions are tender. Add the purée, stock and seasonings. Simmer 2 hours, increasing the heat a little toward the end to thicken the sauce if necessary. Serve hot, with pasta if desired.

WHELK FRITTERS

◆

Yield: Enough to serve 4 to 6

1 Cup flour
½ Teaspoon each salt and baking powder
Cayenne pepper to taste
4 Eggs, beaten
1½ Cups finely minced or ground whelk

2 Tablespoons melted butter
1 Large onion, peeled and finely ground
½ Teaspoon each powdered thyme and marjoram
Oil for deep-frying
Lime wedges

Sift together flour, salt, baking powder and cayenne. Beat in eggs and butter. Stir in whelk, onion, thyme and marjoram. Deep-fry by teaspoonfuls in hot oil until golden brown on both sides, turning once. Serve hot with lime wedges.

SEA URCHINS

Echinoidea

These spiny echinoderms with their beautiful globular shells are almost totally unknown as food in this country, yet the roe of sea urchins is considered a great delicacy and is much prized in other parts of the world, particularly in France, Italy, Japan and the West Indies.

SEA URCHINS AS FOOD: Since the only part of the animal that's eaten is the gonads (roe), both female ovaries and male testes, it follows that the only time for sampling this delicacy is during spawning season. For sea urchins in the vicinity of Long Island, this can take place at any time from late summer to early spring. Commercially, sea urchins are available seasonally at very specialized seafood markets, but because they are highly perishable, they are only shipped during cold months, principally at Christmas. Especially at this time of peak demand, orders must be placed well in advance.

Plan on 6 to 12 sea urchins per person in order to serve enough roe to really taste. Hold each urchin carefully with a thick cloth (or wear a rubber glove) and cut away spines all over the body with a pair of kitchen shears. Turn so the top of the animal is down and its Aristotle's lantern is up, and with scissors or a very sharp knife, begin at the midpoint of the shell and cut off the bottom or mouth half, leaving the top intact. An alternative way to get to the roe, which is firmly attached to the top half of the animal, is to crack the mouth apparatus all around its edges with a hammer. The point is to get at and discard both the interior liquid and fibrous insides, leaving only the 5-branched golden roe. Spoon out the roe, rinse and drain it, then chill well. Serve with lemon quarters, accompanied by crusty French or Italian bread and chilled white wine. Or serve the roe in place in the shell.

DESCRIPTION: Sea urchins (or sea eggs) are close relatives of starfishes and sand dollars, with whom they have many features in common. Atlantic shores are home to only 2 of the 500-odd varieties of sea urchins found world-wide. Most common from Maine to New Jersey is the green sea urchin, whose scientific classification, *Strognylocentrotus drobachiensis*, is a mouthful of Latin for such a small creature. About 2 inches in size and green or greenish-purple in color, it is similar in appearance to a chestnut burr.

The second urchin common along Hampton shores is the one-inch purple sea urchin (*Arbacia punctulata*), in shallow waters where the bottom is pebbly or shell-covered. Color ranges from deep purplish-black to much lighter shades; the thick spines are tipped with brown.

HABIT AND HABITAT: Both green and purple sea urchins are found in rock crevices or under rocks, at any point along the shoreline where they can take shelter from pounding surfs. Gather them during spawning season from late summer to early spring. These are gregarious animals, usually found thickly clustered on rock surfaces or bottoms of tide pools, so once you locate one, finding the rest should pose no problem at all. The sharp spines can cause painful injury, however, so wear heavy rubber or garden gloves when gathering.

CRUSTACEANS

Beneath the serene surface of our East End waters teems an underwater population so vast, so diverse and intricate, as to make our populous neighbor New York City seem uncrowded by comparison.

Some of the most desirable of these tenants are the crustaceans, a profusion of animals in surprising variety of form, each supremely adapted to its unique way of life.

The ecological value of crustaceans is twofold. On the one hand, as scavengers—some exclusively vegetarian, others not—they purify their own marine neighborhoods of dead organic matter. On the other hand, they themselves provide a rich and varied supply of food for other marine wildlife.

From a culinary standpoint, crustaceans are unparalleled. Some of the most delectable and memorable dining experiences are those which feature such eminent crustaceans as lobster, shrimp or crab. All are exceptional. A crustacean by any other name, shape or size would taste as sweet.

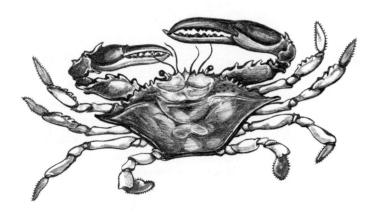

EDIBLE CRABS

Edible crabs, the most highly developed of all crustaceans, are well represented along Long Island's shores. Although they vary surprisingly in size and color, there are only two main types . . .

The *swimming crabs*, with their paddle-shaped final set of legs (these include the blue claw crab, green crab, lady crab and the nonedible fiddler crab) and . . .

The *walking crabs*, with final legs that end in points, enabling them to scuttle quickly over land (rock crab and Jonah crab).

BLUE CLAW CRAB

Callinectes sapidus

These bright-blue and -red scrappers are prized in their hardshell or softshell stages and are second only to lobsters as America's favorite seafood.

BLUE CLAW CRAB AS FOOD / CLEANING AND COOKING BLUE CLAW AND ALL OTHER EDIBLE CRABS: Crabs can live quite a while out of water if they're kept cool and moist and out of the direct sun. If you catch your own, cover with layers of wet seaweed or in a pinch, with wet newspapers. Fresh, uncooked crabs from your fish store should be nice and lively. Avoid crabs that don't respond when prodded.

To cook, plunge live crabs into a kettle of rapidly boiling water to cover, allow the water to return to a boil, then simmer until the shells turn bright red. Drain thoroughly. When cool enough to handle, hold the crab firmly and

- Pry off and discard apron flap underside.
- Pry off and discard top shell.
- Break off large claws and set aside.
- Pry off back areas to expose the membrane covering the crabmeat.
- Hold crab in both hands and break it down the middle so that there are an equal number of legs on each side.
- Remove membrane cover by prying loose with knife or slicing lengthwise through the center of each half.
- Pick out the meat . . . and enjoy.
- Crack the claws and eat the meat in these. There is a little meat in the smaller legs, but many think it's not worth the work it entails to get at it.

If the softshell crab you purchase has not already been cleaned, here's how to do it yourself. Using a sharp knife, lift up and remove the apron on the crab's rear undersurface. Turn the crab over and use scissors to cut off the eyes and the face just back of the eyes, then lift up the pointed sides of the top covering and dig out and discard the spongy gill material underneath. Wash and dry the crab thoroughly before cooking.

Taken commercially in the East End by dredges, trawls, nets, pots, seines and so on, blue claws are sold in both the hardshell and softshell stages, cooked in the shell both fresh and frozen, and the meat alone is sold fresh, frozen and canned as

Lump meat: big, solid chunks of body meat, for use where texture and appearance is important, in cocktails or salads;

Backfin: smaller pieces of the above;

Flake meat: all other white meat, in small flakes or shreds. Flake and lump meat may be combined in same package.

The claw meat, while sweet and delicious, is sometimes tinged with brown and is not generally used in dishes where appearance counts.

As a softshell, the whole crab is not only edible but the soft, white outer covering is high in nutritive value. Market season for softshells usually extends from the end of April through August.

Avoid buying any crab meat that smells of ammonia or has a fishy odor.

Softshell crabs are best bought live; frozen softshells are likely to be soggy and have a wrinkled look.

DESCRIPTION: The multicolored shell color varies from a rich sea-green to a deep blue-green, with legs tinged with bright blue. The spiny forward surface of the shell culminates in the center in two sharp protruding spines tinged with red, and the underbelly is creamy white.

Characteristically, blue claws are almost twice as wide as they are deep, with the shell of the adult reaching 6 to 8 inches across.

HABITS, HABITAT AND SEASON: The blue claw is almost always in a belligerent mood. These are active predators, very scrappy and combative, ready to attack at the slightest provocation not only fellow blue claws but even towering monsters like you.

Favorite habitats are muddy bottoms of inland waters (harbors, bays, inlets, river mouths, preferably brackish) where they swim nimbly about in search of prey or back up into mud, where, with only stalked eyes and great forward claws showing, they wait for unsuspecting prey.

Every crab you catch should be examined to determine whether it is male or female (the female's abdomen is broad, the male's narrow and pointed). If your catch should prove to be an egg-carrying female (eggs are orange to brown), be sure to return her to her home—all local shellfish ordinances prohibit the taking of such blue claw crabs, called "sponge" crabs.

MOLTING: As each crustacean grows, it casts aside its too-small horny chitin covering. While this shedding process goes on, the animal has already begun forming a new shell underneath, so that by the time the old shell splits off, the crab is somewhat protected by the delicate makings of a new set of armor. Since this new shell hardens in about a week, while the animal, defenseless and exhausted, hides out as best he can, the softshell blue claws that do make it to market are usually those caught in the stage just preceding the shedding of their shells. Knowledgeable crabbers spot these "shedders" by their loose shells, which reveal a thin white line of new shell forming underneath. These are isolated in special submerged cages, and sent to market as soon as they shed.

Should your crab catch include several of these soon-to-molters, you can try the same trick. Just make sure that the sea water in which your trophies are confined circulates freely, or they will soon perish from lack of oxygen.

SEASON AND WHERE FOUND: Blue claw crabs can be captured at any time, whenever and wherever you find them. The most productive time of year for taking them is summer through fall; the most productive places, brackish waters near the mouths of estuaries and mud bottoms of harbors, bays and inlets. Docks and other structures with wood pilings are good places to drop your lines or even to crab with a long-handled net, since blue claws often surface to dine on barnacles.

HOW TO CATCH: Blue claws might show up unexpectedly at the end of your line while you're angling for other trophies. They will grab virtually any kind of bait offered for anything, if you are in the right place. Just tie a weighted sinker to your baited line, and drop it into the water. With a little practice, you can keep several lines going at once. Test from time to time by lifting your line until the sinker clears bottom, to see if any blue claws have found your offering worthy of interest. As soon as you hook one, pull him slowly toward you, then scoop him up with a long-handled net. Or, if you're fast enough, and the crabs are plentiful— forget the hook and line and use the long-handled net as a scoop.

Another popular crabbing technique is the use of a folding trap baited with pieces of meat or a fish head tied securely to the middle of the bottom of the trap. Lower the trap into the water with the sides flat. As soon as the crab tiptoes in, pull up the trap, raising its sides and penning the crab. Keep a healthy distance from the claws of any blue claw you catch: even captured specimens will have no compunctions about taking you on, despite the disparity in size.

SHELLFISH ORDINANCES:

Shelter Island prohibits the taking of hard blue claw crabs less than 5 inches point to point, or softshell crabs less than 3 inches point to point. Taking of sponge (egg-bearing) crabs from town land is prohibited at any time.

Southold prohibits taking of blue claw crabs less than 5 inches from point to point of upper shell. No one may take more than ½ bushel (2 pecks) of blue claw crabs for noncommercial purposes in any one day, and no sponge crabs may be taken at any time.

Southampton prohibits the taking of sponge crabs.

ROCK CRAB

Cancer irroratus

Rock crabs and their near kinsmen the Jonah crabs differ from blue claw crabs in being walkers rather than swimmers. Their market value is not nearly as high as the blue claw's, but they are just as delicious.

ROCK CRAB AS FOOD: The meat from these crabs is no different from that you'd pay fancy prices for in your seafood market. Because of their small size these won't provide as much meat as blue claw crabs do, but the first pair of claws yield large chunks of meat, and in large specimens, the second claws may do the same.

DESCRIPTION: These crabs, not surprisingly, mainly frequent rocky beaches, although they are also partial to sandy bottoms. Smaller than either the blue claw or Jonah and slightly oval in shape, their mature size is about 3 inches long and 4 inches wide. The rear legs, nicely adapted for scuttling about on land, are pointed rather than paddle-shaped, and the first pair of claws are short and heavy. Shell color is yellow-brown, festooned with closely-set brown dots.

WHERE FOUND: Between tides, these may be found hiding out beneath the sand or gravel pockets that form on rocks, or seeking the comfort of tidal pools that the retreating tide leaves behind. Mature rock crabs tend to go it alone in deeper waters, while younger specimens will congregate together in tidal pools.

HOW TO CATCH: Notorious bait stealers, rock crabs often show up on the end of your line when your hook is set for some other seafood variety. Reel in your unexpected prize slowly, then lift it from the water with a long-handled net. This latter is also your most efficient tool when you are purposefully setting out to scoop these small but tasty crustaceans from their tidal pools.

JONAH CRAB

Cancer borealis

DESCRIPTION: The Jonah is larger and bulkier than the rock crab, with thickset legs and a rough-textured, brick-colored upper shell and yellowish underbelly.

JONAH CRAB AS FOOD: The meat of the Jonah is equal in quality and flavor to that of any other crab, but its unusually hard shell makes extracting it a chore. Other crabs are marketed whole, but the meat of the Jonah must be extracted before it can be sold to retailers, which diminishes its commercial importance. Jonahs also have some value as bait.

HABITS AND HABITAT: Limited in range to northeast Atlantic shores—eastern Long Island is just about the farthest south it goes—the Jonah is only fairly abundant locally, although there are signs that it may be staging a comeback.

This crab prefers clear, open waters to the muddy, inshore sites favored by the rock crab, and while it is often found scuttling over rocks, it foregoes the safety of rock crevices and it is therefore more often a prey of shore birds.

HOW TO CATCH: Jonahs can be scooped up in long-handled nets from rocky beach areas between tides, or captured by any other method used to snare crabs.

GREEN CRAB

Carcinides maenas

A pugnacious little member of the swimming crab tribe which is equally adept at burrowing into sand. Its last pair of legs are only slightly flattened and are not as paddle-shaped as those of the blue claw, but since they also have points like the walking crabs, green crabs are nicely adapted for either land or water.

GREEN CRAB AS FOOD: While primarily used as bait (particularly for catching blackfish), green crab meat is also quite lovely and, to the crab enthusiast, very much worth the effort it takes to extract it. Cook it as you would any crab. If your booty should include a few potential "shedders," hold them in reserve for a softshell feast. Prepared after molting, the shell is no problem, and the flavor is equal to that of the succulent blue claw crab.

DESCRIPTION: Easy to spot because of its bright-green shell peppered with yellow dots, the green crab is relatively small, about 1½ to 2 inches long and a slight bit wider. An immigrant to Atlantic shores, it has become widespread in range up and down the coast since its evident introduction from Europe to Cape Cod during the early nineteenth century. Because of its fondness for soft clams, it has now achieved considerable status as a major pest of the commercial clam industry.

WHERE FOUND AND HOW TO CATCH: Green crabs are often so abundant that snaring bagfuls of them becomes an easy matter of turning over loose stones, hunting in tidal pools or on rocks around jetties, or of enticing them out of their burrows by scratching the sand with a rake. Watch out for your fingers when handling: despite its small size, the green crab won't hesitate to attack as you approach. Its Latin name, *maenas*, means "frenzy," and frenzied is a perfect description of its scrappiness. Eminently pragmatic in such matters, the French, who appreciate green crab's culinary possibilities, call this tiny aggressor *"crabe enragé."*

LADY CRAB

Ovalipes ocellatus

Also called sand crab or calico crab.

LADY CRAB AS FOOD: The lady crab is very edible despite its small size, although the meat is quite hard to get at. Cook as you would any crab.

DESCRIPTION: Another plentiful and aggressive crab species well suited for its double-life of swimming and scooting about on sand or rocks. The large, menacing pincer claws belie its delicate name. Take care—the lady is capable of inflicting a painful, very unladylike bite on the toes or fingers of unsuspecting crabbers or bathers.

The lady's paddle-shaped back legs that end in tips, plus its thin, pointy side claws (3 to each side) enable this crab to burrow quickly into loose sand, where it remains alert to both food opportunities and danger and is protected from being swept away by the surf.

Size averages about 3 inches in diameter. The white carapace is speckled with red and purple dots, giving it a calico effect. Its favorite foods are clams and small fishes.

WHERE FOUND AND HOW TO CATCH: Look for lady crabs between tides on rocky or sandy beaches below the surf line. Since these are relatively exposed areas, lady crabs can usually be found just below the sand, so take your rake.

STEAMED BLUE CRABS

◆

Yield: Enough to serve 10 to 12

Crabs are perhaps most delicious steamed live, but since this means that they die more slowly, I prefer to plunge them first into boiling water, then withdraw them once they have stopped moving and proceed with the following recipe. If you follow this more humane cooking method, steam the crabs 15 to 20 minutes instead of 20 to 30.

½ Cup crab-boil spice
½ Cup salt
3 Cups white vinegar

3 Cups beer or water
3 Dozen lively blue crabs

Mix the crab-boil, salt, vinegar and beer or water. Arrange half the crabs in a very large pot with a rack and a tight-fitting lid. Pour half the crab-boil over the crabs, add the remaining crabs and remaining crab-boil. Cover tightly and steam 20 to 30 minutes, or until the crabs turn a fiery red. Serve hot with melted butter or cold with your favorite seafood sauce.

GRILLED SOFTSHELL CRABS

◆

12 Softshell crabs, prepared as
  directed on page 288
1 Cup Seafood Marinade

Baste the bottoms of the crabs liberally with marinade. Arrange bottom-side-down on a barbecue grill placed one foot above low coals. Grill 5 minutes, basting the tops of the crabs liberally with marinade. Turn and grill 5 minutes more. Serve immediately.

CHESAPEAKE CRAB GUMBO

◆

Yield: Enough to serve 6

Recipes travel as easily up and down the coast as fishing boats. Captains, who are often excellent cooks themselves, sail the new ideas back to their own kitchens, complete with their special creative touches.

1 Large onion, peeled and coarsely
  chopped
2 Ribs celery, coarsely chopped
3 Large garlic cloves, peeled and
  minced
5 Tablespoons butter
6 Tomatoes, peeled, seeded and
  coarsely chopped

2 Cups okra pieces
½ Teaspoon each leaf thyme and
  chili powder
2 Teaspoons each salt and sugar
¼ Teaspoon black pepper
1 Bay leaf
1 Pound picked-over cooked crabmeat

In a 5-quart soup pot sauté the onion, celery and garlic in butter until the onion is transparent. Add the tomatoes, okra and seasonings. Cover and simmer 1 to 1½ hours, or until the gumbo is thickened. Add the crab and simmer just until heated through. Serve in shallow bowls, over rice.

SEA CAPTAIN'S CRAB CAKES

◆

Yield: 1 dozen cakes

1 Pound picked-over cooked crabmeat
2 Tablespoons lemon juice
2 Eggs
½ Cup Enriched White Sauce
2 Tablespoons mayonnaise
1 Teaspoon dry mustard
1 Tablespoon Worcestershire sauce

½ Cup soft bread crumbs
Salt and pepper
¼ Cup milk
¼ Cup dry bread crumbs
1 Teaspoon paprika
Flour
Oil for frying

Sprinkle crabmeat with lemon juice. Beat 1 egg lightly, then beat in White Sauce, mayonnaise, mustard and Worcestershire sauce. Gently stir in soft bread crumbs and crabmeat. Season to taste with salt and pepper. Chill until firm enough to handle. Shape the crabmeat mixture into 12 cakes.

Beat together the remaining egg and the milk. Mix the dry bread crumbs and paprika. Dip each cake first in flour, then in the egg mixture and finally in the seasoned bread crumbs. Fry to golden brown in ¼-inch hot fat, turning once. Serve hot.

BACKFIN CRABMEAT SAUTÉ

◆

Yield: Enough to serve 4 to 6

1¼ Pounds picked-over, cooked backfin crabmeat
1 Tablespoon lemon juice
¼ Cup shallots, peeled and finely chopped
6–8 Tablespoons sweet butter
Salt and pepper
3 Tablespoons dry sherry

Sprinkle crabmeat with lemon juice. Sauté shallots in the butter until transparent. Do not brown. Add the crabmeat and cook over low heat just until heated through. Sprinkle with salt and pepper to taste. Splash with sherry, then stir quickly but gently. Serve in individual casseroles.

CURRY-CORNCAKES WITH HAM AND CRAB

◆

Yield: Enough to serve 8

⅔ Cup corn meal
2 Cups hot milk
1½ Cups very hot water
¾ Cup melted butter
2¼ Cups flour
1½ Teaspoons baking powder
1 Teaspoon each baking soda, curry powder and salt
1½ Tablespoons sugar
2 Large eggs, beaten
¼ Pound baked ham, very thinly sliced
½ Recipe Backfin Crabmeat Sauté
½–1 Cup White Sauce

Beat corn meal into hot milk and water until smooth and lump-free. Cool to room temperature, then beat in butter, flour, baking powder, soda, curry powder, salt, sugar and eggs. Batter should be thin. Cook 4-inch pancakes on a lightly oiled hot griddle until bubbles appear on the surface.

Top each cake with a slice of ham and a spoonful of sautéed crabmeat mixed with a little cream sauce. Serve flat or rolled up.

CRABMEAT CAKES, HAMPTON BAYS

◆

Yield: Enough to serve 6

1½ Pounds picked-over cooked crabmeat
1½ Cups bread crumbs (or a little more)
3 Eggs, beaten
⅓ Cup chopped pimento
1 Teaspoon dry mustard
½ Teaspoon each fresh thyme and tarragon
Salt and pepper to taste
Flour
Oil for frying
Recipe Sauce Aurore

Mix the crabmeat, bread crumbs, eggs, pimento and seasonings (add more bread crumbs if the mixture doesn't hold together when you form it into cakes). Roll lightly in flour, then fry to a golden brown in hot oil. Drain and serve with Sauce Aurore.

CRABMEAT REMICK

◆

Yield: Enough to serve 6

This dish is rich and satisfying . . . and it takes only minutes to prepare.

1 Pound cooked lump crabmeat, picked over
2 Cups Sauce Mayonnaise
½ Cup chili sauce
½ Teaspoon each dry mustard and paprika

¼ Teaspoon celery salt
Tabasco sauce to taste
6 Strips crisp bacon

Heap crabmeat in 6 scallop shells and heat briefly in the oven. Mix mayonnaise, chili sauce and the seasonings, spoon over the crabmeat and top with bacon. Slide under the broiler for a few minutes to glaze. Serve immediately.

SOUTHAMPTON SEAFOOD SOUFFLÉ

◆

Yield: Enough to serve 4 to 6

3 Tablespoons butter
3 Tablespoons flour
1 Cup cold milk
½ Teaspoon salt
⅛ Teaspoon white pepper
A pinch of nutmeg
A sprinkle of cayenne pepper
4 Egg yolks

6 Egg whites at room temperature
Salt
¾ Cup cooked crabmeat and/or lobster and finely flaked fish, or a mixture of all of these
5 Tablespoons finely grated Swiss cheese

Melt butter in a heavy saucepan over medium heat. Blend in flour, then stir in milk, salt, pepper, nutmeg and cayenne. Cook, stirring continuously, until sauce thickens slightly. Remove the pan from the heat. Beat in the egg yolks, one at a time, until all have been incorporated. Set mixture aside to cool.

Preheat oven to 400 degrees F.

Beat egg whites with a pinch of salt until they are stiff but not dry, and gently fold one cup of these into the cooled white sauce to lighten it. Fold in remaining egg whites and seafood with an up-and-over motion. Butter a soufflé or other deep baking dish, add 3 tablespoons of the cheese and roll the dish until all inner surfaces are covered. Turn the egg mixture into it and bake for 3 minutes, then lower the temperature to 375 degrees F. and bake 35 minutes. Quickly sprinkle the remaining cheese over the soufflé and bake 5 to 10 minutes more, or until set and nicely browned. Serve immediately.

EATON'S NECK SEAFOOD CRÊPES

◆

Yield: Enough to serve 6

An excellent hurry-up Sunday supper, especially if the crêpes are waiting in the freezer.

1 Recipe Crêpes
3 Cups mixed cooked, flaked fish, crabmeat and cooked and chopped shrimp

Hot Enriched White Sauce or Curry Sauce
Grated Parmesan or Swiss cheese

Prepare crêpes as directed. Bind the cooked fish or shellfish with just enough sauce to make a thick mixture and arrange by spoonfuls down the center of each crêpe. Roll up the crêpes as they are filled and place side by side in a lightly buttered flameproof baking dish. Sprinkle generously with cheese and set under the broiler just long enough for the cheese to lightly brown. Serve immediately.

ASPARAGUS SEAFOOD CRÊPES: Follow directions for Eaton's Neck Seafood Crêpes (above), but roll up 2 thin asparagus spears (steamed until barely tender) in each crêpe along with the creamed crab.

COLD CRABMEAT CRÊPES

◆

Yield: Enough to serve 6

1 Recipe Crêpes
1 Recipe Crème Fraîche
2 Cups crabmeat

1 Recipe Carrot Twigs
⅓ Cup thinly sliced scallions
Scallion tops

Prepare crêpes as directed. Cool and spread thinly with the cream. Arrange a little crab, one or 2 Carrot Twigs and sliced scallion down the center of each. Roll up and decorate with a dab of cream and thin strings of scallion top. Serve cold.

◆────────────────────────────◆

LOBSTER

Homarus americanus

◆────────────────────────────◆

This King of Shellfish is the largest of all crustaceans and is justifiably renowned for its unique flavor and the succulence of its meat.

LOBSTERS AS FOOD: Baby lobsters begin life as soft-bodied, transparent green-eyed creatures in that planktonic stew on the water's surface, at the mercy of wind and water currents, dining on and in turn being dined upon by other microscopic marine animals. On Day Two of this tenuous existence, they begin the first of the many molts they will undergo as long as they live, or at least as long as their growth persists. As molt follows molt, lobsters finally reach harvestable size (about 1⅓ pounds), a sign that they are at least 5 years old and have molted roughly 2 dozen times. These lively adolescents are most frequently available, but lobsters can and do grow as large as 45 pounds, with not too discernible loss of tenderness or flavor.

The pincer claws of live lobsters are formidable weapons, so handle with care! Hold the animal from behind when removing it from its trap, then secure the claws with rubber bands or wedge a sharp wooden peg against the elongated half of each pincer, not only to keep your fingers intact but to prevent lobsters confined in close quarters from cannibalizing each other. Never use or buy any lobster you suspect might be dead. Live lobsters are vigorously active. The more gymnastics your prisoner performs, the fresher he probably is. Listless specimens, while safe to eat, have usually been in a holding tank overlong, giving the meat plenty of chance to shrink and lessen in flavor. Aside from the visible presence of roe, a distinguishing characteristic in females is a wider tail; also, the tiny leglike flippers found just under the upper section of the animal's body at the point where the tail and upper body join are thin and featherlike in the female, long, spiny and shell-covered in males.

While perhaps more limited in culinary uses than either crab or shrimp, lobster does lend itself to a stunning variety of preparations. The easiest way to prepare the lobster for serving, or to cook the meat for inclusion in other dishes, is by boiling or steaming.

To boil: Boil enough salted water (or sea water) to cover the number of lobsters you are cooking (for salted water, use one tablespoon salt to each quart water). Plunge the lobsters head-first into the kettle to quickly kill them, then, counting from the time the water returns to a boil, allow 8 to 10 minutes for a one-pound lobster, adding 3 minutes more for each additional quarter-pound of weight. It won't make any difference to the lobster, since the boiling water kills him instantly, but if you're reluctant to boil or steam him alive, you can sever his spinal cord first by inserting the point of a sharp knife into the juncture between the body and tail. His legs might still wriggle as he hits the hot water but he'll be quite dead.

To steam lobsters, place them in a single layer on a rack over 3 inches of boiling water. Cover and cook them the same length of time as above, counting the time from when the steam reappears. If you must steam more lobsters than will fit on one layer, remember that those on the bottom will be ready for eating sooner than those on the top layer.

To prepare boiled or steamed lobster for eating, place the lovely thing on its back, cool it enough to handle, then starting at the head end, split the shell with a sharp knife all the way to the end of the tail (use scissors if you like, to cut the membrane on the tail). Cut away and discard both the small, gritty sac at the back of the head and the long black vein that runs from head to tail. Leave intact the coral roe and/or the brownish-green liver, or tomalley.

An alternate method for splitting cooked lobster is to cut first toward the tail from the place where the tail and body join, then turn and slice through the shell to the head. Clean as above.

Loosen the body meat with a fork and crack the claws with a mallet or nutcracker.

To prepare lobster for broiling, first sever the spinal cord by placing the lively animal on its stomach and cutting into the point between the body and tail. Turn the lobster over and cut through the undershell lengthwise. Remove and discard the black vein and the sac behind the head. Leave the coral and green parts intact. Crack the claws, then arrange the lobster on its back in a broiling pan; brush with melted butter and season to taste with salt and pepper. Broil 7 to 10 minutes for a 1½- to 2-pound lobster, slightly longer for larger.

Lobster can also be split into sections for such dishes as Lobster à l'américaine. To prepare, sever the spinal cord first as directed above, then cut off the tail. Next, crack the pincer claws and cut off the legs on both sides, then cut the body and head into pieces. Be sure to remove the sand sac at the back of the head and the black vein running along the animal's spinal column. Remove and reserve the tomalley.

Precooked lobsters are generally a waste of money unless your dealer is absolutely reliable, and even then you should probably be present to check on the health and vigor of your lobsters before they are killed. The temptation is great, from a profit point of view, to dispose of recently deceased lobsters to customers who don't know (or seem to care) about the quality of the product they are buying. Only if you are desperate for lobster shell for a flavored butter or a sauce should you resort to a precooked specimen . . . and then try first to coax a shell from your fish-store owner before you make the purchase.

DESCRIPTION: A long, cylindrical body with an extended abdomen differentiates the lobster from the edible crabs. A one-piece shell, linking the head and thorax, covers the back. The powerful tail makes a superb swimming tool, propelling the animal quickly backward through the water and also assisting the walking legs and swimmerets when the animal travels in forward. The powerful . . . and dangerous . . . front walking legs (pincers) are held always at ready, claws raised like a boxer with his guard up. Shell color locally is dark green-blue, with the upper surface generally speckled with green-black spots (Maine lobsters tend to be darker than their Long Island cousins); the familiar red color appears during cooking. The animal is common from Labrador to North Carolina.

I went lobsterin'. Five, six years ago I went lobsterin'. But   quit it. They stole your pot and stole your lobsters and put you right out of business. Had to quit. These fellows that come out fishin', they see all these lobster pots around . . . they just follow temptation and take 'em. They drop you in a can of beer once in a while for your trouble. You could do good lobsterin' now if they'd leave your pots alone. Lobsters're still there. Yeah.

If you put your pots offshore the draggers get into 'em. Leastwise they used to. Now they have some kind of a metal thing . . . you can leave it under the water for two or three days an' it comes right up by itself 'bout the time you're ready to come by for it. Like they used to do during prohibition, you know. Say you're comin' in offshore with a helluva lot of liquor and the revenue boats get too close. They'd throw the liquor overboard and weight it down heavy with sugar. When the revenuers got tired of lookin' . . . after so-and-so many hours the sugar would dissolve an' up the liquor would float. You just come around an' pick it up. Well now, they got the same kind of thing for lobster pots. Only of course they don't use sugar.

HABITS, HABITAT AND SEASON: This largest marine invertebrate makes its solitary home in the rocky-bottomed depths and is better at walking than at swimming. A nighttime diner, the lobster shuns daylight, hiding from the sun in the shelter of sand or rocks, then emerging to stalk for prey at night. Any limb injured in battle or by accident repairs itself each time the animal molts, in a kind of spontaneous regenerative process.

Lobsters may be taken at any time in local waters but few, if any, are harvested in winter. Frigid water temperatures cause them to "mud up" (a semidormant state), but come May or June they travel inshore to spawn (fishermen begin setting out their pots at this time). Females are known locally as "eggers" and set free if caught.

Hatchlings that manage to survive the hostile surface environment in which they spend the early weeks of life undergo at least 4 successive moltings before sinking to the ocean floor, where they spend the rest of their lives. At first, these young lobsters stay in relatively shallow waters, hiding out under stones and such, out of sight of hungry bottom-feeding fish, but once they grow to 4 to 5 inches, they venture into deeper waters.

Lobsters offered by fish markets and restaurants during the winter are usually residents of Maine waters, a hardier breed than their East End relatives. These tasty fellows can be found at depths ranging from 10 to 200 feet, but draggers operating at depths of 600 feet also get large hauls.

Local lobstermen tend pots during a season that runs from the end of April right up until late fall, when the pots are gathered to avoid loss or storm damage.

HOW TO CATCH: To catch lobsters, you'll need to set out pots expressly designed for them. These are usually wooden boxlike structures with one or more funnel-shaped netted openings. Each pot is equipped with weights to hold it on the bottom, but new pots might initially need the added weight of a couple of heavy stones or bricks until the wood absorbs water and becomes less buoyant.

Tie a rope to each of your pots and secure its loose end to a marker buoy before lowering it away. Check the pots by pulling them up hand over hand (unless you can afford the motorized winches commercial lobstermen use to lift their pots). Occasionally you may lose a pot to stormy seas or a strong tide, a clear signal to add more weight to keep your pots stationary, but most often any losses are due to poachers, who make off with the lobsters as well as the pots.

Baits: Almost any fish or fish part, alive or dead, will be considered a treat by passing lobsters. Use bunkers, any so-called junk fish (sea robins are popular) or heads and tails from cleaning your fishing catch. Attach your bait with wire to the mouth of the funnel-shaped aperture in the pot. When checking your pots, be sure to take along extra bait in case you find your trap full and your bait gone. Also bring along your gauge (see below).

PERMITS: Before you launch any lobstering enterprise, be advised that New York State law requires you to be a New York State resident and to acquire a state permit. The allowable limit on these crustaceans is 6 per day for noncommercial purposes and a length of 3 and 3/16ths inches, from rear end of eye socket to the end of the body, *without* including the tail in this measurement. You *must* release smaller lobsters. Both the law regarding size and the regulation concerning who may or may not set out pots and how many pots may be set out are strictly enforced.

State law specifies that lobsters may be taken only with pots, traps, otter trawls or similar devices, by skin-diving with scuba equipment, or by hand; in neither of the latter two methods may you use a spear, gig, gaff or other penetrating device.

Three types of permits are now available:

A resident noncommercial permit costs $5—you must be a resident of New York State for at least 6 months to obtain one. The legal limit for setting out lobster pots for individual family use is 5 pots, and only 6 lobsters may be harvested in any one day. If you intend to dive for your catch, you must still get a permit and can take only 6 lobsters daily.

If 5 pots or traps and 6 lobsters daily won't satisfy your family's hankering for this delicacy, or if the thrill of catching them and stocking your own larder turns you into an avid lobsterman, then you must get a commercial license. A Resident Commercial permit costs $50 and allows you to take as many lobsters as you can catch, as long as you use only legal methods.

There is also a non-Resident Commercial permit, costing $75, which allows holders to take lobsters from restricted areas. For permit information, write:

Shellfish Permit Office
New York State Department of Environmental Conservation
Building 40
State University of New York
Stony Brook, N.Y.   11794

Buoys: State law also requires you to attach your pots or traps to buoys or other identification markers, each painted in distinctive color or colors which identifies these pots as yours. Your permit number, painted in a contrasting color, must be plainly visible on each buoy or marker. Poaching has been the biggest problem in recent years. Disturbing other people's traps or pots is a violation punishable by law.

A *gauge* designed to measure the size of your catch is a small piece of metal conveniently notched at 3 and 3/16ths inches. To make sure any lobster you take is of legal size, measure by hooking one end of the gauge into the rear end of the animal's eye socket; as long as the notch touches any point along the main shell (thorax) of the animal without extending out over the segmented tail when the gauge is held in a straight line, you may keep your prize. Should the notch of the gauge extend past this juncture of thorax and tail, you *must* return the animal to the water.

Strict laws also protect egg-carrying female lobsters, so inspect the underside of each of your catches; even if it is of legal harvestable size, an egg-carrying female may *not* be taken.

ORANGE LOBSTER IN CHAMPAGNE

Yield: Enough to serve 4

◆

4 Small lobsters, with spinal cord severed

3 Cups champagne

1½ Cups orange juice, strained

⅓ Cup Cointreau

Blanched fresh tarragon fronds

Simmer the lobsters in their shells in the champagne until the shells are red. Cool slightly. Cut the inside shell of the tail with scissors and carefully remove it without breaking the tail meat or separating it from the shell of the body. Crack the lobster claws and remove without breaking the claw meat or separating it from the arm of the pincer. This should give you an entire lobster with just the claws and tail shelled. Repeat this process with the other 3 lobsters.

Reduce the champagne liquid, orange juice and Cointreau until the sauce is syrupy. Carefully poach the lobsters in the syrup until they are hot and slightly undercooked. Arrange on a platter or individual plate and keep warm. Simmer fronds of fresh tarragon for a second or two in the syrup and arrange attractively all around the lobsters on the platter or plate. Spoon a little hot sauce carefully around the lobsters so as not to disarrange the tarragon. Serve immediately.

LOBSTER PERNOD GOURMET

◆

Yield: Enough to serve 6

6 Lobsters, cut shell and all into 2-inch pieces

2 Cups white wine

6 Tablespoons butter

2 Tablespoons flour

¼ Cup water

¼ Teaspoon each salt and white pepper

½ Cup Pernod

2 Tablespoons each minced fresh tarragon and chervil

Fried Garlic Toast Triangles

Simmer the lobster pieces (without the heads) in the wine in a large chafing dish or kettle until the shellfish are bright red. Set the lobster aside and add the butter and the flour mixed with ¼ cup water to the wine. Add the salt and pepper and stir constantly until the sauce boils and thickens. Float the Pernod on the sauce, and when it warms set it aflame. Stir in the tarragon, chervil and lobster and simmer until the lobster is just cooked through. Serve hot over Garlic Toast.

EAST END PAELLA

◆

Yield: Enough to serve 10

1 Chicken, cut into pieces
½ Cup butter
3 Cloves garlic, peeled and crushed
2 Cups rice
½ Teaspoon each saffron, salt and fennel seed
2 Cups each hot Fish Stock and chicken broth
2 Lobsters cut into 1-inch pieces
2 Dozen each clams, mussels, scallops and shrimps, all in the shell and well scrubbed

1 Chorizo (or other highly seasoned sausage), sliced
1 Cup diced pimento
1 Tablespoon each minced fresh oregano, thyme, marjoram and sage
½ Teaspoon each salt and freshly ground black pepper
3 Tablespoons finely chopped parsley
Lemon wedges

Fry the chicken in the butter and garlic until it is golden brown on all sides. Set the chicken aside, add the rice and stir over medium heat until the rice is golden. Stir in the saffron, salt and fennel seed, Fish Stock and broth and simmer until all the liquid is absorbed and the rice partially cooked.

Preheat the oven to 350 degrees F.

Butter paella pan or deep Dutch oven, arrange in it half the chicken pieces and half the lobster, clams, mussels, scallops, shrimp and sausage. Sprinkle with half the pimento, herbs, salt and pepper. Cover with ¾ of the rice, add the remaining chicken pieces, shellfish, sausage, pimento and herbs. Cover with the remaining rice and bake for 40 to 50 minutes, adding a bit of Fish Stock or broth from time to time if needed. Sprinkle with parsley and serve with lemon wedges.

STOCKS, SOUPS, CHOWDERS AND STEWS

COURT BOUILLON AND FISH STOCK

Once your fish has flipped his tail for the final time in that natural semi-salt or salt soup in which he grew, he must be carefully handled to enhance his "just-caught" goodness. If your fish is to be returned to a liquid environment to prepare him for your table, there are a handful of basics that are important. Although purists insist that a few fish with more distinctive flavors (striped bass, sea bass, etc.) need only a salt/water cooking solution for poaching or for making soups and chowders, to my mind the flavor of the finished dish is considerably enhanced by the judicious use of a combination of liquids.

There are two basic cooking liquids useful in seafood cookery; for the fish aficionado as well as for the angler-cook, mastering both is fundamental. The first is Court Bouillon; the second is Fish Stock or *fumet*.

A Court Bouillon is a seasoned liquid meant not only to add flavor but also to keep the fish cooked in it an appealing color. As the name implies, a *court* ("short") bouillon takes only a short while to cook. It can be made in several different ways, but the basic ingredients are most often water and wine (or vinegar or, occasionally, lemon juice). Other components may be milk, vegetables and seasonings. After the mixture is simmered, skimmed and strained according to directions, the fish poached in it will contribute its own juices. The Court Bouillon can then be reduced to serve as the base for a sauce, or frozen for future use.

A fish stock or *fumet de poisson* is a very rich court bouillon made by including fish bones, heads and other trimmings and usually a much larger proportion of wine to water. The concentrated and flavorful fish essence that results from combining and cooking down fish, wine, water, vegetables and seasonings makes a marvelous base for fish soups and sauces.

Although fresh is best, both court bouillons and stocks may be prepared in advance and stored in your freezer. To prepare for freezing, strain, then pour into pint or half-pint containers, leaving ½ inch of headroom at the top, or freeze in ice-cube trays and place in sealed freezer bags. Freeze at 0 degrees F. or below.

A NOTE ABOUT FISH HEADS AND TRIMMINGS: Fish heads are the basis of many a marvelous fish stock, but unless you are sure these were caught less than 24 hours before, it's best to remove the gills before setting the heads simmering in the stockpot, since these respiratory organs are quickest to take on off-odors and off-tastes. It is also a good idea to avoid using for stock any parts from such strong-flavored fish as mackerel, mullet, dogfish or skate. However, if some fresh shellfish shells are handy, you may include these.

COURT BOUILLON WITH VINEGAR

◆

Yield: Enough to poach a 5-pound fish. Increase in proportion for larger fish

Simplest of all court bouillons is water to which salt is added, and perhaps a bay leaf or two. Only a bit more complex is this well-seasoned version for cold fish.

9 *Cups water*
¾ *Cup white wine vinegar*
2 *Medium-size onions, each peeled and studded with 2 whole cloves*
1 *Leek, white part only, coarsely chopped*
2 *Medium-size carrots, scraped and quartered*

2 *Ribs celery, coarsely chopped*
2 *Sprigs parsley*
1 *Bay leaf*
½ *Teaspoon dried thyme*
2 *Teaspoons salt*
12 *Black peppercorns, cracked*

Combine all ingredients in a large pan or fish poacher and bring to a boil. Skim off scum. Simmer, uncovered, for about 30 minutes. Allow to cool, then strain through a double thickness of dampened cheesecloth.

WHITE WINE COURT BOUILLON

◆

Yield: Enough to poach a 5-pound fish. Increase in proportion for larger fish

8 *Cups water*
2 *Cups dry white wine*
2 *Medium-size onions, peeled and thinly sliced*
2 *Medium-size carrots, scraped and sliced*
1 *Clove garlic, peeled and cut in half*

1 *Large bay leaf, crumbled*
4 *Sprigs parsley*
Salt to taste
½ *Teaspoon dried thyme*
1 *Tablespoon black peppercorns, crushed*

Bring all ingredients to a boil in a large pan or fish poacher, then skim off scum. Simmer, uncovered, for 30 minutes. Cool and strain through a double thickness of dampened cheesecloth.

RED WINE COURT BOUILLON: Follow directions for White Wine Court Bouillon but substitute dry red wine for the white.

COURT BOUILLON WITH MILK

♦

For poaching cod family members and other white-fleshed fish. Combine 4 cups water and one cup milk in a saucepan, season with 1½ teaspoons salt, a pinch of white pepper and one tablespoon lemon juice, then bring mixture just to a simmer and add the fish. If larger amounts of liquid are necessary, increase, using the same proportions of milk to water.

FISH STOCK (FUMET DE POISSON)

♦

Yield: About 2 quarts

2 Tablespoons butter
½ Cup each chopped onions, carrots and celery
2 Pounds fish heads (with gills removed), bones and trimmings

5 Cups water
4 Cups dry white wine
2 Tablespoons chopped parsley, stems only
Salt

Melt the butter in a saucepan and cook the vegetables until soft, without browning. Add the fish parts, water and wine and bring the mixture to a boil, skimming off any scum that rises. Reduce the heat, add the parsley stems and simmer, uncovered, for about 20 minutes. Season to taste with salt and strain through several thicknesses of dampened cheesecloth. Keep refrigerated.

QUICK AND EASY FISH STOCK

♦

Useful in emergencies.
Yield: About 2 cups

1¼ Cups water
1 Cup bottled clam juice
1 Cup dry white wine or dry vermouth

1 Small onion, peeled and thinly sliced
3 Sprigs parsley
Salt (optional)

Combine all ingredients and simmer gently over low heat until liquid reduces in volume by one third. Strain and adjust seasoning before using; clam juice tends to be rather salty.

TO CLARIFY FISH STOCK: To produce a crystal-clear stock suitable for use in aspics, refrigerate the strained stock long enough for any fat particles to rise to the surface, then skim these off. The stock should be completely de-greased for clarification to succeed.

For each 4 cups stock, you will need 2 egg whites and 2 egg shells. Beat the whites until frothy, crush the shells, and add both to the stock. Bring the mixture slowly to just under a boil, stirring continuously. Lower the heat and allow the stock to barely simmer for 15 minutes, then carefully remove from the heat without disturbing the thick surface foam and allow to stand for about 10 minutes. Meanwhile, arrange a dampened linen towel over a colander and place both over a clean pan. Gently push the scummy foam aside and ladle the clear stock into the colander.

ICED FISH, MEAT AND BUTTERMILK SOUP

◆

Yield: Enough to serve 6

One of the most delicious of cold summer soups.

3½ Cups each cold plain yogurt and buttermilk
1 Cup cooked, peeled and chopped shrimp
2 Cups cooked, flaked flounder (or other fine white-fleshed fish)
1 Cup cooked, chopped ham
2 Medium-size cucumbers, peeled, seeded and chopped
5 Scallions with 3 inches green tops, finely chopped

2 Small dill pickles, finely chopped
¼ Cup finely chopped fresh parsley
2 Tablespoons finely chopped fresh fennel
1 Tablespoon minced fresh thyme
2½ Tablespoons lemon juice
Salt and freshly ground black pepper
6 Hard-cooked eggs, sliced
Chopped parsley

Combine the yogurt and buttermilk and mix well. Stir in the shrimp, fish, ham, cucumbers, scallions, pickles, fresh herbs and lemon juice. Season to taste with salt and pepper. Refrigerate for at least 4 hours. Thin with a bit of cold milk if the soup is too thick for your taste. Adjust seasonings. Serve cold, garnished with slices of hard-cooked egg and a sprinkle of chopped parsley.

SPRING GARDEN LEEK AND MONKFISH SOUP

◆

Yield: Enough to serve 6

If the winter is not too severe I generally manage to coddle a crop of late-planted leeks through to early spring. In May, when it's time to contemplate my new garden, I harvest a refrigerator drawer full of both fat and pencil-slim green beauties to squander as wantonly as pleases me. This potent green broth was a result of just such an excess plus a gift of monkfish fillet.

4 ¾-inch-thick leeks, with 5 inches green tops
7 Cups lightly salted water or Fish Stock
1¼ Cups uncooked rice
2 Pounds well-trimmed monkfish, cut into ½-inch dice

2 Medium-size onions, peeled and cut into ½-inch dice
1 Tablespoon minced fresh thyme or ½ teaspoon dried thyme leaves
Salt to taste
A sprinkle of cayenne pepper

Split the leeks, wash them well and cut into ½-inch-thick slices. Bring the water or stock to the boil, add the rice and leeks, lower the heat, cover and cook 10 minutes. Add the fish, onions and thyme. Cover and continue cooking 5 to 10 minutes or until rice is tender and fish flakes. Season to taste with salt and cayenne pepper. Serve immediately. The onions should be a little crisp; the fish should have about the firmness of lobster.

Occasionally I prepare one soup several ways . . . depending upon the fish or shellfish available. In the following variations, serve the shellfish in their shells for a more attractive presentation.

VARIATION I: Substitute 3 dozen scrubbed small littleneck clams for half of the monkfish and cook until the shells open. Stir in 2 tablespoons flamed cognac and serve immediately.

VARIATION II: Substitute 4 dozen scrubbed mussels for the monkfish and cook until the shells open. Stir in 3 tablespoons tomato paste and serve immediately.

VARIATION III: Substitute 3 dozen scrubbed whole scallops in the shell for half the monkfish. Stir in 2 tablespoons Pernod and a pinch of cayenne and serve immediately.

NAPEAGUE CURRIED POTATO-FISH SOUP

◆

Yield: Enough to serve 6

Just the dish to whip up after an afternoon's fishing on a blustery day. Equally delicious served cold, thinned with a little light cream.

5 Cups Fish Stock
5 Medium-size potatoes, peeled and cut in ½-inch dice
2 Medium-size onions, peeled and coarsely chopped
2 Large cloves garlic, peeled and finely chopped
2–3 Teaspoons curry powder
3 Tablespoons minced fresh Chinese parsley (cilantro or coriander) leaves

½ Teaspoon salt
2–3 Cups milk
1 Cup heavy cream
3 Tablespoons butter
½ Teaspoon freshly ground black pepper
1½ Pounds boneless, skinless fish fillets (preferably cod, haddock, sea robin or tilefish) cut in 1-inch pieces

Put the stock in a large saucepan, add the potatoes, onions, garlic, curry, 2 tablespoons of the parsley and the salt, and cook, tightly covered, for 30 minutes. Remove the soup from the heat and press through a strainer, or purée in a food processor or blender. Add enough milk to thin slightly, bring to just under a boil, add the fish and simmer over low heat until fish is just cooked through. Add the cream and reheat. To serve, dot with the butter and sprinkle with pepper and remaining tablespoon parsley.

CREAMY SHRIMP SOUP, HAMPTON BAYS

◆

Yield: Enough to serve 6

4 Large leeks, white part only,
  coarsely chopped
3 Ribs celery, finely chopped
4 Tablespoons butter
4 Tablespoons flour
3½ Cups Fish Stock
3 Cups water
1 Teaspoon salt
1½ 8-ounce packages cream cheese,
  at room temperature

1½ Cups plain yogurt
3 Egg yolks
1½ Pounds shelled shrimp, cut in
  ½-inch pieces
White pepper
2 Tablespoons each finely chopped
  fresh chives and dill

Sauté the leeks and celery in the butter, stirring once or twice, until the vegetables are soft but not brown. Add the flour, blend until smooth, then when golden in color add the stock, water and salt. Cook over high heat, stirring continuously, until the mixture comes to a boil; reduce heat to low and allow the soup to simmer, stirring occasionally, for 15 minutes.

Meanwhile, cream together the cream cheese, yogurt and egg yolks. Remove the soup from the heat and set aside to cool for 5 minutes. Stir in the cream cheese mixture, pressing out any lumps with the back of a spoon, then stir in the shrimp. Return the soup to the heat and allow to barely simmer, stirring constantly, until the soup is piping hot. Do not allow the soup to boil or the egg yolks will curdle. Season to taste with white pepper and additional salt, if necessary. Serve immediately, garnished with the herbs.

AUNT EMILIE'S CREOLE SOUPE DE POISSON

◆

This family recipe adapts beautifully to Hampton ingredients.

2 Tablespoons each olive oil and
  peanut oil (or similar vegetable oil)
2 Medium-size onions, peeled and
  coarsely chopped
1 Medium-size leek, split, thoroughly
  rinsed and finely chopped
4 Medium-size cloves garlic, peeled
  and minced
3 Medium-size carrots, scraped and
  finely chopped
4 Medium-size ribs celery, finely
  chopped
2–3 Tablespoons Pernod
¼ Teaspoon each saffron threads,
  dried thyme, and powdered sage

3 Tablespoons flour
1½ Cups water or Fish Stock
1 Cup white wine
Salt and freshly ground black pepper
  to taste
2 Pounds various skinless fish fillets,
  such as dogfish, sea robin,
  bluefish, blackfish and/or tile, cut
  into 2-inch pieces
½ Cup milk
1 Cup heavy cream
Garlic croutons

Heat the oils in a large, heavy kettle and sauté the onions, leek, garlic, carrots and celery until the onion is golden. Add Pernod and set aflame. Stir in the saffron, thyme, sage and flour. Add the water or stock, mix until smooth, then add the wine and stir until mixture begins to lightly boil. Add salt and pepper. Cover and simmer 10 minutes. Stir in the fish, milk and cream and simmer until fish is barely cooked through. Place a crouton in each soup plate and ladle soup over.

CHEF CORTINO'S FISH SOUP, MADRID

◆

Yield: Enough to serve 6 generously

I acquired this recipe some years ago from a marvelous Spanish chef. Since my Spanish was poor and his English nil, the dish changed but did not seem to suffer in the translation. It has become a favorite spring Sunday night supper.

¼ Cup olive oil
3 Cloves garlic, peeled and crushed
1 Lobster, cut in 1½-inch pieces
1 Pound shrimp, shelled and de-veined
⅓ Cup brandy
1 Large onion, peeled and coarsely chopped
4 Medium-size tomatoes, peeled, seeded and chopped
1½ 6-ounce cans tomato paste
1 8-ounce jar pimento-stuffed olives, drained

1 Teaspoon each *salt and sugar*
1 Tablespoon *minced fresh basil*
¼ Teaspoon *freshly ground black pepper*
6 Cups Fish Stock
1 Cup dry white wine
1½ Pounds tilefish or other firm, white-fleshed fillets, cut in 1½-inch pieces
12 Small hardshell clams, scrubbed

Heat the oil in a large skillet and sauté the garlic for 2 minutes; add the lobster and shrimp pieces and cook over medium heat until the shellfish turn red, about 5 minutes. Sprinkle with the brandy and ignite, shaking the skillet until the flames die. With a slotted spoon, remove the shellfish from the pan and set aside. Add the onions to the oil remaining in the skillet and sauté until golden, then stir in the tomatoes, tomato paste, olives, seasonings, stock and wine. Partially cover the pan and allow the soup to simmer over low heat for 20 minutes.

Add the fish pieces and the clams and cook just long enough for the fish to flake and the clams to open. Return the reserved shellfish to the soup and cook a minute or two, or just long enough to heat through. Adjust seasonings. Serve immediately.

FAR EAST EGG-DROP FISH SOUP

◆

Yield: Enough to serve 6

It's a wonderful luxury to have leeks growing in your own garden all winter, just waiting to team up with those early-spring visitors to our Hampton waters . . . weakfish, blackback flounder and the like.

6 ½-inch-thick leeks with 5 inches green tops
7 Cups lightly salted water or Fish Stock
1¼ Cups uncooked rice
1 Teaspoon cornstarch mixed with ¼ cup water
1 Egg beaten with 2 teaspoons water
2 Pounds weakfish fillet cut into 1-inch cubes
¾ Cup sliced water chestnuts
Soy sauce

Split leeks, wash well and cut into ½-inch-thick slices. Bring water or stock to the boil; stir in rice and leeks. Cover, lower heat and cook 10 minutes. Bring soup back to a boil, stir in cornstarch mixture and continue stirring until the soup is clear and somewhat thickened (about 5 minutes). Pour egg mixture into soup, stirring all the while. Add fish and water chestnuts. Lower heat to simmer and cook five minutes or until fish flakes. Serve immediately with soy sauce.

GRANDFATHER'S FISH AND POTATO SOUP WITH SIEVED CREAM CHEESE

◆

Yield: Enough to serve 8

6 Large potatoes, peeled and cut into ½-inch cubes
2 Medium-size onions, peeled and chopped
5 Cups water
1 Teaspoon salt
4 Tablespoons butter
3 Tablespoons flour
1 Pound boneless, skinless halibut fillets, cut into 1-inch pieces
4 Teaspoons finely chopped fresh dill
1 Tablespoon finely chopped fresh chervil
2 Teaspoons finely chopped fresh mint
2 Cups milk
1½ 8-ounce packages cream cheese
2 Tablespoons finely chopped fresh parsley
1 Tablespoon finely chopped fresh chives

Put the potatoes and onions in a pan with the water, add salt and cook until the potatoes are just tender. Melt the butter in a large soup kettle and stir in the flour until the mixture is well blended, then add the vegetables with their cooking liquid and cook over low heat, stirring constantly, until the soup thickens slightly. Add the halibut, dill, chervil, mint and milk, and simmer for 5 minutes or so or until the fish is just cooked through. Adjust seasonings. Force the cream cheese through a fine sieve with the back of a spoon and divide it equally among the soup bowls. Pour the hot soup over the cheese and garnish with parsley and chives before serving hot.

MON-LING'S SOUTHAMPTON SEAFOOD SOUP WITH MISO

◆

Yield: Enough to serve 6

East End fish meet Far East ingredients. Result: a quick and unusually tasty soup.

8½ Cups Fish Stock
1 Cup white miso
1½ Pounds weakfish fillet, cut in ½-inch cubes
1 Pound shrimp, cooked, peeled, de-veined and coarsely chopped

1 Pound tofu (bean curd), cut into ½-inch cubes
½ Pound well-washed spinach, cut diagonally into ½-inch-wide strips
Togarashi (hot red pepper) or Tabasco

Bring the stock to a boil. Stir one cup of stock into the miso until free of lumps, then gradually return the miso mixture to the soup, stirring it in well. Add the fish, shrimp, tofu and spinach and cook 5 minutes longer. Stir in a few drops of togarashi. Serve piping hot.

LOUSE POINT WHELK CHOWDER

◆

Yield: Enough to serve 6

3 Cups precooked whelk meat cut into ¼-inch-thick strips
Flour
½ Cup bacon, chopped
2 Medium-size onions, peeled and coarsely chopped
6 Tomatoes, peeled, seeded and coarsely chopped

3 Cups Fish Stock or whelk cooking liquid
½ Teaspoon each fennel seed, thyme, oregano and black pepper
3 Large potatoes, peeled and cut into ½-inch cubes
Finely chopped parsley
Finely chopped dill

Dip the whelk in flour and fry with the bacon and onion until lightly browned. Stir in the tomatoes and simmer for 15 minutes. Add the Fish Stock or cooking liquid and the seasonings. Simmer for 2 hours, or until the whelk is tender, adding a bit more liquid if necessary during cooking. Add the potatoes and enough liquid to cover and stew until the potatoes are tender. Adjust the seasonings. Serve with small bowls of parsley and dill to spoon into the chowder.

BACK EAST BLACKFISH CHOWDER

◆

Yield: Enough to serve 6

3 Dozen mussels, well scrubbed
3 Cups white wine
3 Cups Fish Stock
6 Potatoes, peeled and thickly sliced
3 Large onions, peeled and thickly sliced
½ Teaspoon salt
Flour
2 Cups ham, coarsely chopped

2 Tablespoons each fresh, minced dill, Italian parsley and chives
1 Cup each heavy cream and milk
2 Pounds blackfish fillets, cut in 2-inch strips
Butter
Tabasco

Open the mussels by heating briefly in the wine. Reserve the mussels in their shells, then pour the liquid carefully into another pot, leaving any grit behind. Add the Fish Stock to the mussel liquid with the potatoes, onions, salt and ham and cook until the potatoes are nearly tender. Stir in the flour and cook 2 minutes. Add the herbs, cream and milk and bring to just under a boil, stirring constantly. Add the fish, lower the heat and simmer until the fish flakes. Add more salt if necessary. Put a pat of butter, 6 mussels and 2 drops of Tabasco in each bowl as you serve the chowder.

FISHERMAN'S HADDOCK CHOWDER
◆

Yield: Enough to serve 6

The Portuguese ancestry of some Hampton and New England fishermen influences in particular their chowders and stews.

½ Cup salt pork cubes	¼ Teaspoon each white pepper,
1½ Cups chopped onion	saffron and powdered cumin
4 Cups peeled and cubed potatoes	2 Pounds haddock, cod or whiting,
6½ Cups Fish Stock	cut in 2-inch pieces
2 Tablespoons vinegar	Salt to taste

Render the pork over low heat in a deep, heavy soup pot, stirring until cubes are brown on all sides. Remove the pork pieces with a slotted spoon and keep them warm. Add onion, potatoes, Fish Stock, vinegar and seasonings and boil until potatoes are nearly done. Add the fish, lower the heat and continue cooking until the fish flakes. Season to taste. Serve immediately, sprinkled with pork cubes.

SMITHTOWN TOMATO-FISH STEW
◆

Important here are the "hard-edge" potato cubes. These must be cooked through, but the corners should not become too rounded, nor should the cubes become mushy. This may sound picayune—but the chunky counterpoint to the tender fish is quite lovely. Also important is the sweet, fresh taste baking imparts to the tomatoes, a Victorian technique seldom used nowadays.

10 Large fresh tomatoes, peeled and seeded	1½ Teaspoons curry powder
2 Tablespoons sugar	½ Teaspoon each dried thyme and freshly ground black pepper
3 Tablespoons sweet butter	Salt to taste
1 Large (or 2 medium) whole leeks, split and well washed	3 Pounds cod, hake or pollock fillets, or any combination of these, cut into 1½-inch fingers
3 Large potatoes, peeled	Sour cream (optional)
2 Cups Fish Stock or water	

Preheat oven to 400 degrees F. Cut tomatoes into eighths and arrange in a large baking dish so wedges do not overlap too much. Sprinkle with sugar and dot with 1½ tablespoons of butter. Bake 30 minutes. Cool and purée.

Cut the leek, both white and green, into ½-inch pieces and sauté in the remaining butter for 15 minutes or until limp and tender. Cut the potatoes into ½-inch cubes and add with stock or water to the leeks. Cover and bring to a rolling boil, then remove from the heat and let stand, covered for 15 minutes. Add the tomato purée and seasonings and bring the mixture to a boil. Add fish and boil until barely tender. Correct seasoning. Serve hot, with dollops of sour cream if desired.

SAND SHARK STEW, PARMESAN
◆

The sand shark (or dogfish) has skin as rough as emery boards that can make your fingernails disappear like magic during the cleaning process. Once you've passed this barrier, the meat is as sweet as that of any fish. In this recipe, two salty ingredients, anchovies and Parmesan cheese, provide a nice counterpoint.

2 Large onions, peeled and coarsely chopped
3 Tablespoons sweet butter
1 Teaspoon flour
A large pinch of mace
2 Anchovy fillets, minced (or 1 teaspoon anchovy paste)
2 Cups Fish Stock

3 Pounds sand shark, filleted and cut in 1-inch pieces
1 Cup heavy cream
Salt to taste
Black pepper
Grated Parmesan cheese
Cayenne pepper

Sauté the onions in 2 tablespoons of the butter until onions are transparent. Sprinkle flour over and cook, stirring, for 2 minutes. Add mace, anchovies and stock. Bring just to a boil, stirring constantly. Add fish and cream and simmer until the fish is just cooked through (about 8 to 10 minutes). Season to taste with salt and black pepper. Serve steaming hot, with remaining tablespoon of butter, Parmesan cheese and cayenne pepper.

VARIATION I: Add 2 cups peeled, cubed potatoes to the onions and an extra cup of cream to Sand Shark Stew, Parmesan.

VARIATION II: Add 1 tablespoon each minced fresh parsley, thyme and sage in place of the mace and anchovies in Sand Shark Stew, Parmesan.

VENEZUELAN GROUND-ALMOND FISH STEW

◆

Yield: Enough to serve 6

Each country brings its unique set of ingredients to fish cookery and Hamptons residents always seem to be on the lookout for a new approach. The almonds included here furnish a particularly nice texture. An interesting variation would be the substitution of one pound of bay scallops for one pound of the flounder.

2 Pounds flounder fillets
1 Pound whiting fillets
½ Pound shrimp, shelled, cleaned and split lengthwise
2 Medium-size onions, peeled and coarsely chopped
¾ Pound cooked ham, coarsely chopped
2 Tablespoons butter
1½ Quarts Fish Stock or bottled clam juice
3 Cups chicken broth
White wine (or additional stock or broth)

½ Cup uncooked rice
1⅓ Cups ground blanched almonds
1½ Teaspoons salt
1 Teaspoon black pepper
½ Teaspoon saffron threads (or, for the budget-wise, curry powder)
½ Teaspoon thyme leaves
4 Hard-cooked eggs, peeled and chopped
6 Scallions, finely chopped
¼ Cup finely chopped parsley

Cut flounder and whiting into 2-inch strips and set aside with the shrimp. In a soup kettle, sauté onions and ham in butter until onion is translucent. Add stock, broth and wine, and bring to a boil. Lower heat and stir in rice, almonds, salt, pepper, saffron (or curry) and thyme. Cover and cook over low heat for 15 minutes.* When ready to serve add enough wine, stock or broth to bring stew to desired consistency. Add fish and shrimp (or scallops), cover and cook gently, until fish barely flakes. Do not overcook, or fish will fall apart. Serve hot with accompanying small bowls of chopped eggs, scallions and parsley for guests to add as they please.

*The stew may be prepared to this point several hours in advance of serving. In this case more of the liquid will be absorbed by the rice, and larger amounts of wine, stock or broth will be needed.

BASQUE FISHERMAN'S STEW

◆

Yield: Enough to serve 10 to 12

4 Pounds fresh tuna fillets
5 Pounds potatoes, peeled and cut into 1-inch chunks
2 Large onions, peeled and cut into coarse dice
3 Green peppers, seeded and coarsely chopped

5 Large garlic cloves, peeled and minced
½ Cup olive oil
4 Large tomatoes, peeled, seeded and coarsely chopped
Water
Red wine

Cut fish into 2-inch chunks. Sauté the potatoes, onions, peppers and garlic in olive oil until the onion is golden. Mash the tomatoes with a fork and add to the other vegetables with enough water to reach 1 inch above the level of the vegetables. Bring to a boil and cook until potatoes are almost tender. Add tuna, cook over high heat for 5 minutes. Cover the pot, remove it from the heat and let stand 15 minutes. Serve with a splash of red wine stirred into each bowl.

CIOPPINO

◆

Yield: Enough to serve 6

If they are available, the addition of a dozen or so scallops in their shells adds to the flavor and the beauty of this wonderful stew, a California version of bouillabaisse that originated with San Francisco's Portuguese fishermen. The dark body of the scallop encircles the white adductor muscle during cooking and is quite delicious. The open scallop shells fanning up from the broth are particularly attractive.

18 Clams in their shells
18 Mussels in their shells
18 Scallops in their shells (optional)
2 Cups water
6 Tablespoons dried mushrooms
3 Medium-size onions, peeled
2 Large green peppers with pith and seeds removed
5 Cloves garlic, peeled
7 Medium-size tomatoes, peeled and seeded
¾ Cup olive oil
1½ Cups coarsely chopped spinach

1 Tablespoon flour
3 Cups Fish Stock or bottled clam juice
3 Cups tomato purée
3½ Cups red wine
1 Teaspoon each salt and sugar
½ Teaspoon each black pepper and thyme
2½ Pounds sea bass fillets (or striped bass, or both) cut in 2-inch strips
2 Small lobsters cut in 2-inch pieces
½ Pound shrimp shelled, de-veined and split in half lengthwise

Scrub shells of clams, mussels and scallops and let stand several hours in water to cover, changing the water several times. Place 2 cups fresh, cold water in a kettle, add shellfish, cover and steam until shells open. Strain and reserve liquid. Soak mushrooms for 1 hour in water to cover. Drain well.

Mince onions, green peppers and garlic and coarsely chop the tomatoes. Heat the olive oil in a soup kettle and sauté the onions, peppers, garlic and spinach for 5 minutes, stirring occasionally. Stir in flour and cook 2 minutes. Add tomatoes, mushrooms, the reserved hot cooking liquid, the hot fish stock, the tomato purée and the wine. Season with salt, sugar, pepper and thyme, bring to a boil, stirring constantly, then lower the heat and simmer, covered, for 30 minutes. Add the fish, lobster and shrimp and cook for 8 minutes, or until lobster is red. Ladle the soup into a broad serving tureen or dish, but leave 1½ cups liquid in the pan. Heat clams, mussels and scallops for 2 minutes in the pan in the reserved liquid and arrange attractively over the soup. Serve immediately. Additional red wine may be added to each soup bowl at the table if desired.

SEA ROBIN STEW, MEXICANA

◆

Yield: Enough to serve 6

Achiote, the colorful, tangy spice paste (made from annatto seed, lard, chopped coriander, sweet peppers and onion), is used extensively in Caribbean and Mexican cuisines. It lends additional excitement to this unusual Sea Robin Stew. The paste is available in Mexican and Puerto Rican grocery stores.

3 Tablespoons each butter and oil
1 Tablespoon anchovy paste or 8 anchovy fillets, chopped
3 Tablespoons minced fresh parsley
2 Large garlic cloves, peeled and minced
2 Tablespoons flour
1 Tablespoon achiote paste
2½ Cups white wine
2½ Cups tomato juice

2½ Pounds sea robin fillets (or a mixture of other firm white-fleshed fish fillets)
1 Cup carrots cut in fine julienne or coarsely grated
1 Pound sliced mushrooms
1 Tablespoon sugar (optional)
Salt and freshly ground black pepper to taste

Heat 2 tablespoons each butter and oil in a heavy kettle. Add anchovy paste, parsley and garlic and sauté for 2 minutes. Stir in the flour and achiote until smooth, then add the wine and tomato juice. Press out any lumps with the back of a spoon. Poach the sea robin in this mixture until it is barely tender, then transfer carefully to a tureen and keep warm. Add the carrots to the pan liquids and quickly cook until tender. Meanwhile, sauté the mushrooms in one tablespoon each butter and oil until tender. Add mushrooms to the sauce and if it has an acid edge, add the sugar. Season to taste with salt and pepper. Pour over the fish and serve immediately.

FISH JELLY

◆

Yield: About 2 cups

Chilled poached fish is usually masked with clarified poaching liquid fortified with unflavored gelatin.

1 Quart poaching liquid reduced to 2 cups

Egg white and shells
½ Cup unflavored gelatin

Clarify the bouillon with egg white and shells as directed on page 307. Soften the gelatin in one cup cold water, then dissolve in the boiling liquid. Chill until syrupy.

FISH QUENELLES FOR SOUP

◆

Yield: Enough to serve 6

2 Cups non-oily fish fillets, cut into
  1-inch pieces
2 Tablespoons chilled Sauce Velouté
1 Egg white

A pinch of nutmeg
Salt and white pepper
½–⅔ Cup heavy cream
Fish Stock

Purée the fish in a blender or food processor, add the velouté, egg white, nutmeg, and salt and white pepper to taste. Whirl until the mixture is a smooth paste, stopping several times to scrape the mixture down against the blades and adding a little of the cream each time until the fish mixture holds its shape.

Pour enough lukewarm stock into a large, shallow pan to bring the depth of the liquid to ¼ inch. Using a teaspoon, scoop out enough of the quenelle mixture to almost fill the spoon, then dip another teaspoon of equal size into hot water and invert it over the first, molding the quenelle into an oval shape. As you form each quenelle, slip it into the stock, taking care to allow room for each to expand during cooking.

Add enough additional lukewarm stock to barely cover the quenelles; gently poach over low heat for 5 to 7 minutes, or until the quenelles are firm. If the pan is not large enough to contain all the quenelles at once, poach them in successive batches. Serve at once in any fish or seafood soup.

If you wish, you may prepare the quenelles in advance, although they will lack the exquisite lightness of those served immediately after poaching. To hold for later use, poach the quenelles as directed above, then place in cold water to cool. Drain carefully, brush with melted butter (brought to room temperature) to keep quenelles from drying out. Arrange in a flat dish in a single layer. Refrigerate. Reheat by simmering gently for a few minutes in the soup in which they are to be served.

Leftover quenelles are also delicious when lightly browned in Clarified Butter or various fish butters.

FISH DUMPLINGS

◆

Yield: Enough to serve 6

1 Large onion, peeled and finely
  chopped
3 Tablespoons butter
4 Slices stale bread
2 Cups boneless, skinless lean
  white-fleshed fish fillets

2 Eggs
2 Egg yolks
2 Teaspoons minced fresh thyme
Salt
Freshly ground black pepper
Flour

Sauté the onion in the butter until just soft. Soak the bread in water, squeeze as dry as possible, then chop and add to the onion. Sauté for 3 to 4 minutes, remove from the heat and set aside. Put the fish fillets through the fine blade of your grinder, or process in a blender or food processor until finely chopped. Mix well with the onion-bread mixture, eggs, egg yolks, thyme, and salt and pepper to taste. Shape into small dumplings, dust lightly with flour, and simmer gently in boiling salted water to cover for 8 to 10 minutes, or until they are cooked through and firm. Use as is or brown on all sides in butter and serve in any fish soup or stew.

FISHBALLS

◆

Yield: Enough to serve 6

2 Pounds non-oily, white-fleshed fish
2 Medium-size onions, peeled and finely chopped
4 Cloves garlic, peeled and finely chopped
¾ Cup corn meal

1 Egg
3 Tablespoons milk
2½ Teaspoons salt
½ Teaspoon freshly ground black pepper
1½ Teaspoons crushed coriander seed

Clean, skin and bone the fish, reserving the head, skin and bones for stock. Cut the flesh into pieces and put through the fine blade of your food grinder or whirl in your food processor. Mix thoroughly with the other ingredients and shape into one-inch balls; drop into simmering soup and cook for 20 minutes.

SAUCES AND BUTTERS

CRÈME FRAÎCHE

◆

2 Cups heavy cream
1 Cup sour cream

Stir the heavy cream into the sour cream, a spoonful at a time, until smoothly blended. Spoon the cream into a glass jar and place the jar in a dish of warm (80-degree) water. Cover with one layer of cheesecloth and let stand overnight. Stir, cover and refrigerate.

CRÈME FRAÎCHE WITH DILL: Stir 2 tablespoons minced fresh dill into 1 cup Crème Fraîche. Refrigerate.

YOGURT CHEESE

◆

Yield: About 1 cup

2 Cups plain yogurt
1 Tablespoon salt
2 Tablespoons minced fresh herbs
   (dill, marjoram, etc.)

1 Large garlic clove, peeled and
   minced (optional)

Line a large sieve or small colander with several thicknesses of cheesecloth or a piece of muslin. Stir all ingredients together, pour into the sieve or colander, fold the ends lightly over the top and let drain overnight in a deep bowl. Unwrap the cheese and roll it into a ball. Serve with crackers or use in cooking.

SAUCE MAYONNAISE

◆

Yield: About 2 cups

Classic Sauce Mayonnaise, with perhaps one or two of its variations in separate dollops, can transform a platter of fish and/or seafood into beautiful and subtly delicious gourmet fare.

2 *Egg yolks, at room temperature*
1 *Tablespoon Dijon mustard*
¾ *Cup each* olive oil and vegetable oil

1½ *Tablespoons warm vinegar or* lemon juice
Salt and white pepper

Rinse a small bowl with hot water and wipe dry. Place egg yolks and mustard into the warmed bowl, mix well with a wire whisk, then set the bowl over boiling water for just a few seconds, continuing to beat as the mixture thickens slightly. Take care not to beat over the heat too long or the mayonnaise will be too thick.

As soon as the egg mixture is off the heat, mix the oils together and gradually beat into eggs, ½ teaspoon at a time, beating continuously and waiting until each previous addition has been thoroughly incorporated and the mixture is creamy before beating in the next.

When one-third to one-half of the oil has been incorporated, beat in the vinegar, then gradually add the remaining oil in small amounts, beating continuously after each addition. When all the oil has been absorbed, season to taste with salt and pepper. Keep chilled.

SAUCE VERTE (GREEN MAYONNAISE): Coarsely chop one cup mixed greens (spinach, watercress, parsley, dill, chives and/or tarragon) and blanch in boiling water for 2 minutes. Drain, refresh in cold water, then drain again and pat dry between paper towels. Press mixture through a fine sieve, or whirl in a food processor or blender. Blend thoroughly in 2 cups Sauce Mayonnaise. Keep chilled.

SAUCE ANDALOUSE: Mix together 2 cups Sauce Mayonnaise and ½ cup Ripe Tomato Purée. Stir in one finely chopped pimento. Keep chilled.

TARRAGON MAYONNAISE: Mix together one tablespoon finely chopped fresh tarragon (or 1½ teaspoons dried) and one cup Sauce Mayonnaise. Add 1 teaspoon lemon juice, salt and freshly ground black pepper to taste. Keep chilled.

ANCHOVY MAYONNAISE: Combine one tablespoon *each* chopped anchovy fillets and finely chopped shallots with one cup Sauce Mayonnaise. To use for masking cold seafood, such as mussels, adjust thickness by adding 1 or 2 teaspoons liquid in which mussels were cooked. Keep chilled.

CURRY MAYONNAISE: Beat into Sauce Mayonnaise ½ teaspoon curry powder or to taste.

QUICK AIOLI (GARLIC MAYONNAISE)

◆

Yield: About 1 cup

2 Tablespoons bread crumbs

3 Cloves garlic, peeled and coarsely chopped

1 Tablespoon lemon juice

2 Large egg yolks

⅛ Teaspoon each salt and black pepper

¾ Cup olive oil

About 1 tablespoon boiling water

Place bread crumbs in an electric blender or food processor and whirl at high speed for about 5 seconds. Add garlic and lemon juice and blend at high speed until mixture is smooth. Beat in egg yolks and seasonings; continue to beat until mixture is quite stiff. Turn motor on again and gradually add the oil, a few drops at a time at first, then slowly increase amount until oil runs in a thin, steady stream. As soon as half the oil has been absorbed, add 1 teaspoon boiling water to thin the mixture a bit.

Continue blending and adding oil at high speed, stopping the action and adding another teaspoon or so of boiling water only if the mixture becomes too thick for the blender blades to turn easily. When all the oil has been incorporated, sauce will be very thick. Scrape from blender jar with a spatula and turn into a container. Cover and chill before using.

SAUCE GRIBICHE

◆

Yield: About 1½ cups

This mayonnaise made with hard-cooked eggs teams up superbly with poached striped bass or other fish. Prepare it at least 2 hours in advance of serving to bring out the full flavor of the sauce.

3 Hard-cooked eggs

1 Teaspoon dry mustard

½ Teaspoon salt

¼ Teaspoon freshly ground black pepper

1 Cup olive oil

2 Tablespoons white vinegar

2 Tablespoons finely chopped mixed fresh herbs (chervil, chives, parsley, tarragon)

1 Tablespoon each well-drained and chopped sour pickles and capers

Separate the hard-cooked yolks and whites. Cut the whites into fine julienne and set aside. Mash the yolks to a paste in a small bowl and blend in the mustard, salt and pepper. Beat in the oil, ½ teaspoon at a time, beating continuously. When all the oil has been added, beat in the vinegar and stir in the reserved egg whites, herbs, pickles and capers.

SAUCE RAVIGOTE

◆

Yield: About 1 cup

1 Small onion, peeled and finely chopped

2 Tablespoons capers, finely chopped

2 Teaspoons finely chopped fresh chervil

2 Teaspoons each finely chopped fresh chives, parsley and tarragon

½ Cup Sauce Vinaigrette or Vinaigrette à la Moutarde

1 Hard-cooked egg, shelled

Combine onion, capers and herbs with dressing. Force egg through a fine sieve and stir into dressing mixture.

SAUCE RÉMOULADE

Yield: About 2 cups

For a more pronounced flavor, make this shellfish accompaniment about 2 hours in advance of serving.

1¾ Cups Sauce Mayonnaise
2½ Teaspoons French mustard
1 Tablespoon each finely chopped and well-drained sour pickles and capers

1 Tablespoon each finely chopped fresh parsley and tarragon
2 Teaspoons finely chopped fresh chervil
1 Teaspoon anchovy paste

Combine all ingredients and mix well. Chill.

SAUCE RUSSE

Yield: About 1 cup

1 Cup Sauce Mayonnaise
3 Tablespoons chili sauce

1 Tablespoon each chopped pimentos and fresh chives

Beat together mayonnaise and chili sauce, then stir in chopped vegetables. Keep chilled.

SAUCE TARTARE

Yield: About 1½ cups

1 Medium-size onion, peeled and finely chopped
2 Large pimento-stuffed olives, finely chopped
1 Medium-size sweet gherkin, finely chopped

1 Tablespoon each finely chopped fresh parsley and capers
1 Cup cold Sauce Mayonnaise

Just prior to serving, stir into the cold mayonnaise all the other ingredients.

SAUCE VINAIGRETTE

Yield: About 1 cup

¼ Cup wine vinegar
⅛ Teaspoon salt
A generous pinch of freshly ground black pepper

¾ Cup olive oil

In your food processor or blender, or by hand, beat the vinegar and seasonings together until well blended. Add the oil and beat again.

VINAIGRETTE À LA MOUTARDE: Prepare Sauce Vinaigrette as directed, but add one teaspoon dry or 2 teaspoons prepared French mustard when beating the vinegar and seasonings together. Proceed as directed.

MUSTARD GRAVLAX SAUCE

◆

Yield: 1 cup

¼ *Cup each oil and prepared mustard*
2 *Tablespoons each red-wine vinegar and sugar*

½ *Teaspoon salt*
¼ *Teaspoon pepper*
2 *Tablespoons heavy cream*
¼ *Cup minced fresh dill*

Thoroughly mix the oil, mustard, vinegar, sugar, salt and pepper. Stir in the cream and then the dill.

DILL SAUCE

◆

Yield: About ¾ cup

¼ *Cup each oil and Crème Fraîche*
2 *Tablespoons white-wine vinegar*
½ *Teaspoon sugar (optional)*

¼ *Teaspoon each salt and white pepper*
3 *Tablespoons minced fresh dill*

Mix ingredients in order given.

BASIC RICE VINAIGRETTE FOR SALADS

◆

Seafood with cold rice is as delightful as are *fruits de la mer* and hot rice.

1 *Cup long-grain rice*
Water

Salt
Sauce Vinaigrette à la Moutarde

Cook the rice in water following directions on the package. Salt to taste. Toss with the sauce while the rice is warm.

THOUSAND ISLAND DRESSING

◆

Yield: About 1½ cups

3 *Tablespoons chili sauce*
¼ *Cup each finely chopped celery and green pepper*
1 *Hard-cooked egg, shelled and finely chopped*

1 *Cup Sauce Mayonnaise*
1 *Tablespoon each cider vinegar and cream*
½ *Teaspoon paprika*
Salt

Prepare at least 2 hours in advance of serving and keep chilled. Mix the chili sauce, celery, green pepper and hard-cooked egg into the mayonnaise. Stir in the cider vinegar, cream, paprika and salt to taste.

GREEN GODDESS DRESSING

◆

Yield: About 2 cups

½ *Small onion, peeled and finely chopped*
2 *Scallions, green part only, minced*
2 *Cloves garlic, peeled and minced*
4 *Anchovy fillets, finely chopped*
¼ *Cup finely chopped fresh parsley*

1 *Cup Sauce Mayonnaise*
½ *Cup sour cream*
2 *Tablespoons each tarragon vinegar and lemon juice*
¼ *Teaspoon freshly ground black pepper*

Combine all ingredients until thoroughly mixed. Keep chilled.

TOMATO-CREAM SAUCE

◆

Yield: About 2½ cups

8 Ounces cream cheese, at room
  temperature
¾ Cup Ripe Tomato Purée
2 Large cloves garlic, peeled and
  finely chopped
2 Tablespoons finely chopped fresh
  basil

⅛ Teaspoon Tabasco sauce (or more
  to taste)
Salt to taste
⅓ Cup heavy cream

In your food processor or blender or by hand, beat the cream cheese
until fluffy, then blend in the remaining ingredients. Serve cold or heated
through.

APPLE-HORSERADISH CREAM

◆

Yield: About 2 cups

1 2½-inch piece fresh horseradish
  root, scraped
3 Medium-size apples, peeled
  and cored

1½ Cups plain yogurt
1½ Tablespoons honey
Salt

Grate horseradish and apples in your food processor or by hand. Combine
with yogurt and honey and season to taste with salt. Pour mixture into
an ice-cube tray and freeze until mushy, then beat thoroughly with a
fork and refreeze until hard. Soften slightly, scoop out and serve over
cold fish.

BASIC WHITE SAUCE

Yield: 2 cups

This is a simple sauce to make, and one on which many others are based.
The foolproof cold-milk method takes a little longer to cook but is less
likely to lump . . . a good recipe for beginners. For more experienced cooks
the hot-milk technique works well. Simply remove the pan from the heat
and stir in hot milk instead of cold. Return the pan to the heat and stir
until thick.

3 Tablespoons butter
3 Tablespoons flour
2 Cups cold milk

½ Teaspoon salt
White pepper

Melt the butter over medium heat in a heavy saucepan. Stir in the flour
with a wire whisk for 3 or 4 minutes. When the mixture is smooth,
remove from the heat and add the cold milk all at once, stirring until the
mixture is well blended and lump-free. Return to medium heat and cook,
stirring continuously, until the sauce bubbles and is creamy and thick.
Season to taste with salt and white pepper.

For Thin White Sauce—increase milk to 2½ cups. For Thick White
Sauce—reduce the amount of milk to 1¼ cups.

ENRICHED WHITE SAUCE, OR BÉCHAMEL: Prepare as directed above, but sauté one small onion, peeled and thinly sliced, in the butter until the slices soften, then discard onion and blend in the flour. Substitute one cup cream for one cup of the milk and proceed as directed. Strain if necessary.

SAUCE MORNAY (MORNAY SAUCE): Add ¼ cup grated Swiss cheese and ¼ cup grated Parmesan cheese to 2 cups hot Enriched White Sauce. Stir over low heat until the cheeses melt.

CURRY SAUCE (SAUCE CURRIE): Melt butter as directed in Sauce Béchamel. Add one teaspoon curry powder along with flour, then proceed as directed.

EGG AND HERB SAUCE: Prepare Sauce Béchamel as directed. Just before serving, stir in 2 coarsely chopped hard-cooked eggs and 2 tablespoons finely chopped mixed fresh herbs (chervil, marjoram, thyme, etc.)

SAUCE NANTUA
◆

Yield: About 2½ cups

½ Cup heavy cream
2 Cups Enriched White Sauce
Salt and white pepper
3–4 Tablespoons Lobster Butter or
*   Shrimp Butter*

¼ Cup cooked lobster meat or
*   shrimp (optional)*

Scald the heavy cream and mix into the Enriched White Sauce. Strain the mixture through a fine sieve into a heavy saucepan and cook for 5 minutes until well heated, but do not allow the mixture to boil. Remove from heat and season to taste with salt and pepper, then stir in Lobster or Shrimp Butter. If desired, finely chop seafood and add to the sauce. Cool slightly before serving, taking care to remove any butter that rises to the surface.

SAUCE AURORE
◆

Yield: About 2½ cups

This may also be made with Sauce Velouté. It is especially good with fresh mousses.

2 Cups Enriched White Sauce
3 Tablespoons very thick Ripe
*   Tomato Purée*

1 Tablespoon butter

Prepare 2 cups Enriched White Sauce as directed. Just before serving and off the heat, swirl in 3 tablespoons purée and one tablespoon butter.

SAUCE VELOUTÉ

◆

Yield: About 2 cups

3 Tablespoons butter
3 Tablespoons flour

2 Cups hot Fish Stock
Salt and white pepper to taste

Melt the butter over medium heat in a heavy saucepan. Stir in the flour and stir slowly until the roux bubbles and turns golden. Remove from the heat and add the fish stock. Stir until smooth and bubbling. If the sauce is runny, simmer it until it is nicely thickened. Season to taste.

ENRICHED VELOUTÉ: Prepare Sauce Velouté as directed. After gradually adding the hot stock, cook and stir the mixture over low heat for 10 minutes, until smooth and fairly thick. Beat together 2 egg yolks and ½ cup heavy cream in a small bowl, then gradually add ½ cup of the hot velouté, one tablespoon at a time, beating well after each addition. Pour the egg-cream mixture back into the hot velouté, stirring continuously, and continue to stir until the mixture comes almost to a boil. Remove immediately from the heat, continuing to stir until the sauce cools a bit, then strain into a clean pan. Season to taste with salt and white pepper and stir in one tablespoon lemon juice.

SAUCE POULETTE: Just before serving Enriched Velouté, stir in two tablespoons finely chopped fresh parsley.

ONION SAUCE: Heat 2 tablespoons butter and cook 2 medium-size onions, peeled and finely chopped, until soft and transparent. Stir the vegetables into 1½ cups Sauce Velouté and simmer over low heat for 30 minutes. Purée and strain the sauce just before serving, stir in 2 tablespoons heavy cream and season to taste with salt and white pepper.

PARSLEY SAUCE: Blanch ¼ cup finely chopped fresh parsley in boiling water for 2 minutes and drain well; refresh in cold water, drain again and pat dry between paper towels. Stir into 1½ cups Sauce Béchamel and season with lemon juice. Serve over mackerel or salmon.

SAUCE AMÉRICAINE

◆

Yield: About 2 cups

1 Live lobster, about 1½ pounds
4 Tablespoons butter
2 Tablespoons olive oil
2 Shallots, peeled and finely chopped
1 Tablespoon each finely chopped
   fresh chervil and parsley

1 Clove garlic, peeled
1½ Cups Ripe Tomato Purée
1 Teaspoon flour
2 Tablespoons brandy

Kill and clean the lobster and cut it into pieces as directed on page 298. Reserve the liver or tomalley. Heat 2 tablespoons each butter and oil in a large skillet and sauté the lobster pieces until they begin to turn red, about 5 to 7 minutes. Add the shallots, herbs, garlic clove and purée, and simmer until the shallots are tender.

Meanwhile, cream together the tomalley, remaining butter and the flour. Remove lobster pieces and garlic clove from the sauce. Discard the garlic; remove lobster meat from pieces of shell and thinly slice. Stir tomalley mixture into sauce, add sliced lobster meat and brandy, and simmer for 4 or 5 minutes, stirring once or twice, without letting sauce boil.

SAUCE VILLEROI
◆

Traditionally this sauce has two uses: 1) to coat fish or shellfish before rolling them in crumbs preparatory to deep-frying; and 2) to bind together the ingredients for Seafood Croquettes and Fritters. In either case, prepare the sauce just before using.

2 Egg yolks
1 Cup hot Enriched Velouté or
   Enriched White Sauce

Salt

Beat the egg yolks together lightly, add a spoonful or two of the hot sauce and beat again, then turn the mixture back into the remaining sauce. Cook over very low heat (an asbestos pad is useful here) or in the top part of a double boiler, stirring continuously, until the mixture becomes very thick and pulls away from the sides of the pan. Season to taste with salt and cool to room temperature before using to coat or bind seafood. If desired, finely chopped onions or parsley may be added to the hot sauce before the egg yolks are incorporated.

SAUCE CARDINAL
◆

Yield: About 1½ cups

4 Tablespoons Fish Stock
1 Cup hot Enriched Velouté

1 Truffle, coarsely chopped (optional)
4 Tablespoons Lobster Butter

Stir the stock into the hot velouté and add the truffle, if desired. Just before serving, remove the sauce from the heat and swirl in the Lobster Butter.

SAUCE BÉARNAISE
◆

Yield: About 1½ cups

¼ Cup dry white wine
¼ Cup wine vinegar
1 Tablespoon finely chopped shallots
1 Tablespoon finely chopped fresh
   tarragon or 1 teaspoon dried
3 Egg yolks
2 Teaspoons water

¾ Cup melted butter
A pinch each of salt and black pepper
Lemon juice or tarragon vinegar
A pinch of cayenne
1 Teaspoon finely chopped fresh
   tarragon or parsley (optional)

Put the wine, wine vinegar, shallots and tarragon in a small saucepan; boil over medium heat until mixture has reduced to 2 tablespoons. Remove from the heat, strain and set aside to cool. Place the egg yolks and water in the top of a double boiler and beat together. Beat in the wine–wine-vinegar reduction. Set the pan over hot, but not boiling, water; the bottom of the pan should sit at least one inch above the surface of the water. Beat the egg-yolk mixture until it begins to thicken and continue to beat while gradually adding the melted butter, a little at a time. When all the butter has been incorporated, season to taste with salt and pepper, lemon juice or tarragon vinegar and stir in the cayenne and chopped herbs.

SAUCE CHORON: Reduce ⅓ cup Ripe Tomato Purée until it is very thick Stir the paste into 1½ cups Sauce Béarnaise. Serve immediately.

EASY SAUCE HOLLANDAISE
◆

Yield: About 1½ cups

½ Pound (2 sticks) sweet butter
1 Cup hot water
6 Egg yolks

4 Teaspoons lemon juice
A generous pinch each of salt and
white pepper

Melt butter over medium heat. Meanwhile pour the hot water into the container of your food processor or blender and allow to stand one minute, then discard water and dry the container. Place egg yolks, lemon juice and seasonings in warmed container; cover and whirl until well mixed. As soon as butter is very hot, turn on machine and through the opening in the top add in a very thin but steady stream—it is important not to add it too quickly. When all the butter has been incorporated, shut the machine off. Serve sauce at once, or keep warm in a bowl set in a pan of warm, not hot, water.

MOUSSELINE SAUCE: Just before serving, fold an equal amount of whipped cream into Sauce Hollandaise.

HOLLANDAISE WITH EGG WHITE: Just before serving, fold a stiffly beaten egg white into Sauce Hollandaise.

HERB HOLLANDAISE: Just before serving, stir into Sauce Hollandaise 1 to 2 tablespoons finely chopped fresh herbs (parsley, chives, dill, tarragon, etc.)

SNOWPEA SAUCE

◆

A delightful light, garden-fresh sauce.

1 Pound snowpeas (reserve 18 perfect pods for garnish)
2 Cups Fish Stock or chicken broth
2 Tablespoons butter
3 Tablespoons heavy cream
Salt and pepper to taste

Simmer the peas in stock or broth until they are quite tender. Set the peas aside and reduce the stock to ½ cup. Purée the peas (not those to be used as a garnish) with the reduced stock in a food processor. Strain through a coarse strainer. Swirl the purée with the butter in a saucepan until well integrated. Add the cream and simmer 3 minutes or until nicely thickened. Season to taste. Blanche the reserved snowpeas.

LEEK SAUCE

◆

2 Large leeks, trimmed of their roots and all but 2 inches of green tops
2 Cups Fish Stock or chicken broth
2 Tablespoons butter
3 Tablespoons heavy cream
Salt and pepper to taste

Wash the leeks well and cut them into 1-inch lengths. Simmer in stock or broth until tender. Purée in food processor and strain through a coarse strainer. Swirl the purée with the butter until well integrated and nicely thickened. Add the cream and simmer once again until the sauce is creamy. Season to taste.

SWEET AND SOUR SAUCE

◆

Yield: About 3 cups

1 8-Ounce can pineapple chunks
½ 8-Ounce jar (4 ounces) sweet mixed pickles
½ Cup malt vinegar
1 Cup water
3 Tablespoons soy sauce
2 Tablespoons sherry
1 Teaspoon each salt and freshly ground black pepper
3 Tablespoons vegetable oil
3 Slices fresh ginger root, peeled and finely chopped
2 Cloves garlic, peeled and finely chopped
2 Medium-size onions, peeled and thinly sliced
2 Medium-size green peppers, trimmed and thinly sliced
1 Small carrot, scraped and thinly sliced
½ Cup granulated sugar
3 Tablespoons cornstarch

Drain pineapple chunks and pickles, reserving juices. Coarsely chop fruit and pickles, then set aside. Mix together juices, vinegar, ½ cup water, soy sauce, sherry, salt and pepper; set aside.

Heat the oil in a large skillet over high heat and stir-fry the ginger and garlic for one minute. Add the sliced vegetables and stir-fry 3 minutes more, then add the reserved juice–soy sauce mixture and bring to a boil. Mix the sugar and cornstarch into the remaining ½ cup water and stir into the boiling mixture along with the reserved pineapple and pickles. Cook over medium heat, stirring continuously, until sauce is thickened and clear.

RIPE TOMATO PURÉE

◆

Yield: About 2 cups

16–20 Fully ripe tomatoes
1 Tablespoon butter or vegetable oil
½ Teaspoon granulated sugar

Wash the tomatoes and cut into eighths. Heat the butter or oil in a heavy stainless-steel saucepan, add the tomatoes and sugar and cook, uncovered, over medium heat until the juices have evaporated. Force the tomatoes through a food mill or strainer. If the purée seems too watery, return it to the pan and simmer until the remaining juices evaporate and the mixture is quite thick.

The purée may also be prepared in a food processor. Process the fresh tomato wedges until they become liquid, then pour through a strainer into hot butter or oil in a heavy stainless-steel saucepan. Add the sugar and cook over medium heat until the purée simmers down to a nice thick consistency.

If desired, divide the purée among serving-size containers, leaving ½-inch headroom, then seal and freeze.

TAPANADE

◆

Yield: 2 to 3 cups

Your food processor or blender renders this once-difficult recipe easy. It's wonderful to sauce cold fish or as a vegetable dip.

1 7-ounce can oil-packed tuna
3 2-ounce cans oil-packed anchovies
¼ Cup capers, drained
20 Black Greek olives, pitted
3 Cloves garlic, peeled

2½ Tablespoons lemon juice
½ Cup fine olive oil
Cognac
Cayenne pepper to taste
Freshly ground black pepper

Whirl the tuna and anchovies (both with their oil), the capers, the olives, the garlic and the lemon juice until smooth. While the motor is still running add half the olive oil a few drops at a time. Add the remaining oil in a thin stream until the consistency is similar to that of mayonnaise. Stir in the cognac, cayenne and black pepper to taste. Serve at room temperature or lightly chilled. (Don't go overboard on the cognac, or the sauce will be too thin. Two tablespoons or so should be about right.)

CRUNCHY TOMATO-NUT TOPPING

◆

Yield: About 1 cup

The crunch of finely chopped nuts and the slightly acid "zing" of tomato makes this a perfect topping for any soft or oily broiled fish fillet.

1 Tablespoon each soy sauce and Worcestershire sauce
½ Cup minced pecans, almonds or walnuts (black or plain)

2 Tablespoons tomato paste
1–2 Tablespoons sherry
A pinch of sugar

Mix all ingredients. The sauce should be nicely spreadable but thick enough to "stay put" on the fish fillet. If the sauce seems too thick to spread, thin it with a little extra Worcestershire.

CLARIFIED BUTTER

◆

This is butter that has been divested of its milk solids. To prepare, melt a bit more than the amount needed in a small saucepan over low heat. Use a slotted spoon to skim off any foam that rises. Remove from the heat and cool slightly to allow the milky sediment to settle. Skim off any remaining foam, then pour off the clear yellow oil into a container, leaving the sediment behind.

Clarified butter makes the perfect dipping sauce for chunks of hot boiled lobster, crabmeat, or steamed soft clams. It is particularly useful in making the so-called brown or black butters, since its burning point is higher than that of regular butter.

If desired, a large amount of clarified butter can be made at one time, then divided among several containers and frozen for future use. Either salt or sweet butter may be used.

BROWN BUTTER (BEURRE NOISETTE): Place 8 tablespoons Clarified Butter in a pan over medium heat and cook until it takes on a light-brown color. Serve at once over hot fish or use as directed in your recipe.

LEMON BUTTER (BEURRE MEUNIÈRE): In this variation of Beurre Noisette, finish the sauce by swirling in one teaspoon lemon juice and one tablespoon finely chopped fresh parsley.

BLACK BUTTER (BEURRE NOIR): Place 8 tablespoons Clarified Butter in a pan over medium heat and cook until it takes on a rich dark-brown color, then remove from the heat and swirl in one teaspoon wine vinegar. Black butter is the classic sauce for Poached Skate (Raie au Beurre Noir), although it can be used with other fish. To use with skate, add one tablespoon finely chopped fresh parsley to the melting butter, then proceed as above. Top the hot skate with capers before pouring the sauce over.

KNEADED BUTTER (BEURRE MANIÉ): This is a fail-safe culinary means for rescuing thin sauces or cream soups. Knead together with your fingers or a fork equal parts of softened butter and flour. When the mixture is well blended, break off small pieces and drop one piece at a time into the hot liquid, stirring continuously to dissolve each piece before adding the next. Add only as much of the kneaded butter as will thicken the mixture, and cook only long enough for the floury taste to vanish.

COMPOUND BUTTERS

These are easy-to-make seasoned butters, traditionally served in solid form rather than as melted additions. Once the ingredients are well blended, the butters can be shaped into rolls and chilled, then cut into thin slices and allowed to melt over hot fish. Or if you prefer, cut or press the butter into fancy shapes or molds, then chill and serve.

You may cream the ingredients together by hand, pressing them afterward through a fine sieve, but the quickest and most efficient way to prepare any compound butter is in your food processor or blender, where at the flick of a switch and in a matter of seconds, the ingredients will be turned into a smooth, well-blended mixture. However, be sure to start with cold butter cut into pieces, and chill any finished butter until ready for use.

ANCHOVY BUTTER: Cream together until smooth 2 finely chopped anchovy fillets and 6 tablespoons sweet butter.

CAVIAR BUTTER: Mash 4 tablespoons caviar and blend with 8 tablespoons softened butter. The caviar need not be the finest quality beluga or sevruga; black or red lumpfish caviar or the popular red salmon roe are all perfectly acceptable.

DEVILED BUTTER: Cream 6 tablespoons butter until soft; blend in one tablespoon Worcestershire sauce and ½ teaspoon *each* Tabasco sauce, dry mustard, chopped onion and chopped fresh chives.

GARLIC BUTTER: Peel and crush 2 garlic cloves; cream 8 tablespoons butter and blend in garlic and 1½ teaspoons minced fresh parsley. Season to taste with white pepper.

GREEN BUTTER: Combine in a saucepan 6 to 8 fresh spinach leaves, 2 small shallots, peeled and finely chopped, one tablespoon finely chopped fresh parsley and one teaspoon *each* finely chopped fresh chervil and tarragon. Add 2 tablespoons boiling water and simmer 1 to 2 minutes, stirring constantly. Drain and press dry between paper towels. In your food processor cream ingredients together with 8 tablespoons butter.

LOBSTER BUTTER: This butter may be prepared by mashing 3 tablespoons cooked lobster coral to a paste and combining with 8 tablespoons sweet butter, but another method is to dry out a leftover cooked shell from one large lobster in a slow oven, then pound or grind the pieces as fine as possible. Place in the top half of a double boiler with 8 tablespoons butter and 2 tablespoons white wine or water. Cook over boiling water until the butter melts, then simmer the mixture for 10 minutes without letting it boil. Line a fine strainer with cheesecloth, set it over a bowl of ice water, and pour the hot butter mixture through. Place the bowl in the refrigerator until the butter hardens. Lift off the butter, wrap it well and refrigerate. Add remaining liquid to fish stews. For Crab Butter, replace the lobster shell with 1 or 2 cooked leftover crab shells.

MAÎTRE D'HÔTEL BUTTER: Cream 8 tablespoons butter and mash together with ½ teaspoon finely chopped parsley, the juice of ½ lemon, and salt and freshly ground black pepper to taste. For Colbert Butter, add 2 teaspoons meat glaze and bring mixture to room temperature before using.

MUSTARD BUTTER: Cream together 1½ teaspoons French mustard and 8 tablespoons Clarified Butter.

SHRIMP BUTTER: Make the butter according to directions given for Lobster Butter, substituting the shells from one pound of shrimp for the lobster shell.

SMOKED SALMON BUTTER: Finely chop one 2-inch slice smoked salmon and combine with 6 tablespoons sweet butter.

TARRAGON BUTTER: Blanch and blot dry 6 tablespoons (⅓ cup) fresh tarragon leaves as directed in Green Butter, then cream to a paste with 6 tablespoons butter.

WHITE BUTTER: Place ½ cup vinegar and 2 shallots, peeled and finely chopped, in a small saucepan. Cook until the liquid reduces to one-quarter its volume, then set side to cool. Cream together 6 tablespoons butter, one teaspoon finely chopped fresh parsley, and salt and freshly ground black pepper to taste. Add the reduction and blend thoroughly.

SNAIL BUTTER
◆

Yield: 1¼ cups

4 *Cloves garlic, peeled and crushed*
½ *Cup minced parsley*

1 *Cup butter*
Salt to taste

Cream the garlic, parsley, butter and salt together.

CRÊPES, SANDWICHES AND TOASTS

CRÊPES

♦

Yield: Enough to serve 6

4 *Extra-large eggs*
¾ *Cup each milk and water*
¼ *Teaspoon salt*

3 *Tablespoons vegetable or peanut oil*
1 *Cup plus 2 tablespoons flour*
3 *Tablespoons butter or oil*

Beat eggs well, then combine with the milk, water, salt, vegetable oil and flour and blend thoroughly. Refrigerate the mixture for 2 hours.

Using ½ teaspoon butter (or oil), rub the inside of a 6-inch crêpe pan. Set pan over low heat for one minute, then remove from the heat and wipe the pan with paper towels. Return the pan to the heat, add another ½ teaspoon butter, and repeat the process. This seasons the skillet so the pancakes won't stick. Or, if you like, use a 6-inch nonstick skillet and omit this seasoning process.

Stir the cold crêpe batter to make sure it is smooth. Put ¼ teaspoon butter into the seasoned pan; as it melts, tilt the pan as necessary to evenly coat its sides and bottom. Meanwhile have 2 to 3 tablespoons of the batter ready in a ladle to add to the butter as soon as it is hot enough; the idea is to turn out a succession of crêpes that are very thin, yet hold together. Experience—plus the size of your pan—will soon show you just how much batter is needed each time.

To determine whether the pan is hot enough to receive the batter, flick a few drops of water into it. If the water sizzles, pour in the measured batter and quickly rotate the pan from side to side to spread the mixture evenly over the bottom surface. As soon as bubbles appear over the pancake surface, loosen and lift one edge with a spatula. If the bottom is light brown, immediately turn the pancake over and let cook until speckled with brown. Slide the pancake from the pan and set aside on a plate.

Continue making pancakes in the same way, using about ⅛ teaspoon butter for each until they begin to brown nicely without sticking. As you turn them out of the pan, stack them one on top of the other, with foil in between if they begin to stick together, then reheat, if necessary, by setting them on the middle rack of a warm oven.

Despite their fragile appearance, these French pancakes are actually quite sturdy. You can make them well ahead of time, then refrigerate or freeze until needed. To use, bring to room temperature and reheat as directed above.

CURRY CRÊPES: Proceed as for plain crêpes, but first beat ¾ teaspoon curry powder with the eggs.

AVOCADO CRÊPES

◆

Yield: About 2 dozen

Any one of a number of creamy fillings may be rolled into these unusually tasty crêpes. Serve them as a first course or as an elegant luncheon.

1 Medium-size avocado, peeled and pitted	½ Teaspoon salt
	½ Cup water
6 Eggs	¾ Cup milk
¾ Cup flour	Butter

Purée avocado pulp with the eggs, flour and salt. Gradually beat in water and milk. Refrigerate one hour. Stir well. Melt ¼ teaspoon butter in a 7-inch crêpe or nonstick pan. Add 3 to 4 tablespoons batter and tilt the pan to cover the bottom evenly. Brown lightly on both sides. Continue until all batter is used.

Any unused crêpes may be stacked, wrapped in aluminum foil and frozen. To defrost: Remove package from freezer and place in refrigerator to defrost for 2 to 3 hours. To heat: Place in baking dish still wrapped in foil. Heat in 400-degree-F. oven for 15 minutes, then fold back foil and bake 15 minutes more. Serve with Savory Fillings.

CURRY CRÊPE FILLING

◆

3 Cups Enriched White Sauce	Salt and white pepper to taste
1 Tablespoon curry powder (or more or less to your taste)	1 Cup avocado cut into ⅓-inch cubes
	Butter
3 Cups flaked, cooked fish or shellfish (or a combination of these)	6 Tablespoons Swiss cheese, grated

Heat white sauce and work in curry powder until evenly distributed. Stir in fish and/or seafood and avocado. Immediately remove from the heat. Spread a little filling on one half of each crêpe, then roll up and place seam-side-down side-by-side in a well-buttered baking dish. Sprinkle with Swiss cheese, dot with butter and bake at 400 degrees F. for 15 minutes, or until cheese is melted.

SMOKED FISH FILLING: Follow directions for Curry Filling above, but substitute for the curry powder ½ teaspoon dried thyme leaves and for the fish the same amount of smoked fish.

ROE FILLING: Follow directions for Smoked Fish Filling above, but substitute cooked or smoked roe for the smoked fish.

CHEESE AND CRABMEAT FILLING: Follow directions for Curry Filling above, but stir one cup grated Swiss cheese into the white sauce until it is melted and very thick. Substitute one tablespoon Worcestershire sauce for the curry powder, and crabmeat for the fish and/or shellfish.

PICKLED FISH FILLING

◆

3 Cups well-drained pickled fish and
   their onions, coarsely chopped
3 Tablespoons minced fresh dill
Crème Fraîche

Salt and freshly ground black pepper
   to taste
Avocado

Squeeze the fish gently in paper towels to remove excess liquid. Sprinkle with dill and mix in just enough cold Crème Fraîche to bind. Spread the filling on one half of a cold crêpe and roll up. Place, seam-side-down, on cold serving plate or platter. Just before serving, decorate plate with thin slices of peeled avocado. Serve cold.

FISH SALAD FILLING: Follow directions for Pickled Fish Filling above, but substitute cold cooked fish and/or shellfish for the pickled fish.

SMOKED-FISH SALAD FILLING: Follow directions for Pickled Fish Filling above, but substitute cold smoked fish for the pickled fish.

COLD ROE FILLING: Follow directions for Pickled Fish Filling above, but substitute cooked or smoked roe for the fish.

SMOKED SALMON FILLING

◆

Crème Fraîche
24 Slices smoked salmon
3 Tablespoons minced fresh dill

Freshly ground black pepper
Avocado

Spread one half of each cold crêpe with crème fraîche, top with one slice smoked salmon and a sprinkle each of dill and pepper. Roll up crêpe and arrange seam-side-down on a cold serving plate or platter. Decorate plate with thin slices of peeled avocado. Serve cold.

SWEET AVOCADO CRÊPES

◆

Follow directions for Avocado Crêpes, but use only ¼ teaspoon salt and add one teaspoon sugar to the batter. Although sweet avocado crêpes twirled around fresh, sugared fruits and satiny creams do provide a nice change-of-pace dessert for nearly any fish meal, these crêpes are also delightful wraparounds for fruited fish salads.

COLD SHRIMP-HONEYDEW FILLING

◆

1 Cup honeydew, cut into ½-inch
   cubes
Cold Crème Fraîche

½ Cup whipped cream
2 Cups shrimp, cut into ½-inch pieces
1 Cup avocado, cut into ½-inch cubes

Drain honeydew well and press gently between paper towels to remove excess moisture. Fold whipped cream into Crème Fraîche and use just enough to bind the melon, shrimp and avocado. Spread filling on one half of each crêpe, roll up and place on cold serving plate or platter. Serve cold.

COLD FISH SALAD WITH WHITE GRAPES: Follow directions for Cold Shrimp-Honeydew Filling, but substitute peeled halved white grapes for the melon and cold flaked flounder or other fine, white-fleshed fish for the shrimp.

SANDWICH FILLINGS

Lunch-box, teatime and picnic sandwiches are extra-tempting when fish or shellfish is featured in the filling—particularly if those fish have been freshly caught and cooked by you. To use any of the fillings listed below, simply spread over the bread of your choice. And since both seafood and mayonnaise are perishable foods, be sure to keep the fillings well chilled. Serve with lemon and/or lime wedges.

SALMON FILLING

◆

Yield: About 1½ to 2 cups

2 Cups cooked salmon
1 Teaspoon lemon juice
2 Tablespoons finely chopped fresh dill

3 Tablespoons Sauce Mayonnaise
1 Hard-cooked egg, shelled and finely chopped
1 Tablespoon capers

Pick over and flake fish, taking care to remove all bits of skin and bone. Combine with lemon juice, dill and mayonnaise. Stir in egg and capers.

CRABMEAT FILLING

◆

Yield: About 1½ to 2 cups

1½ Cups cooked crabmeat
2 Scallions, with 3 inches green tops, finely chopped
2 Tablespoons finely chopped celery

1 Tablespoon minced fresh thyme
4 Tablespoons Sauce Mayonnaise
Salt and freshly ground black pepper

Pick over the crabmeat and remove any bits of shell or cartilage, then combine with the scallions, celery and thyme. Bind with mayonnaise and season to taste with salt and pepper.

SHRIMP FILLING

◆

Yield: About 1½ to 2 cups

12–16 Cooked, peeled and de-veined shrimp, finely chopped
1 Hard-cooked egg, shelled and finely chopped

1 Tablespoon finely chopped fresh dill
4 Tablespoons Sauce Mayonnaise
Salt and freshly ground black pepper

Mix together the shrimp, egg, dill and mayonnaise. Season to taste with salt and pepper.

SMOKED SALMON FILLING

◆

Yield: About 1 to 1½ cups

8 Ounces cream cheese, at room temperature
2 Ounces smoked salmon, finely chopped

¼ Bermuda onion, finely chopped
2 Tablespoons capers, finely chopped
1 Teaspoon lemon juice
1 Tablespoon heavy cream (optional)

Mash the cream cheese with a fork until creamy and smooth, then blend in the smoked salmon, onion, capers and lemon juice. Thin to spreading consistency with the cream if desired.

To prepare your own smoked fish filling, follow directions for Smoked Salmon Filling, but substitute for the salmon any smoked fish you have prepared as directed.

FISH AND OLIVE FILLING

◆

Yield: About 2½ cups

2 Cups flaked fish
1 Rib celery, finely chopped
2 Tablespoons each finely chopped
   onion and pitted ripe olives
3 Small sweet gherkins, finely
   chopped

1 Teaspoon finely chopped fresh
   parsley
1½ Teaspoons lemon juice
3 Tablespoons Sauce Mayonnaise

Mix fish with remaining ingredients.

LOBSTER FILLING

◆

Yield: About 1½ to 2 cups

1½ Cups cooked, finely chopped
   lobster
1 Rib celery, finely chopped
1 Small tomato, peeled, seeded and
   finely chopped

1 Tablespoon lemon juice
¾ Teaspoon Worcestershire sauce
3 Tablespoons Sauce Mayonnaise
Salt and cayenne pepper

Carefully pick over the lobster meat to eliminate any small bits of shell or cartilage. Mix with celery, tomato, lemon juice, Worcestershire and mayonnaise; season to taste with salt and cayenne pepper.

OPEN-FACED SANDWICHES

Open-faced sandwiches should please the eye as well as the palate. Arrange ingredients attractively and garnish with colorful, tasty bits—pimientos, scallions, halved cherry tomatoes, egg and olive slices, and so forth.

PICKLED FISH SANDWICHES

◆

Mustard Butter
Thinly sliced rye bread
Your own pickled fish

Thin slices of Bermuda onion
Hard-cooked eggs
Lemon wedges

Spread Mustard Butter over the bread slices; drain the fish well and arrange attractively on top. Serve topped with onion slices and garnished with egg quarters and lemon wedges.

SMOKED SALMON SANDWICHES

◆

Thinly sliced pumpernickel bread
Tomato Filling
Smoked salmon slices
Black caviar

Hard-cooked egg yolks
Finely minced scallion, including
   some green tops

Cover one side of the bread slices with Tomato Filling, arrange smoked salmon slices on top, and garnish each sandwich with a bit of black caviar and a sprinkle of sieved hard-cooked egg yolk and minced scallion.

SMOKED WHITING SANDWICHES

◆

Thinly sliced rye bread
Tomato Filling
Smoked whiting fillets (or other
boneless smoked fish)

Thinly sliced onion rings
Thinly sliced sweet pickles

Cover one side of the bread slices with Tomato Filling, arrange fillets on top and garnish each sandwich with onion rings and pickle slices.

TOMATO FILLING

◆

Yield: About 1½ to 2 cups

12 Ounces cream cheese, at room
temperature
3 Medium-size tomatoes, peeled,
seeded and chopped

2 Tablespoons finely chopped fresh
basil
2–3 Tablespoons sour cream
Salt and freshly ground black pepper

Beat the cream cheese until light and fluffy. Blend in the tomatoes, basil and as much of the sour cream as necessary to bring the mixture to a spreading consistency. Season to taste with salt and pepper.

BASIC FISH-FILLED HARD-COOKED EGGS

◆

Yield: 24 egg halves

1 Dozen hard-cooked eggs
1 Cup flaked fish
½ Cup Sauce Mayonnaise

¼ Cup soft sweet butter
Salt and pepper to taste
1½ Tablespoons red caviar (optional)

Carefully cut the eggs in half lengthwise. Reserve the whites. Press half the egg yolks through a sieve and reserve. Coarsely chop the remaining yolks and toss with the fish. Mix the mayonnaise and the butter and stir into the fish mixture. Season to taste. Mound the filling in the halved egg whites, sprinkle with the sieved yolks and garnish with caviar. Chill for two hours. Serve cold.

CURRIED FISH-FILLED HARD-COOKED EGGS: Follow directions for Basic Fish-Filled Hard-Cooked Eggs, but substitute Curry Mayonnaise for Sauce Mayonnaise.

HARD-COOKED EGGS RÉMOULADE: Follow directions for Basic Fish-Filled Hard-Cooked Eggs, but substitute Sauce Rémoulade for Sauce Mayonnaise.

HARD-COOKED EGGS À LA RUSSE: Follow directions for Basic Fish-Filled Hard-Cooked Eggs, but substitute Sauce Russe for Sauce Mayonnaise.

ANCHOVY OLIVES

◆

Yield: 24 Olives

*24 pitted black olives or green olives
with pimento removed*

*Anchovy Butter
Minced parsley*

Drain the olives well and fill with the slightly softened butter. Dip both ends of each olive in the parsley. Chill well. Serve cold.

To prepare Caviar Olives, Lobster Olives, Shrimp Olives and Smoked Salmon Olives, follow directions for Anchovy Olives, but substitute the named butters for the Anchovy Butter.

TOAST TRIANGLES

◆

Yield: 24 Toast Triangles

*6 Slices fine-quality white bread with
crusts trimmed*

Cut the slices into triangles and toast under the broiler. Dry in a slow oven if crisp toasts are desired. These triangles may be cut in half prior to drying if the toasts are to be passed with hors d'oeuvre.

FRIED TOAST TRIANGLES: Cut 6 slices crustless bread into triangles and fry in 6 tablespoons Clarified Butter until golden on both sides. Keep warm.

FRIED GARLIC-TOAST TRIANGLES: Follow directions for Fried Toast Triangles above, but add 2 split garlic cloves to the butter as it warms.

ANCHOVY TOAST TRIANGLES: Toast 6 crustless bread slices lightly and, while they're still hot, spread them with Anchovy Butter. Split 36 canned flat anchovies lengthwise and drain them well. Press 3 hard-cooked egg yolks and whites separately through a sieve. Crisscross the toasts with anchovy, sprinkle with parsley and chill. Cut into triangles with a very sharp knife, then decorate the edges with sieved egg white and yolk. Refrigerate again until ready to serve.

LOBSTER TOAST TRIANGLES: Toast 6 crustless bread slices lightly and, while they're still hot, spread them with Lobster Butter. Bind 3 shelled and minced hard-cooked eggs with 2 to 3 tablespoons mayonnaise and spread this over the toasts. Sprinkle with 2 tablespoons minced dill. Cut each bread slice into 4 triangles. Slice 2 lobster tails into ¼-inch-thick slices and arrange one slice on each triangle. Refrigerate until ready to serve.

SHRIMP TOAST TRIANGLES: Follow directions for Lobster Toast Triangles but substitute Shrimp Butter for the Lobster Butter and shelled, cooked and halved shrimp for the lobster.

FISH TOAST TRIANGLES: Toast 6 crustless bread slices lightly and, while they're still hot, spread them with Lobster Butter. Bind one cup chilled, flaked fish with 3 tablespoons Tomato Filling and spread this over the toasts. Cut into triangles, then decorate the edges with 3 tablespoons minced parsley. Arrange an eighth of a teaspoon of red caviar in the center of each triangle and refrigerate until ready to serve.

FRITTER BATTER WITH BEER

◆

Yield: Enough batter for about 15 to 20 fritters

2 Cups flour
1¼ Cups beer
¼ Cup vegetable cooking oil (not olive)

Salt to taste
2 Egg whites

Sift the flour into a mixing bowl. Lightly beat the beer with the oil and stir into the flour only until the flour is moistened. (There should be a few lumps.) Stir in the salt and let the batter stand 2 to 3 hours in a warm place, covered by a damp dishtowel. When ready to use, beat the egg whites until stiff and fold them in. Dip in fish, shellfish, corn, or whatever is called for in recipe and fry in deep hot oil. Drain on paper towels.

TEMPURA BATTER

◆

1 Cup flour
1 Egg, beaten
1 Cup cold water

Sift flour and use thick chopsticks to beat lightly with egg and water. Do not overmix. Dust fish with flour before dipping in batter. Fry in oil heated to 350 degrees F. (A drop of batter will sink if oil is not hot enough or sizzle on the surface if oil is too hot. If batter floats midway, temperature is correct.)

BASIC PIE PASTRY

◆

Yield: Enough pastry for 1 double-crust pie

No two cooks measure ingredients in precisely the same way . . . one may have a rather heavy hand; another may judge a cup or spoon to be full when it is slightly on the scant side. Then, too, the amount of moisture in the air (and therefore the flour) affects how much or how little liquid you will need to properly moisten your pie dough. For this reason you may occasionally have to make adjustments in dry and liquid ingredients if your dough is too sticky to roll out or too dry to hold together. Hot weather, too, may cause problems by melting the shortening and turning your pie dough into a sticky mass. In this case, work in a little extra flour, and refrigerate the dough before rolling it out.

11–12 Tablespoons (1½ sticks) sweet
   butter and 3 tablespoons cold
   shortening (or for less rich pastry
   use 7 tablespoons each cold
   shortening and butter)

2½ Cups flour
1¼ Teaspoons salt
8 Tablespoons ice water (or a little
   more or less)

Sift together dry ingredients, cut the butter and shortening into pieces and tuck these into the flour. With 2 knives cut the fat into the dry ingredients until the mixture resembles coarse meal (or whirl briefly in your food processor). Stir in the ice water, 2 tablespoons at a time, until the dough forms a ball. Chill for at least 15 minutes before rolling out.

To roll out the dough, divide the dough in half. Roll out each half on a lightly floured pastry board, taking care not to overwork the dough. If a single pie crust is called for in your recipe, refrigerate or freeze the unused portion until needed.

PÂTE À CHOU (PUFF-SHELL DOUGH)
◆

One of the most versatile staples of the gourmet kitchen is *chou* pastry. Small puffs and éclairs may be baked, filled with bits of fish, shellfish or roe and served as hors d'oeuvre, or larger puffed receptacles may be filled with salads or hot creamed fish and/or shellfish mixtures and served forth as tasty light luncheon dishes.

12 Tablespoons butter, cut in ½-inch
   pieces
1 Teaspoon sugar
½ Teaspoon salt

2 Cups water
1½–1¾ Cups flour
6–7 Large eggs

Bring butter, sugar, salt and water slowly to a boil in a small, heavy saucepan. When the butter has melted, beat in the flour all at once until smoothly blended. Return the mixture to low heat and beat briskly with a wooden spoon until the ingredients are thoroughly blended and the mixture pulls away from the sides of the pan.

Beat in the eggs, one at a time, making sure each egg is well incorporated before adding the next. (Your food processor makes this easy.) The finished paste should be smooth and shiny. Use immediately or press plastic wrap directly down on the surface to prevent excess exposure to the air, and refrigerate up to 3 days until needed.

To prepare the pastry, preheat oven to 425 degrees F.

To make small puffs, drop *chou* mixture by teaspoons onto a buttered baking sheet. To make larger puffs or éclairs, force mixture through a pastry bag fitted with a ¾-inch round tube onto a buttered baking sheet, forming 1- or 2-inch circles for the puffs and strips 1 inch wide and 4 inches long for the éclairs. Allow enough room between the puffs and/or éclairs so that they will not touch when they expand.

Bake for 15 minutes, then reduce heat to 375 degrees F. and bake until the puffs or éclairs are a light golden brown, about 15 to 18 minutes. Take care not to over-brown—the sides of the puffs or éclairs should feel rigid when done.

To use, press down centers of each puff or éclair when hot, or cut a small piece or strip from the top of each when cooled, then fill with your choice of hot or cold fillings.

VEGETABLE ACCOMPANI- MENTS

CARROT FLOWERS

◆

Yield: About 3 cups

4 Medium-size carrots, scraped

Make 4 long, shallow V-shaped cuts at equal distances the entire length of each carrot. Cut in ¼-inch-thick crosswise slices to form 4-petaled "flowers."

STEAMED CARROT FLOWERS: Prepare 1 recipe Carrot Flowers and steam over hot water until not quite tender. Serve hot or chilled.

CARROT TWIGS

◆

Yield: 3 cups

Scrape 4 carrots and cut into 2-inch-long, ¼-inch-thick matchstick shapes (3-sided ones will do fine in most recipes). Simmer in chicken broth until not quite tender. Serve hot or chilled.

SWEET PEPPER JULIENNE

◆

Yield: About 3 cups

4 Large whole sweet peppers
  (green or red)

Hold peppers over a flame on a fork until the skin turns black all over. Rinse away the charred skin under running water. Discard the pith and seeds and cut the peppers into julienne strips about ¼ inch wide. Marinate for a few hours in 2 tablespoons mild vinegar. Chill. Just before serving time, toss with a nice fruity olive oil and drain well.

TURNIP TWIGS

◆

Yield: About 3 cups

4 *Medium-size turnips, peeled*
Chicken broth

Cut turnips into ¼-inch-thick julienne. Simmer 2 minutes in chicken broth. Do not overcook, or these will crumble. Serve warm or chilled.

SAUTÉED CUCUMBERS

◆

Yield: Enough to serve 6

4 *Medium-size cucumbers, peeled*
3 *Tablespoons sweet butter*
Boiling water

Salt and pepper to taste
Finely chopped fresh mint (optional)

Halve the cucumbers lengthwise and use a melon baller to remove the seeds. Cut the flesh into ½-inch-wide strips. Blanch 3 minutes in boiling water to cover. Drain well on paper towels. Sauté in butter for 3 minutes without browning. Season with salt and pepper and sprinkle with mint if desired.

SCALLIONS IN FISH STOCK

◆

2 *Dozen trimmed young green*
scallions, about the thickness and
length of a pencil
2 *Cups Fish Stock or clam broth*

2 *Tablespoons butter*
2 *Teaspoons lemon juice*
Salt and white pepper to taste
¾ *Cup minced fresh clams (optional)*

Arrange the scallions in a large skillet, cover with Fish Stock or broth and cook over high flame until barely tender (about 6 or 7 minutes). Remove scallions to a hot plate and keep warm. Reduce the pan liquid to half, stir in the butter, lemon juice and seasonings and boil for 2 minutes. Add the clams and simmer a minute or 2, or until clams are just heated through. Pour over scallions and serve immediately. If the butter is omitted from the sauce, these are also delicious served cold.

SPINACH PURÉE

◆

Yield: About 1½ cups

3 *Pounds well-washed spinach leaves*
with tough stems removed
½ *Cup Sauce Béchamel*

Pinch granulated sugar (optional)
Salt
Nutmeg

Bring salted water to a boil in a large saucepan, add spinach, then cook only long enough for water to return to a boil. Remove from heat and drain well. Cool slightly and then squeeze dry. Purée. Stir in remaining ingredients until well incorporated. Serve hot.

FRIED TOMATO SLICES

◆

Yield: Enough to serve 6

8 Large, firm green or ripe tomatoes
2 Eggs
1½ Teaspoons salt

2½ Cups fine, dry bread crumbs
Vegetable oil or butter for frying

Cut tomatoes into thick slices. In a large, shallow bowl, beat together eggs and salt. Dip each tomato slice in the egg mixture and then in bread crumbs and fry in hot oil or butter until brown on both sides. Arrange on serving plate. Carefully lift off skins if desired. Serve immediately.

DUXELLES

◆

½ Pound fresh, perfect mushrooms
2 Tablespoons butter
1 Shallot, peeled and minced

2 Teaspoons minced parsley
½ Teaspoon salt

Trim mushrooms and wipe with a damp cloth. Mince with a sharp knife or cut in quarters and whirl until finely chopped (5 or 6 seconds) in a food processor. Heat the butter, mushrooms, shallot and parsley until all the moisture has evaporated. Season to taste with salt.

DUCHESSE POTATOES

◆

Yield: Enough to serve 6

8 Medium potatoes, peeled and cut
   in quarters
1 Small egg plus 2 yolks
2 Tablespoons butter

1 Teaspoon salt
Dash each ground nutmeg and white
   pepper

Cook potatoes in water to cover until tender, then drain well. Shake potatoes over low heat for 2 to 3 minutes, or until potatoes are dry. Mash potatoes thoroughly, or whirl in food processor, turning quickly on and off 3 times, removing cover each time to stir potatoes from bottom to top. Add remaining ingredients and beat in thoroughly or whirl in food processor, turning machine rapidly on and off 2 or 3 times until ingredients are well blended, stopping once to scrape down container sides.

Preheat oven to 325 degrees F.

Pipe through a pastry tube to form a decorative border and broil until lightly browned, or force into puffs or mounds on a buttered cookie sheet and bake until nicely browned.

To store any unused Duchesse Potato mixture, brush surface lightly with vegetable oil, then press plastic wrap directly against potato mixture. Refrigerate. To use, reheat in the top of a double boiler over very low heat, stirring constantly until potato mixture reaches proper consistency for shaping.

FRIED PARSLEY

◆

*Yield: Enough to
serve 6 to 8*

1 *Bunch parsley, well washed and
drained*

*Vegetable oil for deep-frying
Salt*

Dry parsley thoroughly between paper towels. Cut off and discard any long, tough stems. Fry the parsley sprigs, a few at a time, in deep hot oil only long enough to crisp. Drain on paper towels and sprinkle with salt.

OLD-FASHIONED POTATO STUFFING

◆

Yield: About 4 cups

3 *Large potatoes, peeled*
3 *Tablespoons milk*
3 *Tablespoons butter*
2 *Cups stale bread crumbs*
1 *Small onion, minced*

½ *Cup dried celery*
1 *Egg, lightly beaten*
½ *Teaspoon each salt and thyme*
A pinch of black pepper
1 *Tablespoon minced chives*

Boil the potatoes until tender and drain well. Mash with milk and 2 tablespoons of the butter. Soak bread crumbs in water to cover, then squeeze out excess moisture. Sauté the onion and celery in the remaining tablespoon butter, until onion is transparent. Toss together the potatoes, bread crumbs, onion, celery, egg, seasonings and chives.

FISH FORCEMEAT

◆

A flavorful stuffing for whole fish or rolled fillets.

1 *Pound fine white, nonoily fish*
3 *Slices white bread, with crusts
removed*
Heavy cream

1 *Egg, separated*
4 *Egg yolks*
*A pinch each of powdered thyme and
tarragon*

Cut fish into 1-inch pieces and whirl in blender or food processor until smooth and creamy (or pound in a mortar). Soak bread several minutes in just enough cream to cover. Add the bread to the blender, processor or mortar and work it into the fish until smooth. Whirl in the egg white, then the egg yolks (one at a time), and finally just enough cream to make a smooth paste that holds its shape.

RIVAL PLEASURES OF SEA-WATER AND FRESH-WATER FISHING

. . . And yet the fisher's steps explore
With equal joy the salt sea shore
Skims in his yacht the breezy bay
Where schools of the leaping bluefish play
Stemming the boiling tides with prow
That cleaves the billows like the plow;
And here he casts the humming line
To snatch the weakfish from the brine.

Off where the tumbling billows roar
Afar from ledge or bar of shore
He drops his anchor, casts his bait
The snap, the nibble to await;
And soon the flapping spoil is won
The sea bass blue, the blackfish dun
And thinks no joys may rival these
The angling pastimes of the seas.

• •

Part Three

F·I·S·H A·N·D

N·U·T·R·I·T·I·O·N

FISH AND NUTRITION

Beyond their intricate beauty, awe-inspiring design and deluxe taste . . . fish are super-nutritious. A mere 4-ounce serving of lean fish, for instance, will supply about half the body's daily protein requirements, with an expenditure of only about 100 calories. What's even better, this is complete protein that contains a larger variety of the essential amino acids the body needs for upkeep and growth than does the protein found in meat. Fish protein is also easier to digest than meat protein, and the small amount of fat it does contain is high in polyunsaturates and low in cholesterol, which means that eating fish (but not shellfish, which tend to be higher in both fat content and cholesterol) can lessen the risk of atherosclerosis.

Fish are also good natural sources of minerals and other useful nutrients. Along with shellfish and roes, all exceptionally mineral-rich, fish provide ample amounts of iron, phosphorus, potassium and calcium, plus traces of copper, magnesium, manganese, cobalt and zinc. Many also supply a fair percentage of the B vitamins the body needs daily, and fish like eel, halibut, mackerel, salmon, sardines and swordfish are particularly rich in Vitamin A.

Salt-water species are a fine source of iodine, and although their habitat is highly saline, these fish are surprisingly low in sodium, which makes them especially valuable to those who must limit their salt intake. Actually, unless salt is introduced through pickling, salting, canning or smoking, the sodium content of fish is, in general, much lower than that of meat.

Fish differ greatly in fat content. Leanest of all is haddock, followed closely by such cod-family kin as codfish, tomcod, pollock, whiting and squirrel hake. Other nonfat fish are, on an ascending scale, tilefish, skate, all the flounders, halibut and redfish (ocean perch).

There are also many tasty and exceptionally nutritious fishes that are neither particularly lean nor particularly fat. These include such popular kinds as striped bass, kingfish, porgy and smelt. In general, fat content can vary even among the same species, depending on age, season, locality, and available diet . . . oily forage fish, insects, plants, etc.

Even really fatty fish are not consistent in their fat content: Atlantic salmon, for example, well-buffered by a thick layer of fat as they begin their perilous annual migration, eat nothing at all enroute and return to the sea considerably slimmed and therefore relatively fat-free. For more specific information consult the following chart.

COMPOSITION OF VARIOUS FISH AND SHELLFISH

The chart on the following pages indicates the nutritional composition of various fish and shellfish, based on an edible portion of 100 grams. Numbers in parentheses denote values imputed—usually from another form of the food or from a similar food. Zero in parenthesis indicates that the amount of a constituent probably is none or is too small to measure. Dashes denote lack of reliable data for a constituent believed to be present in measurable amounts. Calculated values, as those based on a recipe, are not in parentheses.

Note: The nutritive values of fish listed in the following chart are taken from *Handbook of the Nutritional Contents of Food*, prepared for the United States Department of Agriculture (Agriculture Handbook No. 8)

Fish or Shellfish	Food Energy (Calories)	Protein (grams)	Fat (grams)	Carbo-hydrate Total (grams)	Ash (grams)	Calcium (mg)
Albacore						
RAW:	177	25.3	7.6	0	1.3	26
Alewife						
RAW:	127	19.4	4.9	0	1.5	—
CANNED, SOLIDS AND LIQUID:	141	16.2	8.0	0	3.4	—
Anchovy						
PICKLED, WITH AND WITHOUT ADDED OIL, NOT HEAVILY SALTED:	176	19.2	10.3	.3	11.6	168
Bass, black sea						
RAW:	93	19.2	1.2	0	1.2	—
Bass, striped						
RAW:	105	18.9	2.7	0	1.2	—
Blackfish (tautog)						
RAW:	89	18.6	1.1	0	1.1	—
Bluefish						
RAW:	117	20.5	3.3	0	1.2	23
Bonito, Atlantic and Striped						
RAW:	168	24.0	7.3	0	1.4	—
Butterfish						
RAW:	169	18.1	10.2	0	1.4	—
Caviar, Sturgeon						
GRANULAR:	262	26.9	15.0	3.3	8.8	276
PRESSED:	316	34.4	16.7	4.9	8.0	—
Clams, soft						
MEAT AND LIQUID:	49	6.5	.4	4.2	2.7	—
MEAT ONLY:	80	11.1	.9	5.9	2.3	69
Clams, hard						
MEAT AND LIQUID:	49	6.5	.4	4.2	2.7	—
MEAT ONLY:	80	11.1	.9	5.9	2.3	69

Phosphorus (mg)	Iron (mg)	Sodium (mg)	Potassium (mg)	Vitamin A Value (International Units)	Thiamine (mg)	Riboflavin (mg)	Niacin (mg)	Ascorbic Acid (mg)
—	—	40	293	—	—	—	—	5
218	—	—	—	—	—	—	—	—
—	—	—	—	—	—	—	—	—
210	—	—	—	—	—	—	—	—
—	—	68	256	—	—	—	—	—
212	—	—	—	—	—	—	—	—
227	—	—	—	—	—	—	—	—
243	.6	74	—	—	.12	.09	1.9	—
—	—	—	—	—	—	—	—	—
—	—	—	—	—	—	—	—	—
355	11.8	2,200	180	—	—	—	—	—
—	—	—	—	—	—	—	—	—
175	—	—	—	—	—	.13	—	—
151	7.5	205	311	—	—	—	—	—
175	—	—	—	—	—	.13	—	—
151	7.5	205	311	—	—	—	—	—

Fish or Shellfish	Food Energy (Calories)	Protein (grams)	Fat (grams)	Carbo-hydrate Total (grams)	Ash (grams)	Calcium (mg)
Clams						
CANNED, INCLUDING HARD, SOFT, RAZOR AND UNSPECIFIED						
SOLIDS AND LIQUID:	52	7.9	.7	2.8	2.3	55
DRAINED SOLIDS:	98	15.8	2.5	1.9	2.8	—
LIQUOR (BOUILLON OR NECTAR):	19	2.3	.1	2.1	1.9	—
Cod						
RAW:	78	17.6	.3	0	1.2	10
CANNED:	85	19.2	.3	0	1.0	—
DEHYDRATED; LIGHTLY SALTED:	375	81.8	2.8	0	7.0	—
DRIED, SALTED:	130	29.0	.7	0	19.7	225
Crab including blue and rock						
COOKED, STEAMED:	93	17.3	1.9	.5	1.8	43
CANNED:	101	17.4	2.5	1.1	1.8	45
Dogfish, spiny						
RAW:	156	17.6	9.0	0	1.0	—
Eel, American						
RAW:	233	15.9	18.3	0	1.0	18
SMOKED:	330	18.6	27.8	0	2.4	—
Flounder						
RAW:	79	16.7	.8	0	1.2	12
Haddock						
RAW:	79	18.3	.1	0	1.4	23
SMOKED (FINNAN HADDIE):	103	23.2	.4	0	3.1	—
Hake, squirrel						
RAW:	74	16.5	.4	0	1.3	41
Halibut, Atlantic						
RAW:	100	20.9	1.2	0	1.4	13
SMOKED:	224	20.8	15.0	0	15.0	—
Herring, Atlantic						
RAW:	176	17.3	11.3	0	2.1	—
CANNED (PLAIN):	208	19.9	13.6	0	3.7	147

Phosphorus (mg)	Iron (mg)	Sodium (mg)	Potassium (mg)	Vitamin A Value (International Units)	Thiamine (mg)	Riboflavin (mg)	Niacin (mg)	Ascorbic Acid (mg)
137	4.1	—	140	—	.01	.11	1.0	—
—	—	—	—	—	—	—	—	—
—	—	—	—	—	—	—	—	—
194	.4	70	382	0	.06	.07	2.2	2
—	—	—	—	—	—	.08	—	—
891	3.6	8,100	160	0	.08	.45	10.9	—
—	—	—	—	—	—	—	—	—
175	.8	—	—	2,170	.16	.08	2.8	2
182	.8	1,000	110	—	.08	.08	1.9	—
—	—	—	—	—	.05	—	—	—
202	.7	—	—	1,610	.22	.36	1.4	—
—	—	—	—	—	—	—	—	—
195	.8	78	342	—	.05	.05	1.7	—
197	.7	61	304	—	.04	.07	3.0	—
—	—	—	—	—	.06	.05	2.1	—
142	—	74	363	—	.10	.20	—	—
211	.7	54	449	440	.07	.07	8.3	—
—	—	—	—	—	—	—	—	—
256	1.1	—	—	110	.02	.15	3.6	—
297	1.8	—	—	—	—	.18	—	—

Fish or Shellfish	Food Energy (Calories)	Protein (grams)	Fat (grams)	Carbo-hydrate Total (grams)	Ash (grams)	Calcium (mg)
Herring, Atlantic (continued)						
CANNED (IN TOMATO SAUCE):	176	15.8	10.5	3.7	3.3	—
PICKLED, BISMARCK-TYPE:	223	20.4	15.1	0	4.0	—
SALTED OR BRINED:	218	19.0	15.2	0	12.0	—
SMOKED (BLOATERS):	196	19.6	12.4	0	3.2	—
SMOKED (HARD):	300	36.9	15.8	0	13.2	—
SMOKED (KIPPERED):	211	22.2	12.9	0	4.0	66
Kingfish (Northern)	105	18.3	3.0	0	1.3	—
Lobster (whole)	91	16.9	1.9	.5	2.2	29
COOKED OR CANNED:	95	18.7	1.5	.3	2.7	65
Mackerel, Atlantic						
RAW:	191	19.0	12.2	0	1.6	5
CANNED, SOLIDS AND LIQUID:	183	19.3	11.1	0	3.2	185
SALTED:	305	18.5	25.1	0	13.0	—
SMOKED:	219	23.8	13.0	0	2.0	—
Menhaden (bunkerfish)						
CANNED, SOLIDS AND LIQUID:	172	18.7	10.2	0	3.8	—
Mullet, Striped						
RAW:	146	19.6	6.9	0	1.3	26
Mussels, Atlantic						
MEAT AND LIQUID:	66	9.6	1.4	3.1	2.1	—
MEAT ONLY:	95	14.4	2.2	3.3	1.5	88
Oysters, Eastern						
MEAT ONLY:	66	8.4	1.8	3.4	1.8	94
CANNED, SOLIDS AND LIQUID:	76	8.5	2.2	4.9	2.2	28
Porgy						
RAW:	112	19.0	3.4	0	1.3	54
Redfish (Ocean perch)						
RAW:	88	18.0	1.2	0	1.1	20
Roe						
COD, HADDOCK, HERRING, SHAD:	130	24.4	2.3	1.5	1.7	—
SALMON AND STURGEON:	207	25.2	10.4	1.4	1.7	—

Phosphorus (mg)	Iron (mg)	Sodium (mg)	Potassium (mg)	Vitamin A Value (International Units)	Thiamine (mg)	Riboflavin (mg)	Niacin (mg)	Ascorbic Acid (mg)
243	—	—	—	—	—	.11	3.5	—
—	—	—	—	—	—	—	—	—
—	.	—	—	—	—	.19	—	—
—	—	—	—	—	—	—	—	—
—	—	6,231	157	—	—	—	—	—
254	1.4	—	—	30	—	.28	3.3	—
—	—	83	250	—	—	—	—	—
183	.6	—	—	—	.40	.05	1.5	—
192	.8	210	180	—	.10	.07	—	—
239	1.0	—	—	(450)	.15	.33	8.2	—
274	2.1	—	—	430	.06	.21	5.8	—
—	—	—	—	—	—	—	—	—
—	—	—	—	—	—	—	—	—
—	1.3	—	—	—	—	—	—	—
220	1.8	81	292	—	.07	.08	5.2	—
—	—	—	—	—	—	—	—	—
236	3.4	289	315	—	.16	.21	—	—
143	5.5	73	121	310	.14	.18	2.5	—
124	5.6	—	70	—	.02	.20	.8	—
250	—	63	287	—	—	—	—	—
207	1.0	79	269	—	.10	.08	1.9	—
—	.6	—	—	—	.10	.76	1.4	14
—	—	—	—	—	.38	.72	2.3	18

Fish or Shellfish	Food Energy (Calories)	Protein (grams)	Fat (grams)	Carbo-hydrate Total (grams)	Ash (grams)	Calcium (mg)
Salmon, Atlantic						
RAW:	217	22.5	13.4	0	1.4	79
Salmon, chinook (king)						
RAW:	222	19.1	15.6	0	1.1	—
CANNED, SOLIDS AND LIQUID:	210	19.6	14.0	0	2.0	154*
Salmon, Chum						
CANNED, SOLIDS AND LIQUID:	139	21.5	5.2	0	2.6	249*
Salmon, coro (silver)						
RAW:	—	—	—	—	—	175
CANNED, SOLIDS AND LIQUID:	153	20.8	7.1	0	2.4	244*
Salmon, pink						
CANNED, SOLIDS AND LIQUID:	141	20.5	5.9	0	2.3	196*
Salmon, sockeye (red)						
CANNED, SOLIDS AND LIQUID:	171	20.3	9.3	0	2.7	259*
Salmon, smoked	176	21.6	9.3	0	9.4	14
Sardines, Atlantic						
CANNED IN OIL, SOLIDS AND LIQUID:	311	20.6	24.4	.6	3.8	354
CANNED, DRAINED SOLIDS:	203	24.0	11.1	—	3.1	437†
Scallops, bay and sea						
RAW:	81	15.3	.2	3.3	1.4	26
Shad, American						
RAW:	170	18.6	10.0	0	1.3	20
CANNED, SOLIDS AND LIQUID:	152	16.9	8.8	0	2.8	—
Sheepshead, Atlantic						
RAW:	113	20.6	2.8	0	1.3	—

*Based on total contents of can. If bones are discarded, value will be greatly reduced.

†Values for sardines without skin and bones canned in oil are: calcium 54 mg per 100 grams; phosphorus 319 mg per 100 grams.

Phosphorus (mg)	Iron (mg)	Sodium (mg)	Potassium (mg)	Vitamin A Value (International Units)	Thiamine (mg)	Riboflavin (mg)	Niacin (mg)	Ascorbic Acid (mg)
186	.9	—	—	—	—	.08	7.2	9
301	—	45	399	310	.10	.23	—	—
289	.9	—**	366	230	.03	.14	7.3	—
352	.7	—**	336	60	.02	.16	7.1	—
231		48	421	—	.09	.11	—	1
288	.9	351**	339	80	.03	.18	7.4	—
286	.8	387**	361	70	.03	.18	8.0	—
344	1.2	522**	344	230	.04	.16	7.3	—
245	—	—	—	—	—	—	—	—
434	3.5	510	560	180	.02	.16	4.4	—
499†	2.9	823	590	220	.03	.20	5.4	—
208	1.8	255‡	396‡	—	—	—	—	—
260	.5	54	330	—	.15	.24	8.4	—
—	.7	—	—	—	—	.16	—	—
197	—	101	234	—	—	—	—	—

**For product canned without salt, value is approximately the same as for raw salmon.

†Based on frozen scallops, possibly brined.

‡One sample with salt added contained 875 mg of sodium per 100 grams and 275 mg of potassium.

Fish or Shellfish	Food Energy (Calories)	Protein (grams)	Fat (grams)	Carbo-hydrate Total (grams)	Ash (grams)	Calcium (mg)
Shrimp						
RAW:	91	18.1	.8	1.5	1.4	63
CANNED, WET PACK, SOLIDS AND LIQUID:	80	16.2	.8	.8	4.0	59
CANNED, DRY PACK OR DRAINED SOLIDS OF WET PACK:	116	24.2	1.1	.7	3.6	115
Skate						
RAW:	98	21.5	.7	0	1.2	—
Smelt						
RAW:	98	18.6	2.1	0	1.1	—
CANNED, SOLIDS AND LIQUID:	200	18.4	13.5	0	5.4	358
Squid						
RAW:	84	16.4	.9	1.5	1.0	12
Sturgeon						
RAW:	94	18.1	1.9	0	1.4	—
SMOKED:	149	31.2	1.8	0	1.9	—
Swordfish						
RAW:	118	19.2	4.0	0	1.3	19
Tilefish						
RAW:	79	17.5	.5	0	1.4	—
Tomcod, Atlantic						
RAW:	77	17.2	.4	0	1.0	—
Tuna, Bluefin						
RAW:	145	25.2	4.1	0	1.3	—
Tuna, yellowfin						
RAW:	133	24.7	3.0	0	1.4	—
Tuna						
CANNED IN OIL, SOLIDS AND LIQUID:	288	24.2	20.5	0	2.4	6
CANNED IN OIL, DRAINED, SOLID:	197	28.8	8.2	0	2.0	(8)

Phosphorus (mg)	Iron (mg)	Sodium (mg)	Potassium (mg)	Vitamin A Value (International Units)	Thiamine (mg)	Riboflavin (mg)	Niacin (mg)	Ascorbic Acid (mg)
166	1.6	140	220	—	.02	.03	3.2	—
152	1.8	—	—	50	.01	.03	1.5	—
263	3.1	—	122	60	.01	.03	1.8	—
—	—	—	—	—	.02	—	—	—
272	.4	—	—	—	.01	.12	1.4	—
370	1.7	—	—	—	—	—	—	—
119	.5	—	—	—	.02	.12	—	—
—	—	—	—	—	—	—	—	—
—	—	—	—	—	—	—	—	—
195	.9	—	—	1,580	.05	.05	8.0	—
—	—	—	—	—	—	—	—	—
—	—	—	—	—	—	.17	—	—
—	1.3	—	—	—	—	—	—	—
—	—	37	—	—	—	—	—	—
294	1.1	800	301	90	.04	.09	10.1	—
234	1.9	—	—	80	.05	.12	11.9	—

Fish or Shellfish	Food Energy (Calories)	Protein (grams)	Fat (grams)	Carbo-hydrate Total (grams)	Ash (grams)	Calcium (mg)
Tuna CANNED IN WATER, SOLIDS AND LIQUID:	127	28.0	.8	0	1.2	16
Weakfish RAW:	121	16.5	5.6	0	1.2	—
White perch RAW:	118	19.3	4.0	0	1.2	—
Whiting (silver hake) RAW:	74	16.5	.4	0	1.3	41

Phosphorus (mg)	Iron (mg)	Sodium (mg)	Potassium (mg)	Vitamin A Value (International Units)	Thiamine (mg)	Riboflavin (mg)	Niacin (mg)	Ascorbic Acid (mg)
190	1.6	41§	279§	—	—	.10	13.3	—
—	—	75	317	—	.09	.06	2.7	—
192	—	—	—	—	—	—	—	—
142	—	74	363	—	.10	.20	—	—

§ One sample with salt added contained 875 mg of sodium per 100 grams of 275 mg of potassium.

I·N·D·E·X

for white perch, 183
for whiting, 117–18
techniques, of American Indians, 58–59
see also Names of fish
Flambéed Whole Striped Bass with Dried
Herb Branches, 87
Flatfish
to prepare for stuffing, 18
to clean, 18
Creamed, Baked Corn and (with
variations), 151
family, described, 137–38
Fillets
à l'Américaine, 148
with Anchovies, 149
with Anchovies and Olives, 148
with Asparagus Tips, Hollandaise,
148
with Asparagus Tips, Parmesan, 148
Bannaro, 148
with Finger-Length Zucchini, 147
Marguery, 148
with Mushrooms (with variations),
147
with New Potatoes and Green
Butter, 147
Poached, 146
Poached, Rolled, 150
with Roe, 147
Sautéed, Amandine, 149
Sautéed, with Eggplant and Tomato,
148
Sautéed, with Orange Slices, 149
with Sweet Peppers and Thyme, 149
to fillet, 20
Grilled, 150
Turbans
Poached, 150
Chilled, on Rice Salad, 152
with Lobster and Oysters, 152
see also Names of flatfish
Flesh, firmness of, as sign of freshness in
fish, 12
Flounder
in Aku Aku Seviche, 38
in Baked Corn and Creamed Flatfish
(with variations), 151
to cut, for Sashimi, 64
fillets. *See* Flatfish
and Fluke, An Unusual Preparation
for, 66
Grilled, 150
in Maggie Young's Flatfish Croquettes,
152
in Iced Fish, Meat and Buttermilk
Soup, 308
in North Shore Fish Pudding, 193
roe, 68
Dip, Peconic, 69
in Salt-Water Gefilte Fish, 179
in Seviche II, 38
vs. sole, 138

turbans of. *See* Flatfish
in Venezuelan Ground-Almond Fish
Stew, 316
witch, 143
yellowtail, 142–43
Fluke
in Aku Aku Seviche, 38
as bait, 99, 145
in Baked Corn and Creamed Flatfish,
151
to catch, 144–45
described, 144
fillets. *See* Flatfish
Flounder and, An Unusual Preparation
for, 66
as food, 144
Grilled, 150
habits, habitat and season, 144
in Maggie Young's Flatfish Croquettes,
152
turbans of. *See* Flatfish
Forcemeat, Fish, 350
Fourspots, 142
Foxey Bogue Minced Clam Appetizer,
249
Fragrance, fresh, as sign of freshness in
fish, 12, 13
Freezing, as method of preserving fish
and shellfish, 49–51
Fresh Cod "Sounds" and Tongues,
Montauk Lighthouse, 123
Fresh Eel Soup, 135
Fresh Herring and Anchovy Pudding, Old
Cove Mill, 164
Fried Garlic-Toast Triangles, 343
Fried Haddock Fingers in Golden Cream,
127
Fried Mullet and Oysters with Tomato
Cream, 182
Fried Oysters, Villeroi, 266
Fried Parsley, 350
Fried Skate Wings, 208
Fried Toast Triangles, 343
Fried Tomato Slices, 349
Frittata, Scrod (with variations), 119
Fritter(s)
Batter with Beer, 344
Clam, Old-Time North Shore, 252
Whelk, 285
Frittered Mussels, 258
Fritto Misto Mare, 239
Frosted Butterfish, 110
Fruit, Pan-Fried Blackfish with, 93
Frying. *See* Pan-frying; Deep-frying

Gardiner's Bay Sweet and Sour Porgies,
39
Garlic
butter. *See* Butters
-Toast Triangles, Fried, 343
-Tomato Sauce, Eels in, 136
Gefilte Fish, Salt-Water, 179

ABOUT THE AUTHOR

Yvonne Young Tarr is a veteran cookbook writer.
Her books include *The Up-with-Wholesome, Down-with-Store-Bought Book of Recipes and Household Formulas, The Ten Minute Gourmet Cookbook, The Ten Minute Gourmet Diet Cookbook, 101 Desserts to Make You Famous, Love Portions, The New York Times Natural Foods Dieting Book, The Complete Outdoor Cookbook, The New York Times Bread and Soup Cookbook, The Farmhouse Cookbook, The Tomato Book, The Squash Cookbook, The Great Food Processor Cookbook, Super-Easy Step-by-Step Cheesemaking, Super-Easy Step-by-Step Winemaking, Super-Easy Step-by-Step Sausage-making, Super-Easy Step-by-Step Book of Special Breads.*
She is married to sculptor William Tarr. They have two
children, Jonathan and Nicholas.